WITHDRAWN

BRECHT: THE MAN AND HIS WORK

MARTIN ESSLIN was born in Hungary, but while he was still an infant his family left the country as political refugees and settled in Vienna. He majored in English and philosophy at the University of Vienna and attended the Reinhardt (Theatrical) Seminar, where he studied to be a director. Just as he was on the point of starting his theatrical career in 1938, the Nazis moved into Vienna and he was forced to flee. He spent a year in Brussels and then managed to get to England where he joined the BBC in 1940. He is now head of the BBC Radio Drama Department. He is also author of *The Theatre of the Absurd* (A279), *Reflections: Essays on Modern Theatre* and *The Peopled Wound: The Work of Harold Pinter*.

MARTIN ESSLIN

BRECHT

THE MAN AND HIS WORK

NEW REVISED EDITION

ANCHOR BOOKS

DOUBLEDAY & COMPANY, INC.

GARDEN CITY, NEW YORK

CONTENTS

PART FIVE: FOR REFERENCE

FOREWORD TO THE NEW EDITION

This book first appeared in England in 1959, in the United States in 1960. At that time Brecht was still barely known in the English-speaking world. Today he has become a recognized classic, one of the great masters of twentieth-century literature. And there has been a steady stream of books and articles on the man and his work.

Moreover, in the fourteen years since Brecht died many of his previously unpublished works have appeared, and a good deal of information about his life and circumstances, letters and documents have become public. Clearly a book which had been one of the first to attempt only three years after he had died a survey of the man and the artist, the theoretician of drama and the political personality, and for which there seemed a steady continuing demand from students of Brecht and the general public, was in need of revision.

Yet, on rereading what I had written in 1957 and 1958, with an eye on what might have become out of date or been superseded by the new material, I was surprised to what extent the material I had then laboriously assembled has stood up to the test of time. The enormous mass of newly available biographical material and unpublished writings that have recently come to light have, indeed, filled out much that had been reported on the basis of personal reminiscences from friends—and enemies—of Brecht, or from hints contained in newspaper reports of the time. But the basic facts, the basic structure of Brecht's life and personality, the basic outline of his artistic and political profile remain unaffected.

Of course, there has been an immense amount of discus-

sion and often bitter controversy about Brecht; and this boo
has often been in the center of such disputes. But here too
in surveying what has been said for and against my point o
view, I can merely repeat what I wrote in the foreword t
the first paperback edition of the book, in 1960:

"That a study of a highly unorthodox Communist poe
which is appreciative of his genius but critical of his politica
convictions, would find little understanding in orthodo
Communist quarters was only to be expected. There is littl
point in arguing with criticism on the intellectual level o
say, the London *Daily Worker*. One might as well engage in
debate with a parrot. But there has been another, and ou
wardly more plausible, line of attack from similar, or at lea
closely related, quarters which certainly demands strong an
categorical refutation.

"I have been accused of wanting to 'denigrate' Brecht, th
man, and of presenting a 'repulsive' picture of a great, an
defenseless, artist. That such a view is a grotesque misunde
standing, and misrepresentation, of this book should be ap
parent to any attentive reader. How could such a misconcep
tion arise? By applying to Brecht a system of ethics to whic
he himself never subscribed. It has, for example, been sug
gested that I have cast doubt on his honor by reporting tha
after his exile in 1933, Brecht did not accept an invitation t
work in the Soviet Union and even emigrated to America i
1941 by crossing its whole territory from Finland to Vladivos
tok. Did this not imply that he betrayed his faith for the sak
of the fleshpots of Hollywood? I am accused of having pre
sented Brecht as a coward and opportunist because I did noth
ing to explain away, or minimize, the otherwise undoubted
and unquestionable facts that before deciding to go back t
East Germany, Brecht applied for an Austrian passport an
secured a West German publisher and a Swiss bank account
and that in making this decision the prospect of at last ob
taining control of a richly subsidized theatre was at least as
important as his devotion to the interests of the party. Did
this not ascribe the basest motives to a pure believer in the
cause? I am attacked for trying to find an explanation for the
paradox that Brecht *was* a Communist, but that much of his
work was unacceptable to the party as Communist propa-

anda; for searching to establish the connection between
Brecht's political convictions and the structure of his mind
revealed in the imagery of his poetry. Is this not tantamount
to questioning the purity of his motives?

"The fallacy of this approach lies in the naïveté of its underlying, but never openly acknowledged, assumptions. It presupposes that there could not possibly be a moral or ethical
dilemma in being a Communist, even for a man of Brecht's
deep sensitivity and penetrating intellect; that for a Communist all decisions would automatically flow from the basic
equation that everything that is good for the party is good
for all its believers, and that thus, for example, a Communist
could not possibly hesitate before deciding to settle in East
Germany, or make some arrangements to safeguard his political independence; and that it is sacrilege to suggest that
there may be a conflict between the poet's instinct for truth
and the party's propaganda requirements. These, however,
are the basic assumptions of the most puerile level of Communist hagiography which, admittedly, form the foundation
of the terrifyingly simple-minded picture of Brecht as a latter-
day Communist classic painted by the same East German
propagandists who attacked him in his lifetime as a dangerous
formalist and revisionist. To turn a complexly motivated human being into a cardboard poster seems to me a far more
reprehensible and repulsive act of denigration than an honest
and objective assessment of his personality. I admire Brecht
for being a shrewd and realistic person who pursued a policy
of enlightened self-interest, because he felt that he had something important to say and therefore ought to do his best to
survive in his troubled times rather than indulge in empty
heroic gestures. He never tires of praising the unheroic heroes
like Schweik or Azdak who manage to achieve what they set
out to do even at the cost of occasionally appearing less than
brave, virtuous, or truthful. This was the system of ethics
taught by Brecht's alter ego, the charming and worldly wise
Mr. Keuner:

'The bearer of knowledge must not get involved in fights;
nor speak the truth; nor fail to eat; nor refuse honors;

nor be recognizable. The bearer of truth has, of all virtues only one: that he carries the truth within him,' said
Mr. Keuner.*

And Brecht certainly regarded himself as the bearer of an im
portant truth. Is it really an insult to suggest that for its sak
he sometimes did not refuse honors like the Stalin Prize, tha
sometimes he tried to make his real motives unrecognizable
that for its sake he refused to starve, that for its sake he some
times retreated when challenged to a fight? Those who throv
up their hands in horror when confronted with the image o
Brecht as a complex, contradictory, modern, and therefore fa
from guiltless, human being, instead of their own oversimpli
fied comic-strip conception of a superman hero, do in fact be
tray an amazing insensitivity toward the truly heroic, becaus
tragically ambivalent, aspect of their idol. It is, of course
fully understandable that the family and immediate circle o
a great man would rather see some aspects of his character
his meanness in money matters perhaps, or the multiplicity
of his love affairs, glossed over. But, in the long run, the 'offi
cial, authorized' biographies of great men usually do mor
harm to their memories than the most irreverent. Even th
failings of a great poet are valuable: they may reveal th
sources of his poetry.

"There is only one other misunderstanding I should like to
clear up. It concerns my method. In his brilliant, and deeply
perceptive, essay,† Ernest Borneman criticizes me for—o
compliments me on?—the fact that the way I build up my
picture of Brecht from his biography and background towar
a psychological and critical appreciation of the man and artist
amounts to my using a Marxist, or crypto-Marxist, approach
This is a very penetrating observation, but it is valid only i
the term 'Marxist' is taken in its very widest sense, if, in fact
Marx could claim to be the only philosopher who insisted
that all arguments should proceed from a foundation of solid
fact. Marx may have been convinced that he had discovered
the application of the scientific method to social (and per-

* "Von den Traegern des Wissens," Versuche 1.
† "Two Brechtians," The Kenyon Review, Summer 1960.

⟶aps also literary) analysis, but that does not mean that the ⟶cientific method was discovered by Marx. It is quite true ⟶hat the argument of this book does proceed in a somewhat ⟶lialectical fashion. But this is inherent in the character of ⟶3recht, who was a personality of contradictions and para⟶loxes, rather than in the method of the argument. In fact, ⟶3recht's divided nature, in its alternation between anarchy ⟶nd discipline, is the key to his deeply felt affinity to the ⟶Iegelian and Marxist dialectic. Moreover, as Borneman ⟶ightly points out, my book also relies on the use of modern ⟶sychological concepts and employs a system of philosophical ⟶nd literary categories and values that would be anathema ⟶o Marx himself, let alone the scholastic dogmatists who ⟶laim to be the champions of Marxism today. Although I ⟶tart from the facts of Brecht's life and background, my ⟶concern is to explain the relationship between Brecht's poetic ⟶enius and political convictions through an analysis of the ⟶sychological foundations of his personality revealed in the ⟶magery of his poetry; a genuinely Marxist approach would ⟶e in the diametrically opposite direction: from his social ⟶nd class background toward his psychology. Nor is my final ⟶conclusion, as Borneman would have it, that 'the sole therapy ⟶or creative artists of Brecht's stamp . . . is to submit to ⟶Communist discipline,' but, on the contrary, that conversion ⟶o Communism may often be the symptom of that pro⟶found psychological disturbance, the wound of the poet, for ⟶which his *creative genius* provides the therapy."

So much for what I wrote in answer to criticism of this book in 1960. I stand by it today.

This new edition thus presents the same point of view as the first version of the book; but I have added a good deal of detail to my arguments from the material now available.

The bibliography has been brought up to date by the inclusion of many books on Brecht. The list of articles from periodicals, on the other hand, remains substantially the same as in the earlier edition: the inclusion of all the articles written about Brecht in the last ten years would have burst the bounds of a single volume; and besides, it would be futile to include anything other than material which I had actually used in writing my book.

On the other hand, I have given an extensive table of contents of the new collected Suhrkamp edition of Brecht (1967) and have listed the translations of Brecht's work most readily available in the English-speaking world.

My thanks are due to the numerous friends who drew my attention to errors and omissions, and especially to Eric Bentley, whose vast knowledge of Brecht was always at my disposal and whose enthusiasm and generosity played a vital part in getting this book—and its new edition—published.

M.E.

London, May 1970

INTRODUCTION

There can be little doubt that Bertolt Brecht is one of the most significant writers of this century.

German literature, unlike that of France, Italy, pre-revolutionary Russia, or Scandinavia, is on the whole so remote from the taste and aesthetic conventions of the English-speaking world that its influence does not often make itself felt. Yet occasionally an author writing in German imposes himself and leaves a lasting impression. Kafka was one of these, Brecht is another. His influence on the theatre may well prove as powerful as that of Kafka on the novel.

It is an influence that has already left its mark; it did so long before Brecht's name itself was ever mentioned. Auden and Isherwood's early plays, and a good many of the poems of their left-wing phase, clearly owe a debt to the early Brecht. In an entirely different sphere, the contemporary American musical with its blending of serious purpose in the book with popular tunes certainly derives to some extent from Brecht's experiments in *The Threepenny Opera*.

This first, anonymous and unacknowledged impact of Brecht's ideas was followed, after an interval, by a second, more direct wave of his influence. This spread from Brecht's own theatre in East Berlin, which gave him an opportunity to demonstrate the full range of his powers. His fame as a theatrical reformer was carried to western Europe by visitors to Berlin and led to triumphant appearances of Brecht's Berliner Ensemble in Paris and London. Brecht's name became a household word, the daily coinage of drama critics. His theories were quoted in support of a multitude of contradictory causes. And his adherence to the East German Communist regime further confused the issue. Some argued that his greatness as a director, backed by subsidies received from a Communist government, proved the cultural superiority of the Eastern camp, while others condemned him on the ground that he was a Communist propagandist and therefore could not be a great artist.

But Brecht's case defies such simplifications. It is far more complex and constitutes a curious paradox: Brecht was a Communist and also a great poet. But while the West liked his poetry and distrusted his Communism, the Communists exploited his political convictions while they regarded his artistic aims and achievements with suspicion. To understand this paradox it is necessary not only to examine Brecht's professed opinions, his background, and his works, but also to subject them to an objective, critical analysis.

This book attempts to be such a factual, yet critical, study of Brecht's artistic personality. It is not primarily a biography. The time is not yet ripe for a full-scale story of Brecht's life. He died in 1956. Much of the material essential for a full account of his personal fortunes will not be available for a long time to come. His life was rich in love affairs and acrimonious disputes. Most of the documents about these cannot as yet be accessible to objective scrutiny. But enough about Brecht and his public persona is known to draw a fairly circumstantial picture of his character and the main events of his life, which will suffice to elucidate some of the more puzzling aspects of his colorful and contradictory personality.

Brecht's importance transcends his significance as a dramatist, poet, or amusing personality. He is above all an epitome of his times. Most of the crosscurrents and contradictions, moral and political dilemmas, artistic and literary trends of our time are focused and exemplified in Brecht's life and its vicissitudes. Through his commitment to a political cause, through his participation in the struggles of pre-Hitler Germany, his experience as an exiled writer in Europe and America, and his plunge back into the drab but fascinating half-light of East Berlin, Brecht was more deeply involved in the conflicts of his age than most of his contemporaries. His experiences concentrate and distill its basic issues: the reaction

f the generation of the First World War to the collapse of
heir entire civilization; the dilemmas facing a sensitive and
passionate personality in an age of declining faith; the dangers that beset an artist whose indignation about the social
evils of his society drives him into the arms of totalitarian
orces; the theoretical and practical difficulties encountered
by a writer of genius in a rigidly authoritarian society; the
choice between lavishly subsidized but severely restricted
working conditions in a Communist state and the limitations
mposed on the artist by a free, but commercial, society.

However the most intriguing question posed—and largely
answered—by Brecht's experience is: how far is it possible for
a great writer to adhere to a creed so rigidly dogmatic, so
far divorced from the reality of human experience as our
latter-day brand of Communism, without doing violence to
his talent?

An analysis of Brecht's case will, I believe, put this problem in a new light by presenting the factual evidence of a
concrete case of a committed major writer. It should help to
explain why the most important Communist writer of his
time was virtually banned within the Communist orbit at the
same time that he was being used to impress Western intellectuals with the achievements of Marxist culture.

And finally, although the main strength of Brecht's poetic
power derives from his highly individual use of the German
language, an attempt can be made at a critical survey of his
work. His theory of the "epic theatre," which he himself
expounded in a most confusing manner and which has since
been further confounded by commentators hypnotized by the
intriguing technical terms he invented, can be summarized
in simple language and its real content and significance as-
sessed. The real themes of his writing, which lie behind the
surface of commitment and social purpose, can be laid bare
and traced through the bewildering changes of style and tone
of Brecht's Protean œuvre. This in turn sheds further light
on Brecht's personality and helps to explain the motives
which made him an anarchist, nihilist and cynic on the one
hand, and a fervent believer in the collective virtues of discipline embodied in Marxist Communism on the other.

To avoid wearying the reader with lengthy summaries of

plays, novels, short stories and poems which would interrupt the argument if they had to be inserted into the critical as sessment of Brecht's work, a descriptive list of his writings is included in the reference section at the end of the book. This can be consulted as the need arises or studied separately at leisure. A short chronology of the main events of Brecht's career is also provided.

References to books and articles in periodicals and news papers quoted are given in the notes at the end of each chap ter, but in some cases titles have been abbreviated, e.g. Ernst Schumacher's massive study *Die dramatischen Versuche Bertolt Brechts 1918–1933* is referred to as "Schumacher." Full details of the more important sources used are given in the bibliography at the end of the book.

It is impossible to discuss a major writer without quoting from his works. To have given the quotations in the original German would have been both pedantic and discourteous to the general reader. Brecht's poetry is peculiarly difficult to translate, but the quotations are nevertheless given in trans lated form. The translations are my own throughout the book. They make no pretense at giving more than a sugges tion of the meaning and the mood of the passages in ques tion. Readers who know German are referred to the original; exact references to the passages concerned are provided.

As the book was designed to be a *critical* study of Brecht, and an objective account of his political convictions and the resulting tangled relations with the Communist party and au thorities in East Germany, it was impossible to approach his family and collaborators there without running the risk of later involving them in all kinds of embarrassment—and worse. Fortunately this was not necessary. The whole story can be told by studying the ample material contained in newspapers and publications originating in East Germany and presenting the story in irreproachable "official" form. Where personal accounts of events have been used, they were never accepted without rigorous cross-checking against the published facts and other independent sources.

For personal reminiscences of Brecht I am greatly in debted to Prof. Alfred Kantorowicz, Mr. Ernest Borneman, Mr. R. A. Harrison, Mr. Melvin J. Lasky, Dr. F. Wendhousen, and many others. I am particularly grateful to Mr. Eric Bentley for his help with information about Brecht's stay in America. My thanks are also due to Mr. Walter Nubel, New York, for permission to use the list compiled by him of productions of Brecht's plays in America from 1931 to 1956.

Rare books and other valuable material were kindly put at my disposal by Frau M. Dobrozemsky of the National Library, Vienna, Mr. Clemens Heller, Dr. C. Brinitzer, Dr. R. Weil, and others.

Miss A. Scherman helped me in finding my way through the East German Press, and I am most grateful to the Wiener Library, London, which gave me access to their files of newspaper clippings and their collection of periodicals of the German emigration between 1933 and 1945, and also obtained for me material from Germany on microfilm.

I am grateful to Messrs. Suhrkamp of Frankfurt on Main for permission to include quotations from Max Frisch's *Tagebuch 1946–1949*.

Part One: THE MAN

Part One: The Mask

CHAPTER I

FROM AUGSBURG TO BERLIN

(1898–1924)

> I, Bertolt Brecht, am from the black forests.
> My mother carried me, as in her womb I lay,
> Into the cities. And the chill of the forests
> Will stay within me to my dying day.
> BRECHT, *Of poor B.B.*

Throughout his life Brecht loved to picture himself as representative of tormented twentieth-century man—a child of nature exiled to the barren asphalt and concrete cities of the industrial age. Yet the place where he was born and grew up was far from being such a monstrous megalopolis.

The city of Augsburg—*Augusta Vindelicorum*—had indeed once been one of the centers of European trade. But that was a long time ago, when the great merchant princes of the Renaissance, the Fuggers and the Welsers who vied with the Medici in splendor and acted as bankers to emperors and kings, had their headquarters there. By the time Brecht was born on February 10, 1898, Augsburg had long lost its position as one of the dominant centers of the German-speaking world and become a provincial Bavarian backwater, a sleepy place with some ninety thousand inhabitants, a sizable textile manufacture, some paper mills, and a small but rapidly expanding engineering industry. But it had also remained a market town to which the farmers of the surrounding countryside brought their produce.

It was all very quiet and idyllic. Brecht says:

Past my father's house there ran an avenue of chestnut trees along the old city moat; on the other side there lay the city wall with the remnants of ancient fortifications. Swans swam in the water that was like a pond. The chestnuts shed their yellow leaves. . . .[1]

Once a year the farmers came to amuse themselves, and the town put on a show for them:

I often visited the Herbstplaerrer ["autumn barker"], an annual fair of booths on the "little drill ground" with the music of many merry-go-rounds, and "panoramas" that displayed crude pictures of historical events, like "The Shooting of the Anarchist Ferrer at Madrid" or "Nero Surveys the Fire of Rome" or "The Bavarian Lions Storm the Defenses at Dueppel" or "The Flight of Charles the Bold after the Battle of Murten." I remember the horse of Charles the Bold. It had enormous frightened eyes, as though it felt the horror of the historical situation.[2]

Brecht's father was a respected and well-to-do citizen, the managing director of a paper mill. His mother was the daughter of a civil servant from the Black Forest. Theirs was a mixed Catholic-Protestant marriage, and young Eugen Berthold Friedrich Brecht was christened in the Protestant faith of his mother. It would be easy to speculate on the influence of the conflict of faiths in his family on Brecht's ambivalent and self-contradictory character, but there is no evidence to support such an assumption, beyond the fact that his Protestant upbringing accounts for the strong influence the language of Luther's Bible exercised on him. As to the three names he had been given, he later rejected them all, avoiding Eugen and Friedrich with their patriotic overtones, and amending Berthold as the mood took him by shortening it to Bert or hardening the rather sentimental syllable "-hold" (which can mean "lovely") into Bertolt.

He was a sensitive and taciturn child, nonconformist and rebellious in a quiet, negative way. It may be of some significance that his younger brother was the one who followed

closely in his father's footsteps and showed such interest in
the problems of paper-making that he later became Professor
of Paper Manufacture at the Technical University of Darmstadt. Be that as it may, Brecht himself always saw himself
as a rebel and a traitor to his bourgeois background:

> I grew up as the son
> Of well-to-do people. My parents
> Put a collar round my neck and taught me
> The habit of being waited on
> And the art of giving orders. But
> When I had grown up and looked around me
> I did not like the people of my own class
>
> And I left my own class and joined
> The common people. . . .[3]

There is a hint in one of Brecht's later short stories[4] that his
revolt against the respectability of his parents may have been
inspired by the example of his grandmother: at the age of
seventy-two, when her husband died, this old lady suddenly
shocked the family by abandoning the dull, cramped conventions of petty bourgeois gentility and consorting with all sorts
of queer and not quite respectable people. Contempt for respectability in any shape or form and a strong and largely
unfulfilled yearning for the company of "plebeian" people
certainly became dominant features of Brecht's whole life
and character.

On both his father's and his mother's side his ancestors
had been shrewd, hardheaded peasants from Baden. His
friends have often attributed his calculated, cunning and in-
direct approach to intellectual as well as business matters
to his descent from a long line of sly, suspicious country people with their ingrained distrust of city slickers, their scepti-
cism about anything that sounds highflown or pompous.
Brecht's horror of all sentiment and phrase-making, his love
of irony and parody, and his often proclaimed faith in the
wisdom of cowardice may well have had their origins in his
canny peasant blood. That he was already master of this

oblique, "dialectical" approach in his early years is shown by
an often quoted story for which we have the authority of one
of his school-fellows:

> For Brecht and one of his classmates a great deal de-
> pended on their success in the end-of-term test papers in
> French and Latin respectively. Brecht's French was as
> weak as his friend's Latin, and both papers came back
> with numerous corrections in red ink—and bad marks.
> Brecht's friend tried to retrieve the situation by erasing
> some of the corrected mistakes, substituting the correct
> versions and complaining to the Latin master that his
> paper had received too low a marking. But the Latin
> master held the paper up against the light and imme-
> diately saw that it had been tampered with. Brecht had
> a far subtler plan: he liberally inserted additional red
> marks in places where his translation had been quite cor-
> rect, then went to his French master and very tactfully
> and humbly queried some of these corrections. The mas-
> ter was highly embarrassed at having absent-mindedly
> faulted some perfectly correct phrases, apologized, and
> hastened to give Brecht's paper a much higher marking.[5]

Always a rebel, Brecht maintained that he learned more
from opposition than emulation in his schooldays. As he put
it:

> Elementary school bored me for four years. During my
> nine years at the Augsburg Realgymnasium [high school]
> I did not succeed in imparting any worthwhile education
> to my teachers. My sense of leisure and independence
> was tirelessly fostered by them. . . . By indulgence in
> all kinds of sport I acquired some heart trouble which in-
> troduced me to the mysteries of metaphysics. . . .[6]

Brecht was sixteen when the First World War broke out,
and he soon got into trouble with the authorities in his Real-
gymnasium by voicing violently pacifist views in an essay on
the theme of *"Dulce et decorum est pro patria mori. . . ."*

Only the intercession of one of his teachers who pleaded that the war must have completely upset the sensitive boy's mind saved him from being expelled. At this time he was already contributing occasional book reviews and poems to a local newspaper under the pen name "Berthold Eugen." The journalist who helped him to get his first efforts printed later described him as "a shy, reserved young man, only able to speak after the clockwork inside him had been wound up."[7]

He can hardly have been as tongue-tied in the company of his schoolmates, for he became the center of a circle of faithful friends who remained loyal to him all his life, chief among them Caspar Neher, the eminent painter and stage designer, whose work was always closely linked with Brecht's.

In 1916 he left school and moved to Munich, where he began to read medicine and science at the university. But after a few terms he had to interrupt his studies. It was wartime and he was called up. Being a medical student, he became a medical orderly in a military hospital.

There can be no doubt that this was one of the decisive events of his life.

I was mobilized in the war [he told Sergei Tretyakov] and placed in a hospital. I dressed wounds, applied iodine, gave enemas, performed blood-transfusions. If the doctor ordered me: "Amputate a leg, Brecht!" I would answer: "Yes, Your Excellency!" and cut off the leg. If I was told: "Make a trepanning!" I opened the man's skull and tinkered with his brains. I saw how they patched people up in order to ship them back to the front as soon as possible.[8]

In fact it is most unlikely that Brecht did any of these things. It now appears certain that, when he started his service as a medical orderly in the fall of 1918, he was assigned to department D which specialized in venereal disease. He took his service very easy, moreover, and occasionally appeared in the hospital dressed in civilian clothes of a very dandified kind. When, however, one evening he sent his parents' maid to give his superior, a kindly dermatologist, the

daily report on his charges in the VD ward, he had gone too
far and was severely admonished.

But whether he actually helped in operations or merely
saw the casualties of war from a safe distance, there can be
no doubt that Brecht was deeply affected by the sufferings he
encountered in the military hospital. His poetry is haunted
by images of dismembered bodies, a fanatical pacifism became the basis of all his political thought, and his implacably
violent attitude clearly sprang from the impotent rage of the
helpless bystander, yearning to inflict the same cruel treatment upon all those he felt responsible for such senseless
mutilation. Even Brecht's ostentatious display of defiant
toughness in later life, the disgusted rejection of anything
even remotely smacking of high-minded sentiment, whether
religious or patriotic, can be seen as the reaction of a basically
tender mind shaken to its core by the sheer horror of existence in a world where such suffering was allowed to happen.
Whether he had been religious or not in any conventional
sense, the blatant cynicism of his public persona in later life
is all too obviously the mask of one whose faith has been
shattered and who had decided to meet the world on its own
inhuman terms.

This is the experience behind Brecht's first characteristically Brechtian poem, *The Legend of the Dead Soldier*, a
ballad about a dead body that is dug up and solemnly pronounced fit for military service in the fifth year of the war,
because the Kaiser needs more cannon-fodder:

> *They poured some brandy down his throat*
> *The rotten corpse to rouse.*
> *Two hefty nurses grabbed his arms,*
> *And his half-naked spouse.*
>
> *Because the rotten body stank,*
> *A parson limped ahead*
> *And over him his incense swung*
> *To cover the stench of the dead.*[9]

And so the dead soldier is paraded through the streets in solemn procession:

The band in the van with rum-tum-tum
Played him a rousing march.
The soldier as he had been drilled
Kicked his legs high from his arse.[9]

The determination to shock, to be as coarse and crass as possible, is only too clear. But so is the shattered faith behind the defiance and despair:

You could not see him for the crowd
Thronging round him with hurrahs!
One might have seen him from on high:
But nothing was there—but the stars.[10]

When the revolution came in November 1918 and was followed by a brief spell of Communism in Bavaria, Brecht was wholeheartedly on the side of the revolutionaries. As he told the audience in the Kremlin when he was given the Stalin Peace Prize in 1955:

I was . . . twenty when I saw the reflection of the great fire [of the Russian Revolution] in my own home town. I was a medical orderly in an Augsburg military hospital. The barracks and even the military hospitals emptied, the ancient city suddenly filled up with new people, who came in large numbers from the outskirts. . . .[11]

Twenty years earlier he had related the same episode in somewhat less idealized terms to Sergei Tretyakov:

I was a member of the Augsburg Revolutionary Committee. The hospital was the only military unit in the town. It elected me. . . . We did not boast a single Red Guardsman. We didn't have time to issue a single decree or to nationalize a single bank or to close a single church. After two days General Epp's troops came to town on their way to Munich. One of the members of the revolutionary committee hid at my house until he managed to escape.[12]

Soon the whole revolutionary episode was forgotten. Brecht returned to the Bohemian life of a medical student in Munich. He had started to write plays. Characteristically his very first effort originated in his fury about an existing play, *Der Einsame* by Hanns Johst (later the leading poet of Nazi Germany), which had been published in 1917. This is a dramatic biography of the German poet Grabbe, who was an outsider and drunkard but a genius. Brecht, discussing the play with his school friend George Pfanzelt, criticized the false idealism and sentimentality with which Johst had presented the life of a dissolute character. When challenged to do better, he wagered with Pfanzelt that he would write a better play on a similar theme in four days. And he did, although it seems unlikely that he took no more than four days to do it. Dieter Schmidt, who has devoted an excellent book to the origins, background and varying versions of Brecht's first play, comes to the conclusion that it took him approximately five weeks to complete the first version.

Baal like Johst's play tells the story of a poet, an antisocial outsider who seduces women, throws them to the dogs afterwards, and finally murders his best friend in a fit of homosexual jealousy reminiscent of Verlaine's attack on Rimbaud. The play is preceded by an orgiastic ballad in the style of *The Legend of the Dead Soldier*. *Baal* is a wild and extravagant effusion in the tradition of Buechner's *Woyzeck*, episodic and disjointed but carried along by a torrent of powerful images that unmistakably bear the marks of genius.

Brecht knew that *Baal* had little chance of being performed. So he wrote another play, with an eye to the requirements of the moment. Lion Feuchtwanger, the novelist, playwright, and man of letters, then thirty-five and already an established author, has described how Brecht came to see him with this play:

At the turn of the year 1918, shortly after the outbreak of the so-called German Revolution, a very young man came to my Munich apartment, thin, badly shaved, and unkempt in appearance. He slunk around the walls, spoke Swabian dialect, had written a play, and was called Bertolt Brecht. The play was called *Spartakus*.

Unlike most young authors, who on handing over their manuscripts have a habit of pointing to their bleeding hearts from which their work has been torn, this young man stressed that he had written his play *Spartakus* exclusively to make money.[13]

Feuchtwanger read the play. It was about a soldier who had come back from the war and was drawn into the revolutionary troubles of the "Spartakus" uprising in Berlin. He was impressed.

> I . . . telephoned the unkempt young man and asked him why he had lied to me; he could not possibly have written this play merely out of material necessity. At this the young author became very violent and dialectical almost to the point of incoherence and declared that he had indeed written this play for money's sake only; but that he had another play as well, which was really good and he would bring it to me. He brought it. It was called *Baal* . . . and turned out to be an even wilder, even more extravagant and very splendid piece of work.[14]

Feuchtwanger, who was fourteen years older than Brecht, helped him with his plays, and *Spartakus*, renamed *Trommeln in der Nacht* (*Drums in the Night*), later became Brecht's first stage success.

But that was almost four years later. In the meantime Brecht led the life of a student who was gradually drifting into the world of the theatre and literature, a world of smoke-filled cafés and taverns, endless discussions, and a great deal of dissipation. Brecht would sing the *Ballad of Baal* and *The Legend of the Dead Soldier* in taverns and coffee houses, accompanying himself on the guitar or banjo and bawling out the verse in his high-pitched voice. Often some living ex-soldiers with patriotic sympathies would take exception to the sentiments expressed in the ballad about the dead soldier and give the young bard a good hiding.

But he also made interesting acquaintances in this way. Peter Suhrkamp, who became his firm friend and later his publisher, has described how he met him in some rural Ba-

varian tavern, singing his ballads to a group of coachmen and
carters.[15] And the strange young vagabond poet also had a
fascination for women when he sang his ballads. In his novel
Erfolg (Success), Feuchtwanger describes young Brecht
thinly disguised as Kaspar Proeckl, a motorcar designer, a
casting a peculiar spell on women:

> Of course, this fellow was always unshaven. But the way
> he made his hair grow over his forehead had a kind of
> naïve coquettishness. He smelt like soldiers on the
> march. Nor did his angular, malicious sense of humour
> seem the right thing for the ladies. There was an un-
> mistakable odour of revolution about him. Clearly it was
> his way of singing his crude ballads that did it. When he
> sang them with his shrill voice women swooned. . . .[16]

And Brecht's schoolmate and fellow medical student, Otto
Muellereisert, later said about Brecht's singing: "He got
ninety per cent of his women that way."[17]

The times were troubled and manners rough. In the ups
and downs of revolution and counterrevolution politics often
came between friends. A story, later told by Muellereisert,
shows that in spite of his violently left-wing views Brecht retained his own special sardonic sense of humor: one day
Muellereisert decided to join one of the bands of right-wing
irregulars, the *Freikorps*, that harassed the Allied armies in
Germany at the time. He wrote Brecht about it. Brecht angrily replied that their friendship was at an end and that he
would not even come to his funeral if Muellereisert were
killed. But a week later he wrote another letter: he had
changed his mind. Stupidity, after all, was not a ground for
divorce. He had reached the conclusion that he would attend
his funeral after all. Muellereisert never joined the *Freikorps*.

In October 1919, while continuing his studies and his Bohemian existence in Munich, Brecht began to commute to
Augsburg to act as theatre critic for *Der Volkswille*, the local
organ of the extreme left-wing Independent Socialist party.
His notices were distinguished mainly by their rudeness:

The man who has leased the Augsburg Municipal Theatre as his milch-cow knows today, after so many years,
about as much about literature as an engine driver knows
about geography.[18]

The personnel of the theatre protested in an open letter
against the tone of these criticisms—only to be rebuked in
even ruder terms. Brecht continued to belabor the management and actors of this no doubt miserable provincial company until the beginning of 1921.

By this time his medical studies had lapsed. Brecht had
finally entered the world of the stage, in the capacity in which
most young dramatists in the German-speaking theatre begin
to make their living: as a "Dramaturg." This post, non-
existent in the Anglo-Saxon theatre, combines the position
of a resident playwright and play-adapter with those of a
reader, literary adviser of the management, editor of the program brochure, and public relations officer. Brecht became
one of the Dramaturgen of the Munich Kammerspiele, whose
manager, Otto Falckenberg, had been impressed by his plays
and was planning to put on *Drums in the Night*. But while
doing a certain amount of work for Falckenberg, Brecht also
tried to place his plays elsewhere, to find a publisher and
perhaps to gain a foothold in the capital city of the German
theatre—Berlin.

In the course of the year 1921 he went to Berlin several
times for this purpose. And there, early in 1922, he met
Arnolt Bronnen. Bronnen (1895–1959) is one of the most
extraordinary, and most controversial, figures of contemporary
German literature. The son of a Jewish-Austrian schoolmaster called Bronner, he rose to fame as one of the leaders of
the Expressionist movement, but later abandoned his left-
wing friends and put his very considerable talents at the
service of the Nazis—having established his racial purity by
making his mother testify in court that he was not her husband's son. Towards the end of the Second World War he
joined the anti-Nazi underground movement, became a Communist, was burgomaster of a mountain village for a time,
and moved to East Germany after the Soviet troops left
Austria.

In 1922 Bronnen was trying to make his way as an autho
while working as a clerk in a Berlin department store. He ha
described how one afternoon, in the apartment of Ott
Zarek, the writer and journalist, who had invited him to te
to meet some literary friends, he had left the drawing roon
and was exploring the large flat:

From one of the rooms I could hear guitar music. . . . I
went in. It was rather dark there; at first I could only
hear a croaking voice. . . . Then I saw the singer: an
emaciated young man of twenty-four with steel-rimmed
glasses and untidy dark hair that fell over his forehead.
I stared at him. I was as if under a spell. I experienced
a sensation which perhaps is only given to very lonely
human beings: to be suddenly confronted with man in
all the richness of his being. He sang, he spoke, he read
aloud, there were four other young people in the room;
I did not see them. I only stared at this one young man.
Later Otto Zarek told me that his name was Bert
Brecht.[19]

Soon Brecht and Bronnen were firm friends. Bronnen's
play *Vatermord* had just been accepted by Moritz Seeler, the
pioneer of Expressionist drama who ran an experimental matinee theatre, Junge Buehne. Brecht insisted that he was the
only person who could direct Bronnen's play. Bronnen agreed.
But Brecht was so undernourished that he fell seriously ill
and had to be taken to the hospital. Bronnen tried to help
him financially as far as his own meager means permitted
and impatiently waited for him to be well enough to start
rehearsals.

Seeler had secured two very distinguished artists for the
main parts in the play—Heinrich George and Agnes Straub.
These already famous actors were horrified when the young
unknown director hurled strings of obscene invective at them
in his marked Bavarian accent. Bronnen's play was written in
the explosive, declamatory style of the Expressionists. But
Brecht wanted to produce it quietly and realistically. Already
at this early stage he hated noisy, emotional tantrums in the
theatre. The stars insisted that the text demanded such out-

bursts. And so the day came when Heinrich George threw his part away with such force that it landed in the fifteenth row of the stalls and Agnes Straub had to be taken away in hysterics. The world première of *Vatermord* was off. Brecht congratulated Bronnen: "It would not have been a success with these actors."

Brecht returned to Munich, having, as Bronnen claimed, plagiarized part of his name: Bronnen had hardened his Christian name Arnold into the more archaic-looking and more original Arnolt, and this, he claims, gave Brecht the idea of turning his own first name Berthold into Bertolt. While Bronnen's play was being performed in Frankfurt and produced by another, more diplomatic director in Berlin as well, Brecht's *Drums in the Night* was also to have its world première. In a letter dated September 22, 1922, Brecht asked the influential Berlin critic Herbert Ihering to come to Munich for the first night

which will be on 29 September (Friday). I know exactly how much I am asking, but very much indeed depends on it for me. Since Berlin has ceased to make experiments, it has become extremely difficult to obtain decent criticism at a time when one needs it most.[20]

The first night at the Kammerspiele was a great success. The audience had been greeted by streamers with inscriptions like "DON'T STARE SO ROMANTICALLY" and "EVERY MAN FEELS BEST INSIDE HIS OWN SKIN." They saw the action taking place in a non-realistic setting, with the picture of the city rising up behind the screens that suggested the walls of the rooms where the soldier Kragler made his decision to marry his shop-soiled bride and turn his back on the revolution, while a red moon hung above like a Chinese lantern.

Ihering *had* gone to Munich. His review in the *Berliner Boersen-Courier* was enthusiastic and brilliantly perceptive:

The twenty-four-year-old poet Bert Brecht has changed the literary physiognomy of Germany overnight. With Bert Brecht a new tone, a new melody, a new vision has entered our time. . . . Brecht is impregnated with the

horror of this age in his nerves, in his blood. This horror
creates a pallid atmosphere, a half-light round men and
things. . . . Brecht physically feels the chaos and putrid
decay of the times. Hence the unparalleled force of his
images. This language can be felt on the tongue, on the
palate, in one's ears, in one's spine. . . . It is brutally
sensuous and melancholically tender. It contains malice
and bottomless sadness, grim wit and plaintive lyricism. . . .[21]

As it happened Ihering acted as adjudicator for the Kleist
Prize, an annual award to the best young dramatic talent, for
the year 1922. Originally he had intended to divide the prize
between Bronnen and Brecht. But in the end he gave it to
Brecht alone. Brecht's reputation as a rising dramatist was
established.

But the road to success was far from smooth. Germany's
leading theatre, Reinhardt's Deutsches Theater, was planning to produce *Drums in the Night* in December 1922.
Brecht returned to Berlin and filled himself up with the un-
limited number of rolls served free with even the cheapest
dish in the Aschinger chain of restaurants. He was so careful
with his money that Bronnen had great difficulty in persuad-
ing him to take an occasional tram. He resisted these se-
ductions by pointing out that extravagance usually leads to
ruin: "The tramride will end in a pauper's grave," he said.[22]

The great Max Reinhardt himself was so fascinated by
Brecht's play that he attended the rehearsals of *Drums in the
Night* every day for three weeks, quietly sitting in the back of
the theatre. But there were difficulties about the casting and
décor, and Brecht greatly disagreed with Felix Hollaender,
who was managing the Deutsches Theater for Reinhardt at
the time. Eventually *Drums in the Night* was a failure in
Berlin. Brecht wrote to Ihering from Munich:

So Hollaender has murdered the *Drums*. What a black
heart that man has in his chest. God will sit in judgment
over him. That will be unpleasant for him. But I too
shall sit in judgment over him. And that will be even
more unpleasant.[23]

In Munich the State Theatre was about to produce an-
ther new play by Brecht: *Im Dickicht* (later revised as *Im
Dickicht der Staedte—In the Jungle of the Cities*). This curious play, with its "motiveless action" which foreshadows
Beckett, Ionesco or Adamov, puzzled the audience when it
was performed in May 1923. And Brecht's earliest effort,
Baal, which had its first stage performance in Leipzig in
December, caused a veritable scandal. One critic called the
play a "mud-bath" and added: "It would have been wiser
and in better taste if the municipal theatre had left this
boy's *tour-de-force*' to people who liked to read this kind of
thing and had spared us, Brecht, and itself this wild evening."[24]

Undaunted, Brecht was already working on a new play. His
contract with the Munich Kammerspiele also required him
to direct. He was asked to tackle *Macbeth*, but felt that such
a task would be beyond him. So he decided to try his hand
on a lesser Elizabethan dramatist, and chose Marlowe's *Edward II*. As he did not like the existing translation he began
to make an adaptation of his own. Lion Feuchtwanger helped
him with this work. Brecht would bring him his version, and
Feuchtwanger would tighten the construction and roughen
the verse when it ran too smoothly. In the end, the play,
while following Marlowe's plot fairly closely, had become an
entirely original work through its unusual form and language:
a balladesque chronicle play in the naïve style of the historical paintings Brecht had seen in the "panoramas" of the Augsburg fairground. Brecht himself directed *Edward II*, which
was first performed in March 1924. In many ways this was
the debut of Brecht's "epic theatre," a production naïvely
sophisticated yet highly stylized. In later years Brecht used
to tell the story of how he had been in difficulties with a
battle scene. He had asked everyone for advice and finally had
come to Karl Valentin, the famous clown of the Munich
beer halls, whom he greatly admired as a folk artist of naïve
profundity. "What do soldiers do in a battle?" Brecht asked
the lanky, quixotic comedian. Valentin replied: "They are
afraid." And so Brecht made his soldiers appear in the battle
with their faces made up chalk-white. The scene produced an
unforgettable effect.

Brecht's artistic personality was already clearly formed i:
these early days in Munich and Berlin. On May 1, 192C
his mother had died and there can be little doubt that thi
was an event as traumatic as his glimpses of the suffering
of war in the military hospital.

In her lifetime Brecht had been a rebellious son. In ai
early poem, "Auslassungen eines Maertyrers" (Effusions of .
Martyr), for example, Brecht describes how he was "playin;
billiards" in the attic where the washing was hanging up t(
dry, and his mother scolded him for getting "pornographic'
thoughts on seeing the dripping underwear—

> . . . and then she cries of course and says: From the
>   washing! And that I would be her death
> And the day would come where I would want to dig
>   her up with my fingernails
> And then it would be too late and that I would realize
> What I had had in her, but I should have thought about
>   that sooner . . .

There is a direct reference to this ironic and frivolous poen
in another which he wrote on hearing the news of her death:

> . . . Many go from us without our holding them back.
> We had told them all, there had been nothing left be-
> tween us, our faces had hardened on saying goodbye.
> But the important things we have not said to each
> other, but have economised with what is most essen-
> tial . . .
> Now my mother has died, last night, on the evening
> of May 1st!
> Now I cannot dig her up with my fingernails!

The mother figures in Brecht's plays, the strange mixture of
irony and violence, the hardboiled disdain for sentiment and
tenderness which pervades his dramatic and lyrical work, all
may be better understood from this kind of reaction to his
mother, his rebelliousness to her, and the guilt feelings produced by her early death.

Brecht's outward persona in those early years remained

at suggested by the cynical first poem on his mother: the
orldly-wise, unsentimental anti-establishment writer. Out-
ardly at least Brecht appeared as the exact opposite of the
nventional German idea of a poet—anything but a with-
rawn individualist who spins the sacred essence of his per-
nality out of himself in the secrecy of some lonely garret.
e was a collective being, always the center of a crowd of
llaborators, asking advice and accepting it from anyone who
red to offer it. Even while lying in a state of collapse in
e Berlin Charité Hospital, Brecht, as Bronnen reported,
as never alone, but "always in a whirl of heads, from which
is own head stood out. . . ."[25] Bronnen describes Brecht's
ethod of work as based on complete relaxation:

> comfortably puffing his cigar Brecht stalked through the
> room listening to arguments and counter-arguments
> from dozens of people, cracked jokes, but stuck unshak-
> ably to his main line of work. He rode his thought until,
> magnificently formulated, he could dictate it to the
> miniature audience of his ever-present aides.[26]

As he regarded his work not as the emanation of some
metaphysical experience but as the product of trial and error,
Brecht was always ready to change and amend his writings.
According to Feuchtwanger

> he rewrites his work countless times, in twenty, thirty
> different versions to suit the needs of any insignificant
> provincial theatre. He attaches no importance whatever
> to the fact that a piece of work is finished. Even if it
> has been printed ten times, the last version always turns
> out to have been the last but one. He is the despair of
> publishers and producers. If his attention is drawn to
> some inner inconsistency, he does not hesitate to throw
> out the work of a whole year; but he would not devote
> a minute to the correction of some blatant error in ex-
> ternal probability. He leaves that to the director, or to
> his secretary, or to Mr. X.[27]

Bernhard Reich, who worked with Brecht at the Munich

Kammerspiele, confirms that this attitude extended to h
own work as a director:

> If the director Brecht liked an actor, the actor had to be
> shown to greater advantage. The poet Brecht immedi-
> ately took a piece of paper from his pocket and wrote
> new text for the actor. The director Brecht discovered
> that the author's intention could not in practice be real-
> ized on the stage. So the poet Brecht arrived the next
> morning with a rewritten and changed text. As the dress
> rehearsal approached, Brecht became more and more
> busy, handing up whole reams of new text to the actors
> from the auditorium. . . .[28]

The power to gather a circle around him testifies t
Brecht's genius for friendship. It is remarkable how, startin
with his schoolmates at Augsburg, all those to whom he gav
his friendship remained his firm friends to the end, often i
spite of political disagreement and across the East–West bar
rier. And yet the same slight, thin young man, unkempt an
unshaven, with his cheap steel-rimmed glasses, his leathe
coat and leather cap, and his rudeness, terrified other people
out of their wits as a sinister individual, sullen, hard, an
disgusting. This dual nature of Brecht's was apparent ever
to his friends. The first edition of his *Hauspostille (Domestic
Breviary)* contains a drawing of Brecht by his friend Caspa
Neher. Underneath it is a revealing inscription in schoolboy'
dog-Latin:

> Iste erat Hydatopyranthropos/ vivens Augustis Vindeli-
> corum/ per unum saeculum/ 1898–1998/ . . . / major
> nisi Himalaya tamen certe Monte Blanco/ Caput Bene-
> volentiae Integritatis/ semper aequam servans mentem/
> pueris puellisque amicus/ inimicis terror. . . .

This touching tribute with its wish that he might live a hundred years and its insistence on Brecht's friendliness and integrity and his friendship for boys and girls recognizes the
inner contradiction of his character by labeling him *Hyda-*

pyranthropos—a man compounded of fire and water—and
terror to his enemies.

In the character of Kaspar Proeckl in *Success* Feuchtwan-
er reveals the deeper layers of Brecht's personality that had
een so terribly hurt by his wartime experience.

That Brecht had stood model for Proeckl was publicly ac-
nowledged by all concerned when passages from the novel
ere linked to a radio portrait of Brecht, broadcast in De-
mber 1930. It is significant that Feuchtwanger has made
roeckl not a poet but an engineer, the designer of a peo-
le's car, an expression of Brecht's attitude to art as a kind
f mental engineering. Proeckl, like Brecht, is talkative, yet
eticent about his own personality and thoughts.

> . . . he had made up a theory for himself, according to
> which he only spoke with people he met about *their*
> affairs, never about his own or about general topics. For
> people usually are well informed only about their own
> affairs, and only on those matters can you learn anything
> worth while from them. . . .[29]

But behind this severely rational attitude of Proeckl-Brecht
es a substratum of sentiment. People do not know, Proeckl
ells himself in a moment of emotional tension, "how much
costs him to suppress sentiment by clear, hard rational-
ty."[30] And another character in the book insists that Proeckl
s driven into a collective, social frame of mind by certain
eep deficiencies within him:

> That you have been taken in by Communism . . . is due
> to the fact that from birth you have been singularly de-
> ficient in social instincts. What for others is a matter of
> course, instinct . . . overwhelms you by its novelty, by
> its scientific façade. You are a poor creature. You are
> unable to feel yourself into other people. You cannot
> have sympathy with others; that is why you are trying
> to get things by artificial means. . . . And on top of
> that—you are a puritan. You lack the most important
> human organs: senses capable of pleasure and a charita-
> ble heart.[31]

This view, which in the novel comes from a character with a strong emotional bias, may be unjust to Brecht, but it shows one side of his nature: a person basically tender, driven to suppress his emotion, to appear hard and rational, a human being so deeply hurt that he has become afraid of being involved in the feelings of others, and therefore appears incapable of sympathy—and empathy. All this is highly relevant to the complex character of the young Brecht. The whole theory of his "epic theatre" is based on the rejection of empathy and of the emotional involvement of the audience with the characters on the stage.

Young Brecht was indeed "compounded of fire and water," a bundle of apparent contradictions: lonely, almost incapable of communicating his deeper emotions, yet constantly surrounded by a circle of friends, admirers, and collaborators; a sensualist and Don Juan, yet a puritan who seemed incapable of real sensual pleasure; an ugly and unkempt figure to some, highly attractive to others, men and women; the soul of courtesy, tact, and friendliness to some, intolerably rude and repulsive to others.

In Feuchtwanger's novel, which presents a wide canvas of Munich life and society at the time of the first Hitler *Putsch* of November 1923, the young motor engineer Proeckl finally leaves Munich—for Moscow. In real life Brecht also left Munich after the beer-cellar *Putsch*. But *he* went to Berlin.

NOTES

1. Brecht, "Bei Durchsicht meiner ersten Stuecke," *Stuecke* (Aufbau Verlag), pp. 12, 13.
2. Ibid.
3. Brecht, "Verjagt mit gutem Grund," *Hundert Gedichte*, East Berlin, 1951, p. 298.
4. Brecht, "Die Unwuerdige Greisin" ("The Unworthy Old Woman") in *Kalendergeschichten*.
5. Told by Herbert Ihering in "Der Volksdramatiker," *Sinn und Form*, First Special Brecht Issue, 1949, p. 5.
6. Brecht in a letter to Herbert Ihering (1922), published in *Sinn und Form*, 1958/I, p. 31.

7. Wilhelm Bruestle, "Wie ich Brecht entdeckte," *Neue Zeitung*, unich, 11.27.1948. Quoted by Schumacher, p. 26.

8. Sergei Tretyakov, "Bert Brecht," *International Literature*, Mos-w, May 1937.

9. Brecht, "Legende vom Toten Soldaten," *Hauspostille*, Berlin, 27, p. 127.

10. Ibid., p. 129.

11. Brecht, Speech on receiving the Stalin (later Lenin) Peace ize, Moscow, 1955, *Versuche* 15, p. 146.

12. Sergei Tretyakov, "Bert Brecht," *International Literature*, oscow, May 1937.

13. L. Feuchtwanger, "Bertolt Brecht, dargestellt fuer Englaen-r," *Die Weltbuehne*, Berlin, 9.4.1928.

14. Ibid.

15. Peter Suhrkamp, "Introduction to Brecht, *Gedichte und ieder*," Berlin and Frankfurt, 1956, p. 5.

16. L. Feuchtwanger, *Erfolg*, Berlin, 1930, vol. I, p. 179.

17. *Der Spiegel*, Hamburg, 9.13.1950.

18. Brecht writing in *Volkswille*, Augsburg, 10.13.1920. Reprinted Sinn und Form, Second Special Brecht Issue, 1957, p. 220.

19. *Arnolt Bronnen gibt zu Protokoll*, Hamburg, 1954, pp. 97–98.

20. Letter from Brecht to Ihering, *Sinn und Form*, 1958/I, p. 29.

21. Herbert Ihering, "Der Dramatiker Bert Brecht," *Berliner oersen-Courier*, 10.5.1922. Reprinted in *Sinn und Form*, Second pecial Brecht Issue, 1957, pp. 230–31.

22. Bronnen, op. cit., p. 110.

23. Letter from Brecht to Ihering dated February 1923, *Sinn und orm*, 1958/I, p. 32.

24. *Leipziger Neueste Nachrichten*, 12.10.1923. Quoted by Schu-acher, p. 42.

25. Bronnen, op. cit., p. 98.

26. Ibid., p. 109.

27. L. Feuchtwanger, "Bertolt Brecht, dargestellt fuer Englaen-er," *Die Weltbuehne*, Berlin, 9.4.1928.

28. Bernhard Reich, "Erinnerungen an den jungen Brecht," *Sinn nd Form*, Second Special Brecht Issue, 1957, p. 432.

29. Feuchtwanger, *Erfolg*, Berlin, 1930, vol. I, p. 170.

30. Ibid., vol. II, p. 266.

31. Ibid., vol. I, pp. 422–23.

CHAPTER II

BERLIN
(1924–1933)

Into the cities I came in the time of disorder. . . .
BRECHT, *An die Nachgeborenen*

Berlin had always attracted Brecht. It really was the moder
megalopolis he so loved to hate; the vast pile of stone, cor
crete, and asphalt so many of his poems speak of, where ma
is lost as in a jungle; the seething cauldron of lust, greed, an
corruption that for him summed up the twentieth-centur
world: dreadful, doomed—and magnificent. As one of his le
ters to Bronnen, written around 1923,[1] shows, Brecht ha
nicknamed Berlin "Mahagonny," so it is clear that Mahag
onny, the town whose rise and fall he made the subject c
an opera, stands for Berlin. And in fact the mythical pionee
city of Mahagonny, a jerry-built jumble of brothels and sa
loons somewhere between the California of the forty-niner
and the Alaska of the Klondike gold rush, where everythin
is to be had for money and the only capital crime is lack o
cash, seems a very apt symbol for the Berlin of the middl
twenties and early thirties.

Berlin was the place where a young man of Brecht's bound
less ambition had to make his way to become famous and t
acquire influence. And Brecht wanted to have influence. Ac
cording to Bernhard Reich, Brecht at that time

> believed that he would have to create for himself a net
> work of followers and believers that would cover the

whole of Germany, people who would work for a new art
of the theatre from key positions—in theatres, publishing
houses, and newspapers. He saw himself as the chieftain
of this band.[2]

he German theatre could be transformed and renewed only
om the center—and the center of the German theatre was
ndoubtedly Berlin.

Brecht moved to Berlin late in 1924. His play *In the Jungle*
as due to be performed at the Deutsches Theater in Oc-
ober of that year, and *Edward II* was to follow at the Prus-
an State Theatre in December. Moreover, he had landed
job as Dramaturg of the Deutsches Theater, which could
fford a number of such literary editors and advisers. Carl
uckmayer, who was one of Brecht's colleagues in this office,
as described how in that dismal and hungry post-inflation
inter he himself would come to his office every morning,
erely to collect the pile of coal briquettes that had been put
readiness by the stove, pack them in his briefcase, and
ave again, accompanied by the approving nods of the porter,
ho was duly impressed by the amount of work the Herr
Oramaturg had taken home again in his bulging briefcase.
s for Brecht

he only rarely put in an appearance in his loose leather
jacket that made him look like a cross between a truck
driver and a Jesuit seminarist. He demanded that full
powers be transferred to himself so that he could mold
the repertoire entirely according to his own ideas and re-
name the Reinhardt theatres "epic smoking theatres";
for he was of the opinion that people might be more inclined to think if they were allowed to smoke in the
theatre. As these demands were rejected, he confined his
activity to occasional appearances to collect his salary.[3]

All the more energetically he plunged into the bustling
activity of projects and counterprojects, endless discussions,
plots and counterplots of the life of the Berlin theatrical and
literary world.

The Berlin theatre at that time was dominated by three

great producers: Max Reinhardt, Leopold Jessner, and Erw
Piscator. Reinhardt had created a colorful style of his own
cross between realism and romanticism, but at that time
was looking for new worlds to conquer: vast spectacles
circuses and giant halls or open-air productions involvi
whole towns, like his *Everyman* at the Salzburg Festival. Le
pold Jessner at the Staatstheater (Prussian State Theatr
was the exponent of Expressionism as applied to the classi
highly stylized productions built around huge staircases. A
finally there was the radically left-wing Agitprop theatre
Piscator, who regarded the stage as above all an instrume
for mobilizing the masses. Piscator relegated the author to
relatively minor position and was often content to comp
his productions out of newspaper reports or documentary m
terial. He put these spectacles on a constructivist stage a
used graphs of statistics, explanatory captions, lantern slid
of photographs or documents, newsreels, and documenta
film sequences to convey the political or sociological bac
ground of the play, while the propaganda lesson was draw
by choruses, spoken or sung, on stage or in the auditoriu
so that the spectators were inevitably drawn into the actio
His aim was a theatre that would be political, technological
and *epic*. By the latter term he meant a drama that would l
utterly different from the conventional "well-made" play-
kind of illustrated lecture or newspaper report on a politic
or social theme, loosely constructed in the shape of a serio
revue, a sequence of musical numbers, sketches, film, an
declamation, sometimes linked by one or several narrators.

Piscator produced the first play billed as an "epic drama
Fahnen (Flags) by Alfons Paquet, a dramatization of tl
Chicago anarchists' trial of 1886. In this production, whic
opened Piscator's tenure of the Volksbuehne in 1924, phot
graphs of the historical figures appearing in the play we
projected onto a screen during the prologue, and after eac
scene a written commentary on the action appeared on tw
boards on either side of the stage. Piscator claimed that "i
a certain sense *Fahnen* represented the first Marxist dram
and the production the first attempt at laying bare the m
terialist motive forces of the action. . . ."[4]

Brecht's later theories of the "epic theatre" certainly we

eatly influenced by Piscator's conception. Brecht also
anted a scientific, Marxist drama, loosely constructed so as
 make it possible to explain the wider social and historical
ackground of the play—"he grew very angry if this invention
f his was explained by his lack of sense for dramatic con-
ruction"[5]—and he, too, used posters and placards, songs,
nd choruses. But while Piscator attached little importance to
urely literary values, Brecht laid great stress on the poetic
spects of such a drama. And so, although Brecht became a
lose collaborator of Piscator's, although he worked on many
daptations of plays for his theatre and they discussed several
oint projects, Piscator never tackled one of Brecht's own
lays.

Both Brecht's and Piscator's efforts on behalf of a modern,
Marxist theatre were, incidentally, viewed with suspicion by
he Communist party, whose interests they were intended to
erve. Brecht had his own difficulties with the party, which
re dealt with elsewhere in this book.[6] As for Piscator, when
socialist realism" became the ruling aesthetic creed in Rus-
ia, his theory and practice were rejected by the Communists
nd classed as formalist aberrations no less heinous than
hose of Kerzhentsev's Proletkult theatre in the Soviet Union.

If Reinhardt, Jessner and Piscator formed the hard artistic
:ore of the Berlin theatre of that period, around them re-
volved a kaleidoscope of lesser lights, ranging from the vul-
;arly commercial boulevardiers who produced cheap farces,
drawing-room comedies, or musical shows—the operetta mer-
chants, as Brecht called them with contempt—to the young
ind struggling *avant-gardists*, talented and untalented, backed
ind without backing, who were trying to come to the fore.
Competition was intense and the tone was decidedly rough.
Rows and scandals, angry accusations and counteraccusations
were the order of the day. In the autumn of 1924 Brecht was
accused of plagiarism. Somebody had discovered that a number of lines in *The Jungle* were taken from a German translation of Rimbaud's *Une saison en enfer*. Brecht cleared himself by pointing out that these lines appeared in quotation
marks in the text and were in fact being quoted by the char-

acter. It was not the last accusation of plagiarism he had
rebut. At another time right-wing circles tried to have
action for blasphemy brought against him for a Christm
poem of his that cast doubt on the divinity of Jesus. T
public prosecutor was reported as having the matter on
agenda. Although Brecht's friend, the painter and cartoon
George Grosz, who had shown Christ crucified wearing a
mask, was brought to trial, the matter did not reach t
courts in Brecht's case. But Brecht gave as good as he g
He and Bronnen vigorously hit back at their main criti
opponent, Alfred Kerr, the doyen of Berlin critics who wr
his exquisite notices in the *Berliner Tageblatt*. Kerr, hims
a poet, was a great believer in the "beautiful," a categc
wholly rejected and detested by Brecht, and never missed
opportunity for voicing his dislike of such dramatic iconocla
and vulgar exhibitionists as Brecht and Bronnen. When Bro
nen's play *Die Katalaunische Schlacht* (*The Battle of t
Catalaunian Plains*) was badly reviewed by Kerr, Brecht
plied in a poem that compared Kerr to the opponents
railways at the time of their invention who had objected
them on the grounds that "they had no tails and ate
oats. . . . Who had ever seen a locomotive producing hors
droppings?" But if Kerr was stubbornly against Brecht, t
other leading Berlin critic, Herbert Ihering, his discovere
staunchly supported him in the *Berliner Boersen-Courier*.

The rows and scandals were by no means confined to t
columns of the newspapers. When Brecht's *Baal* reached t
Berlin stage early in 1926, the first night audience, aware
the play's reputation as strong, scandalous stuff, was ten
with expectation. An eyewitness has described how the stor
suddenly broke loose:

People whistled, shrieked, booed, applauded. The actress
who happened to be on stage by herself jumped onto the
piano and began to bang the keys with her feet, singing:
"*Allons enfants de la patrie!*" The noise grew deafening
. . . and was kept up until the instigators of the scandal
were utterly exhausted. Suddenly everything was quiet
again. Only from one of the galleries one could hear the
words "You aren't *really* shocked, you are only pretend-

ing . . ." followed by the loud noise of a face being slapped. Then applause started, rose to a climax and the performance went on. . . .[7]

A few weeks later Brecht was in the center of another scandal. The Dresden State Opera was producing Verdi's *La forza del Destino* with an entirely new libretto by the poet Franz Werfel. This was considered an event in the history of opera and to mark it, it was decided to invite representatives of the new generation of German literature. Brecht, Bronnen and the novelist Alfred Doeblin were chosen for this honor, and very proudly they traveled down to Dresden in March 1926, to bask in the sun of public recognition and to read from their own works at a special Sunday matinee arranged for them at the Dresden State Theatre on the morning after the first night of *Forza del Destino*. But when the three emissaries of the new generation arrived in the offices of the Saxon State Theatres the bureaucrats there treated them rather haughtily and handed them three seats somewhere on the side in the upper gallery. And there was no invitation to the official reception after the performance. The three young authors were speechless. Solemnly they tore up the gallery tickets and placed them in an envelope to be handed back to the "Herr Generalintendant" of the Saxon State Theatres. Then they left and were not seen again all evening. The next morning they were just about to leave their hotel to take the train to Berlin when the envoys of the authorities came dancing in, apologizing for the mistake that had been made and begging them not to leave them in the lurch with the public already eagerly awaiting their appearance in the sold-out State Theatre.

Gentle, kind-hearted Alfred Doeblin [Bronnen reports in his memoirs] was immediately moved to pity for these eunuchs. . . . Brecht had already got rid of his fury in a little allegorical ballad he had composed and looked upon the proceedings with sovereign disdain. Only I was boiling, and I continued to boil while we were being escorted in triumph to the theatre. . . .[8]

The matinee started well enough. Doeblin read from
works quietly and at great length. Brecht recited his bal
on the incident. It was about three gods who had been
vited to the city of Alibi on the River Alibe (Elbe) to hor
the great Alea (*alea* means dice, and dice in German
Wuerfel, which suggests Werfel), but

> *when they arrived, only the rain had come*
> *To receive them. . . .*[9]

and when they came into the great hall of the city

> *They saw their chairs standing*
> *Where coats are hung up and rotten eggs are boiled.*[9]

And not a crumb fell for them from the table of great Al
Finally the gods had to be prevailed upon not to drown t
city in a great flood. This poem too was received in silence,
the audience did not understand its allusions, and Brecht p
ceeded to read some of his other works. Then it was Bronne
turn, and Bronnen was known for his hot temper. One of t
Saxon bureaucrats was so terrified at what would happen th
he whispered in his ear: "If you keep quiet we'll put on yo
next play!" This attempt to bribe him so enraged Bronn
that he launched into a violent and obscene diatribe agair
the shameful way he had been treated. The uproar that f
lowed is said to have been beyond description.

Brecht's poem about the three gods became the germ tha
at a much later date, burgeoned into the three gods of *D
Gute Mensch von Sezuan* (literally, *The Good Human Bei
of Setzuan*, produced in America under the title *The Go
Woman of Setzuan*.)

Brecht greatly enjoyed these scandals. He disliked the p
lite aesthetic atmosphere of educated and respectable socie
and wanted the theatre to become more like a sports aren
He elaborated this idea in a number of articles and favorab
compared the genuine enthusiasm and technical expertise
be found on the sports ground with the pallid and inexpe

reactions of audiences in the theatre. But, of course, a new
kind of theatre needed a new kind of play and a new kind of
building.

> In the old kind of theatre [Brecht said in 1926] we are
> as out of place with our plays as Jack Dempsey would be
> unable to show his skill in a tavern brawl, where some-
> one could knock him out by hitting him over the head
> with a chair. . . .[10]

To show his disdain for the effete world of the intellectuals
Brecht sought the company of boxers and racing cyclists. Paul
Samson-Koerner, the German light-heavyweight champion,
became his friend and constant companion. In July 1926
Brecht announced that he was writing Samson-Koerner's biography. And when the film of the Dempsey-Tunney fight of
1926 was shown at a Berlin cinema, the performance was
preceded by a poem by Brecht, recited by the well-known
actor, Fritz Kortner.[11]

Brecht's rejection of the over-refined attitude of the aes-
thete in favor of a boisterous sportsmanlike approach led to
another notable scandal of which he became the protagonist.
In the autumn of 1926 a leading literary review asked Brecht
to act as judge in a competition for a poetry prize it was organizing. Brecht accepted and four hundred young poets
sent in their work. In February 1927 Brecht published the
result. He declared himself unable to award any prize at all:
none of the poems received struck him as serving any useful
purpose whatever—and in his view poetry had to be of some
practical use.

> Poetry [he said in his report on the competition] must
> surely be capable of being examined from the point of
> view of its practical value. . . . All great poems have the
> value of documents. They show how their author, a sig-
> nificant human being, expressed himself.[12]

The young poets who had taken part in the contest, however,
had shown themselves as nothing but decadent and uninter-
esting specimens of contemporary youth

whose acquaintance [Brecht rudely declared] I should
much more profitably have been without. . . . Here we
have them once more, those quiet, gentle, dreamy creatures, the sensitive section of a used-up *bourgeoisie*, with
whom I do not want to have anything to do. . . .[12]

And so having refused to award a prize to, or even print, any
of the exquisitely sensitive poems that had been submitted
to indicate what he meant by poetry that *was* of some practical use, Brecht printed a poem that had not been entered in
the competition at all, a very naïve and crude piece of doggerel in praise of a six-day bicycle racing hero of the time,
Reggie MacNamara, which he had found in a cycling paper.
It has the title (in English): *He! He! The Iron Man!*

The uproar created by this decision, and the calculated insult implied by the choice of this poem, can be imagined.
Brecht was accused of various base motives, above all, envy
and jealousy of the superior talent of the poets he was to have
judged. High-minded defenders of the most sacred values of
German literature reproached him with deliberately wanting
to debase the refined and respectable traditions of the nation's poetic patrimony and dragging it down to the level of
vulgar fair-ground jingles. This, of course, was precisely the
reaction Brecht had intended. To destroy the existing values
of ossified sentiment was his aim, and *Épatez les bourgeois!*
his slogan.

And yet certain representatives of an older and more gra-
cious tradition of letters—and manners—recognized Brecht's
importance from the very beginning. One of his earliest sup-
porters among them was Hugo von Hofmannsthal, the gentle
and aristocratic writer of exquisitely melancholy verse, author
of *Der Rosenkavalier* and other delicately constructed Viennese comedies. "He had a high opinion of Brecht and even
admired him in a certain sense, but spoke of him . . . as of
a somewhat sinister person. . . ."[13]

Hofmannsthal wrote a dramatic prologue to the performance of *Baal* by the experimental studio of the *Theater in der
Josefstadt* in Vienna on March 21, 1926. This charming little
piece, which has become a bibliographical rarity, shows members of the company discussing the strange new play they are

about to perform. Each of the actors appears as himself. Oscar Homolka, well known in later years in Hollywood, London, and New York who played Baal in the performance, is made the spokesman of the new drama:

> A play like this represents the ultimate in dramatic unity. These are not just cleverly thought-out words pasted onto a cleverly thought-out plot. Gesture and word have become one. Pent-up forces of the soul break forth and create a new kind of living-space which they fill with themselves.[14]

Behind his gentle mockery of the grandiloquence and exuberant language of Brecht's *Baal*, Hofmannsthal admits, with a gesture of amused resignation, that in the new era that is about to dawn the whole concept of character and of the sacred integrity and unity of human personality will have to be abandoned—on the stage as in life:

> Our time is unredeemed; and do you know what it wants to be redeemed from? . . . The individual. . . . Our age groans too heavily under the weight of this child of the sixteenth century that the nineteenth fed to monstrous size. . . . We are anonymous forces. Potentialities of the soul. Individuality is an arabesque we have discarded. . . . I should go so far as to assert that all the ominous events we have been witnessing in the last twelve years are nothing but a very awkward and long-winded way of burying the concept of the European individual in the grave it has dug for itself. . . .[14]

And so, with a gesture, deprecating yet politely acknowledging his importance, ironic, sardonic, yet with a tinge of horror in his smile, Hofmannsthal introduced the playwright of the violent new age of impersonal collective forces to the Viennese public.

In spite of rows and scandals and other time-wasting activities, Brecht worked with astounding energy in those years.

He had acquired a secretary, who became far more than
secretary to him—Elisabeth Hauptmann, co-author of man
of his plays and a loyal friend beyond the grave. Some note
from her diary for 1926 that have been published shov
Brecht not only writing short stories—mainly to make mone
—but also putting the finishing touches to his comedy *Man
ist Mann* (*Man Equals Man*) prior to its first performanc
in Darmstadt, attending the rehearsals for the production o
Baal that caused the Berlin theatre scandal mentioned above
and pursuing a remarkable number of projects that were t
remain unfinished: a comedy about juvenile delinquents,
play on Charles the Bold, whose picture he had seen in th
"panoramas" of the Augsburg fair grounds of his youth,
revue for Reinhardt, a novel, a play entitled *Dan Drew an
the Erie Railroad,* and another on the machinations of whea
speculators on the Chicago stock market, which later de
veloped into *Die Heilige Johanna der Schlachthoefe* (*St
Joan of the Stockyards*). Over and above all this, Brecht wa
assembling his first major collection of poems, which wa
published in the course of 1926 in an edition limited to onl
twenty-five copies under the title *Taschenpostille* (*Pocke
Breviary*). This book, which contains some pretty scandalou
poems, was made up to look exactly like a prayer book, boun
in flexible black leather and printed on Bible paper ir
two columns with titles in red and the lines of the poem
running on like Bible verses. The ordinary edition of thi
book was published in 1927 under the title *Hauspostille
(Domestic Breviary*), looking like a conventional volume o
poems.

Apart from all this literary activity Brecht continued t
work on his own education. His project of a play about grain
speculators had led him to study economics. It also brough
him face to face with the problem of how the theatre coulc
deal with the workings of high finance and commerce. Elisa
beth Hauptmann notes in her diary that he began to think

> that the forms of drama as they had existed hitherto
> were not suitable for the exposition of such modern
> processes as the world distribution of wheat, nor for the
> presentation of the life story of present-day human be-

ings. "These things," he said, "are not dramatic in the
accepted sense and if you try to translate them into
poetic terms they are no longer true. . . . But if it is
realized that the present-day world does not fit the established dramatic form, then that dramatic form is no
longer suitable for our world."[15]

After the first night of *Man Equals Man* Brecht took a holiday, which he spent studying *Das Kapital*. The man who
played the most important part in Brecht's development as
a Marxist and to whom Brecht himself used to refer as his
"teacher" was Karl Korsch, who, ironically and significantly,
had been expelled from the German Communist Party as
early as 1926. Korsch (1886–1961) was undoubtedly one of
the most important Marxist thinkers and theoreticians of
his generation. He had been a university teacher, member
of the Reichstag, Minister of Justice in the socialist state
government in Thuringia, and had written important books
on Marxist theory. It was to Korsch, who had remained a
Marxist but was in bitter opposition to the German Communist Party's line, and later to Stalin, that Brecht turned,
throughout his later life, when grappling with problems of
Marxist theory.

As important for Brecht's subsequent development as his
encounter with *Das Kapital*, Karl Marx and Karl Korsch was
the beginning of his collaboration with the composer Kurt
Weill (1900–50), which dates from this time.
Brecht had always sung his own ballads to the guitar; he
composed the music with the words. Later he also made up
his own music for any songs or ballads that occurred in his
plays. In 1926 he and Elisabeth Hauptmann improvised the
music for the production of *Man Equals Man*, basing the
theme song on *Madame Butterfly*.[16] However amateurish
and primitive this Brechtian music may have been, it had an
unmistakable personal touch, which shines through the musical treatment of his poetry by composers as individually different and original as Weill, Hanns Eisler, and Paul Dessau,

and which springs from the highly personal music of Brecht ian verse as well as from the more direct effect of Brecht' assistance and advice in working with the composer.

Brecht's attitude to music was highly idiosyncratic. He hated Beethoven and the sound of violins, but liked Bach and Mozart. But above all he disliked the atmosphere of concerts: the spectacle of frock-coated gentlemen sawing away at their instruments, of polite and educated people gently bored and pretending to be moved. So great was Brecht's contempt for this kind of music that he rejected the term itself and designated the music he liked by a new generic term he had invented for himself: *misuk*. Brecht's composer friend Hanns Eisler finds it difficult to define *misuk*. "It is above all popular," he says, "and it is best described as reminiscent of the singing of working women in the backyards of tenements on Sunday afternoons. . . ."[17]

Brecht had known Kurt Weill since the early twenties. Nicolas Nabokov has described how he, together with Isadora Duncan, the Russian poet Essenin, Brecht, and Weill, had "sniggered indecently" at the old-fashioned Russian world presented to them by Stanislavsky's Moscow Art Theatre at a performance of *The Three Sisters* in Berlin in 1922 or 1923.[18]

Weill, a pupil of Busoni, shared Brecht's contempt for the polite neo-Romanticism of the still dominant style of music in Germany. He too wanted to return to a popular, modern form of musical expression that would be free from the overelaboration of the large orchestra wallowing in beautiful sound, and be harsh, topical in catching the mood of its time, and serve a purpose in fitting into the everyday life of the people.

The sequence of "Mahagonny Songs" in the *Domestic Breviary* gave Weill an opportunity to try out his ideas. His operatic cantata *Mahagonny* was performed at the Baden-Baden festival of modern music in 1927. This short work formed the germ of the full-length opera *Rise and Fall of the City of Mahagonny* and was the beginning of an association that produced Brecht's—and Weill's—greatest success: *Die Dreigroschenoper* (*The Threepenny Opera*). In the course of their co-operation in this and a great many other projects Brecht and Weill mutually influenced each other. Brecht's theory of the function of opera and of the "epic theatre" in general owes a great deal to Weill's ideas.

Another influence, entirely different in kind but no less important, that Brecht encountered at this time was that of a great character of fiction: Jaroslav Hašek's *Good Soldier Schweik*.

Piscator planned a production of this great comic novel of the First World War, but the only authorized adaptation did not meet his requirements. So he called in a team of new adapters—the Communist playwright Gasbarra, Leo Lania, and Brecht—to make a new version, while the names of the authorized adapters remained on the program for reasons of copyright.

Piscator's production of the *Good Soldier Schweik*, which opened in January 1928, was one of his most notable achievements. The great Austrian comedian Max Pallenberg, one of the outstanding comic actors of his day, played Schweik, round-faced, genial in his simulated simplicity, coarse and gentle at the same time. This character moved through a brilliantly conceived comic world, designed by the most bitter of German postwar satirical artists, George Grosz. Or, rather, the scenery moved round Schweik. As the good soldier's "anabasis" proceeded, the backdrop behind him showed the landscape passing as he marched, and the houses, sheds, privies, railway stations, taverns and trees he encountered came rolling onto the stage as he approached them.

Schweik is more than a mere character; he represents a basic human attitude. Schweik defeats the powers that be, the whole universe in all its absurdity, not by opposing but by complying with them. He is so servile, so eager to please and to carry out the letter of any regulation or command, that in the end the stupidity of the authorities, the idiocy of the law are ruthlessly exposed. Brecht not only entered into the ways of thought of Hašek's immortal character so completely that twenty years later he could reproduce the authentic ac-

cents of the little soldier in his own play, *Schweik in the
Second World War;* he also made the Schweikian attitude
his own. Many of the characters in his later plays show features of this ironic servility: the hired man Matti in *Puntila,*
the rascally judge Azdak in *The Caucasian Chalk Circle,* the
great Galileo himself. And these characters are all, in some
way, self-portraits of Brecht. So also is Brecht's perhaps most
completely Schweikian character, Herr Keuner, the hero of a
collection of short anecdotes Brecht started to write in the
late twenties to illustrate his attitude to issues of conduct
and ethics. These Keuner stories provide a key to Brecht's
character. Many of his later actions that have puzzled and
antagonized public opinion become intelligible if seen in the
light of Keuner's, and Brecht's, Schweikian philosophy, based
as it is on the idea that it is often wisest to purchase one's
peace and quiet by a show of compliance and even cheerful
servility towards even the most absurd authorities, regardless
of whether they are the U. S. Committee on Un-American
Activities or the Communist bureaucrats of East Germany.

Brecht's own basic attitude had always contained Schweikian elements, inherited from the Black Forest peasantry to
which his ancestors belonged. But his work on Schweik helped
him to crystallize these instinctive features of his nature into
a coherent and conscious philosophy—a philosophy of enlightened self-interest based on the conviction that survival and
success are more important than the striking of heroic attitudes. Long before this philosophy was put to the test in
Brecht's dealings with Nazis and Communists he summed it
up in one of his most revealing Keuner stories, *Measures
Against Violence.*

In this story Keuner behaves in a rather cowardly manner
when faced with the threat of violence. His disciples ask him
if he has no backbone. He replies: "I have no backbone to be
smashed. I, of all people, must outlive violence."[19] And to
show what he means by this reply, Keuner tells the story of a
man whose home was invaded by an agent of authority who
asked him: "Will you serve me?" Without saying a word the
man served the agent of violence for seven years until the in-
truder finally got so fat that he died. The man wrapped his

body in an old blanket and threw it out of the house. "Then he washed the bedstead, whitewashed the walls, breathed a sigh of relief and answered: 'No.' "[19]

The year 1928, which had started with Piscator's triumphant *Good Soldier Schweik*, was Brecht's *annus mirabilis*. In December he won the first prize in a short-story competition organized by the *Berliner Illustrirte Zeitung*—three thousand marks, at that time a very considerable sum. But by that time he was no longer impressed by such amounts of money. For in the summer he had scored his greatest success: *The Threepenny Opera* had had its first night on August 31 and had made Brecht and Weill famous.

The tremendous success of Nigel Playfair's London revival of Gay's *Beggar's Opera* had drawn the attention of stage circles throughout Europe to this evergreen work. Brecht's secretary and collaborator, Elisabeth Hauptmann, made a translation of the *Beggar's Opera* that so fascinated Brecht that he began to adapt it. In the end the adaptation bore very little resemblance to the original. He transposed the action into seedy Edwardian costume, added songs and ballads based on Villon and Kipling, and made the play into a bitter satire on the bourgeois society of postwar Germany. Weill wrote a brilliant musical score, one of the first attempts to make jazz into an idiom for a serious composer.

The Theater am Schiffbauerdamm decided to take the risk of putting on a play so novel and unusual, but in the course of the rehearsals, which were beset by all kinds of misfortune, leading members of the cast falling ill and having to be replaced at short notice, the management developed serious doubts about the whole venture and was inclined to call it off at the last moment. Eventually the first night did take place, and *The Threepenny Opera* was an immediate success —even if only a *succès de scandale* for some sections of the press and public. It became one of the longest runs in the history of the Berlin theatre, the rare case of a play intended as a work of serious *avant-garde* art achieving genuine popular success. Performances throughout the world, including the phenomenally successful New York revival of the fifties—

although it must be confessed that this adaptation by Marc Blitzstein differs considerably from the original—have proved its immense vitality.

Brecht would not have been Brecht and Berlin not Berlin if the success of *The Threepenny Opera* had not brought its own quota of scandals in its wake. His sudden success made Brecht cocky. He began to suspect the motives of critics who failed to join in the general chorus of praise, particularly if they belonged to the left, whom he regarded as natural allies. The critic of the intellectual progressive weekly *Die Welt-buehne*, Harry Kahn, found *The Threepenny Opera* disappointing, ". . . a green room rag put on with excellent and lavish means. . . ."[20] Brecht countered this with a characteristically mean letter addressed to the critic:

Dear sir, I am compelled to confess that I have made a mistake. When, before the twenty-fifth performance of *The Threepenny Opera* . . . you rushed towards me with the request that I should get you a better seat, I should not have refused it. It was pure *hubris* on my part. Probably success had gone to my head: you said that in the interests of objective criticism it was important to get you a seat farther to the front. I thought at the time that your seat was not too far back for objective criticism. But I have been wrong. It was. . . .[21]

This foolish outburst exposed Brecht to a deserved rebuff. Kahn ironically remarked that of course he had only attacked Brecht's previous play *Man Equals Man* (which in fact he had highly praised) because he had not received a free portion of sausages in the intermission on the first night.

But *The Threepenny Opera* caused more serious rows. On May 3, 1929 Brecht's old enemy, Alfred Kerr, attacked Brecht in the *Berliner Tageblatt* for having plagiarized an existing translation of Villon's ballads by using whole passages from it without acknowledgment in *The Threepenny Opera*. The translation in question was by K. L. Ammer and had been out of print since 1909. Kerr's discovery caused a storm; there were only too many people in literary circles who were delighted to see the successful young poet exposed as a thief of literary property. Brecht defended himself with studied nonchalance. He published a short statement that merely said:

> A Berlin newspaper has somewhat belatedly noticed that in the Kiepenheuer edition of *Songs from the Threepenny Opera* the name of the translator Ammer has been omitted next to that of Villon, although in fact 25 out of my total of 625 lines are identical with Ammer's excellent version. I am asked for an explanation. I therefore truthfully declare that I have, alas, forgotten to mention Ammer's name. This in turn I explain by my basic laxity in matters of literary property.[22]

A chorus of indignation greeted this boastful admission of "laxity." A literary periodical pontificated: "Basic laxity—that in fact means the most sinister determination to get rich at the expense of others. This is fully in accordance with the views of that section of the nation who allow themselves to be amused by Bert Brecht."[23] *Die Weltbuehne* published one of Brecht's poems with a different author's name and added in a footnote: "In spite of his basic laxity in matters of literary property the author of this poem does not lay claim to a fee. . . ."[24] On the other hand, Kerr's attack brought Brecht unexpected allies. The great Viennese satirist Karl Kraus, one of the most brilliant polemical writers of his time, who had been waging an endless feud against Kerr, regarded all of Kerr's *bêtes noires* as his special friends. He came out with a withering attack on Kerr's pettiness in which he declared that in spite of his "immoral sanity" Brecht had "more in common with the real world of poetry and the stage than all the horrid ephemeral crew that have now started yapping round his heels."[25]

All this scandal had an excellent effect on the run of *The Threepenny Opera*. K. L. Ammer's translation of Villon became so famous that it was reprinted, preceded by a sonnet by Brecht in which he gaily confessed that he had "helped himself" to some of it. And, of course, K. L. Ammer, an Austrian officer called Klammer, was given a share in the royalties. According to a recent newspaper account he was still drawing his share of the takings in 1958.[26]

The biggest row in the wake of *The Threepenny Opera's* success, however, concerned the film version.

A film company, Nero-Film, paid Brecht and Weill forty thousand marks for the film rights. But both the author and the composer insisted that they must retain control of the adaptation of book and music. For their work in this respect Brecht and Weill were to be paid separately. Brecht was to receive fourteen thousand marks for the screenplay. The film was to be directed by G. W. Pabst.

In June 1930 Pabst and the writer Leo Lania, who had worked with Brecht on the adaptation of *Schweik* for Piscator and was to collaborate with him on the screenplay of *The Threepenny Opera*, visited Brecht, who was on holiday in Le Lavandou, to discuss the film. It soon became clear that Brecht's views differed so radically from Pabst's that collaboration would be well-nigh impossible. Nevertheless, on August 3, 1930 the film company agreed to Brecht's furnishing the story outline for the film and to his retaining the right to suggest reasonable alterations in the final screenplay. But in due course the company came to the conclusion that it could not follow Brecht's outline. Since he had written the stage version Brecht had become much more radically Marxist in his views, and he insisted on giving the story a far more openly anti-capitalist twist, with Macheath ending up as the president of a bank. The company offered to pay Brecht his full fee for the story if he would consent to withdraw from the work of adaptation altogether. Brecht refused. In the meantime work on the film had already started and the company was investing the at that time enormous sum of eight hundred thousand marks in the project.

While the film was being shot Brecht and Weill sued the company for breach of contract and demanded an injunction against its being shown. This was not only a sensational *coup de théâtre* but also aroused interest as involving the principle of how far the author of an original work could insist on its being filmed according to his views, rather than being treated like any other piece of goods that passes into the hands of a buyer outright after he has paid the purchase price.

The hearings of the case on October 17 and 20, 1930 in Berlin were a social occasion. Everyone wanted to see the famous author of *The Threepenny Opera* pleading his cause. And the sessions certainly were stormy. Brecht theatrically refused an offer by the company's lawyer to renounce all further rights for twenty-five thousand marks. At one point he angrily left the courtroom. The opposing lawyers argued that Brecht himself had shown little regard for literary property in purloining Ammer's translations of Villon. Brecht retorted that in this matter he was not concerned with his own rights but the *rights of the public,* who were entitled to be shown a film version of a play faithful to the author's intentions rather than to have fobbed off on them an inferior product bearing the name of a famous and respected literary work. The Schiffbauerdamm Theatre, where the run of *The Threepenny Opera* had come to an end, dutifully revived the stage version to allow the court to judge the literary merits of the play for themselves.

But it was all in vain. Brecht's demand for an injunction against the company was rejected, largely on the ground that he had never shown sufficient readiness to get down to serious work on the film version instead of merely criticizing the company's version. Weill, on the other hand, won his case; the company had to remove alterations of his score they had introduced and he was given the right to supervise the music of the film.

Nevertheless, Brecht with his native shrewdness fared by no means badly in the end. The company was afraid that he might appeal against the decision of the lower court. To guard itself against the complications any prolongation of the case might cause after the completion of the film, it offered Brecht a settlement if he undertook not to appeal against the decision. In return for a payment of sixteen thousand marks (nine thousand still owed to him for his story outline and seven thousand towards his costs), and the company's undertaking that the film rights would revert to him after only two years, he agreed.

The film was finished and was immensely successful. It incorporated a good deal of Brecht's new story line, but in

Brecht's view in far too prettified a form. And the quarrel
spread. Brecht's staunch friend and supporter, Herbert Ihering, bitterly attacked the well-known Communist script
writer Bela Balazs for having betrayed the left-wing cause in
having gaily stepped into Brecht's shoes and helped to complete the emasculation of a left-wing work in the interests of
the capitalists. Balazs countered by claiming that he had in
fact saved a left-wing work of art from going by default, and
that he had taken the job precisely because he wanted to
preserve the message of the original. To which Ihering retorted by quoting a right-wing paper to the effect that the
story of *The Threepenny Opera* film "has such a fairy-tale-like
effect and is told with such charm and humor that in the
end one completely disregards the intended meaning and just
enjoys the story. . . ."27

Brecht was accused of having once more caused a scandal
for the sake of personal publicity and of having emerged from
it both in a martyr's pose and considerably richer than before. To explain his own case and to show why he had gone
to law, Brecht not only published his own story outline under the title *Die Beule* (*The Lump on the Head*) but also
wrote a long and pretentious essay in which the whole case
was described as a valuable "social experiment" designed to
demonstrate the fact that in a capitalist society it was unthinkable that an industrial project, involving an investment
of eight hundred thousand marks, could ever be stopped just
because the author's rights had been violated. In this experiment he claimed complete success. He had demonstrated
that "justice, freedom, character have all become conditional
upon the process of production. . . ." As to the reproach
that he had settled the action out of court rather than appealing, Brecht argued: "The case aimed at publicly proving
the impossibility of collaboration with the film industry,
even with contractual guarantees. This aim has been fulfilled. . . ." And in any case he had acted not in his own
interest, but in that of the public.

The public was entitled to our trying to obtain justice,
for we had the duty towards the public of making sure

that the spiritual attitude of our work, which is an oppositional attitude, should be preserved in every shape or
form this work might assume. . . .[28]

It will be noticed that in this case Brecht adopted his
Schweikian attitude of pretended servility and ironical ob-
sequiousness not towards the authorities but towards the
public.

It is one of the ironies of Brecht's life that, having written
this lengthy essay to prove that his difficulties in connection
with *The Threepenny Opera* film were due to the inherent
evil of capitalist society, twenty-five years later he was involved in an equally acrimonious dispute about the filming
of another work of his, *Mother Courage,* but this time with
the State-controlled film production company of Communist
East Germany. And in that case he had no opportunity to
seek redress in the courts.

In the meantime, while the various disputes arising from
The Threepenny Opera had run their course, Brecht had been
exceedingly active. He had not only tried to repeat the success of *The Threepenny Opera* but had set out to conquer
entirely new spheres.

The attempt to produce another *Threepenny Opera*
proved a dismal failure. It took the form of a musical play,
Happy End, billed as an adaptation by Elisabeth Hauptmann
"from a short story by Dorothy Lane published in the *J. L.
Weekly,* Saint Louis," with lyrics by Brecht and music by
Kurt Weill. The imitation of the pattern of *The Threepenny
Opera* is only too obvious: an Anglo-Saxon original, adapted
by Elisabeth Hauptmann with poetry by Brecht. The subject of *Happy End* concerns the efforts of a Salvation Army
girl to save the souls of some Chicago gangsters. To win their
confidence she has to become something like a gangster's moll
herself. The American source was pure invention, intended
to give the play the cachet of authenticity and the prestige
of a transatlantic original.

Happy End opened the autumn season at the Schiffbauerdamm theatre in September 1929. The first night ended in a
scandal and the play was immediately withdrawn.

Brecht has often been reproached with having launched this weak play under the name of his secretary. Although h certainly never published *Happy End* in any of the collecte editions he supervised, there can be little doubt that his sha in it was greater than the mere writing of the lyrics. On th other hand, his method of work had always been a collectiv one, and no doubt in this case he had contributed somewha less than in others. He certainly used some of the basic mc tives and situations of *Happy End* in one of his masterpiece: *St. Joan of the Stockyards*, which is also laid in Chicago an also has a Salvation Army girl as heroine.

While *Happy End* was obviously put together with the lef hand, very serious work went into a number of other join efforts with Kurt Weill that marked the beginning of a nev phase in Brecht's development—the *Lehrstuecke* (didacti plays).

If Brecht had started in an exuberant, poetic vein, whicl expressed his anarchic nihilism in strings of extravagant anc earthy images, his preoccupation with Marxism was chang ing his outlook to one of austerity, economy of expression and strictly utilitarian aims. This was wholly in the spirit o the times. Functionalism, the admiration for the beauty o useful objects, the machinery, skyscrapers, and motorcars o America, had produced the movement called "*Neue Sachlich keit*" (New Objectiveness). This opposed the functiona beauty of machinery to the traditional romantic bombast of German literature. Poets were to become social engineers, their work was to be useful in a very practical and concrete sense by stimulating desirable social attitudes. This was the age of "*Gebrauchslyrik*" (Utilitarian Poetry) as of "*Gebrauchsmusik*" (Utilitarian Music). The functional ideal of "*Neue Sachlichkeit*," combined with Marxism and Watson's Behaviorism, which rejected all introspective psychology and confined itself to the study of observable human reactions, led Brecht and Weill to formulate the theory of a new kind of musical drama that would not even try to arouse emotion by depicting the fate of individuals but would teach social attitudes by showing the highly formalized actions of abstract social types. What is more, this kind of musical drama would aim not so much at educating an audience as at educating those participating in the performance itself. Such a musical drama would be a teaching aid rather than an entertainment; it would therefore have to go into the schools rather than the theatre, hence the idea to write *Schulopern* (school operas).

Brecht's first two attempts in this genre were brought before the public during the Baden-Baden Festival of Modern Music in 1929. *Der Flug der Lindberghs* (*The Flight of the Lindberghs*) was described as "a didactic radio play for boys and girls." To avoid even the suggestion of individual hero-worship the part of the heroic airman, Charles Lindbergh, was played by a whole choir of Lindberghs. The music for this dramatic cantata was written jointly by Weill and Paul Hindemith. Brecht's other *Lehrstueck*, presented at Baden-Baden, with music by Hindemith, had a similar theme and was in some ways an extension and elaboration of *The Flight of the Lindberghs*. It has the cryptic title *Das Badener Lehrstueck vom Einverstaendnis* (*The Didactic Play of Baden: On Consent*) and deals with the fate of a group of transatlantic flyers whose aircraft has crashed. While the pilot rebels against his fate, the mechanics consent to die in the cause of human progress. In the course of an interlude, designed to demonstrate man's inhumanity to man, a huge figure on stilts has his arms and legs sawed off by two clowns. During the first performance of the *Badener Lehrstueck* members of the audience fainted during the course of this gruesome scene with its reminiscence of Brecht's experiences in the Augsburg military hospital. The then grand old man of the German theatre, Gerhart Hauptmann, left in disgust.

Brecht's preoccupation with the theme of consent, which in this context means the individual's willingness to sink his private feelings in the common cause of human progress and to agree to become part of an anonymous and disciplined mass, reflects his own difficulties in the face of his decision to throw in his lot with the Communist party. The immoralist, anarchist and nihilist Brecht felt that he *must* find a positive creed. And in those years when the new barbarism of the Nazi movement already loomed on the horizon, the Communists seemed to many German intellectuals the only effective counterforce. That is why the need for the individual to divest himself of his freedom in the interests of a higher cause forms the recurring theme of the *Lehrstuecke*. For Brecht this decision always had the emotional color of a religious act. His next *Lehrstueck*, the school opera *Der Jasager* (*He Who Says Yes*), openly derives the individual's consent from a Japanese religious ritual. This short opera, for which Weill also wrote the music, is based on Arthur Waley's translation of a Japanese Nō play, *Taniko*. During a journey through the mountains a boy falls ill and thereby endangers his traveling companions. In accordance with an ancient tradition, he consents to be killed rather than slow down their progress.

Ironically enough, when this school opera was presented in Berlin in 1930, it was enthusiastically received by circles that saw it as a tract in favor of the Prussian virtues of obedience, discipline, and self-sacrifice. Brecht and Weill visited a number of schools that were rehearsing the play and changed the text according to the wishes and suggestions of the children. The pupils of the Karl Marx Schule pointed out that there was no need for the boy in the play to be killed. Characteristically, Brecht let himself be convinced. He rewrote the play as *Der Neinsager* (*He Who Says No*) and turned it into a passionate plea for the rethinking of ossified beliefs:

> The answer that I gave was false, but your question was even more false. He who says A does not have to say B. He can also recognize that A was wrong. . . . And as for the great ancient custom, I see no reason in it. Instead I require a great new custom, which we must introduce forthwith, namely the custom to think anew in any new situation. . . .[29]

Brecht's decision to alter the *Jasager* into the *Neinsager* at the request of a group of schoolboys shows that he genuinely tried to keep an open mind and that he wanted to resist the temptation of becoming dogmatic. However, when he took up the same theme for the third time, transferring the action from ancient Japan to Communist agitators in modern China, the hero again consented to be killed. The ancient custom of discipline and obedience to orders prevailed, whether the discipline was Prussian, Samurai, or Stalinist, the orders those of an ancient religious rite or Communist policy. On this play *Die Massnahme* (*The Measures Taken*)—one of Brecht's greatest achievements—he worked with a different composer, Hanns Eisler.

The culmination of Brecht's collaboration with Kurt Weill was undoubtedly the opera *Aufstieg und Fall der Stadt Mahagonny* (*Rise and Fall of the City of Mahagonny*), which had its first performance at Leipzig in March 1930. This opera was intended to put an end to the era of mere enjoyment in the opera house. It was an attack against the whole conception of opera as a pleasure of the senses. Bourgeois society, which made these pleasures its sole preoccupation, was depicted as a lawless frontier town, where everything is permitted according to the principle of *laissez-faire* and the only crime is lack of money. At the climax of the action, when the hero is sentenced to death for having failed to pay his debts, the bourgeois public was directly addressed by an inscription flashed on a screen:

MANY AMONG YOU MAY WATCH THE FOLLOWING EXECUTION OF PAUL ACKERMANN WITH DISTASTE. BUT YOU TOO IN OUR OPINION WOULD NOT WANT TO PAY HIS DEBTS. SO HIGHLY IS MONEY ESTEEMED IN OUR TIME.[30]

The first night in the Leipzig opera house again produced a first-class scandal, one of the most memorable in the history of the German theatre. The critic Alfred Polgar has immortalized it in the following description:

Here, there, above, below in the electrically charged theatre contradictions flashed like lightning and aroused further contradictions which in turn gave rise to more contradictions in geometrical progression. And soon the epic form of the theatre spread from the stage to the

auditorium. . . . The woman on my left had a heart
attack and wanted to leave. But when it was pointed
out to her that this was a historic moment she stayed.
. . . A man behind me on the right was heard to observe: "I'll only wait till that fellow Brecht turns up!"
He smacked his lips. Readiness is all. War cries echoed
through the auditorium. In places hand-to-hand fighting
broke out. Hissing, applause, which sounded grimly like
faces being slapped. . . . And in the end: the *levée en
masse* of the malcontents, smashed by thunderous applause. There were impressive episodes: a worthy gentle-
man with the face of a boiled lobster had taken out his
bunch of keys and waged a heroic struggle against the
epic theatre . . . he had pressed one of the keys against
his lower lip and caused streams of air of an extremely
high rate of vibration to pass over the hole at its end.
The noise which this instrument produced had an implacable quality. It cut right through one's stomach. Nor
did his spouse desert him in this hour of trial; a large,
round woman, she was the ride of the Valkyries all over,
with a bun and a blue dress with yellow flounces. This
lady had put two fat fingers into her mouth; she closed
her eyes, blew up her cheeks, and produced a whistle
louder than the key. . . .[31]

This pattern was repeated in a number of other provincial
cities where *Mahagonny* was performed. The political atmosphere of the times was already tense, and here the bourgeois
public felt themselves personally attacked. They did not expect to be insulted in an opera house, of all places. Instead
of uplift they were given a picture of immorality, and then
told that this was an image of their own society. In the provincial parliament of Oldenburg the caucus of the National
Socialist party demanded the cancellation of the scheduled
performance in the local theatre, because *Mahagonny* was a
"concoction of vile and immoral content."[32] But the left was
equally dissatisfied with *Mahagonny*. *Die Weltbuehne* attacked it for its negative attitude and its lack of relevance to
the problems of the moment: "Life is not like that, not even

in the Klondike of yesteryear, certainly not in the America of today, and the relevance of it all to the Germany of 1930 is very thin. This is stylized Bavaria. . . ."[33]

And so *Mahagonny*, however successful it might have been as a satirical spectacle and a musical experiment, failed as an expression of Marxism on the stage.

Brecht, who had become so fascinated with the Marxist philosophy that he had conscientiously attended lectures of the Marxist Workers' College (*Marxistische Arbeiter Schule*) in Berlin throughout 1928 and 1929, decided to tackle a more directly Marxist subject. What fascinated him most about the Communist party was the problem of the subordination of the individual to the collective will. And so he fused the theme of the Japanese schoolboy from *He Who Says Yes* with reports of the Communist party's attempt to organize the workers of China and produced *The Measures Taken*. Brecht got the idea for it from Hanns Eisler's brother Gerhard, who had been sent to China by the Comintern a few years earlier.

The Measures Taken, which is discussed at greater length elsewhere in this book, was originally intended for the "New Music" Festival in Berlin in the summer of 1930. But the committee of the "New Music," to which Paul Hindemith belonged, had qualms about putting on so openly political a work and demanded to see the text. Brecht and Eisler indignantly refused. This led to a breach between Hindemith and Brecht, and so *The Measures Taken* was first performed by the Greater Berlin Workers' Choir (*Arbeiterchor Grossberlin*) on December 10, 1930. The oratorio, which depicted the liquidation of a deviationist by a group of Communist party workers, aroused a storm of indignation—not only among the non-Communists but in Communist party circles as well.[34]

Brecht's conversion to an austere didactic creed also expressed itself in the form in which he now began to publish

his works. His earlier poems and plays had appeared in gay
little volumes. From 1930 on, Brecht issued his current work
in consecutively numbered gray brochures, made to look like
the drabber kind of school primer and entitled *Versuche*
(which can mean "drafts" or "essays" or "experiments" and
was intended to allude to all three of these meanings). Most
issues of *Versuche* contained more than one work by Brecht;
the series was something like a periodical appearing at irregular intervals and devoted to the continuous publication
of Brecht's work in progress. Each separate play, essay or cycle
of poems in the series was numbered, on the pattern of opus
numbers of the works of composers. To show the collective
nature of the work, each item was signed in characters of
equal size with the names of the collaborators: "Brecht.
Hauptmann. Caspar Neher. Weill" (in the case of *Mahagonny*); "Brecht. Suhrkamp" (Note on *Mahagonny*); etc. That
this fiction of collective authorship was largely affectation is
shown, however, by the title page of each issue, which laconi-
cally proclaims the author and contents as BRECHT: VERSUCHE.

Seven numbers of *Versuche* appeared between 1930 and
1933. In 1949 Brecht resumed publication of these gray brochures. Number 15, the last, came out shortly after he died.

In spite of the rather pained reception of *The Measures
Taken* by the Communists, Brecht resolutely continued to
work for the party. With a loyalty and readiness to accept
criticism, most remarkable in a professed cynic and immoralist, he resolved to learn from the "mistakes" of his first attempt and to do better next time. The result was his adaptation of Gorky's *The Mother*, which had its first performance
early in 1932. This play was too openly designed as propaganda to be judged as a work of art by the non-Communist
press. Nor was it intended for a more general public. Neher
had designed sets that could easily be transported and re-
erected in public houses or local halls, and *The Mother* began
to move from one district party center to the next through
the Berlin working-class quarters. The government of the day
tried to stop these performances, even if only on the ground

that the halls in question had not been passed for theatrical performances and did not comply with fire regulations. This led to the actors' giving mere readings of the play, closely watched by the police lest they begin to impersonate the characters. Brecht was delighted. The effect of mere reading was as great if not greater than that of a fully acted performance—conclusive proof of his pet theory that the actors should not even try to pretend to be the characters they impersonate. Despite its propagandist purpose *The Mother* is a moving and impressive play. Hanns Eisler again wrote very effective music for it.

His attempts to make the film version of *The Threepenny Opera* a vehicle of left-wing propaganda having failed, Brecht was eager to make a real Communist propaganda film. With the help of various Communist organizations he succeeded in producing *Kuhle Wampe* in 1932. *Kuhle Wampe* is the name of an area on the working-class outskirts of Berlin where the unemployed lived in shacks. The film was written by Brecht and Ernst Ottwalt. The music was by Hanns Eisler, and Brecht's friend, the young Bulgarian film director Slatan Dudow, directed it.

Kuhle Wampe describes the plight of the unemployed during the great economic crisis and, among other things, bitterly attacks the Social Democrats for their old-fashioned, petty bourgeois outlook. After showing the demoralization of some young workers by idleness and hopeless waiting for jobs, it ends in a surge of optimism and activity symbolized by a workers' sports rally.

Kuhle Wampe immediately ran into trouble. The government banned the film on the ground that it offended the President of the Republic by linking a young worker's suicide with the appearance of a presidential emergency decree; that it maligned the administration of justice in depicting the eviction of a family by the police; and that it exposed religion to ridicule by showing naked youths plunging into the river to the sound of church bells.

In a posthumously published account Brecht has described

the interview between the producers of the film, himself,
Eisler and Dudow, and the censor. The censor criticized the
film because it neglected the individual features of the characters and showed them as generalized types. The young
worker who committed suicide appeared not as an individual
but as the representative of all young workers who were denied the right to live, etc. "No, gentlemen," he exclaimed,
"you have not acted as artists. You were not concerned in
showing a tragic individual case. We would never have denied
you the right to do that!"[35]

The makers of *Kuhle Wampe* were pained. The censor had
very precisely summed up their original intention. They had
done their work too well and had been found out. Brecht,
with his usual cynicism, came to the rescue:

I rose and, in spite of my revulsion against speeches, I
made a speech. I stuck strictly to the untruth. I quoted
the individual features we had given our unemployed,
for example, that he had put away his wristwatch before
jumping out of the window. . . . I protested against the
horrible accusation that we had not acted strictly as artists . . . and I shamelessly asserted that my honor as an
artist had been called into question. . . .[35]

In the end this cynical maneuver succeeded. The film was
passed with a few minor cuts. Brecht noted:

Leaving the building we did not conceal our high opinion of the censor. He had penetrated the essence of our
artistic intentions with far greater sagacity than our most
benevolent critics.[35]

Kuhle Wampe, which was shown in America under the
title *Whither Germany?*, was the only Communist film ever
produced in the Weimar Republic.

In the winter of 1930–31, when unemployment was at its
peak in Berlin, Brecht and Elisabeth Hauptmann had roamed

the soup kitchens of the Salvation Army. Ever since 1926 Brecht had wanted to write a play on the workings of capitalist society. The writings of Lincoln Steffens and other muckraking American authors, Upton Sinclair's *The Jungle* and accounts of the destruction of coffee and wheat to raise prices contributed to the somewhat crude idea he had formed of the great buccaneers of capitalism like Dan Drew and Commodore Vanderbilt. His original idea of a play on the wheat speculators of the Chicago Stock Exchange had come to nothing. Another play, *Der Brotladen* (*The Bread Shop*), which uses a chorus of unemployed (who rhapsodize on the mysterious actions of the rich with their unfathomable consequences for the poor in the same vein as the chorus in a Greek tragedy would bewail the equally unfathomable workings of fate), also remained unfinished. In this play Brecht had introduced a Salvation Army girl to show the absurdity of wanting to solve economic problems by mere charity. This character, Miss Hippler, coalesced with the Salvation Army girl in the abortive musical *Happy End* into Joan Dark (i.e. d'Arc), the heroine of *St. Joan of the Stockyards*.

St. Joan of the Stockyards is one of Brecht's greatest and most characteristic works. Like all his best plays, it moves on several levels. On one of these levels it is a devastating parody of German classical drama, above all of one of the silliest plays in the German classical canon, Schiller's *Maid of Orleans*, and of Goethe's *Faust*. The meat-packers of the Chicago stockyards talk in the bombastic blank verse of Schiller's romantic heroes:

> *Remember, Cridle, how some days ago*
> *We crossed the stockyard as the evening fell*
> *And standing by the newest canning plant*
> *Remember, Cridle, how we saw that ox*
> *Great, blond and sullen looking at the sky*
> *As it received the deathblow: oh, I felt*
> *It had been meant for me; oh Cridle, Cridle,*
> *Ours is a bloody business. . . .*[36]

It is also an attempt, and a rather naïve one, to look behind the scenes of big business and stock-exchange operations. And thirdly, *St. Joan of the Stockyards* returns to the question of ends and means. The capitalist Pierpont Mauler is shown with the hardly concealed admiration that Brecht, like Shaw, had for the ruthless millionaire operator. In fact, *St. Joan of the Stockyards* combines features of Shaw's *St. Joan* and *Major Barbara*.

It was a portent of the times that by 1932 Brecht, although an acknowledged and famous playwright, could not get a theatre to put on *St. Joan of the Stockyards*. Apart from a shortened radio version, broadcast from Berlin in the spring of 1932, *St. Joan of the Stockyards* remained unperformed until April 30, 1959, when it had its first stage performance in Hamburg.

Throughout the eight years of this first Berlin period Brecht retained the public persona of the literary *enfant terrible*. At the height of his fame and prosperity he continued to sport his highly personal getup; he wore waistcoats with cloth sleeves, a leather tie, a mechanic's or lorry driver's leather jacket and a dirty visored cap. He was still unshaven. But some of the more malicious observers of the time alleged that he wore exquisite silk shirts under this proletarian costume. His hair was combed forward in a fringe, and the steel-rimmed glasses of a minor civil servant or village schoolmaster were the most prominent feature of his face. He drove round Berlin at great speed and considerable risk to himself and his passengers in an open Steyr car, earned by writing an advertising jingle for the makers—a mercenary act for which the defenders of the romantic view of the German poet's ethereal and spiritual mission held him in contempt.

With his strange appearance and studied arrogance Brecht aroused feelings of physical disgust and violent loathing in the breasts of many respectable people—which was precisely what he intended. He loved being taken for a very "dangerous fellow," and enjoyed paining worthy literary critics by remarking in a condescending tone: "I have nothing against Ibsen or Schnitzler. They are very good—for their own time and their own class."[37] But what disconcerted his detractors most

was his exasperating habit of switching his standpoint in the
middle of a discussion and suddenly agreeing with everything
his opponents had said, pointing out that precisely this had
always been his opinion, so that in the end one did not know
whether he really agreed or was merely exercising a subtle
form of derisive irony.

Much of this was part of a systematic attempt to destroy
the idea of the poet that Stefan George and Rilke had tried
to embody: romantic beings singled out by Providence, too
delicate to soil themselves by contact with the real world, the
secret kings and priestly lawgivers of the nation. Hence
Brecht's ostentatiously unromantic and businesslike air. As
his friend George Grosz once said:

> In spite of the fact that he was anything but a colorless
> person, he loved the color gray, not the opaque gray of
> obscurity, but the sober gray of the theoretician, com-
> mentator, and schoolmaster. He clearly would have liked
> to have had a sensitive electric computer in the place of
> his heart and in place of his legs the spokes of a motor-
> car's wheel. . . .[38]

In his desire to destroy the legend of the poet's mysterious
and lonely act of creation Brecht liked to work surrounded by
crowds of friends.

> On a long table by the window his typewriter stood al-
> ways open and ready for work surrounded by numerous
> folders containing cuttings from European and Ameri-
> can papers. If a visitor came Brecht regarded this as
> excellent for his work—he read out a difficult passage to
> test the quality of the writing against the visitor's reac-
> tion, or discussed it with him at length. Immediately he
> rushed to the typewriter to write down a new version.
> He believed that it was good for his work if many people
> participated in it. And so he collected young people
> around him as collaborators. They did research, dis-
> cussed his plans with him, made suggestions for altera-
> tions and amendments. In the printed versions of his
> works they appear as his co-authors.[39]

His influence on these young people was so strong that they all began to look like Brecht:

> Brecht, Klabund, Dudow, Caspar Neher, and Paul Samson Koerner (the boxer), all sported exactly identical haircuts . . . the hair was sliced off abruptly all around the head after two or three inches' growth, and hung down vaguely like the coiffure you see on busts of Roman emperors.[40]

It was a closely knit circle. Carola Neher, one of Brecht's favorite leading ladies and one of the great loves of his life (in spite of her name no relative of Caspar Neher, the designer), was the wife of Brecht's friend, the consumptive poet Klabund. The character of Polly in *The Threepenny Opera* and *St. Joan of the Stockyards* had been written for her. Kurt Weill was married to Lotte Lenya, another of the leading ladies of *The Threepenny Opera* and *Mahagonny*.

Brecht himself, whose first brief marriage to Marianne Zoff, the sister of the writer Otto Zoff, had ended in divorce, was by this time married to the actress Helene Weigel, who had played the feminine lead in the 1927 Berlin production of *Man Equals Man*. Two years younger than Brecht, Helene Weigel, who came from Vienna, was the product of a famous girls' school run by a militant suffragette, resolved to prove that she could produce girls more intelligent and intellectual than the best boys' school. A whole generation of brilliant girls, Helene Weigel among them, was evidence that this had not been an empty boast. Helene Weigel combines the emotional intensity of a great, though always intellectual, actress, with an acute and cultivated mind and prodigious organizing ability. At the same time she was always a good housewife and mother. Her loyalty and devotion to Brecht never faltered. In spite of his inveterate and irrepressible polygamous tendencies Brecht and she remained devoted to each other for thirty years.

Inside the circle of his own admirers Brecht lost the sinister air he liked to wear in public. He became kind, gentle and genial, bubbling over with ideas. The Russian writer Sergei Tretyakov, who met Brecht repeatedly in 1931 and

1932, has left a vivid picture of his conversation at the time.
Puffing the poisonous cheap cigars he smoked incessantly and
resembling "a note blown through a slender clarinet, his
hooked-nosed face recalling that of Voltaire or Rameses"[41] he
would hold forth on the German character, tells stories of
his early life, throw out ideas for dozens of new plays, or
develop his project for a new kind of theatre, that would

> function like a court room. Two trials an evening, each
> lasting an hour and a quarter. For example, the trial of
> Socrates, a witches' trial, the trial of Karl Marx's *Neue
> Rheinische Zeitung*, the trial of George Grosz on the
> charge of blasphemy for his cartoon of Christ in a gas-
> mask. Brecht was carried away by his enthusiasm. He
> began to elaborate: "Let us suppose that the trial of
> Socrates is over. We organize a short witches' trial, where
> the judges are armored knights who condemn the witch
> to the stake. Then the trial of George Grosz begins, but
> we forget to remove the knights from the stage. When
> the indignant prosecutor storms at the artist for having
> insulted our mild and compassionate God . . . the
> knights . . . are moved to applause. . . ."[42]

In January 1933 Anatoly Lunacharsky—until 1929 Soviet
Commissar for Education—came to Berlin for an eye operation. He had met Brecht on earlier occasions and went to
visit him. Lunacharsky's widow has described how the conversation circled round the impending catastrophe: Hitler's
rise to power. The members of Brecht's circle who were present spoke of the probable need to emigrate, and Lunacharsky
tried to comfort Brecht by pointing out that, after all, he
could continue to write his plays even in exile. "One of the
actresses laughed: 'Brecht can't live without a theatre . . . he
would rather work as a prompter than be without one!'—'He
would even be ready to become the backstage fireman!' said
someone else."[43]

A few weeks later Hitler had come to power. On February
27 fire broke out in the Reichstag building, and stormtroop-
ers started rounding up Communists and left-wing intellectuals. On the following day Brecht went into exile.

NOTES

1. *Arnolt Bronnen gibt zu Protokoll*, Hamburg, 1954, p. 117.
2. Bernhard Reich, "Erinnerungen an den jungen Brecht," *Sinn und Form*, Second Special Brecht Issue, 1957, p. 434.
3. C. Zuckmayer, "Drei Jahre" in *Theaterstadt Berlin, Ein Almanach*, ed. Herbert Ihering, Berlin, 1948, pp. 87–89.
4. E. Piscator, *Das politische Theater*, Berlin, 1929, p. 57.
5. Feuchtwanger, "Bertolt Brecht, dargestellt fuer Englaender," *Die Weltbuehne*, 9.4.1928.
6. See Chapter VII.
7. Hans Henny Jahnn, "Vom armen B.B.," *Sinn und Form*, Second Special Brecht Issue, 1957, p. 425.
8. *Arnolt Bronnen gibt zu Protokoll*, Hamburg, 1954, pp. 158–59.
9. Brecht, "Matinée in Dresden," *Berliner Boersen-Courier*, 3.23.1926. Reprinted in Hans Meyer, "Gelegenheitsdichtung des jungen Brecht," *Sinn und Form*, 1958/II, p. 287.
10. Elisabeth Hauptmann, "Notizen ueber Brechts Arbeit 1926," *Sinn und Form*, Second Special Brecht Issue, 1957, p. 241.
11. PEM, *Heimweh nach dem Kurfuerstendamm*, Berlin, 1952, p. 205.
12. Brecht, "Kurzer Bericht ueber 400 (Vierhundert) Junge Lyriker," *Die Literarische Welt*, Berlin, 2.4.1927.
13. Willy Haas, *Bert Brecht*, Berlin, 1958, p. 11.
14. Hugo von Hofmannsthal, *Das Theater des Neuen*, Vienna, 1947.
15. Elisabeth Hauptmann, "Notizen ueber Brechts Arbeit 1926," *Sinn und Form*, Second Special Brecht Issue, 1957, p. 243.
16. Schumacher, p. 117.
17. Hanns Eisler, "Bertolt Brecht und die Musik," *Sinn und Form*, Second Special Brecht Issue, 1957, pp. 440–41.
18. Nicolas Nabokov, "Time in Reverse." Talk in BBC Third Programme, broadcast, 6.11.1958.
19. Brecht, "Massnahmen gegen die Gewalt," *Versuche* 1, pp. 22–23.
20. Harry Kahn, "Traum und Erwachen," *Die Weltbuehne*, 10.2.1928.
21. Brecht, Letter to *Die Weltbuehne*, 11.20.1928.
22. Brecht in *Berliner Boersen-Courier*, 5.6.1929. Quoted by Schumacher, p. 242.
23. *Die schoene Literatur*. Quoted by Schumacher, p. 242.
24. Egon Jacobsohn, "Kanonen-Song," *Die Weltbuehne*, 5.28.1929.
25. Karl Kraus, "Kerrs Enthuellung," *Die Fackel*, August 1929. Reprinted in Kraus, *Widerschein der Fackel*, Munich, 1956, p. 405.
26. *Manchester Guardian*, 7.29.1958.

27. This account of the lawsuit about *The Threepenny Opera* film based on:

Archiv fuer Urheber—Film- und Theaterrecht, Berlin, vol. IV, no. 1, 2.14.1931, pp. 73 ff.

Lotte H. Eisner, "Sur le procès de l'Opéra de Quat' sous," *Europe*, Paris, January/February 1957, pp. 111 ff.

Die Weltbuehne, 2.10.1931. Ibid., 2.17.1931. Ibid., 2.24.1931. Ibid., 3.3.1931.

Brecht, "Der Dreigroschenprozess," *Versuche* 3, pp. 256–306.

28. Brecht, "Der Dreigroschenprozess," *Versuche* 3, pp. 256–306.

29. Brecht, *Der Neinsager*, *Versuche* 4, p. 324.

30. Brecht, *Aufstieg und Fall der Stadt Mahagonny*, *Versuche* 2, p. 98.

31. Alfred Polgar, "Theaterskandal" in *Handbuch des Kritikers*, Zurich, 1938, p. 32.

32. Schumacher, p. 275.

33. Peter Panter (i.e. Kurt Tucholsky), "Proteste gegen die Dreigroschenoper," *Die Weltbuehne*, 4.8.1930.

34. See Chapter VII.

35. Brecht, "Kleiner Beitrag zum Thema Realismus," *Der Sonntag*, East Berlin, no. 6, 1958, p. 9.

36. Brecht, *Die Heilige Johanna der Schlachthoefe*, *Versuche* 5, p. 362.

37. Willy Haas, *Die Literarische Welt*, Hamburg, 1955, p. 134.

38. George Grosz, *Ein kleines Ja und ein grosses Nein*, Hamburg, 1955, p. 181.

39. Bernhard Reich, "Erinnerungen an den jungen Brecht," *Sinn und Form*, Second Special Brecht Issue, 1957, pp. 434–35.

40. Ernest Borneman, "The Real Brecht," *Encore*, London, July/August 1958, p. 26. Also in *The Kenyon Review*, Spring 1959.

41. S. Tretyakov, "Bert Brecht," *International Literature*, Moscow, May 1937.

42. Ibid.

43. Natalya Rosenel, "Brecht und Lunatscharsky," *Neues Deutschland*, East Berlin, 2.8.1958.

CHAPTER III

EXILE

(1933–1948)

. . . changing countries more often than shoes. . . .
BRECHT, *An die Nachgeborenen*

> *To teach without pupils*
> *To write without fame*
> *Is difficult. . . .*
> BRECHT, *Ueber das Lehren*
> *ohne Schueler* (1935)

In our age of political and racial persecution, passport chican-
ery, and labor permits, the fate of the refugee is hard enough
in itself. But that of the refugee writer, suddenly cut off from
the medium of his skill—his language—is harder still.

Brecht's case was particularly cruel. He was not merely a
poet, dependent on his mastery of his language, but also an
experimenter and innovator in the theatre; to do his work
and to widen his range he needed a stage, scenery, actors—
and a public. At the age of thirty-five, just when he had
achieved fame—or at least notoriety—and financial success, his
career had suddenly come to a virtual end.

He might have derived certain hopes from the success of
The Threepenny Opera outside the German-speaking world,
brought about to a large extent, and ironically, by Pabst's
film, which had been produced simultaneously in French and
German versions. *The Threepenny Opera* was also produced

n the stage in the main capitals of Europe and even in New
'ork (in 1933—with little success), and the royalties from
he musical numbers brought Brecht a certain income, right
p to the outbreak of war. But his chances of writing and
roducing new works were greatly reduced; to rely on transla-
ions for launching new plays is to ensure failure. And the
ossibilities of getting new plays produced in German were
drastically diminished.

There were still a few countries, not yet controlled by Hit-
er, that had a German-speaking population and some outlets
or German artists: Austria, Switzerland, and certain areas of
Czechoslovakia, some places in the Balkans and even in Soviet
Russia, where the Volga Germans had their own autonomous
egion, much publicized at the time. But with the exception
of Vienna, Prague, or Zurich, these places were largely provincial in their tastes and standards. And even in Vienna,
Prague, and Zurich the possibilities were strictly limited and
ar too small for the sudden influx of writers, producers, com-
osers, actors and journalists from Hitler's Reich.

Some refugee writers had the courage and the ability to
ettison their own language and master another; but these
(Arthur Koestler, Robert Neumann, and a few others) were
exceptions. The remainder had to rely on the few publishers
outside the Nazi orbit who were prepared to risk losing the
German market by publishing writers persecuted by Hitler,
and on the numerous but ephemeral anti-Nazi literary magazines that sprang up in Vienna, Prague, Amsterdam, and
Paris. They spent their days planning and launching such
ventures in the cafés of Europe. In the beginning they still
hoped for the sudden collapse of Hitler's regime. Later they
tried to convince themselves, with steadily diminishing success, that the great powers would not stand idly by while
Hitler openly planned the war against them. But the years
went by and nothing effective was done. It was a truly terrible
situation in which these intellectuals found themselves; they
knew Hitler and they knew what was going to happen, but
were condemned to pour out their warnings in unread refugee periodicals, to have their rousing plays, designed to open
the world's eyes, performed in the back rooms of cafés, where

only other refugees who did not need to be converted came to see them, to move among people unaware of their former importance or fame, and to beg for grants from charitable organizations. It is not surprising that many of these German refugee writers committed suicide or drank themselves to death.

On the day after the Reichstag fire Brecht fled to Vienna, accompanied by his wife and his little son, Stefan. His name had always been high up in the Nazis' liquidation lists; as early as 1923, at the time of the first Hitler *Putsch*, Brecht figured as number five on the list of people to be arrested—mainly for having besmirched the honor of the German front line soldier in his *The Legend of the Dead Soldier*. When the Nazis burned the books of their chief opponents soon after they had come to power, Brecht's books were among the first to be thrown into the flames. Later he was deprived of his German citizenship—again as the author of *The Legend of the Dead Soldier*.

Making it more serious, the younger of his and Helene Weigel's two children, the two-year-old Barbara, had been left behind in Germany, in the care of Brecht's father. In the course of March 1933 rumors reached Vienna that the Nazis intended to use the child as a means to blackmail Brecht into returning to Germany. An Englishwoman who was doing welfare work in Vienna heard about this dangerous situation and offered to smuggle the little girl out of Germany. On April 1, 1933 this rescue operation was successfully, if precariously, carried out. Little Barbara was picked up in the country outside Augsburg and put on a train that took her to Switzerland, where her parents had in the meantime gone.

In the months that followed Brecht, like so many of his fellow-writers, was traveling through Europe in search of a place to live and a chance to work. Prague, Vienna, Paris were the conventional stopping places on these depressing prospecting tours. In the spring of 1933 a group of prominent anti-Nazi writers held a kind of council of war at Sanary-sur-Mer to discuss their plight. There were Thomas and Heinrich Mann, Feuchtwanger, Arnold Zweig, Thomas Mann's son

Klaus, Ernst Toller, and Brecht. It was the first of innumerable similar gatherings, all devoted to the earnest and searching examination of the problem of what writers could do to help bring about the downfall of Hitler. To keep their self-respect and their sanity they had to believe that their efforts mattered a great deal. In fact, they mattered little.

A few weeks after Whitsun, Brecht went to Denmark on the invitation of the Danish novelist, Karin Michaelis. He decided to make Denmark his base, and Karin Michaelis helped him to find a temporary home there. Denmark was remote from the centers of the emigration, with their depressing cliques and distracting and futile intrigues and bogus projects. And Denmark was relatively near to Germany. Brecht liked to think of himself as taking part in the underground struggle of the German workers, a myth to which he and so many of his colleagues stubbornly clung, although very little corresponded to it in reality:

> *Escaped beneath the Danish thatched roof, friends,*
> *I follow your struggle. . . .*[1]

The Danish thatched roof was that of a farmhouse at Skovbostrand near the city of Svendborg on the island of Funen. The former stables had been whitewashed and turned into a workroom for Brecht. An immensely long table ran along one of the walls, beneath the window, where he would sit by his typewriter, tapping out satirical poems, plays, essays and articles on his favorite gray tissue paper; meticulously pasting corrections over the discarded passages; and cutting out piles of pictures and news photographs from illustrated magazines and newspapers—material for future work. Brecht believed in documentation and collected voluminous scrapbooks filled with images of human folly. After the war he published one of these: *Kriegsfibel* (*Primer of War*); it consists of photographs from a number of papers—*Life* magazine occurs most frequently—each of them accompanied by a bitter, biting quatrain.

On one of the oak beams supporting the roof of the former stable he had fixed an inscription that proclaimed in large

letters the first article of his artistic and philosophical cree
THE TRUTH IS CONCRETE. And

. . . in front of the whitewashed wall
There stands the black soldier's suitcase with the manuscrip
On it the smoking utensils with the copper ashtrays.
The Chinese scroll that shows the doubter
Hangs above it. . . .[2]

These were his favorite possessions, which he carried rou
the world with him: his manuscripts, his smoking things, ar
the scroll with the painting of a Chinese philosopher, pro
ably Confucius.

From the courtyard he could hear the voices of his childre
playing on their swing. But however idyllic it might appea
he never saw himself as settled, but ever prepared and read
to be on the move again——

. . . the house has four doors from which to escape. . .

From this base in Denmark Brecht carried out his varie
almost feverish, but never very profitable activities.

In Paris in the spring of 1933 he and Kurt Weill had wri
ten a ballet, *Die sieben Todsuenden* (*The Seven Dead*
Sins), designed as a vehicle for Weill's wife, Lotte Leny
George Balanchine's company, "Les Ballets 1933," presente
it at the Théâtre des Champs-Elysées in June of that yea
The ballet tells the story of an American girl who goes ou
into the world to make money and has to avoid the seve
deadly sins—the indulgence of her own natural instincts—tha
might prevent her from achieving her objective. Anna
shown as a split personality; her emotional side is dance
(Tilly Losch created this part) while her rational side (Lott
Lenya) admonishes her in song. Caspar Neher came to Par
to design the décor. But the performance achieved hardl
more than a *succès d'éstime*. From July 1 to 15 the balle
was presented at the Savoy Theatre in London under th
title *Anna Anna*. Here too it was found impressive, but *Th*
Dancing Times criticized it for abandoning "the Latinity o
style from which ballet has culled so much beauty" and con
plained that there was "nothing to clarify or elucidate th

ɩeavy darkness of the Germano-American text. . . ."[4] This ɩas only the first of a long series of painful reminders that uccess outside Germany was not merely a matter of trans-ɩating Brecht's words from German into English or French. ɩt was the spirit of his work, his whole approach, that ap-ɔeared alien and incomprehensible to a non-German public.

In spite of this Brecht repeatedly returned to Paris and London to discuss the possibility of having one of his plays ɔerformed. Towards the end of 1935 the left-wing Theatre ɩnion in New York decided to put on *The Mother*, and he ɩvent to New York, mainly to try to stop the enthusiastic ɔompany from laboriously changing his "epic" style into a ɔonventional one by putting in all the things he had pur-ɔosely left out: the kitchen smells and the naturalistic detail. ɩHe did not quite succeed, the performance fell between two ɩstools, and the critics confessed that they were puzzled by it ɩll.

In 1936 Brecht became co-editor of a newly founded anti-ɩfascist literary review, *Das Wort*, published in Moscow. The ɩother two editors were Lion Feuchtwanger and Willi Bredel. ɩThe appearance of Brecht's name on the title page of *Das Wort* has led many people, and some compilers of reference ɩbooks, to assume that he lived in Moscow at that time. In ɩfact, in the years of his exile he visited Moscow only on a few ɩoccasions and never for longer than a few days. Considering ɩthat Feuchtwanger did not stay in Moscow much longer and ɩthat Willi Bredel was fighting in the Spanish Civil War, *Das Wort* must have been edited by a peculiar postal method. ɩBrecht published a certain amount of his current output in ɩthe paper, but otherwise there is little trace of his editorial ɩinfluence to be noticed in its policy or contents—some of ɩthe writers he most detested were among the regular con-ɩtributors. On the other hand, this editorship gave him a cer-ɩtain financial security.

At the time of the Nazi-Soviet pact in the summer of 1939 *Das Wort* came to an inglorious end.

To make ends meet Brecht had to work hard; he is even said to have written the shooting script of a film version of

I Pagliacci with Richard Tauber. "The film was almost cat:
strophically bad, but it still showed the touch of the master :
such unlikely scenes as the epilogue in which Tauber su
denly turned to address the audience like a commissar in
Lehrstueck."[5] But this was not the only way in which th
situation militated against his real talent. Even in his mo:
serious work the feeling that he must in some way play h
part in the day-to-day struggle against Hitler led him both 1
make speeches at congresses of anti-fascist writers and to pr
duce a whole series of political *pièces d'occasion*, poetry an
plays, many of them skillful and witty, yet always marke
by the ephemeral quality and inevitable mediocrity of th
kind of writing. The *German Satires*, a group of poems wri
ten for broadcasting by the anti-Nazi "German Freedom St:
tion," for example, are interesting as experiments in an e:
tremely free kind of free verse, but they have worn badl
Today they appear not only dated but politically naïv
Brecht's Communist views hindered rather than helped hi
to penetrate to the true nature of National Socialism; he re
garded it as a kind of conspiracy of the rich against the poo
and completely overlooked the genuinely revolutionary an
really frightening side of the Nazis, who were by no mean
merely the stooges of the generals or the industrialists whon
they used and also ruthlessly betrayed. Brecht not only misse
this point but misunderstood many of the more sinister as
pects of totalitarianism, such as the efficacy of its propaganda
which made the people actually love their oppressors. In ac
cordance with the Communist party line he continued t
depict the German working class as filled with sullen hate
against the "rulers," and concentrated a good deal of his fir
on such relatively unimportant symptoms as the shortage o
butter or oranges. There, as in so many other instances, Marx
ism proved an extremely fallible tool of social analysis. Th
Ribbentrop-Molotov pact finally shattered Brecht's, and
many of his fellow-refugee writers', naïve views on the phe
nomenon of totalitarian dictatorship.

This political *naïveté* also mars the plays Brecht wrote be
tween 1933 and 1938: *Die Rundkoepfe und die Spitzkoepfe*
(*The Roundheads and the Peakheads*), a tract against racialism, and a series of one-act plays and short sketches collected

nder the title *Furcht und Elend des Dritten Reiches* (*Fear
nd Misery of the Third Reich*). A version of this was pro-
uced in the United States in 1945 as *The Private Life of the
Master Race*. Some of its scenes are brilliant proof that Brecht
ould write in the conventional, naturalistic style. But most
of them fail to convince. To do his duty in the Spanish Civil
War, Brecht wrote another play in the conventional dramatic
orm he so despised, *Die Gewehre der Frau Carrar* (*Señora
Carrar's Rifles*), which was performed in German by refugee
actors in Paris in 1937. Helene Weigel played the title role.
This play (vaguely based on Synge's *Riders to the Sea*) is
very effective theatre, but is rather oversimplified politically
and clearly a potboiler. Brecht himself acknowledged this
fact in a note in the collected edition of his plays, which insists that this

> is Aristotelian (empathy) playwriting. The drawbacks of
> this technique can be compensated for, up to a point, by
> presenting the play together with a documentary film on
> the events in Spain, or by linking it with some propa-
> gandistic occasion.[6]

Brecht's only large-scale novel, *Dreigroschenroman* (*Threepenny Novel*), published in Amsterdam in 1934 and in an
English translation in 1937, and in America in 1938, also
suffers from political oversimplification. A long elaboration
of the unused screen story for *The Threepenny Opera* film,
the book gallantly attempts to unmask the workings of capitalist society. It contains many brilliantly written passages
and much bitter satire in the vein of Swift's *Modest Proposal*,
but its competing chains of multiple shops that sell only
stolen goods and syndicates of respectable businessmen who
get rid of rotten hulls to the Admiralty for troop transports,
knowing that they cannot keep afloat, simply cannot be accepted as valid images of the real workings of the capitalist
system.

But as if to make up for the dry, ephemeral and oversimplified nature of all this political pamphleteering, in these years
of exile Brecht also wrote some of his most moving poetry. He
had planned to publish most of this in the fourth volume of a

collected edition, of which two volumes only appeare
printed in Prague in 1938 but with the publisher's impri
"Malik Verlag/London." The third volume was in the pre
when Czechoslovakia fell, and only a small number of copi
of the *Svendborger Gedichte* (*Svendborg Poems*) appeared
an advance extract from the abortive volume four of this co
lected edition. It contains what is perhaps Brecht's most pe
sonal poem—*An die Nachgeborenen* (*To Posterity*) in whic
he begs the generations of a happier age to forgive him fc
the harshness of his writing——

> *For we know:*
> *Even the hatred of evil*
> *Distorts the features,*
> *And anger over injustice*
> *Also hoarsens the voice. Alas, we*
> *Who wanted to prepare the ground for friendliness*
> *Could not ourselves be friendly. . . .*[7]

As the illusion that he could influence the course of event
by his writing receded, Brecht returned to his deeper an
more poetical vein of playwriting. Those who had followe
his development only in what he published in the refuge
magazines had almost written him off as a real poet and be
lieved that he had not fulfilled the promise of his earlie
works. They could not know that from 1937 onwards Brech
had thrown off the shackles of political propaganda and hac
begun to write a series of plays that showed his talent no
only undiminished but considerably matured and purged o
the more puerile antics of his *enfant terrible* period: *Galile*
(1937–38); *The Trial of Lucullus* (1938); *The Good Woma*
of Setzuan (1938–40); *Mother Courage* (1938–39). It i
significant that all these plays were written at a time whe
the situation had grown so bad that political pamphleteerin
had quite clearly become futile, when war was imminent
and when the alliance between the Nazis and Stalin hac
damped the spirit of even the most ardent German Com
munists.

Even in exile Brecht gathered a circle around him. He
could not live without working in the theatre, so he took an

active part in the amateur dramatics of the Danish left wing. *The Roundheads and the Peakheads* had its first performance in Copenhagen in 1936 by actors of the Danish working-class theatre movement, and among Brecht's theoretical writings on the art of acting is a long didactic poem, *Speech to Danish Working-class Actors on the Art of Observation.*

In Denmark, Brecht added two more names to the list of his loyal women friends. One of them, Margarete Steffin, appears as co-author of *Fear and Misery of the Third Reich, The Good Woman of Setzuan, The Trial of Lucullus,* and *Arturo Ui.* Together with her, Brecht translated Martin Andersen-Nexoe's story of his childhood into German. Margarete Steffin also translated Nordahl Grieg's play on the Paris Commune, *The Defeat,* which Brecht published in *Das Wort* and which later gave rise to his counterplay, *The Days of the Commune.*

The Danish actress Ruth Berlau not only appears as collaborator on *The Days of the Commune, The Caucasian Chalk Circle,* and *The Good Woman of Setzuan,* etc., but also became the photographer who created the complete pictorial records of Brecht's productions, which formed the basis of his "model books."

In the summer of 1939, when war had become inevitable and Denmark appeared more and more unsafe, Brecht moved to Sweden. After the German invasion of Denmark and Norway, however, Europe could not offer any real safety to a man as hated by the Nazis as Brecht. So in the course of 1940 he again moved his family—and some of his helpers and collaborators—to Finland, where for some reason it seemed easier to get an American visa. In Finland he was the guest of the writer Hella Wuolijoki, one of whose plays he used as the basis for his play *Herr Puntila und sein Knecht Matti* (*Mr. Puntila and his Hired Man Matti*), later the cause of another accusation of plagiarism. In preparation for America he was also working hard to complete a play with which he wanted to conquer the U.S. stage: *Der Aufhaltsame Aufstieg des Arturo Ui* (*The Resistible Rise of Arturo Ui*), a transposition of the rise of Hitler into a Chicago gangster milieu. On

March 10 Brecht noted the idea in his diary; by March 2
the whole play, except for one scene, had been completed.

On May 3, 1941 the U. S. Vice-Consul in Helsinki issue
Brecht a quota immigration visa. At the beginning of June h
and his family and some of the members of his circle set ou
on the long journey to America—from Finland across the en
tire Soviet Union to Vladivostok by the Siberian Express
They interrupted their journey briefly in Moscow. Bernhar
Reich, who had been one of the artistic directors of th
Munich Kammerspiele in the early twenties and now live
in the Soviet Union, visited the travelers in the Hotel Metro
pole: "Everywhere there lay suitcases and parcels. In the rock
ing chair the boy Steff (Stefan Brecht). In a corner crouche
Barbara; Helli (Helene Weigel) put some order into th
luggage. Somewhere, quite forlorn, sat Margarete Steffin
Brecht occupied a table. A family of migrants! When, year
earlier, we had lightheartedly laughed about the Chaplin film
we had no inkling of the prophetic relevance of this movi
parable." Margarete Steffin, who had difficulty in obtainin
an American entry visa and was suffering from consumption
had to remain behind in Moscow and died there soon after
wards.

Ten days after the party left Vladivostok aboard a Swedish
ship Hitler's troops invaded Russia and Finland entered th
war as an ally of Germany. While Brecht was preparing t
leave, the country had already been swarming with Germa
troops. It had been a last-minute escape.

After a long sea voyage, of which he later liked to remem
ber the porpoises playing in the sea of Japan and the littl
horsecarts in the streets of Manila (soon to be overrun b
the Japanese), Brecht arrived at San Pedro, California, o
July 21, 1941.

He settled on the fringe of Hollywood, where so man
other Central European writers were sitting out the times o
war and exile. Many of his old friends had preceded him
Lion Feuchtwanger, after an adventurous and dangerous jour
ney through German-occupied France; the composer Hann
Eisler; the Austrian poet and producer Berthold Viertel,
fiery and kind-hearted genius whom Christopher Isherwoo
has immortalized in *Prater Violet*; and many others. But i

spite of the help and support of these friends, the times were hard and the atmosphere was anything but congenial:

> *Every morning to earn my bread*
> *I go to the market, where they buy lies. . . .*[8]

The highflown hopes that some of his plays might be performed on the American stage had come to nothing. The gangsters of *Arturo Ui* were far too unlike the originals to give that ambitious play a chance. Apart from a performance of some of the scenes of *Fear and Misery of the Third Reich*, by a group of refugee actors under Berthold Viertel's direction in New York in May 1942, there seemed as yet no chance of gaining a foothold in the American theatre. And so Brecht's time was spent in trying to think up plots that might be sold to a film studio. This was the period of films on the underground struggle in occupied Europe, and Brecht was working on a number of projects of this type. On the struggle of occupied France he and Feuchtwanger were planning a modern version of the story of Joan of Arc, which later crystallized into a novel by Feuchtwanger and Brecht's *Die Gesichte der Simone Machard (The Visions of Simone Machard)*, one of his most tender plays, whose little resistance heroine has clumsily naïve visions of herself as an anachronistic Joan of Arc.

In the end Brecht did succeed in selling a story; it dealt with the assassination of Heydrich by Czech patriots and was filmed by Fritz Lang under the title *Hangmen Also Die*. Hanns Eisler wrote the music. But the final product bore little resemblance to Brecht's outline and he dissociated himself from it.

Far away in Zurich, the gallant band of anti-Nazi actors who made the Schauspielhaus the chief exponent of the free German theatre gave Brecht the only reason to feel himself not completely forgotten. They scored great success with three of the plays he had written in Denmark: *Mother Courage*, *The Good Woman of Setzuan*, and *Galileo*. In his American exile, however, he could not find anyone to print his poems, so that he had to issue some of his *Gedichte im Exil (Poems in Exile)* in typewritten and photostated form for distribution to a few of his friends. But he continued to write: his new version of Schweik, *Schweik im Zweiten Weltkrieg* (*Schweik in the Second World War*) and *Der Kaukasische Kreidekreis* (*The Caucasian Chalk Circle*).

At this time Brecht lived in Santa Monica. He was now in his middle forties and had mellowed considerably, but he had adapted his favorite costume to Californian conditions only in so far as he now wore trousers and jackets of blue denim and tieless, open shirts. Instead of German "Virginias" he now smoked American five-cent cigars and stubbornly refused to have anything to do with more expensive varieties, even when he received whole boxes of them as gifts.

He astonished his Hollywood friends by managing always to appear with a two days' growth of beard; never clean shaven, but never a three days' growth either. Nobody could explain how he did it.

He moved largely in the narrow world of German and Austrian refugee intellectuals and was frequently at loggerheads with those American circles one would have thought most likely to appeal to him: the many left-wing, fellow-traveling and Communist Americans of Hollywood. But these actors, writers and producers were largely under the spell of the Russian theatre and enthusiastic followers of the Stanislavsky method, which was a red rag to Brecht. Artistic contradictions cut across possible political affinities.

And so he remained the center of a mainly German-speaking circle. Ironically enough, Brecht, whose writing in his youth had centered around a mythical conception of an Anglo-Saxon, and largely American, world, found very little contact with the real America. After he had set foot on American soil, the American scene, which had dominated his early works, disappeared from his writing. While he admired the productive achievements of the United States, he had no contact with its cultural climate; distrusted its politics, wrongly believing that after the war the country would inevitably relapse into isolationism; and disliked its cooking. When served some fanciful American dish he would push it away, saying "We don't eat that kind of thing in Augsburg." As for the beauties of the Californian landscape. . . . A friend once took him on a drive along the coast road through the most breathtaking scenery. Brecht remained silent and morose. But when the car turned into the disreputable quarters of the Los Angeles waterfront his face lit up. "What beautiful scenery!" he said. And he meant it. Brecht, whose early poetry was full of ecstatic praise of the beauties of nature, had come to fear them as a temptation that might lure him away from his duties as a social critic.

He continued to consult his friends while writing his plays or poems and spent hours discussing the course of the war with them. To make himself clear he would act out any situation: what he imagined Roosevelt might have said to Stalin or Hitler to Himmler. Thus he turned abstract, political argument into his own kind of dramatic reality. To him truth was always concrete. The slogan that had adorned the oak beams of Svendborg also greeted the visitor from the wall of his apartment at Santa Monica. Always striving for Confucian politeness, Brecht would occasionally lose his temper, particularly if he was reminded of painful facts that did not fit into his political scheme of things, such as the Moscow trials and the Stalinist terror. When his composer friends, Hanns Eisler and Paul Dessau, whom he had met during a visit to New York in 1942, came to see him, there would be a great deal of rambunctious music-making and sometimes Brecht himself would sing his ballads in his high, thin voice, just as he had sung them in his youth in the taverns of Bavaria.

Slowly, gradually, nevertheless, Brecht gained a foothold in the United States. His name had been known to a few enthusiasts for a new kind of theatre since the early thirties, and in spite of the failures of the first New York productions of *The Threepenny Opera* (1933) and *The Mother* (1935) he had retained some followers. Mordecai Gorelik, who had been present at the Copenhagen production of *The Roundheads and the Peakheads*, had written about the "epic theatre" in *Theatre Workshop* as early as 1937. Clement Greenberg had drawn attention to Brecht's poetry in *Partisan Review* a few months before Brecht's arrival in America.

Shortly after he had settled in California he met Eric Bentley, who was to become his chief advocate among the academic and theatrical *avant-garde*. As Bentley himself has described it: "I met Brecht late 1941 or early 1942. I was just out of graduate school. . . . I asked Brecht to help me with my translation of . . . Stefan George. He read me his own poems and I started translating."[9] Other translators were equally keen on presenting his works to a new audience; in 1943 H. R. Hays published his impressive translation of *The Trial of Lucullus*, which was later set to music by Roger Sessions. (Brecht and Dessau based another opera on the original German text in 1951.)

The conquest of the American stage was more difficult. As early as 1942 Max Reinhardt, Brecht's former employer and now a fellow exile in Hollywood, had planned a performance of *Furcht und Elend des Dritten Reiches*, which Bentley translated as *The Private Life of the Master Race*. Brecht had written a very effective framework for the short, unconnected scenes and sketches—an armored troop carrier rolling through wartime Europe with its load of Nazi soldiers was to link groups of scenes illustrating the environment from which the German troops had emerged to ravage Europe. Nothing came of Reinhardt's project. But Bentley's translation was performed at Black Mountain College during the war—the first of a long line of performances of Brecht's plays in American colleges and universities. It is significant that Brecht, who remained consistently unsuccessful on the commercial and professional stage, should have established himself in America through such amateur performances by student players, even at a time when his political views were widely frowned upon throughout the country.

The Private Life of the Master Race reached the professional New York stage in June 1945. Originally Piscator was to have directed it, but shortly before opening night he dropped out and Berthold Viertel took over. A number of the leading roles were played by German refugee actors whose command of English left much to be desired. Brecht tried to improve things by making longer and longer cuts, until some of the scenes became unintelligible. And he added some weird touches that further confused the audience. A Negro actor who appeared in the part of an S.S. man, for example, was given dead-white make-up. No wonder that the first-night reception was a pained one. The New York *Times* gave the production a lukewarm but fairly favorable notice. Burton Rascoe in the New York *World-Telegram* summed up the other camp's point of view in the succinct phrase, "It was perfectly awful."

Nevertheless, by the time the war in Europe ended, there seemed to be a good chance that Brecht might yet make his mark in America. Like most German refugees he was none too eager to hasten back to a devastated Germany with its ruined cities, its hate-ridden population, its misery, and its black markets. Brecht felt that it was worth his while to bide his time and see whether he might not, after all, succeed in creating a place for himself in the United States. He had taken out first citizenship papers immediately after his arrival in 1941, and he now considered applying for a Guggenheim Fellowship.

To bring out their own works in German for the reviving German market, a group of German refugee writers founded a publishing house in New York, the Aurora Verlag. Brecht, Doeblin, Feuchtwanger, Heinrich Mann, Viertel and F. C. Weiskopf were among the partners in this venture.

And for Brecht the pace quickened. Reynal and Hitchcock was interested in publishing a translation of his collected works. Eric and Maja Bentley completed their translation of *The Caucasian Chalk Circle*, which was produced at Carleton College, Minnesota, in 1948, and *The Good Woman of Setzuan*. H. R. Hays was bringing out a volume of translations of Brecht's *Selected Poems* and, most important of all, Brecht himself was working on an English version of his *Galileo* with Charles Laughton, who wanted to play the name part.

As far back as 1943 Orson Welles and Mike Todd had planned a joint production of *Galileo* with Laughton. This plan had come to grief when the clash of these two strong temperaments led to the inevitable quarrel. But Laughton's interest had been aroused. In 1945 he asked Brainerd Duffield and Emerson Crocker to prepare an acting version from an existing literal translation. The two young men retired to the country and emerged with a text that pleased Laughton. But in the meantime Brecht had begun to reshape the play, and eventually he and Laughton embarked on a joint revision

so radical and enjoyable that they completely lost sight of
the existence of other translators or translations. Brecht himself later suggested an almost miraculous process of collaboration through mutual inspiration: "The unfortunate circum-
stance that one of the translators knew no German and the
other only little English forced us from the start into play-
acting as a method of translation."[10]

Brecht admired Laughton as a very great actor and was
amazed at his intuition of the underlying reality of the historical situation and the deeper layers of the character. "So
great was his desire to show things as they really are that, in
spite of his indifference, even timidity, in all political matters, he would demand considerably sharper formulations, or
even suggest them himself, in more than a few places; merely
because he regarded these passages as 'somehow weak,' by
which he meant that they did not do justice to things as they
really are."[10] The two collaborators met at Laughton's house,
"overlooking the Pacific Ocean, because the catalogues of syn-
onyms were too heavy to carry about. . . . [Laughton] used
these heavy tomes much and with untiring patience."[10] To
illustrate a point of translation Laughton would read from
the Bible, Aesop, Molière, or Shakespeare. "We used to work
in L.'s small library, in the mornings. But L. rushed to meet
me in the garden, running out in his shirt and trousers, bare-
foot, across the wet lawn. . . ."[11] While the translation was
still in progress the externals of the production were increasingly discussed in ever more meticulous detail. "When L.
heard about the delicate sketches of scenes that Caspar Neher
used to make so that the actors could group themselves according to the designs of a great artist, he immediately asked
an excellent artist of the Walt Disney Studios to make such
sketches. They turned out somewhat malicious; L. used
them, but with caution."[12]

The production of *Galileo* was Brecht's greatest chance to
break into the American theatre. All his former efforts had
failed. He had tried to persuade Thornton Wilder to adapt
The Good Woman of Setzuan, but had met with a rebuff. He
had adapted *The Duchess of Malfi* for Elisabeth Bergner, together with H. R. Hays and W. H. Auden, but when Bergner
finally did the play on Broadway Brecht's version was not

used. Now a great star of the stage and screen had recognized Brecht's importance and was ready to launch him. Moreover, Galileo was a great play, and highly topical as well. The dropping of the first atom bomb had made the problem of the scientist's responsibility to society one of the most burning issues of the day.

On July 30, 1947, Galileo, directed by Joseph Losey, opened at the Coronet Theatre in Beverly Hills. "L.'s main worry was the heat. . . . He demanded that trucks full of ice blocks should be placed around the theatre and that the ventilators should be turned on so that 'the audience should be able to think.' "[13] But whether the ice was placed around the theatre or not, the public remained cool towards the whole enterprise. Laughton was robustly magnificent. But the unusual, cerebral play was lost on an audience unprepared for a new kind of dramatic convention. Not knowing Brecht's views about a theatre without mounting climaxes and "well-constructed" scenes, they had come expecting the usual effects of suspense and emotional intensity and were not prepared for a loosely strung together sequence of dialogues on a stage of Spartan simplicity. As Variety remarked, the "script" did not seem to make the grade and left an overall impression of dullness. There was still another chance: Galileo was to go to New York as well. But Brecht's thoughts had already turned to Europe.

This was not simply because he had failed to gain success and appreciation; existence on the fringes of American society and intellectual life was becoming less and less comfortable for foreigners with pronounced left-wing views. The cold war was on. Subversion was being suspected in all kinds of places. Hollywood was one of them. Communist infiltration of the motion-picture industry was on the agenda.

In the course of September 1947 Brecht received a subpoena to appear before the Committee on Un-American Activities to testify on this subject.

While some of the members of his circle were terrified by the prospect and suggested ways and means to avoid his having to face the ordeal, Brecht himself was only too eager to pit

his impertinence and Schweikian servility against what he
considered the darkest and most evil forces in the country.
He had always enjoyed such encounters and delighted in mis-
leading pompous representatives of authority by "sticking
strictly to the untruth," as he had done when summoned
before the censor of his film *Kuhle Wampe*.

On Thursday, October 30, 1947, he faced the Committee
on Un-American Activities under the chairmanship of Representative J. Parnell Thomas.

The record of the proceedings on that morning is a curious
document. Anyone who approached it with the expectation of
finding the full horrors of the witch-hunt in it would be
greatly disappointed. What is most striking is the utter innocence of the investigators, their inability to understand an
intellectual, and, even more puzzling, the sketchiness of the
preparation of their case. One might have expected that if
one wanted to prove the Communist sympathies of a world-
famous writer, someone might have been found to read his
works in the original, so that he could confront him with his
own words and opinions. But nothing of the sort had been
done. The few scattered poems or plays of Brecht's that had
been translated or had found their way into American Communist literature seem to have been the main basis of the
Committee's knowledge of Brecht, together with one or two
articles about him that were available in English. This gave
Brecht the opportunity of roundly denying any Communist
tendency in the poems quoted to him by insisting that the
translation had changed his meaning. And when he noticed
that none of the members of the Committee had any real
knowledge of his writings, Brecht subtly misled them even
on those points where they most clearly had a case.

For example, Mr. Robert E. Stripling, the Chief Investigator of the Committee, read him a passage from *The Measures
Taken* and asked:

> Now, Mr. Brecht, will you tell the Committee whether
> or not one of the characters in this play was murdered by
> his comrades because it was in the best interests of the
> party, of the Communist Party; is that true?[14]

This, though it may be somewhat crudely put, is indeed the plot of *The Measures Taken*. But Brecht calmly confused the issue. He replied:

> No, it is not quite according to the story. . . . You will find when you read it carefully like in the old Japanese play where other ideas were at stake, this young man who died was convinced that he had done damage to the mission he believed in and he agreed to that, and he was about ready to die in order not to make greater such damage. So he asks his comrades to help him, and all of them together help him to die. He jumps into an abyss and they lead him tenderly to that abyss and that is the story.[14]

In fact, the three Communists in *The Measures Taken* say quite categorically:

> *Then we shot him and*
> *Threw him into a lime pit.* . . .[15]

But Brecht intentionally confused *The Measures Taken* with the earlier play *He Who Says Yes*, which *was* based on a Japanese legend and had been a kind of preliminary study for *The Measures Taken*. In that play the young man concerned *did* jump into an abyss. If challenged, Brecht could always have excused himself with simply having confused two of his plays that have much in common. But the Committee, of course, did not know the facts. The chairman merely remarked:

> I gather from your remarks . . . that he was just killed, he was not murdered.
> Brecht: He wanted to die.
> Chairman: So they kill him?
> Brecht: No; they did not kill him—not in this story. He killed himself. . . .[16]

And there the matter rested. The Chief Investigator gallantly returned to the charge. He read out at length the article about Brecht by Sergei Tretyakov in the Moscow periodical *International Literature*, in which Brecht was quoted as openly sympathizing with the Communists (as indeed he had since 1928). Triumphantly as the Chief Investigator turned to Brecht:

> Do you recall that interview, Mr. Brecht?
> Brecht: No. [Laughter.] It must have been written twenty years ago or so. . . . I do not recall the interview in exact. I think it is a more or less journalistic summary of talks or discussions about many things.

The Chief Investigator shifted his ground again:

> Have many of your writings been based upon the philosophy of Lenin and Marx?

Ever since 1930 Brecht had openly based all his writing on a Marxist standpoint. But he replied with complete confidence in the ignorance of the Committee:

> No. I don't think that is quite correct. But of course I studied; I had to study as a playwright who wrote historical plays; I, of course, had to study Marx's ideas about history. I do not think intelligent plays today can be written without such study. Also history now, written now, is vitally influenced by the studies of Marx about history.[16]

Again the Committee was left speechless, and this point too went by default. When asked point-blank whether he had ever applied to join the Communist party, Brecht denied it. The Committee produced some more of Brecht's openly Communist marching songs from an American Communist songbook.

> Did you write that, Mr. Brecht?
> No, I wrote a German poem, but that is very different from this. [Laughter.]

Whereupon there remained nothing for the chairman to do
but to close the proceedings:

> Chairman: Thank you very much, Mr. Brecht. You are a
> good example to the witnesses of Mr. Kenny and Mr.
> Crum.[17]

And so Brecht left Washington with the thanks of the Committee on Un-American Activities for his exemplary behavior
as a co-operative witness. No wonder that his friends were in
raptures. As one of them put it, it had been as though a zo-
ologist had been cross-examined by apes.

To his chagrin Brecht had not been allowed to read the
prepared statement he had brought with him to Washington.
This, later published in Mr. Gordon Kahn's book *Hollywood
on Trial*, is a very typical exercise in Brechtian irony and
Schweikian subservience. It begins by describing his career in
the twenties:

> . . . in Germany voices could already be heard that free
> artistic expression and free speech should be silenced.
> Humanist, socialist, even Christian ideas were called
> "un-deutsch" (un-German), a word which I can hardly
> think of without Hitler's wolfish intonation. . . .[18]

After thus openly equating Hitler's attacks on "un-German"
activities with the chauvinism of the "un-American" witch-
hunt, Brecht proceeded to list the places he had passed
through during his exile: Denmark, Finland, Manila, all of
which were afterwards submerged in the tides of authoritarian
invasion. The implication was clear that the same thing was
now happening in the United States. And he went on:

> My activities, even those against Hitler, have always
> been purely literary activities of a strictly independent
> nature. As a guest of the United States I refrained from
> political activities concerning this country even in a lit-
> erary form. . . . Being called before the Un-American
> Activities Committee, however, I feel free for the first
> time to say a few words about American matters: look-

ing back at my experiences as a playwright and a poet in the Europe of the last two decades, I wish to say that the great American people would lose much and risk much if they allowed anybody to restrict free competition of ideas in cultural fields, or to interfere with art, which must be free in order to be art. . . .[19]

When Brecht had asked to read this statement into the record of the Committee, the chairman had demanded to see it, had read it, and had replied:

Mr. Brecht, the Committee has carefully gone over this statement. It is a very interesting story of German life, but it is not at all pertinent to this inquiry. Therefore we do not care to have you read the statement.[20]

Brecht had gone to Washington with the reservation for his flight to Europe in his pocket. Shortly after he got back to New York from his excursion to Washington he left America.

A friend who ran into him in Paris a few days later expressed surprise at seeing him back in Europe. Brecht replied: "When they accused me of wanting to steal the Empire State Building, I thought it was high time for me to leave."

And so, having traveled right around the world in the course of his exile, Brecht was back in Europe, with his suitcase containing his manuscripts on microfilm, a recording of his testimony before the Un-American Activities Committee, and the scroll with the picture of the cheerful, sceptical Chinese sage.

But he was in no hurry to return to Germany. In his sly, cautious way he took his time getting the feel of things, surveying the ground and weighing the pros and cons before finally making up his mind.

At first he went to Switzerland. Zurich was undoubtedly the most favorable vantage point for such a reconnaissance— on the very borders of Germany with easy access not only to West Germany but also to the Soviet zone and within easy reach of Austria. Moreover, it had sufficient German-speaking theatres to give Brecht a chance to work, at least for a while.

He took an apartment at Herrliberg outside Zurich, on the top floor of a gardener's cottage. In the main room he set up his workshop as he had done at so many transitory stopping places in the years of exile. The typewriter stood by the window from which he could look out over the lake, the scroll depicting the Chinese sage was unrolled on the wall, and folders with news photographs cut out of magazines littered the room.

From Herrliberg one can take the train right to the center of Zurich. Not far from the station, at the Café Odeon, one was at that time at the very center of the intellectual life of Central Europe.

The Zurich Schauspielhaus, which had held high the honor of the German-speaking theatre throughout the years of Hitlerism and war, was reviving *Mother Courage* and preparing the world première of *Puntila*. The Municipal Theatre at Chur (Coire), the capital of Grisons, invited Brecht to put on his adaptation of the *Antigone* of Sophocles, which he had freely based on Hoelderlin's great translation. His old schoolmate and friend Caspar Neher came to design the set. Helene Weigel played Antigone, and the performance was a memorable demonstration of the Brechtian style of production. Ruth Berlau has made a detailed photographic record of it.[21]

This healthy and pleasurable plunge back into Brecht's favorite element, practical work in the theatre, also stimulated his theoretical activity. He composed a summary of his beliefs on the "non-Aristotelian" drama in seventy-seven tersely formulated paragraphs, the *Little Organon for the Theatre*. And he began to write a play, *Die Tage der Kommune* (*The Days of the Commune*). It was the last play he completed.

The Swiss novelist, dramatist and architect, Max Frisch, who spent a good deal of time with Brecht in those months in Zurich, has given us a memorable and sensitive picture of Brecht at that time:

reading poems to his guests in the quiet, matter-of-fact tone of a man showing you words as one would show

interesting stones, pieces of cloth, or other things that
have to speak for themselves; in the attitude of a man
who, smoking his cigar, feels impelled to read out a text,
merely because it is not generally available, as one would
read a letter: in the tone of *communication*. He is not
disturbed when the door-bell rings, or a further visitor
enters the room. . . . "I am," he says to the new arrival,
"reading a poem; it is called *To Posterity*." He says this
to make the new arrival wait for a moment before starting on his conversation, and in the voice of sober communication continues to read what he wants to tell
posterity. . . .[22]

Frisch was fascinated by his discussions with Brecht, by his
seriousness and dedicated loyalty to his Marxist creed, which
made him reject any social order existing at present and
wholly align himself with the future.

Christians are aligned with a beyond; Brecht is aligned
with this world. That is one of the differences between
him and those priests to whom he bears no little resemblance, however much he may . . . mock them; the doctrine of the ends that sanctify the means produces similar features even when the ends are diametrically
opposed. Materialist Jesuits also exist. . . .[23]

When it was time to go Brecht would sometimes take
Frisch to the station:

He waits till I have got on the train, makes a spare, somewhat shy gesture with his hand, without taking off his
gray cloth cap; that would be out of style; avoiding the
crowd, he leaves the platform with rapid, short, rather
light steps, his arms hardly swinging, his head held
slightly sideways, his cap drawn into the forehead as if to
conceal his face, half conspiratorially, half bashfully. If
you look at him like that, he gives the impression of a
workman, a metal worker; yet he is too slight, too graceful for a workman, too much awake for a peasant, altogether far more volatile than the local breed of people;

reserved, yet observant, a refugee who has left innumerable stations, too shy for a man of the world, too knowing
not to be anxious, a stateless person . . . a passer-by of
our time, a man called Brecht, a scientist, a poet without incense. . . .[24]

NOTES

1. Motto to *Svendborger Gedichte*, London, 1939.
2. Brecht, "Auf der Flucht," *Lieder und Gedichte*, West Berlin
und Frankfurt, p. 102.
3. Brecht, "Zufluchtsstaette," ibid., p. 103.
4. *The Dancing Times*, London, August 1933.
5. Ernest Borneman, "The Real Brecht," *Encore*, London, July/
August 1958, also published in *The Kenyon Review*, Spring 1959.
6. Brecht, *Stuecke VII*, p. 60.
7. Brecht, "An die Nachgeborenen," *Svendborger Gedichte*, p. 60.
8. Brecht, "Hollywood," *Hundert Gedichte*, East Berlin, 1951,
p. 308.
9. Eric Bentley in a letter to the author.
10. Brecht, *Aufbau einer Rolle: Laughtons Galileo*, East Berlin,
1958.
11. Ibid., p. 9.
12. The artist was John Hubley. Some of his sketches are repro-
duced in *Aufbau einer Rolle*, also with the translation in *From the
Modern Repertoire*, Series Two, ed., Eric Bentley, Indiana University Press, 1952.
13. Brecht, *Aufbau einer Rolle: Laughtons Galileo*, p. 13.
14. *Hearings Regarding the Communist Infiltration of the Motion
Picture Industry*, Washington, 1947, pp. 491–504.
15. Brecht, *Versuche 4*, p. 358.
16. *Hearings Regarding the Communist Infiltration of the Motion
Picture Industry*, Washington, 1947, pp. 491–504.
17. Ibid.
18. Gordon Kahn, *Hollywood on Trial*, New York, 1948, pp. 121–
29.
19. Ibid., pp. 121–29.
20. *Hearings Regarding the Communist Infiltration of the Motion Picture Industry*, Washington, 1947, pp. 491–504.
21. Brecht and Neher, *Antigonemodell 1948*, East Berlin, 1949.
22. Max Frisch, *Tagebuch 1946–1949*, Frankfurt, 1950, p. 226.
23. Ibid., p. 288.
24. Ibid., pp. 292–93.

CHAPTER IV

EAST BERLIN

(1948–1956)

> . . . *Before me come the bombers. Deadly swarms*
> *Announce my return. Raging fires*
> *Precede the son.*
>
> BRECHT, Rueckkehr[1]

> . . . *I do not like the place I have come from*
> *I do not like the place I am going to.* . . .
> BRECHT, Der Radwechsel (1953)[2]

On October 22, 1948 Brecht arrived back in Berlin. To reach the Soviet Zone, and the East Sector of Berlin, he had been compelled to travel from Zurich via Prague. But he was not, by any means, certain that he wanted to stay.

On the morning after his arrival he went out by himself and wandered through the ruins. "I went to the Reich Chancellery to smoke a cigar there," he wrote in his diary.[3] A reporter wanted to know what his impressions were: "Before I say anything, I want to see what it is like . . . ," he replied.[4]

The Communist Kulturbund gave a reception in his honor. There were long speeches. Brecht, who was sitting between the East German Communist leader Wilhelm Pieck (who later became President of the "German Democratic Republic") and the Soviet Political Officer, Colonel Tulpanov, patiently listened to the long and fulsome orations. When his turn came to reply, Brecht rose and

with his bird's head slightly stretched forward he blinkingly eyed the expectant circle of faces, then with a wide, sweeping gesture solemnly shook hands first with Pieck, then with Tulpanov, sat down again, and started to eat his soup. . . .[5]

Brecht had been invited to East Berlin to produce *Mother Courage* at the Deutsches Theater, where Reinhardt had once watched the rehearsals of *Drums in the Night*. Erich Engel, who had produced *In the Jungle* in Berlin back in 1924, was to be his coproducer. Helene Weigel was to play Mother Courage. After long rehearsals the play opened on January 11, 1949. It was a brilliant performance and one of Brecht's greatest triumphs as director and author. This, if not formally, was in fact the birth of the Berliner Ensemble.

Brecht returned to Zurich. Now he had to make up his mind. It was difficult for him to stay in Switzerland permanently. East Germany offered the possibility of obtaining what he had wanted all his life: a theatre of his own and lavish means to experiment to his heart's content. But still he hesitated. He, who had refused the invitation to settle in Moscow at the beginning of his exile, still had some doubts as to the advisability of moving too far into the Soviet orbit. Only after the Soviet blockade of West Berlin had been defeated by the Allied airlift and the prospect of a more normal life in East Berlin, with relatively free access to the West, seemed assured for at least a while, did he finally make up his mind.

For a man in Brecht's situation, and of Brecht's convictions, the decision to throw in his lot with the Communist part of Germany seems natural enough. In the West he had failed to make his mark, and he felt that America had both rejected him as an artist and proscribed him as politically undesirable. And America seemed the dominant force in the Western half of Germany. Moreover, Brecht had always followed the Communist party line in believing that Nazism had been merely a front for the magnates of German industry. To the adherents of this dogmatic view the Western powers' efforts to put German industry—private industry—back on its feet were bound to appear as an attempt to restore the forces of German nationalism. Brecht's long poem *Freiheit und Democracy* (*Freedom and Democracy*), a ballad modeled on Shelley's *Mask of Anarchy*, written in 1947, expressed this conviction: under the banner of Anglo-Saxon freedom and democracy, militarism and chauvinism return to Germany followed by all the motley crew of their erstwhile adherents.

On the other hand, Brecht had no illusions as to the danger and hardship of life in the Soviet Zone. In his characteristically sly and circumspect manner he took precautions to make himself independent of some of the main drawbacks of life in the East.

Brecht never allowed his political convictions and socialist ideals to interfere with his healthy peasant sense of thrift; there are many instances of his preferring to put a play of his into the hands of a rich entrepreneur rather than some poor struggling left-wing collective that would have needed his support to establish itself. When his financial advantage was at stake, these considerations simply ceased to exist. And so at the very moment he moved to East Germany, he put the copyright of his works into the hands of a West German publisher, Peter Suhrkamp, his old friend and collaborator on *Mahagonny*, who had become one of West Germany's leading publishers. This put Brecht outside the effective range of East German censorship and gave him a source of Western currency, a financial bridgehead in the non-Communist world that made him, up to a point, independent of his new Eastern patrons. To this day East German editions of Brecht's plays have to carry the imprint: "By permission of Suhrkamp Verlag, Frankfurt on Main."

Another proof of Brecht's circumspect approach to the question of his final domicile in Europe emerges from the efforts he made to secure a foothold in a German-speaking area that would have saved him from the necessity of deciding between West and East Germany. It was clear that Switzerland could not provide such a permanent residence. But shortly after his arrival in Zurich, Brecht had been approached by the Austrian composer Gottfried von Einem, at that time one of the most active promoters of the Salzburg Festival, to inquire whether he would be interested in lending his name to that famous but then tarnished institution. Von Einem, whom Caspar Neher, designer of many productions at Salzburg, had introduced to Brecht, felt that he might become for postwar Salzburg what Max Reinhardt, the great director, and Hugo von Hofmannsthal, the author of the *Everyman* play annually performed in front of the cathedral, had been in the twenties. Brecht was to come and live in Salzburg and be one of the artistic directors of the festival. He was greatly interested by the project and began to sketch out a *Salzburg Dance of Death* as a successor to the *Everyman*. 1949 was also the bicentenary of Goethe's birth: there was discussion of a *Faust* adaptation by Brecht.

In a letter dated May 23, 1948—six months before Brecht's first visit to East Berlin—Brecht wrote to von Einem: ". . . I persist in my firm intention to come, if the matter can be arranged at Salzburg." In the fall of 1948 Brecht went to East Berlin. But after his return to Zurich in April 1949, he again wrote to von Einem: ". . . I am sitting here with Cas [Caspar Neher] and we have been talking about the festival play; it looks as though that would work. And I now also know of a reward, worth more to me than any advance of whatever kind: that would be a place of sanctuary, in other words a passport. If this were at all possible, it should be done, of course, without any publicity. And perhaps one way to do it, like the following, would be best: Helli [Helene Weigel] is after all a born Austrian—Viennese—and like myself stateless since 1933, and now there exists no German government. Could she get an Austrian passport back? And could I then get one, simply as her husband? You understand: I don't know the legal way. But, indeed, a passport would be of immense importance. I cannot, after all, settle in one part of Germany and then be dead for the other part. . . ."

Von Einem advised Brecht that he would have to apply formally for Austrian citizenship. The Austrian authorities were at that time prepared to grant naturalization fairly easily to distinguished artists, writers and scientists who wanted to settle in that small, newly independent country. Austrians have always been conscious of the value of their cultural prestige and saw this as an opportunity to reestablish their country as a cultural center. But applications of this kind *had* to come from people who already lived in Austria. Brecht had no address in Austria, so his application is dated as from von Einem's residence in Salzburg. In his official application Brecht explained his desire to become an Austrian citizen in these terms: "My longing for Austria is by no means due to external circumstances but can be explained by the fact that I, who have now reached the age of fifty, want to do my intellectual work in a country which can offer me a suitable atmosphere. Austria is such a country. . . . I should like to stress that I feel myself only a poet and do not want to serve any particular political ideology, nor do I especially want to be represented as the exponent of such an ideology. For certain specific reasons I refuse to be repatriated to Germany."

This application was written before Brecht's return to East Berlin in the fall of 1949. It is not clear whether he had already decided to settle in East Germany and merely wanted to obtain an Austrian passport as a safeguard and a means to travel in the West, or whether he had not yet made up his mind. What is certain, however, is that *after* the foundation of the Berliner Ensemble and after his final settlement in East Berlin Brecht continued to press for his naturalization in Austria. On March 2, 1950—at a time when the German Democratic Republic already officially existed and he could easily have become its citizen—Brecht wrote to von Einem: ". . . Believe me I am as much interested as before, even more so. You *must* help me. So much depends on it for my artistic work (and collaboration with others), as many countries, including West Germany, could not be visited without a travel paper. . . ."

In April 1950 Brecht's application for Austrian citizenship was finally granted. The formalities to obtain the passport itself took some time. He obtained his Austrian passport in the fall of 1950. By that time the whole episode of his application for naturalization had become known in Austria and had caused a public scandal, as anti-Communist circles reproached the government for having been taken in by a

well-known Communist. There was even, for a time, a boycott of Brecht's plays in Austria, outside of the Soviet sector
of Vienna. But he retained his Austrian nationality to the
end. With his Austrian passport he could freely travel in the
many countries that did not recognize the East German
regime. If any Western visitor inquired whether Brecht might
be able to come to a performance of his plays or a congress
in Western Europe, Brecht would break into a broad grin and
say with his most Schweikian expression: "But of course; I
have an Austrian passport. . . ."[6]

Moreover, the Berliner Ensemble, which emerged from the
company that had appeared in Brecht's and Engel's production of *Mother Courage* at the Deutsches Theater, was at
first planned as a mobile, touring company. In the first years
of its existence the Berliner Ensemble, while it was given excellent rehearsal accommodation and ample financial means,
had no permanent home of its own; it appeared as a fleeting
tenant of the stage of the Deutsches Theater and spent a
good deal of time on the road. In the autumn of 1949, before
the Berliner Ensemble was formally constituted, *Mother
Courage* had toured West Germany. The East German authorities clearly regarded the *avant-gardist* style of Brecht's
theatre as even more useful for propaganda purposes in the
West than within their own sphere, where Brecht's theories
and practice were regarded with some suspicion as formalism.
But the East German authorities' aim suited Brecht admira-
bly; it gave him, at least in theory, the best of both worlds:
East German money to put on his plays and ample opportunity for travel and acclaim in the West.

What is more, in East Germany he felt that he could
exercise a real influence on the course of events. His prestige
as an internationally famous figure who had thrown in his lot
with the regime, the very fact that his presence was being
used for purposes of propaganda, seemed to give him an opportunity to make his views count. He knew many of the
leading figures of the regime from his years of exile, so that he
was sure he would always have access to the authorities. In
the West he would have been only an artist and intellectual
on the fringe of affairs. In the East he would be in the very
center of things. In the words of Brecht's *alter ego* Herr

Keuner, the city of B was preferable to the city of A, because "in the city of A they asked me to dine; but in the city of B they asked me into the kitchen."[7]

In the autumn of 1949 Brecht finally moved to Berlin to become "artistic adviser" to the Berliner Ensemble, which was placed under the direction of his wife, Helene Weigel. After thirteen preliminary and forty-eight stage rehearsals the new company's first production, Mr. Puntila and His Hired Man Matti, opened on November 8, 1949.

Brecht, who had left Berlin as the *enfant terrible* of his time, now returned to it as the grand old man of German literature. He found it difficult to fill that role adequately. Considerable efforts were made to give him a tidier and better groomed appearance, but without much success. On one occasion, when he turned up for a reception at the House of Soviet Culture, shabbily dressed and unshaven, he was turned away at the door as unworthy of gracing so respectable a gathering of dignitaries. Hastily, and much relieved, he hurried away before his identity might be discovered.

With his austere gray suit cut on the lines of a workman's overall and his cloth cap, he did not look like a person of weight. One day when he had to get papers stamped at some ministry, the minor official at the door made him feel the power of authority by having him fill in a long document with all the details of where he wanted to go and whom he wanted to see. Scrutinizing this document, he spelled out the applicant's name—" 'Bertolt Brecht. Are you a relative of Bert Brecht?' he asked. 'Yes, I am my own son,' said Brecht and disappeared, muttering: 'In every hole you still find a Kaiser William II.' "[8]

He refused to make use of a sumptuous official car and drove around in an old Steyr cabriolet, exactly like the one he had earned in the twenties by writing a publicity poem. And this car he had *bought* and paid for himself. If, as he drove up in his car, the porter hastened to hold the car door open for him, he ostentatiously got out on the other side.

Yet he did not refuse some of the other, more solid benefits and privileges enjoyed by members of the ruling circle of a Communist country: a flat in town and a country house at Buckow on the shore of the Scharmuetzelsee, with a large park surrounding the villa that had once belonged to a rich Berlin businessman. Brecht himself preferred to stay in the gardener's cottage.

The flat in town was at the back of an old building in the Chausséestrasse. It overlooked the Huguenot cemetery, where Hegel is buried. Helene Weigel had a separate flat on the floor below where she lived with her daughter Barbara, an actress in the Berlin Ensemble. Brecht's son had stayed behind in the United States.

Now that Brecht could indulge his tastes, he surrounded himself with objects he liked:

> . . . Curiously shaped chairs that did not match, very small tables, a minute harmonium, a portable typewriter. Half-smoked cigars were lying on pewter plates; on the walls an engraving, Oriental masks, and two little old photographs, one of Marx when his beard was still black, the other of Engels in his early youth; all horizontal areas were covered by mountains of paper: music, manuscripts, letters, posters, books. . . .[9]

The clock on the wall of one of the rooms had a case made of an old copper saucepan. For Brecht loved old, well-worn things:

> *Of all the works of man I love most*
> *Those that are much used.*
> *Copper vessels, dented, buckled, with flattened rims;*
> *Knives and forks with wooden handles*
> *Worn smooth by many hands: such forms*
> *I thought most noble. . . .*[10]

And in his own surroundings as much as in the theatre he disliked any attempt to cover up the workings of machinery by hiding it behind genteel disguises. When he asked one of the decorators of the Berliner Ensemble to fix him some cur-

tain wire in his study at Buckow, the workman hid the wire
behind a beautiful oak pelmet. Brecht was horrified:
"Fischer," he said to the man, "you are covering up the technical apparatus. One must be able to see how things
work. . . ."11

So Brecht created an island for himself to which he could
withdraw from the strains and stresses of the outside world.
He was appalled by what he found on his return to Germany:
the bureaucracy of the authorities, the vulgar, petty bourgeois tastes of the population, the horrible tastelessness of the
goods offered for sale—and eagerly bought by the people.
Where was the upsurge of good taste the left-wing intellectuals of the twenties had always associated with the coming
of the revolution? Now Brecht had to explain it all away by
the argument that people of a class that has just come to
power desire first an abundance of the things they had seen
in the homes of the class they displaced. The trouble was,
however, that the working class of East Germany did *not*
feel that it had come to power. It merely wanted any con-
sumer goods it could get hold of, whether they were ugly or
not.

But from these realities the members of the ruling clique
in East Germany were mercifully isolated; they had no contact with the people or with popular feeling. The immense
difference in their way of living completely cut off the few,
with their town flats and country houses, their cars and their
privilege of free travel—and shopping—in the West from the
downtrodden, fear-ridden mass of the people. The intellectuals within this narrow ruling class had little in common
with the hardboiled party functionaries. They had to fall back
on the even narrower circle of their fellow intellectuals. For
Brecht in many ways this became a replica of the equally
isolated world of the German *émigrés* in the United States.
Hanns Eisler and Paul Dessau, who had been among Brecht's
closest friends in America, belonged to this circle; Arnold
Zweig had also returned from exile; Herbert Ihering, Brecht's
discoverer and champion among the critics, had kept his
position under Hitler and had now landed on his feet in the
Soviet Zone as well.

For Brecht the main escape from this parochial world of

uperannuated intellectuals was his work with the young
members of his theatre and with the young writers who
were his pupils in the German Academy of Arts. In these
young people Brecht inspired a fanatical devotion, and among
them he found a considerable number of brilliant talents.
Manfred Wekwerth, Hans Joachim Bunge, Peter Palitzsch,
Kaethe Ruelicke, Egon Monk, and a number of other members of the literary and production staff of the Berliner Ensemble formed the nucleus of a band of disciples who more
than once provoked the wrath of the party stalwarts by their
unorthodox views and their unorthodox and somewhat uni-
form appearance. Among the young writers with whom
Brecht worked or who followed his teaching from a distance
were some of the outstanding talents of the younger generation: the poets Heinz Kahlau and Guenter Kunert, and the
young dramatist Peter Hacks, now the main exponent of
Brechtian drama in Germany. It is significant that these
young writers are all considered to belong to the opposition
against the hide-bound party orthodoxy of the old guard intellectuals. They have often been the target of attacks from
the inner circles of the party and have sometimes bravely hit
back. Monk and Palitzsch left East Germany and for many
years have been working in West Germany where they have
been responsible for the transplanting and continuation of
the Brechtian style of production and revolutionary political
approach to the theatre.

In 1954 the Berliner Ensemble was given its own theatre;
the Theater am Schiffbauerdamm, which had seen some of
Brecht's greatest triumphs in the twenties, became its permanent home. A startling poster designed by Picasso invited the
people of East Berlin to the opening performance and immediately aroused a storm of protest from people who considered it a typical example of formalistic, bourgeois art.

The Schiffbauerdamm theatre had been modernized and
brought up to date. Brecht was so grateful to the technicians
that he wrote them a letter in which he asked them to remind
him of the debt he owed them, if and when he should become
too rude during rehearsals. The technicians, remembering

many terrible rows that Brecht had made, painted the rele
vant sentence from Brecht's letter on an enormous streame
that always hung in the flies, to be lowered into view at the
appropriate moment should Brecht ever become too angry
But it was never used.

Now that Brecht was master of his own theatre he had
achieved one of the greatest ambitions of his life: a company
of about sixty actors and actresses, a total personnel of more
than two hundred and fifty—actors, designers, directors,
Dramaturgen, mechanics, musicians, scene painters—was at
his disposal. New productions could be rehearsed for periods
from three to five months, and Brecht could indulge his
habit of trying out everything in practice before rejecting or
adopting it. Half jokingly but half seriously, he had often
maintained that he considered himself the greatest director
in the world—with the single exception of Charlie Chaplin.
Now he could put this boast to the test. In the few years that
were left to him, he proved his claim. When the Berliner
Ensemble visited Paris—in 1954 with *Mother Courage* and in
1955 with *The Caucasian Chalk Circle*—its European fame
was assured. Visitors from all over Europe came to East
Berlin to watch Brecht at work as he sat in his special director's chair in the front row of the auditorium, quietly watching the rehearsal and weighing the many different ways in
which a single gesture could be performed until the only one
that was really right was found. In his last years every word
he said during rehearsals was reverently tape-recorded by his
disciples. He had indeed become a grand old man.

But in spite of this outward success, membership in the
Academy of Arts, the award of the National Prize First Class
for Art and Literature and later the Stalin Peace Prize, relations between Brecht and the East German Communist authorities were by no means smooth. However isolated the
privileged class of artists and intellectuals may have been
from the downtrodden and long-suffering population, who
showed their true feelings by crossing the border into West
Germany by the thousands,[12] reality broke in upon them in
the uprising of June 17, 1953. Nor could Brecht, who did not
suffer fools gladly, remain unaffected by the stupidity and
low intellectual caliber of many of the bureaucrats with

vhom he came into contact: the party and state function-
ries responsible for allocating paper, passing the plans for
he theatre's future repertoire, etc. Having become a Communist in protest against the empty nationalism of the German bourgeoisie, he was now supporting a regime that was
indulging in propaganda even more violently chauvinistic and
hollow. This clash between the reality of the Communist
state and the ideal picture he had believed in presented
Brecht with a continuous conflict of conscience, which is described in greater detail elsewhere in this book.[13] The difficulties he had with his and Paul Dessau's opera *The Trial of
Lucullus* were followed by a ban on his play about the Paris
Commune, *The Days of the Commune,* which the authorities
considered too defeatist; his *Primer of War,* the fruit of his
collection of news photographs, was at first refused the im-
primatur of the authorities as being too pacifist. Only when
Brecht threatened to bring the whole matter before the
World Peace Council was permission finally granted.[14]

Even more grotesque, in the light of Brecht's previous struggle with capitalist film makers to protect *The Threepenny
Opera* from being distorted in its film version, was the conflict in which he was involved in connection with a projected
film of *Mother Courage.* The East German State film concern DEFA planned *Mother Courage* as a monster Cinemascope epic in color. Work on the film, which was to be
directed by Wolfgang Staudte, then East Germany's leading
director (he has since fled to the West), was started in the
autumn of 1954. Brecht insisted that the actors of the Berliner Ensemble should appear in the film in the parts they
had played on the stage. Staudte refused and work was sus-
pended. But in the summer of 1955 the project was taken up
again. To increase the film's appeal in the West, Staudte had
invited two leading French stars (Simone Signoret and Bernard Blier) to appear in *Mother Courage.* A three-cornered
fight ensued among Brecht, who still wanted Helene Weigel
to play the name part, Staudte, who preferred another actress,
and the party authorities, who insisted on various changes in
the text, designed to make the film conform with the current political line. Both Brecht and Staudte tried to resist
party interference. On the other hand, Brecht made such a

nuisance of himself by demanding a say in all kinds of detail of the filming, right down to the historical authenticity of the shoes the characters should wear, that the director obtained an order banning Brecht from the precincts of the studios.

After much wrangling and deadlock the film was abandoned for the time being. Having sat idly in Berlin for weeks, Simone Signoret and Bernard Blier returned to Paris. Some years later—after Brecht's death—a less ambitious film version of *Mother Courage* was completed; this was, essentially, a transfer of the Berliner Ensemble's production, with the Berliner Ensemble's actors, to the screen. Helene Weigel played Mother Courage. But this film, important as it is as a record of the great stage production, achieved only moderate success.

In spite of all these difficulties and annoyances Brecht loyally continued to lend the East German Communists his support. Cynic that he was, he still felt under an obligation to repay the financial support he received from the authorities. Talking to a Swiss newspaper man about his troubles with *Lucullus* he once said: "Let Adenauer put the means for so far-reaching an experiment at my disposal! After all, the patrons have a right to make their wishes felt. . . ."[15] In this spirit Brecht played his part in the various campaigns of the East German authorities. He sent telegrams to Einstein and other famous Americans when the campaign to obtain a reprieve for the Rosenbergs was at its height, and repeatedly addressed appeals to West German intellectuals during the agitation against the rearmament of the Federal Republic. From time to time he appeared on the platform at press conferences arranged by the East German propaganda authorities for the benefit of Western journalists. Looking much older than his age and having grown somewhat fat and flabby, he would inveigh with particular venom against the "warmongers" of the West. There can be no doubt that on this point he was sincere; he had succeeded in making himself believe that the old militarists were being helped back into the saddle in West Germany by the Americans, and with his memories of the horrors he had seen in the military hospital of the First World War this conviction enabled him to overlook the most blatant sins of the East German regime—including their rearmament started on the best Prussian lines long before a West German defense contribution had even been discussed.

But despite his valiant efforts to make propaganda for them, the East German regime often let him down. During a discussion with Western intellectuals attended by Brecht and the East German Minister for Culture, Johannes R. Becher, Melvin J. Lasky, then editor of the liberal West Berlin monthly *Der Monat*, offered Brecht space in his magazine to put his views before a Western audience—provided the same privilege was granted Lasky in an East German publication. Brecht laughed off any suggestion that the East German authorities would not dare to have any article of Lasky's published and eventually, if somewhat reluctantly, accepted the challenge. But no article from Brecht arrived. Clearly he had overestimated the liberalism of his political friends. And so he had to undergo the humiliation of seeing *Der Monat* appear with a blank page—reserved for Brecht's article on artistic freedom.[16]

No wonder Brecht looked tired and worn in these years of his greatest outward success. The poems he wrote in this period show a deep feeling of guilt, malaise, and a nostalgic, tender yearning for the Augsburg of his youth. Was it this tiredness that kept him from writing anything of major significance after his return to East Berlin? Was it the oppressive lack of freedom? Or was it, as has been argued by some defenders of the East German regime, merely that Brecht was too eager to see his old plays staged to write any new ones? All these factors undoubtedly contributed to Brecht's sterility. That he was just too busy seems difficult to believe; not only did he work extremely fast, when he came to grips with an idea, but he spent a great deal of time adapting existing plays: Lenz's *Der Hofmeister* (*The Private Tutor*), a combined version of two comedies by Gerhart Hauptmann, *Biberpelz* (*The Beaver Fur*) and *Roter Hahn* (*The Red Cock*), an adaptation of Farquhar's *Recruiting Officer* (*Pauken und Trompeten*), and a version of *Coriolanus*. For Brecht working on an adaptation of this kind was hardly less arduous than writing a new play of his own. On the other hand, it was safer to work on existing material. The East German authorities were constantly urging him to write a propaganda play on one of the great contemporary issues of the Communist transformation of their republic. And it is known that Brecht was in fact working on one such play, which was to have dealt with the life of the shock worker Hans Garbe. But it is also known that he abandoned work on it when it became clear that his way of treating the subject would not meet with the approval of the party authorities. Brecht confined his literary support of the regime to a number of political marching songs, an anti-Adenauer cantata (*Report on Herrnburg*), and a long poem on the improvement of the growing of millet in the Soviet Union (*The Nurture of Millet*).

When he died Brecht left an almost completed but unrevised play, *Turandot oder der Kongress der Weisswaescher* (*Turandot or the Congress of Whitewashers*), a satire in a Chinese setting directed against intellectuals who defend the capitalist system. He is also reported to have been planning a counterplay to Beckett's *Waiting for Godot*.

Helped by his Austrian passport, Brecht took every opportunity to travel in the West, whether it was to a PEN Congress in Amsterdam or a guest appearance of the Berliner Ensemble in Paris, a première of one of his plays in West Germany, a production of *The Threepenny Opera* in Milan, or some East-West discussion in West Berlin.

He particularly enjoyed his visits to Paris; France and French culture had always been his particular love. Vladimir Pozner has described one of these visits to Paris: Brecht buying mountains of paper-back crime stories in English (his favorite reading) or inhaling the delicious odors of a large plate of cheeses in a restaurant. "I should like to exhibit this plate of cheese in the foyer of my theatre in Berlin," he said, "to teach the Germans the meaning of culture!"[17]

In the spring of 1955 Brecht fell seriously ill. Henceforth he was haunted by forebodings of death. When his Swiss friend Max Frisch came to visit him in the summer of that year, Brecht asked him about the chances of buying a small house on Lake Geneva to which he could retire.

He did not look ill, but exhausted . . . and his politeness, a very individual kind of graceful courtesy which
he maintained even after the most heated discussions,
this time only accompanied me to the door of his apartment, so that I had to look for the way out of the house
by myself. Real discussion, the open cut and thrust of
conflicting views—that had been buried long ago. . . .[18]

On his fifty-eighth birthday, on February 10, 1956, Brecht
was in Milan to attend the first night of Giorgio Strehler's
production of *The Threepenny Opera* at the Piccolo Teatro.
Talking to an old acquaintance about his heart, he said with
a smile: "At least one knows that death will be easy. A slight
knock at the windowpane, and then. . . ."
Shortly afterwards his old school friend and favorite stage
designer, Caspar Neher, came to see him. They talked about
the adaptation of *Coriolanus* on which they were working,
and Neher quoted the Roman custom of appearing in sack-
cloth and ashes—*"in luctu et squalore"*—when applying for
public office. Brecht pointed to the cemetery under his window and said: "Soon you will stand down there *in luctu et
squalore*. . . ."[19]
The Berliner Ensemble were rehearsing for their London
season, which was to start on August 27, 1956. On August 5
one of the young directors of the Ensemble, Manfred Wekwerth, had gone to visit Brecht at his country place and found
him in the best of spirits. He typed out a brief note to the
actors on how to succeed with the British: ". . . in England
there is an old fear that German art (literature, painting, music) is terribly weighty, long-winded, complicated, and pedes-
trian. Therefore we must play in a fast, light, and vigorous
manner. . . ."[20] Wekwerth also discussed at length the problem of the production of *The Days of the Commune*, which
had at last been passed by the authorities and which Wekwerth was to produce at Karl-Marx-Stadt (Chemnitz).
Brecht talked about the importance of naïveté in his conception of aesthetics. "The naïve," he said, "is an aesthetic cate-
gory, the most concrete of all." And he mentioned the
paintings of Breughel, which had always influenced his ideas
of décor and grouping, as good examples of what he meant by

the truly naïve in art. "The opposite of a naïve approach is naturalism."[21]

On August 10 Brecht attended a rehearsal at the theatre. He felt very tired afterwards, and his condition gradually deteriorated. During the night from the 13th to the 14th of August it became critical. He died of coronary thrombosis at a quarter to midnight on August 14, 1956. Among the four doctors who signed the medical bulletin on his death was Dr. Muellereisert, his schoolmate at Augsburg.

Brecht was buried, as he had requested, in the old Huguenot cemetery beneath the window of his last apartment. He had specifically forbidden any speech-making at the funeral. So the speeches had to be made at a ceremony in the Schiffbauerdamm theatre.

Today the apartment in the Chausséestrasse has become the Brecht archive. Brecht's enormous mass of manuscripts, draft plays, diaries, and jottings of all sorts is being microfilmed and sorted by devoted disciples. A complete critical edition of all his works which had been promised, has thus far failed to materialize. There can be no doubt whatever that the loyal band of Brechtians in charge of this work is determined to carry it through with the utmost faithfulness to the text and to publish every scrap Brecht ever wrote. But whether such a publication will in fact ever be possible in the present circumstances in East Germany is another, and an open, question.

NOTES

1. *Hundert Gedichte*, East Berlin, 1957, p. 313.
2. *Sinn und Form*, Second Special Brecht Issue, 1957, p. 340.
3. Arnolt Bronnen, "Bertolt Brecht und Berlin," *Berliner Zeitung*, East Berlin, 2.9.1958.
4. H. C. Meier, "Gespraech mit Brecht," *Hamburger Freie Presse*, 11.6.1948.

5. Gody Suter, "Brecht," *Tagesanzeiger*, Zurich, 9.1.1956.
6. On Brecht's Austrian citizenship, cf. letters by von Einem and others reprinted in *Aktion*, Vienna, 10.17.1953; "Warum wurde Brecht Oesterreicher?" *Die Presse*, Vienna, 9.30.1951.
7. Brecht, "Zwei Staedte," *Versuche 12*, p. 154.
8. Ruth Berlau, "Wie war Bert Brecht?" *Das Magazin*, East Berlin, February 1958.
9. V. Pozner, "bb," *Sinn und Form*, Second Special Brecht Issue, p. 453.
10. Brecht, "Von allen Werken," *Gedichte und Lieder*, p. 46.
11. "Dreizehn Buehnentechniker erzaehlen," *Sinn und Form*, Second Special Brecht Issue, 1957, p. 476.
12. 199,000 in 1950; 165,000 in 1951; 182,000 in 1952; 331,000 in 1953; 184,000 in 1954; 242,000 in 1955; 279,000 in 1956.
13. See Chapter VII.
14. "Brecht—beinahe verboten," *Frankfurter Allgemeine Zeitung*, 11.19.1955.
15. Gody Suter, "Brecht," *Tagesanzeiger*, Zurich, 9.1.1956.
16. *Der Monat*, West Berlin, January 1955.
17. Vladimir Pozner, "bb," *Europe*, January/February 1957, p. 30.
18. Max Frisch, "Brecht ist tot," *Die Weltwoche*, Zurich, 8.24.1956.
19. Caspar Neher, "Dem Gedaechtnis meines Freundes," *Sinn und Form*, Second Special Brecht Issue, 1957, p. 437.
20. Brecht, "Zum Londoner Gastspiel." Leaflet in program of London Season of Berliner Ensemble (1956).
21. M. Wekwerth, "Auffinden einer Aesthetischen Kategorie," *Sinn und Form*, Second Special Brecht Issue, 1957, p. 267.

Part Two: THE ARTIST

CHAPTER V

THE POET: BRECHT'S LANGUAGE AND ITS SOURCES

Brecht was a poet, first and foremost. However much interest his writings may have aroused as expressions of the problems and anxieties of the age, as political pamphlets, manifestoes of stage reform, or social documents, their chief distinction lies in their being "memorable speech." This is their primary significance. It underlies, and from it derives, any other significance they may possess.

Brecht's plays may be discussed and imitated as examples of a new kind of dramatic construction or stage technique. Nevertheless their main importance lies in their poetic quality. The new dramatic convention they represent lives above all through the grace of their language and the poetic vision of the world it conveys. Without the stamp of greatness impressed upon them by their poetry, these plays could never have exercised such an influence. They would not even have been noticed. And so it is with Brecht's ideas in other fields. They become important only as the ideas of a major poet.

But this also makes any discussion of Brecht particularly difficult outside his own linguistic sphere. While writers like Sartre or Thomas Mann lose relatively little by translation and their ideas come across in any language, Brecht's ideas, in their own way as significant as theirs, are so intimately bound up with the manner in which they are expressed that any account of Brecht's work which has to ignore this quality becomes unreal. Hence the champions of Brecht in the English-speaking world often appear to be overstating their case. Brecht's poetry does not translate well. Its power, to a large extent, lies in its directness and simplicity, in the bold use o hackneyed words in unhackneyed contexts. Inevitably in trans lation simplicity often turns into mere simple-mindedness o banality and the common word subtly used into the mere commonplace.

It is clearly futile to try to *describe* the beauties of a poet style at second hand. Yet an attempt must be made here t convey, without deeper analysis of Brecht's use of words, syn tax, and imagery, some of the features that account for it impact, and to trace the varied sources and influences that li behind it.

Literary German, and above all stage German, is essentiall an artificial, dead language. While standard English, standard French, and standard American are spoken, if not by th whole population at least by important sections of it, standard German exists only on paper and on the stage. In ordinary life even the most educated Germans have a clearly defined re gional accent and vocabulary. It is thus far more difficult i German to write dramatic dialogue that sounds like rea speech and that is free from the local overtones and limita tions of mere dialect. Some of the greatest achievements o German dramatic literature are in fact dialect plays and con fined to a limited area: the Viennese folk theatre of Raimund and Nestroy, or the Darmstadt comedies of Niebergall. When naturalism reached the German stage, its first successful ex ponent, Gerhart Hauptmann, wrote his early plays in Silesian and later in Berlin dialect. He turned to standard "poetic' German only when he took up a vague and bloodless ro manticism.

In poetry, even more than in the drama, the language used tends to diverge from real speech and to assume a highly formalized hieratic tone, which some poets like Stefan George and Rilke have used with consummate skill and great effect, but which tends to degenerate into empty and abstract phrase-making in the hand of lesser men.

Brecht, however, achieved the rare feat of creating in his poetry and plays a language all his own, which suggested the rhythms and gave the feeling of real speech without being tied to any particular regional dialect. It is still not a language spoken by anyone in reality—with the exception perhaps of Brecht himself. But while it is a synthesis, it is such a vital and original synthesis, so deeply rooted in a number of different traditions, that it creates the illusion of real speech.

This was the quality that overwhelmed the audience even in Brecht's first chaotic plays. As one critic said at that time:

> If it weren't for Brecht's diction! Again and again it simply forces you to listen. His characters may talk the silliest stuff for quarters of an hour on end. In parts what they say is completely devoid of sense. But the point is: *how* they say it! No other writer has caught the speech of the masses of the people as Brecht has. In comparison Toller's leading-article-German is ridiculous; even Hauptmann sounds like reams of paper beside him. . . . For Brecht language is no longer a secondary, indirect matter, no longer merely a question of intellectual expression, but something elementary, a function of the body. . . . This language rises up from depths in which the conscious self only flickers as a far-off, little taper. It is no coincidence that in Brecht's plays there are so many drunkards, and that almost all his characters are good drinkers: *in vino veritas*. This language never lies, there is not the least bit of padding in it. All rational inhibitions are here dissolved. . . . The choice of words itself is *banal*, but the way they are put together almost amounts to genius. . . .[1]

This intensely personal idiom, chaotic and uncontrolled in his early years, disciplined into severe and monumental simplicity later on, is the product of the fusion of many diverse and disparate elements.

Ernest Borneman has most perceptively isolated the four main sources of Brecht's language:

> 1—the daily speech of southern Germany; 2—an anti-metaphorical poetry of colors, textures, and other concrete images; 3—bureaucratic jargon; 4—Anglicisms and exotic expressions.[2]

These elements, which are already clearly present in Brecht's earliest published writings, are the basis of his personal idiom; the regional Bavarian accent is always to be detected, but never lapses into mere local color. It is stylized and fused with archaic elements from an earlier, baroque layer of the German language. The use of phrases and constructions from the jargon of the civil service is in itself a somewhat baroque device. The stilted locutions of the bureaucrats are to a large extent historical relics, and Brecht used their dusty flavor and demented pedantry not only as parody but somehow turned it into poetic imagery through which the desiccated, fossilized clichés suddenly sprang into new and unexpected life.

Brecht's language also has a firm basis in the chief source of modern standard German. Once, when asked by a magazine to name the strongest literary influence in his life, Brecht replied in a single sentence: "You will laugh: the Bible!"[3] And in fact the vigorous, outspoken language of Luther's Bible pervades the writings of the atheist and blasphemer Brecht. He made masterly use of Biblical constructions: the juxtaposition of contrasted half-sentences, parallelism, repetition, and inversion.

Equally marked throughout Brecht's life was the influence of the street ballad, the *Moritat* (morality), as it was sung by balladmongers at country fairs—lurid accounts of murders and executions couched in the strident language of lachrymose sentiment and naïve horror. Brecht turned to this "vulgar" style in protest against the gentility and respectability of the bourgeois society he abhorred. Disgusted by the insipid classical poetry taught at school, he reveled in the powerful emotions and garish colors of the entertainments of the common people, the songs of kitchen maids and the pleasures offered by the sideshows of fair grounds and beer gardens.

In protesting against the canons and conventions of German poetry, the stately idealism of Goethe or Schiller which he had been taught at school, Brecht returned to the last relics of an older tradition which these reformers of the German language and purgers of its "coarseness" and "irregularity" had tried to eradicate. Goethe and Schiller had been the crowning glory of the literary movement of the eighteenth century, whose aim it had been to base the greatness of the united German nation they sought to create upon the sure foundation of a German national literature as respectable and regular, as elegant and polite as the literatures of France and England. To achieve this aim the exuberance of the baroque, the earthiness of the folk tradition had to be banished from polite society. The victory of the reformers seemed complete. Yet among the comics of the beer gardens, in the peep-shows and fair-ground "panoramas" the old German baroque drama, the earlier traditions of Hans Sachs, the Austrian and Bavarian forms of the Italian commedia dell' arte, and even some relics of the mystery plays of the Middle Ages were still alive when Brecht was young.

The Austrian and Bavarian folk theatre, which reached its peak in the Viennese popular drama of the late eighteenth and early nineteenth centuries, is a branch of the same tradition that also survives in English pantomime. The only example of the genre which has achieved international fame is Schikaneder's *Magic Flute*, carried to immortality by Mozart's music. If one imagines *The Magic Flute* with the music much reduced in weight, it can serve as a good example of its type. The main plot is a fantastic fairy tale with a strong moral lesson, but parallel to it there always runs a coarsely comic plot that parodies and debunks the highfalutin antics of the noble lovers and matches their ethereal sentiments with earthy common sense. While the "high" plot is intended as historical drama, the "low" plot lapses into constant anachronisms. The spoken dialogue is interrupted by musical numbers—"couplets" with recurring refrains that resemble the comic character songs of the Victorian music hall.

This is a genuinely common, "plebeian" kind of theatre. As the romantic plot is no longer taken seriously, the higher world of upper-class sentiments is presented from the ruthless viewpoint of the common people. The heroes are seen through the eyes of their valets and chambermaids. This produces a characteristic duality of language: the high-flown bombast of the "noble" characters stands against the homely, vigorous common sense of the people.

The sketches that Brecht's greatly admired friend Karl Valentin performed in the beer gardens of Munich were direct descendants of this tradition. He was the last in a long line of great clowns and Hans Wursts stretching back to the eighteenth century.

Brecht's theatre with its use of fairy-tale elements, musical numbers, and broadly comical characters is a continuation of this old and once despised tradition and has re-established it as a vehicle for the expression of ideas. His language drew much of its vigor and force from the earthy speech of clowns who never failed to call a spade a spade.

The affinities between this comico-heroic drama and Shakespeare are clear enough, and the early Brecht was deeply indebted to the Elizabethans, both directly, and indirectly through their greatest follower in German literature, Georg Buechner, the author of *Woyzeck* and *Danton's Death*. Brecht regarded Buechner as the greatest German dramatist and modeled his early plays on him. In *Baal* and *Drums in the Night* we find the same feverish, rhythmic prose, tender and coarse in turn, direct and daring in its images:

And love is like letting one's naked arm swim in the water of a pond, with weeds between one's fingers; like the torment of which the drunken tree begins to sing as it creaks when the wild wind rides it; like drowning in the wine you gulp down on a hot day, and her body pours into you like very cool wine and penetrates every fold of your skin; soft like plants in the winds are the joints; and the force of the impact to which you yield is like flying against a storm and her body tumbles over you like cool gravel. . . .⁴

This ecstatic prose of Brecht's first play also shows the influence of another great rebel among German dramatists, Frank Wedekind (1864–1918), another follower of Buechner, who spent his life struggling for the sexual liberation of mankind like D. H. Lawrence after him, acted in his own plays, and sang his ballads in the Munich cabarets.

Brecht saw himself as one of this band of outsiders. He was fascinated by all the *poètes maudits* of world literature: François Villon, whose ballads he used in *The Threepenny*

Opera, Baudelaire, Verlaine, and Rimbaud. The plot of *Baal* contains echoes of the relationship between Rimbaud and Verlaine, and so does another early play, *In the Jungle of the Cities*, in which Brecht quotes extensively from *Une saison en enfer* in K. L. Ammer's translation. Many of the poems in Brecht's first published collection, the *Domestic Breviary*, are modeled on Rimbaud's language.

Surprising as it may seem at first sight, Brecht was at least as strongly influenced by a poet of an entirely different stamp: Rudyard Kipling. The same impulse that drove him from the drab respectability of provincial society to the vagabonds among the poets, street entertainers, and fair-ground comics also made Brecht dream of the wide, wide world he found in the *Barrack-Room Ballads*. There too he met a vigorous plebeian language—spiced with deliciously exotic names of places and things that breathed an air of boundless freedom and adventure.

Kipling was the main source of the exotic, mythical Anglo-Saxon world which forms the background to a great deal of Brecht's earlier writing. Other elements in it come from Swift and Gay, Upton Sinclair, Jack London, the Chicago stories of the Danish novelist J. V. Jensen (*The Wheel*), Dickens, innumerable crime stories, and gangster films. This world, in which English and American elements are inextricably mixed up, is as unlike real England or America as it could possibly be. It is a world inhabited by huge, hard-drinking lumberjacks from the Yukon *en route* for Benares, laden with gold and ready to spend it; a world where Chicago merges into Soho and John Gay's rogues and highwaymen are blood-brothers to bootleggers and gangsters. This is the world of *The Threepenny Opera*: eighteenth-century London inhabited by highwaymen, whores, and Victorian bankers, ruled by the police chief Brown, who is addressed as "Sheriff" and has served with Macheath in the Indian Army, where they freely made mincemeat out of any brown or yellow race they met between "the Cape and Cooch Behar." Chicago, on the other hand, is the home of the demonic merchant Shlink in *In the*

Jungle, who happens to be a Malay from Yokohama and is hounded by a lynching mob for having lived with a white girl. In Chicago too we find, in *St. Joan of the Stockyards,* the mighty canned-meat king Pierpont Mauler, in whose factories careless workers disappear into the mincing machines to reappear in the form of meatloaf; Pierpont Mauler, who ruins whole industries by his ruthlessness on the Stock Exchange and has his starving locked-out workers beaten up by the police. Everything in this mythical Anglo-Saxon empire, which extends from Alaska to the South Seas, is bigger than life-size, savage, adventurous, and free. Brecht was so fascinated by it that he even wrote a number of "songs" in his own peculiar English, which he thought could alone express its flavor:

> *There is no whisky in this town*
> *There is no bar to sit us down*
> *Oh!*
> *Where is the telephone?*
> *Is here no telephone?*
> *Oh Sir, God damn me:*
> *No!*
> *Let's go to Benares*
> *Where the sun is shining*
> *Let's go to Benares!*
> *Johnny, let us go.*[5]

Brecht's ostensible loathing of the capitalist ruthlessness of this dreamland can never quite conceal the magnetic attraction its size, freedom and adventurousness had for him. The drunken pirates of the *Ballade von den Seeraeubern* (*Ballad of the Pirates*), who murder and rape their way across a boundless azure sea, the Kiplingesque soldiers of *Man Equals Man,* who ransack the treasures of ancient pagodas if they want to pay for a pint of beer and storm the mountain fastnesses of Tibet, are the symbols of Brecht's passionate protest against the respectability of small-town bourgeois life in a landlocked country. His love for these images springs from precisely the same roots as his anti-bourgeois, anti-capitalist politics. Even at a later stage of his development, in so openly political a poem as the one in which at the time of the great depression he somewhat prematurely mourned the *Forgotten Glories of the Giant City of New York*, we can detect an undertone of awe and nostalgia:

. . . Harmonious sounds at evening time of the waters of Miami!
Irresistible gaiety of generations driving fast along unending highways!
Powerful sorrows of singing women, hopefully bewailing Broad-chested men, but still surrounded by Broad-chested men![6]

Such was the curious mixture of influences that shaped Brecht's early poetry and the tense, extravagant prose of his first plays. While the Expressionist fashion of the period also left some superficial traces in his style, his basic attitude remained fundamentally different from that of the Expressionists. They were entirely preoccupied with their own ego and projected their own personal emotions onto a cosmic plane, while Brecht's poetry, even in its wildest effusions of riotous imagery, remains strangely impersonal. Like the ballads of the street singers, whose strident tones he tried to reproduce, most of his poems are reports on the accidents and crimes of other people, or dramatic monologues whose first person singular or plural is clearly that of historical or imagined characters. The only really personal poems in Brecht's first published volume of poetry, *Domestic Breviary*, are relegated to an appendix, headed "Of poor B.B." (an echo of "*pauvre François Villon*"), and even here the lyrical self-portrait of the author is put forward in the exhibitionist tone of a music-hall performer presenting a character sketch, masking the private emotion by the posturing of a public performance.

The publication of the *Domestic Breviary* marks the transition to an even more impersonal approach than that represented by many of the early poems collected in that book. By the time Brecht published these poems (1926) his attitude had become austere and didactic. He had made himself one of the main exponents of *Gebrauchslyrik*, the view that poetry should not be an outlet of private emotions but should be judged solely by its social usefulness. Hence the arrangement of the *Domestic Breviary* on the model of a religious breviary as a kind of blasphemous prayer book, in which each poem is designed for use in a certain situation. The collection is prefaced by a detailed "Direction for Use of the Lessons contained in this Book," which starts with the injunction:

This domestic breviary is designed for the use of readers. It must not be gobbled up in a senseless manner.[7]

Detailed indications follow as to the situations in which the poems should be used:

Chapter 2 ("Ballad on Many Ships") is to be read in hours of danger. . . . Chapter 6 ("Ballad of the Pirates") is mainly designed for the light nights of June; but the second part of this ballad, as far as it deals with the sinking of the ship, can still be sung in October, etc.[8]

This is parody, but behind the jest there was a serious and growing conviction. As the frenzy of the Expressionist era died down and the fooleries of Dadaism lost their novelty, many of the younger poets and artists in Germany tried to get away from the fruitless preoccupation with their own selves to the real problems of the age. The plush curtains and ornamental bric-a-brac of the previous, now discredited generation had been torn down and cast aside. The new beauty of the machine, its economy of outline resulting from perfect adaptation to the function for which it had been created, now became the ideal before the artist. This was the creed of a movement labeled *Neue Sachlichkeit*. If social usefulness, however, was to be the new criterion of beauty, literature and the stage also would have to be didactic and to serve the community by teaching it how to live.

And so Brecht's language cast off all ornament and became functional and austere. The *Lehrstuecke* and "school operas" are meant to be "teaching aids" rather than art, and their language is severely factual. In *The Flight of the Lindberghs*, for example, the chorus, which embodies the collective personality of the hero, introduces itself:

> My name is Charles Lindbergh
> I am twenty-five years old
> My grandfather was Swedish
> I am American.
> I have picked my aircraft myself
> Its name is "Spirit of St. Louis"
> The Ryan Aircraft works in San Diego
> Have built it in sixty days. . . .[9]

The poetry of facts and figures is extracted from the most unpromising material:

> I carry with me:
> 2 electric torches
> 1 coil of rope
> 1 roll of string
> 1 hunting knife
> 4 red flares, sealed in rubber tubes
> 1 waterproof box of matches, etc., etc.[9]

It is a measure of Brecht's stature as a poet that he did succeed in achieving the effect of functional elegance he aimed at and that some of the later *Lehrstuecke* have a monolithic, stark beauty of their own. The sudden rejection of the anarchic exuberance of his early style reflects Brecht's yearning for discipline and order, which led him to Marxism, and it is significant that one of the models for his new didactic style was provided by a civilization that followed a pattern of equally strict military discipline: the Japan of the samurai. The school operas *He Who Says Yes* and *He Who Says No* are based on a Japanese Nō play, *Taniko*, in Arthur Waley's translation, and Brecht's most important didactic play, *The Measures Taken*, also derives from this Japanese model.

Arthur Waley's translations of Chinese poetry made a deep impression on Brecht in his next, more mellowed and relaxed stage of development. The Confucian urbanity and courtesy, the quietly ironical tone and free rhythm of these translations became a decisive influence in his progress towards maturity simplicity. The gentle politeness of the Chinese, the undogmatic authority of their classical teachers, represented for him the ultimate socialist ideal of friendliness as the basis of human relations. Brecht made German versions of a number of Waley's Chinese poems, and some of his most successful later verse is clearly modeled on them. In one of these poems, which relates a dream vision of a visit to the once exiled poets in the land of the dead, Brecht sees himself in the company of the shades of Po Chü-i and Tu-fu, together with those of Villon, Dante, Heine, Voltaire, Shakespeare (exiled to Stratford by James I!), Euripides, and Ovid.

Brecht, who knew his own facility in writing verse, deliberately attempted to get away from smooth, easy rhythms. "I needed a heightened language, but I was repelled by the oily smoothness of the usual iambic pentameter,"[10] he writes in his essay *On Unrhymed Verse with Irregular Rhythms*, in which he describes his efforts to find a style that could dispense with rhymes and regular rhythms and yet remain poetry, a poetry expressing the disharmonies of society.

> As a consequence, apart from ballads and rhymed (political) songs for the masses, I wrote more and more poems without rhyme in irregular rhythms. It must be remembered that my main work was done for the stage; I always thought of the spoken word. And I had worked out a special technique for the speaking of prose or verse. I called it *gestisch*. . . .

i.e., a language in which the words already contain the gesture that must accompany them. Characteristically Brecht illustrates what he means by quoting the Bible. To say "pluck out the eye that offends thee" is far less effective than "If thine eye offend thee, pluck it out." Here the language itself implies and compels the corresponding action. Brecht argues that it is this element of implied gesture which can make unrhymed, irregular verse still keep the quality of poetry. He describes how he discovered the power of such irregular rhythms in the slogans shouted in unison by demonstrating masses of unemployed workers and in the headlines called out by news vendors on the street corners of Berlin.

Apart from political marching songs, for which he used a rhymed stereotype of German "folk song," and some of the songs in his plays, most of Brecht's later poetry is in this unrhymed, irregular verse, the rhythmic subtleties of which he compared to those of the syncopations of jazz or tap-dancing. This highly personal style is equally effective in the robust anti-Nazi *German Satires* he wrote for broadcasting from the "German Freedom Station" before the war and the elegiac poetry of his exile as well as in the very short, epigrammatic poems resembling Japanese Haiku he composed with masterly economy of words in the last years of his life.

But it is in the great plays he wrote between 1937 and 1947 that the overflowing richness of his early language and the didactic severity of the phase that followed are blended in a masterly idiom unequaled by any other German dramatist of this century. The Biblical allusions, the Bavarian local accent, the exotic names, the archaisms, and the garish rhythms of the street ballad are still there, but controlled and put into their place by the conciseness and economy acquired in the austere atmosphere of the didactic plays and mellowed and relaxed by the influence of the Chinese example. Each play has its own individual tone: *Mother Courage* the earthy flavor of seventeenth-century German and the picaresque novels of Grimmelshausen, *Puntila* a racy folk language, *Galileo* the richness of baroque scientific and religious disputation, *The Good Woman of Setzuan* a Confucian urbanity, *The Caucasian Chalk Circle* a different blend of Oriental colors, and *Schweik in the Second World War* a brilliant pastiche of the language of Hašek's novel.

The various and openly acknowledged influences which shaped Brecht's work throughout his life have inevitably led to his being accused of plagiarism and lack of originality. In fact, his originality consisted of his uncanny ability to absorb and assimilate the most diverse and seemingly incompatible elements. Under the influence of the Romantics an even greater value is attached in Germany than elsewhere to the quality of uniqueness, the originality, which is said to be the essence of genius. Brecht thought little of this cult of originality. In one of his Keuner stories he makes his alter ego quote the example of the Chinese philosopher Chuang Tzu, who wrote a book of a hundred thousand words, nine-tenths of which consisted of extracts from other books.

> Such books can no longer be written in our country, because we have not enough intelligence. That is why we manufacture ideas only in our own workshops. Anyone who is unable to put enough of them together feels that he is lazy. That is why there are no ideas worth taking up, and no phrases worth quoting. . . . They build their huts without help and with nothing but the miserable amount of material a single person can carry. They know no larger buildings than those one man can build by himself![11]

Brecht loved to adapt and to modify the work of others. He needed the challenge of another mind to get the best from his own talent. He based many of his plays on existing originals—Marlowe's *Edward II*, Gay's *Beggar's Opera*, Hašek's *Schweik*, old Japanese or Chinese legends. Again and again he drew on motifs from Shakespeare. His satire against racialism, *The Roundheads and the Peakheads*, contains elements from the plot of *Measure for Measure*; in *Arturo Ui*, in which the rise of Hitler is parodied through that of a Chicago gangster, the character of the villainous hero is modeled on Richard III, so that the murder of Roehm echoes the downfall of Buckingham and the Hitler character woos the widow of one of his victims. But while the Shakespearean models are used with reverence and admiration, the German classics are always ruthlessly parodied. Brecht even went so far as to parody the Bible: Macheath, for example, is betrayed by a kiss on a Thursday evening.

Besides reverent adaptation or cruel parody, Brecht had a third way of assimilating the work of others: the counterplay, written as a reply to, or refutation of, an existing work. His first play, *Baal*, was written to show how Johst's *Der Einsame* could be bettered. *The Days of the Commune* was a reply to

Nordahl Grieg, and at the time of his death Brecht planned a counterplay to Beckett's *Waiting for Godot*.

It would be tedious to pursue the countless literary parallels, concealed quotations, and examples of pastiche and parody in Brecht's work. This will provide employment for generations of students to come. Brecht shares his predilection for literary allusion with writers like T. S. Eliot, Ezra Pound, and James Joyce. It marks him as an intellectual, in spite of his sincere attempts and avowed intention to write for the common people. The use of parody, moreover, particularly the iconoclastic mockery of the German classics, the Bible, and religious hymns and anthems, reveals Brecht's ambivalent attitude towards these models. Parody gave Brecht an opportunity to fulfill an unconscious desire to emulate and follow these examples. Under the cover of ridicule he could indulge the "high-minded," even religious impulses which his rational, cynical self would not allow him to acknowledge. In his later phase, when he had found a positive framework of belief and had attained recognition as a classic of his own time, the tendency to parody great literary examples disappeared, while his love for open adaptation and imitation continued unabated.

Brecht's readiness to sink his own personality in the work of his predecessors and contemporaries, to use the whole storehouse of past literature as so much material for his own handiwork, was in accordance with his views about the nature of poetry itself and the poet's function in society. Here, too, he rejected the mystical, romantic view of the poet as the vessel of divinely inspired intuitions, called upon to fulfill and express his unique personality. To him the poet was a craftsman serving the community and relying on his reason and acquired skill, a man among men, not a being set apart by virtue of some special quality or power. That is why Brecht was ready to accept the advice of numerous collaborators, whom he conscientiously named when his works were published. As he did not consider the work of art divinely inspired, he never hesitated to alter, and often debase, his own work, according to the circumstances of the moment.

After the banning of the operatic version of *The Trial of Lucullus* Brecht told a Swiss journalist that he regarded the indignation of his Western admirers about the interference of the authorities with an artist's work as sheer hypocrisy. After all, the authorities had paid for his opera, so they could demand alterations from the craftsman they employed. "When princes commissioned works of art, they too interfered a great deal with the artists."[12]

Within his own sphere of craftsmanship, however, Brecht never suffered from undue humility. Lion Feuchtwanger tells how he used to counter criticisms of his often very unorthodox use of grammar by saying: "*Ego, poeta Germanus, supra Grammaticos sto.*"[13] And when during his stay in the United States someone drew his attention to a literal translation of an English idiom, pointing out that such a phrase did not exist in German, Brecht replied: "All right. So it exists from now on!"[14]

But this arrogance remained confined to the sphere in which he regarded himself as a craftsman, an expert. It never led him to regard the poet as a higher being. For, as he said in a poem dedicated to the Danish writer Andersen-Nexoe, the time will come when the works of the most exquisite poets will be looked at with different eyes:

> . . . *not for their elevated thoughts*
> *Will their books be searched through; but*
> *Some casual sentence, which allows conclusions*
> *As to some feature of those who were weavers of coats,*
> *Will be read with interest. . . .*[15]

NOTES

1. Harry Kahn, "Bert Brecht," *Die Weltbuehne*, Berlin, 1.17. 1928.

2. E. Borneman, "Ein Epitaph fuer Bertolt Brecht," *Sinn und Form*, Second Special Brecht Issue, 1957, p. 142; also in *The Kenyon Review*, Spring 1959.

3. *Die Dame*, Berlin, 10.1.1928.

4. *Baal. Erste Stuecke I*, p. 18.

5. "Benares Song," *Hauspostille*, Berlin, 1927, p. 42.

6. "Verschollener Ruhm der Riesenstadt New York," *Hundert Gedichte*, East Berlin, 1951, p. 130.

7. *Hauspostille*, Berlin, 1927, p. ix.

8. Ibid., p. xi.

9. *Der Flug der Lindberghs*, *Versuche* 1, p. 3.

10. "Ueber Reimlose Lyrik mit unregelmaessigen Rhythmen," *Versuche* 12, p. 143.

11. "Herr Keuner und die Originalitaet," *Versuche* 5, p. 456.

12. Gody Suter, "Brecht," *Tagesanzeiger*, Zurich, 9.1.1956.

13. Lion Feuchtwanger, "Bertolt Brecht," *Sinn und Form*, Second Special Brecht Issue, 1957, p. 106.

14. H. Winge, "Brecht en privé," *Europe*, January/February 1957, p. 46.

15. "Die Literatur wird durchforscht werden," *Hundert Gedichte*, East Berlin, 1951, p. 173.

CHAPTER VI

THE BRECHTIAN THEATRE—ITS
THEORY AND PRACTICE

Terms like "epic theatre," "non-Aristotelian drama,"
"*Verfremdungseffekt*" (alienation effect, abbreviated into
V-effect), and other catch phrases from Brecht's theoretical
writings have become more widely known than any of his
creative work (with the possible exception of the song "Mac
the Knife"). Taken up by enthusiasts of theatre reform on
both sides of the Atlantic, they have found their way into
the currency of daily and weekly theatrical criticism and must
have puzzled countless readers who have never heard of
Brecht, let alone seen any of his plays.

Such Teutonic neologisms seem to exercise a powerful spell
even on Anglo-Saxon minds, not excluding those who appreciate their usefulness in the sphere of lifemanship; from Kant
to Marx down to our own times the difficulty and obscurity
of a specialized and impenetrable jargon has contributed
much to the success and influence of German ideologies.
Brecht, unwittingly, achieved a similar result in his own,
more modest theorizing. Even he, the clearest and most concrete of writers in his poetry and plays, often succumbed to
the ponderous tradition of German aesthetic philosophy
when he tried to expound the underlying principles of his
work.

Basically these principles are neither very complicated nor
very new, however stimulating and revivifying their influence
may yet prove in the present-day theatre. Towards the end
of his life Brecht made repeated efforts to dissipate the fog
of the Brechtian theories he himself had created in his youth.

The accounts [of my theatre] and many of the assess-
ments based on them are applicable not to the theatre
that I myself produce, but to the theatre that my critics
imagine from reading my treatises. . . . My theories
are altogether far more naïve than one might think—
more naïve than my way of expressing them might allow
one to suspect.[1]

Brecht has always acknowledged his debt to a wide range
of old theatrical conventions and traditions: the Elizabethan,
Chinese, Japanese and Indian theatre, the use of the chorus
in Greek tragedy, the techniques of clowns and fair-ground
entertainers, the Austrian and Bavarian folk play, and many
others. Yet he somehow created the impression that he was
advocating something radically new and entirely revolutionary—perhaps by the dogmatic and didactic tone of his earlier
pronouncements, perhaps by his often excessive insistence
that *his* was the only stage theory to meet the needs of a new,
revolutionary, scientific age.

What perhaps adds to the confusion is that the Brechtian
theory of the drama was not a single, homogeneous body of
doctrine. Throughout his life it changed, developed, and finally mellowed in accordance with the changes in his styles
of writing and stage production. The primary factor was always his creative work; the theories he put forward were post-
scripts to plays or poems rather than *a priori* principles on
which these had been based. The rationalist Brecht deeply
distrusted inspirations and intuitions. So he constructed his
theories as rationalizations of changes in his style, taste, or
stage practice. That is why so much of the discussion of these
theories as general principles has proved barren and unreal.
It is yet to be proved that they have any validity apart from
Brecht's own works—and productions—which they were intended to explain and justify.

Brecht was a rebel. The Brechtian theatre can be understood only in the light of what he rebelled against: the theatre as he found it in Germany around 1920 and as it still
remains in many parts of the world to this day—a theatre in
which bombastic productions of the classics alternate with
empty photographic replicas of everyday life, whether in

melodrama or drawing-room comedy; a theatre that oscillates between emotional uplift and after-dinner entertainment.

We are so used to the concept of the stage as a faithful representation of the world that we tend to forget how recent a growth the naturalistic theatre really is. Before the second half of the nineteenth century, before the introduction of modern lighting techniques and stage machinery, historically accurate costumes, and three-dimensional properties, the theatre could not even pretend to create a complete illusion of actual life, observed through a missing fourth wall. On the earlier stage styles of acting had to be kept openly theatrical to match the surrounding scenery and lighting. Declamation, asides and monologues formed part of a convention never intended to convey the illusion of real happenings on which the audience was merely eavesdropping.

So great was the effect of the new stage techniques that emerged from the efforts of directors like the Duke of Saxe-Meiningen, Stanislavsky, Antoine, Brahm, Granville-Barker, and Reinhardt, that the naturalistic theatre in the widest sense had become accepted as the only possible stage convention by the time Brecht was born. The previous convention survived only in the form of parody (as it does to this day in the skits on Shakespeare and Victorian melodrama one still sees in English music halls).

The reaction against this theatrical convention, which had to come, is entirely analogous to the reaction against representational painting that came at the same time. For centuries painters had tried to get nearer and nearer to reality; the Impressionists had finally captured the very flicker of daylight, just as the naturalistic stage could simulate the changing light from the blazing sun of noon to the bluish tints of the moon at night. Such perfection having been attained, the next step *had* to be a new beginning, the initiation of an entirely different line of development—in painting away from nature into the realms of the primitive and the abstract, in the theatre away from the illusion of eavesdropping on real events.

Brecht belonged to the generation which had to make this new beginning, and his solution is one of many that were put forward by his contemporaries. German Expressionism, the poetic drama of T. S. Eliot, the satires of Mayakovsky, the Russian theatre of Meyerhold and Tairov, the monster pantomimes of Max Reinhardt, Piscator's political theatre with its use of film and posters are all part of the same striving to overcome the limitations of the "theatre of illusion."

When Brecht began to formulate his ideas in the late twenties he had already experimented with a variety of techniques. He had written plays that showed the influence of the Expressionist trend in their loose construction, their treatment of the characters as types rather than individuals, and their highly concentrated, poetic language; and he had worked in close collaboration with Erwin Piscator, whose stage made use of every new technique in order to turn the theatre into a forum for the discussion of current affairs.

Brecht's theories show the influence of all these experiments. He, too, was convinced that the theatre must become a tool of social engineering, a laboratory of social change.

> Today [he wrote in 1931] when human character must be understood as the "totality of all social conditions" the epic form is the only one that can comprehend all the processes which could serve the drama as materials for a fully representative picture of the world.[2]

Why did Brecht consider the existing stage convention incapable of providing such a picture of the world? His objections against the theatre of illusion concern both the means employed and the uses to which these means are put.

In formulating his theory of "epic" theatre Brecht was reacting against the German classics' theory of drama: in 1797 Goethe and Schiller, the two giants of the German tradition, had jointly presented their point of view in an essay, "On Epic and Dramatic Poetry." It is against this specific theory that Brecht offered his counter-theory.

Goethe and Schiller had described the distinction between the epic and dramatic genres of poetry as follows: "Their great essential difference lies in the fact that the epic poet presents the event as totally past, while the dramatic poet presents it as totally present." Goethe and Schiller had urged their readers "always to keep before (their) mental eyes a rhapsodic singer and an actor, both being poets: the one surrounded by a circle of quiet listeners, the other by impatiently watching and listening spectators." Thus the epic poet, the rhapsodic singer, has happened in calm contemplation ". . . he will freely range forward and backward in time. . . . The actor, on the other hand, is in exactly the opposite position: he represents himself as a definite individual; he wants the spectators to participate . . . in his action, to feel the sufferings of his soul and of his body with him, share his embarrassments and forget their own personalities for the sake of his. . . . The spectator must not be allowed to rise to thoughtful contemplation; he must passionately follow the action; his imagination is completely silenced. . . ."

It was this conception that Brecht abhorred, and that he called, knowing that Goethe and Schiller had based their theory on Aristotle's *Poetics*, the Aristotelian concept of drama, the drama of catharsis by terror and pity, the drama of spectator-identification with the actors, the drama of illusion, which tries to create magical effects by conjuring up events which are represented as "totally present," while palpably they are not. Such a theatre therefore was a fraud. Brecht, the rationalist, demanded a theatre of calm contemplation and detachment, a theatre of critical thoughtfulness; in other words, a theatre to correspond to the mood described by Goethe and Schiller and an attribute of the rhapsodic singer of epic poetry: an *epic* theatre.

Brecht regarded a theatre of illusion and identification as downright obscene:

looking around one discovers more or less motionless bodies in a curious state—they seem to be contracting their muscles in a strong physical effort, or else to have relaxed them after violent strain . . . they have their eyes open, but they don't look, they stare . . . they stare at the stage as if *spellbound*, which is an expression from the Middle Ages, an age of witches and obscurantists. . . .[3]

Identification with the characters on the stage appeared equally indecent to Brecht:

> How long are our souls going to have to leave our "gross" bodies under cover of darkness to penetrate into those dream figures up there on the rostrum, in order to share their transports that would otherwise be denied to us?[4]

Such an audience, Brecht argues, may indeed leave the theatre purged by its vicarious emotions, but it will have remained uninstructed and unimproved. For them the theatre will be a means of mental refreshment in the same sense as a good meal, which is consumed with enjoyment, provides physical refreshment, but leaves no lasting trace behind. Brecht regarded the art of the theatre as more than a mere article of consumption and despised what he called the "culinary theatre," the theatre which merely provides mental foodstuffs, to be gobbled up and then forgotten. The audience in his view should not be made to feel emotions, they should be made to *think*. But identification with the characters of the play makes thinking almost impossible; the audience whose souls have crept into that of the hero will see the action entirely from *his* point of view, and as they are breathlessly following a course of events which, in suspension of disbelief, they accept as really happening before their very eyes, they have neither the time nor the detachment to sit back and reflect in a truly critical spirit on the social and moral implications of the play. And all this because the author, the director and the actors have conspired to create so powerful an illusion of reality!

Brecht's answer is clear: the theatre must do its best to destroy in the bud any illusion of reality, which will continuously, and mischievously, tend to arise.

It must at all times be made apparent to the spectators that they are not witnessing real events happening before their very eyes at *this very moment*, but that they are sitting in a theatre, listening to an account (however vividly presented) of things that have happened in the *past* at a certain time in a certain place. They are to sit back, relax, and reflect on the lessons to be learned from those events of long ago, like the audience of the bards who sang of the deeds of heroes in the houses of Greek kings or Saxon earls, while the guests ate and drank. Hence the term *epic* theatre. While the theatre of illusion is trying to re-create a spurious present by pretending that the events of the play are actually taking place at the time of each performance, the "epic" theatre is strictly *historical*; it constantly reminds the audience that they are merely getting a report of past events.

Moreover, the audience must be *discouraged* from losing their critical detachment by *identification* with one or more of the characters. The opposite of identification is the maintenance of a separate existence by being kept apart, alien, strange—therefore the director must strive to produce by all the means at his disposal effects that will keep the audience separate, estranged, alienated from the action. That is the meaning of the famous "*Verfremdungseffekt*," a term that has never been successfully rendered in English because terms like alienation or estrangement have entirely different, and unfortunate, emotional overtones. In French *distantiation* is a happier term.

The abolition of the old theatre of illusion, which Brecht once described as having sunk to the level of a "branch of the bourgeois drug traffic," frees the critical faculty of the audience and absolves the playwright from being cramped by the narrow and rigid conventions that the pretense of presenting real happenings imposes. In the realistic convention one can show only the action of the characters themselves; it is quite impossible to supply the sociological background of their actions or to comment on them from a higher viewpoint than their own. In the "epic" theatre the author is able to dispense with the tedious ritual of the naturalist exposition through which the characters laboriously have to establish their names and relationships in the framework of seemingly casual, "natural" conversation; he can now make them introduce themselves directly to the audience, or flash their names on a screen. He can go further: he can tell the audience in advance how the play will end, freeing their minds from the distraction of suspense; he can supply background material of all kinds by letting a narrator describe the thoughts and motives of the characters or, as in Brecht's adaptation of Gorky's *The Mother*, by flashing the prices of basic foodstuffs onto the backdrop during a scene in which the cost of living is mentioned in the dialogue. Brecht claimed that the "epic" theatre alone could present the complexity of the human condition in an age in which the life of individuals could no longer be understood in isolation from the powerful trend of social, economical and historical forces affecting the lives of millions.

By abandoning the pretense that the audience is eavesdropping on actual events, by openly admitting that the theatre is a theatre and not the world itself, the Brechtian stage approximates the lecture hall, to which audiences come in the expectation that they will be informed, and also the circus arena, where an audience, without identification or illusion, watches performers exhibit their special skills. What distinguishes the theatre from the lecture room or the circus, however, is the fact that it "produces living illustrations of historical or imaginary happenings among human beings."[5]

To what purpose are these happenings re-created? It is in this respect that Brecht's thought changed most radically between his earlier and later periods. In the beginning Brecht proclaimed his conviction that the theatre had to be strictly didactic; he saw it as his task "to develop the article of consumption into a teaching aid and to refashion certain institutions from places of entertainment into organs of information."[6] In this period of the didactic plays and school operas the austerity of Brecht's conception was such that he wrote plays that were to serve for the instruction of the *participants alone*. "They need no audience."[7]

By 1948 he had mellowed to the extent of openly repudiating much of this severity of approach:

Let us therefore recant . . . our intention of emigrating from the realm of the pleasing and let us . . . proclaim our intention of settling in this realm. Let us treat the theatre as a place of entertainment. . . . But let us inquire what kind of entertainment we regard as acceptable.[8]

Brecht answered this question by rejecting the old idea of

entertainment through emotional catharsis. The pleasure that his theatre was now permitted to give was the pleasure we feel when we discover new truths, the exhilaration we experience when we enlarge our understanding. In this scientific age Brecht wanted his audience to experience some of the exaltation felt by the scientist who has uncovered one of the mysteries of the universe. For Brecht, whose own curiosity and thirst for knowledge were boundless, regarded the "instinct of inquiry as a social phenomenon not less pleasurable, nor less imperious, than the instinct of procreation."[9]

To keep the audience relaxed and yet receptive, to stimulate their critical faculties, and to make them think, the "epic" theatre employs a variety of means. In Brecht's view, the abolition of the dramatic illusion alone removes a good many of the less desirable implications of the "Aristotelian" theatre. The very fact that the action was each time assumed to be happening anew before the eyes of the audience implied that the passions and attitudes of the characters were unchangeable expressions of a fixed "human nature"; the dynamic, tautly logical construction of such plays indicated the relentless course of fate and made it appear unfathomable and incapable of being influenced by human initiative. In the "epic" theatre, therefore, there is no attempt to create fixed, highly individualized characters. Character emerges from the social function of the individual and changes with that function. As Brecht once put it, character

should not be regarded like a stain of grease on a pair of trousers, which, however much you try to rub and wipe it away, will always come up again. In actual fact the question is always how a given person is going to act in a specified set of circumstances and conditions.[10]

The plays of the "epic" theatre, which rejects the logically built, well-made drama, are free from the need of creating suspense, loosely knit, and episodic; instead of mounting to a dynamic climax, the story unfolds in a number of separate situations, each rounded and complete in itself. The total effect of the play is built up through the juxtaposition and "montage" of contrasting episodes. While the "Aristotelian" drama can be understood only as a whole, the "epic" drama can be cut into slices that will continue to make sense and give pleasure, like the favorite chapters of a novel that can be read by themselves, or the extracts from plays of great length that are performed as self-contained units in the Chinese classical theatre.

Just as isolated episodes of the play retain their individual significance even if taken out of the context of the play as a whole, the non-literary elements of the production—décor, music, and choreography—also retain their independence; instead of serving as mere auxiliaries of the text, reinforcing it by stressing some of its features, and painting in atmosphere, mood, or descriptive details, they are raised to the level of autonomous elements; instead of pulling in the same direction as the words, they enter into a dialectical, contrapuntal relationship with them. The musical numbers are no longer smuggled in at the point when the emotional charge of a scene rises to a climax and speech merges into song, but are introduced as entirely distinct ingredients of the play, which interrupt its flow, break the illusion, and thereby render the action "strange." And within the musical numbers themselves the music does not merely express the mood of the words; it often stands in contradiction to them, comments on them, or reveals the falsity of the sentiments they express.

The stage designer, who is no longer bound by the necessity of trying to create the illusion of a real locality in which the action takes place, is now free to supply his own, independent contribution to the play by providing background material of all kinds (in *Galileo* Caspar Neher backed the action by projections of maps, documents, and works of art of the Renaissance) or even by duplicating the action by showing it from a different angle (in the first production of *Mahagonny* the scene in which greedy Jakob eats himself to death was played in front of a backdrop showing a large portrait of Jakob eating, so that the audience saw the episode split in two).

Thus the "epic" theatre does not use décor and music to produce a Wagnerian *Gesamtkunstwerk* with its, in Brecht's

view, diabolically strong narcotic and hypnotic effect and con-
certed onslaught on the senses, but to destroy the illusion of
reality. As Brecht put it, *"Sie verfremden sich gegenseitig"*
("they mutually make each other appear strange").

The destruction of stage illusion, however, is not an end in
itself. The *Verfremdungseffekt* has its positive side. By inhibiting the process of identification between the spectator
and the characters, by creating a distance between them and
enabling the audience to look at the action in a detached and
critical spirit, familiar things, attitudes and situations appear
in a new and strange light and create, through astonishment
and wonder, a new understanding of the human situation.
The great discoveries of mankind, Brecht points out, were
made by men who looked at familiar things as if they had
never seen them before—Newton at the falling apple, Galileo
at the swinging chandelier—and in the same way the theatre
public should be taught to look at the relationships between
men with the critical "estranged" eye of the discoverer. "The
natural must be made to look surprising."[11]

This is how Brecht has summed up the distinction between
the old convention and his own conception of the theatre:

The spectator of the *dramatic* theatre says: "Yes, I have
felt the same. — I am just like this. — This is only natural.
— It will always be like this. — This human being's suffering moves me, because there is no way out for him. —
This is great art: it bears the mark of the inevitable. — I
am weeping with those who weep on the stage, laughing
with those who laugh."

The spectator of the *epic* theatre says: "I should never
have thought so. — That is not the way to do it. — This
is most surprising, hardly credible. — This will have to
stop. — This human being's suffering moves me, because
there would have been a way out for him. — This is great
art: nothing here seems inevitable. — I am laughing
about those who weep on the stage, weeping about those
who laugh."[12]

Brecht has written a great deal about the methods of production and the technique of acting he required to translate these theories into practice. And he has left detailed records of some of his most successful productions in the form of "model books"—scene-by-scene descriptions of the performances illustrated by photographs of every movement on the stage.

The basis of the Brechtian technique of acting is the conception that the actor should not regard himself as impersonating the character so much as *narrating* the actions of another person at a definite time in the past. To illustrate these actions and to make them fully understood by the audience he goes through the motions the character made, imitates the tone of his voice, repeats his facial expression, but only to the extent of *quoting* them. The Brechtian style of acting is acting in quotation marks.

Brecht liked to illustrate his basic concept of acting by the example of an everyday occurrence one might observe in any large town. A street accident has happened. A crowd has collected on the scene, and an eyewitness is telling the bystanders what has taken place: he wants to indicate that the old man who has been run over walked very slowly, so he will imitate his gait to show exactly what he means. He is in fact *quoting* the old man's walk. And he is quoting only *those elements* of the old man's movements which are *relevant* to the situation he wants to describe. The eyewitness concerned is far from wanting to *impersonate* the victim: "He never forgets, nor does he allow anyone to forget, that he is not the one whose action is being demonstrated, but the one who demonstrates it."[13] The character who is being shown and the actor who demonstrates him remain clearly differentiated. And the actor retains his freedom to *comment* on the actions of the person whose behavior he is displaying.

A theatre that aims at preventing the identification of the audience with the characters cannot allow the identification of the actor with the character either. Brecht was fully aware of the contagious nature of anything that takes place on the stage, which is the essence of the mystery and magic of the theatre. He did not deny the teaching of Stanislavsky in this respect: if the actor believes that he is Lear, the audience will also believe it and will share his emotions. But Brecht did not want the audience to be taken in. For the "epic" actor, he says, the assertion: "he did not merely act Lear, he *was* Lear," would be a devastating criticism.[14]

As the "epic" actor does not intend to put his audience into a trance, he must also keep *himself* free from any state of trance.

> His muscles must remain relaxed, for even a turn of the head with tensed muscles "magically" carries away with it the eyes, and even the heads of the spectators—and this would reduce their ability to reflect or feel emotion about this gesture. . . . Even if playing one possessed, the actor must not appear possessed himself: how else could the spectators find out what it is that possesses the possessed?[15]

These views express Brecht's revulsion against the cramped and convulsive style of acting that is still widely prevalent in the German theatre, where actors tend to be rated according to the violence and frenetic intensity of the emotions they portray. The frantic *Ausbruch* (outburst) represents the highest peak of acting to the adherents of this style. The Brechtian actor is always loose-limbed and relaxed, always clearly in control of himself and his emotions. In Brecht's view the actor's task is far wider, and far more complex, than the mere identification with the character postulated by Stanislavsky. At one stage in his preparatory work the Brechtian actor also has to feel himself into the character, but the results of this process of empathy are only one of a number of elements which fuse in the final performance on the stage. They must be supplemented by acute and fully rational observations, by implied comment on the character's actions so that the audience can see the actor's approval or disapproval, his pity or contempt, for the character. The actor must also show that he is never taken by surprise by the character's experiences, that, in fact, he knows exactly where the character's conduct will eventually lead him. And he must be able to suggest to the audience that the character's behavior is by no means the only possible course of action, that there are always alternatives. The actor must be able to suggest at suitable moments

apart from what he does, something else . . . he does *not* do: i.e., he acts in such a manner that one can see the alternative course of action, so that the acting allows the audience to detect the other possibilities, so that any given action can be seen as only one among a number of variants.[16]

In other words, the actor's attitude must always be so conscious, so fully rational and demonstrative, that he is in fact telling the public: "I have decided to go left rather than right. I could have gone to the right, but I am going to the left and *not* to the right." This implies a deliberateness of action, a consciousness of the presence of the audience, which are diametrically opposed to Stanislavsky's ideal of an actor who is completely alone, completely wrapped up in himself and unaware of being observed. In fact, Brecht compares the style of acting he advocates to the manner in which the director would demonstrate an intonation to his cast. He too, by the deliberateness of his demonstration, says in effect: "I want it done this way and not *that* way." Nor can there be any question of the actor's thought or action arising spontaneously from the situation; there must be nothing improvised in the delivery of the lines. As Brecht puts it: "The actor's performance must present an attitude that denotes the delivery of a finished product."[17]

Like all attempts to describe a style of acting in theory, these maxims appear more complicated than they are in fact. The villain as he was acted in Victorian melodrama is the perfect example of a style of acting without identification between the actor and the character he portrays. There, too, the audience is never left in doubt as to what the actor thinks of the character, nor that he knows that he will come to a bad end, nor that he enjoys the virtuosity with which he portrays wickedness, nor that he behaves in a manner to which there would be a clear and obvious alternative. And this applies to some extent to all the villains in drama. As Brecht pointed

out: "Why is the principal negative character so much mo:
interesting than the positive hero? Because he is performed i
a spirit of criticism."[18]

In the theatre of illusion and identification the actor worl
through introspection. He delves into the character he is t
portray and tries to merge with him. Only after this work
accomplished are the characters brought into relation wit
each other. The nature of the characters determines the
relationships. The basic unit of such a theatre is the singl
character.

Brecht's theatre, on the other hand, is extrovert. The inne
life of the characters is irrelevant to him except in so far as i
is expressed in their outward attitudes and actions. "For th
smallest social unit is not one human being, but two humav
beings."[19] The eyewitness in the example of the street acc:
dent

derives his characters wholly from their actions. He imitates what they have done and thus permits inferences
as to their nature. A theatre which follows him will to a
large extent break with the habit of the conventional
theatre, which derives its action from the nature of the
characters. . . .[20]

The study of human *nature* is thus replaced by that o
human *relations*. Not the characters but the story in whicl
they are involved becomes the main concern of the epic, nar
rative, historical theatre. "Everything depends on the *story*
it is the centerpiece of the performance."[21] The *story*
(Brecht uses the German word *Fabel*, with its didactic over
tones) is the sequence of events that constitutes the socia
experiment of the play; it provides the dialectical field fo:
the interplay of social forces from which the lesson of the pla
will be seen to emerge.

Characters acting and reacting upon each other are the
basic unit of the Brechtian theatre. The basic attitudes of
human beings are expressed by what Brecht called *Gestus,*
a term that means not merely "gesture" but covers the whole

range of the outward signs of social relationships, including "deportment, intonation, facial expression."[22] Each scene of a play has its *basic Gestus* (*Grundgestus*).

By his emphasis on *Gestus*—the clear and stylized expression of the social behavior of human beings towards each other—Brecht shifts the emphasis from the inner life of the characters towards the way in which they *behave* towards each other: the way in which the downtrodden tutor in *Der Hofmeister* bows to his master, the way in which the kindly prostitute of Setzuan moves differently when she turns into her ruthless cousin, assumes a greater importance than the supposed inner life or emotions of these characters. Brecht wanted to arrive at a *Gestus* so simple and expressive that it could be quoted with the same ease as a well-turned line of dialogue is quoted. And he placed great emphasis on writing dialogue which would contain the appropriate *Gestus* and almost force the actor to assume the correct stance, movement, and tone of voice. He himself was a master of this "*gestische Sprache*" (gestic language). His sentences, with their contrapuntal construction, subtle rhythms, and cunningly placed pauses, their Biblical parallelism and sudden changes of cadence, compel the speaker to follow the author's intentions and to act as he utters them.

Brecht's songs also have this gestic character. They are even more pronounced, even more clearly magnified *exhibits of basic attitudes*, for the music makes the fusion of words and gesture even more compelling. Brecht used to point to the way street singers render the more vulgar kind of popular song with large and simple gestures. His own songs were designed to achieve a similar effect on actor and audience alike by crystallizing an essential, fundamental attitude and exhibiting it with the utmost clarity: despair or resignation, defiance or submission.

The fundamental importance of the *Gestus* determines the method by which actors and director tackle the play. By analyzing the action they determine the basic story line (*Fabel*), which is then broken down into smaller and smaller elements until each scene appears as the expression of one simple, basic action that can be translated into a single sentence (e.g. "Richard Gloucester woos the widow of his victim" or "God wagers against the devil for the soul of Dr. Faustus" or "Woyzeck buys a cheap knife to kill his wife"). This sentence contains the basic *Gestus* of the scene that the director and the actors have to put on the stage. The arrangement and grouping of the actors, their manner of speaking and moving, must be made to convey all the implications of this basic *Gestus* with the greatest possible expressiveness, elegance, and economy of means. It is entirely irrelevant what the scene concerned might have looked like in real life, the director is concerned only with bringing out its social content and significance.

> The new theatre uses the simplest kind of grouping which will express the meaning of the action in the clearest possible manner. Any "accidental" grouping which might try to simulate "real life" . . . is to be avoided. The stage does not reflect the "natural disorder" of things. The opposite of "natural disorder" which it aims at is "natural order." The point of view adopted to achieve this order is historical and sociological.[23]

Once the basic elements of the story have been isolated, they must be linked together again, but not in such a way that they imperceptibly merge into each other. The links between the separate sections must be clearly marked, so that the audience has time to use its judgment instead of drifting helplessly through the story. The component parts have to be carefully juxtaposed to set each other off, preferably by the use of written chapter headings which will not only indicate what will happen next (and thereby inhibit suspense) but also set the tone of the ensuing scene by the way in which they are phrased—"In the style of a chronicle or a ballad or a newspaper or a description of manners and customs."[24]

As Brecht sought to banish trance, illusion, magical effects, and orgies of emotion from the theatre, he tried to replace them by lucidity, rationality, and elegance. The numerous and varied devices by which the illusion of reality was to be dispelled must bear the hallmark of honest craftsmanship, the

perfection that comes from the unpretentious use of undisguised materials.

Above all, the stage must be bathed in light:

Give us light on the stage, lighting engineer! How can we,
Playwrights and actors, present our images of the world
In semi-darkness? Nebulous twilight
Lulls to sleep. But we need the spectators'
Wakefulness, even watchfulness. Let them dream
In blazing clarity![25]

Brecht was against the use of lighting effects to create atmosphere and mood. The coming of night was indicated, in
his theatre as in that of the Elizabethans, by properties like
lamps or the appearance of a moon disk, not by a dimming of
the uniformly bright light in which his stage was bathed. To
dispel any illusion of reality he insisted that the sources of
light should remain visible to the public. "Nobody would
expect the spotlights over a boxing ring to be hidden,"[26] why,
should they therefore be concealed in the theatre?

Nor was the curtain to be used to allow illusions to be prepared in secret:

> *. . . and make*
> *My curtain half-high, don't seal off the stage!*
> *Leaning back in his chair, let the spectator*
> *Be aware of busy preparations, made for him*
> *Cunningly; he sees a tinfoil moon*
> *Float down, or a tiled roof*
> *Being carried in; do not show him too much,*
> *But show him something! And let him notice*
> *That you are not wizards,*
> *Friends, but workers. . . .*[27]

The curtain often also serves to show the projected titles
of the scenes. When it parts, it reveals sets that suggest the
locale of the action rather than depicting it. Brecht's favorite
designers—Caspar Neher, Teo Otto, and Karl von Appen—
each in his individual way leave much to the imagination of
the spectator. The backdrops are often intentionally two-

dimensional and derived from known pictorial models (old prints in *The Private Tutor*, or Persian miniatures in *The Caucasian Chalk Circle*, etc.). The use of décor to supply independent comment on the action has already been mentioned.

Just as the sources of light remain unconcealed, the source of any music also must remain visible. Often the musicians are placed on the stage itself.

The musical numbers and songs are used to interrupt the action and to give the audience an opportunity to reflect. The coming of such an interruption is usually announced beforehand by some visible change on the stage: the title of the song may flash on a screen, special lights may be put on, or a symbolic emblem (e.g. flags and trumpets) may come down from the flies.

These mechanical devices may help in creating the *Verfremdungseffekt*, but the brunt of the work of "making things strange to the audience" is left to the actors. The temptation to identify himself with the character must always remain strong for the actor. Brecht used a variety of techniques to enable him to overcome this.

During rehearsals the actors were invited to translate their text into the third person, so that they were made to relate the story of the actions and speeches of the characters they were later to act. Brecht has published a number of examples of this technique. In scene three of his adaptation of *The Private Tutor* there occurs the following passage:

> (*Enter Count Wermuth. After a few silent compliments he sits down on the sofa.*)
> COUNT: Has Your Excellency seen the new dancing master who has arrived from Dresden? He is a Marchese from Florence. His name is. . . . On all my travels I have only met two dancers I would put above him. . . .[28]

During rehearsals the actor who played the count was made to say:

Then Count Wermuth entered. After a few silent com-

pliments he sat down on the sofa and asked whether
Madame had seen the new dancing master, who had
arrived from Dresden. He was a Marchese from Florence. . . . The Count made a slight pause, as his memory failed him. He nimbly added that on all his travels
he had only met two dancers whom he would put above
him . . . etc.[29]

Another device for inhibiting the identification of actor
and character is the inclusion of all stage directions in the
text spoken during rehearsals. For his production of *Antigone*
at Chur in 1948 Brecht composed linking passages in hex-
ameter, which the characters spoke during rehearsals and
which transformed the tragedy into the recitation of an epic
poem. In this production the actors who were not involved
in the action sat in a semicircle at the back of the stage.
Brecht advised them that "they could read, freely make
small movements, put on their make-up, or leave the stage
quietly."[30]

Brecht also wrote *Practice Scenes for Actors.* These include
"parallel scenes" by which the actors are to be made to see
hackneyed classical situations in a new—estranged—light (the
murder scene in *Macbeth* is equated with the pangs of conscience of a concierge's wife who has broken off the head of a
china statue belonging to the lady of the house and finally
blames the deed on a passing beggar); and "bridge scenes,"
to be acted during rehearsal but omitted in performance
(Hamlet learns that Claudius has ceded a strip of land to
Norway in return for a trade agreement that guarantees the
sale of Danish salted herrings to Norway; this puts him in the
right mood to hear of Fortinbras's expedition to Poland
and explains his change of mind in "How all occasions do in-
form against me"). But as Brecht never tackled *Macbeth,
Hamlet,* or any of the other plays for which he wrote these
practice scenes, they remain expressions of his love of debunk-
ing and parody rather than constructive contributions to the
art of acting.

In his own work as a director with the Berliner Ensemble,
Brecht refrained from expounding his theories to the actors.
For an author of copious theoretical writings on the act of

acting, he was surprisingly empirical. Leading actors who
worked with him found little difference in his approach from
that of other directors with a literary background, except that
he was perhaps more patient and ready to listen to suggestions
than most. As one observer of rehearsals of the Berliner Ensemble put it:

> In this theatre everyone is allowed to state his opinion.
> The actors make all sorts of suggestions to the director.
> The director is all ears and greatly praises the sugges-
> tions. But in the end it is done as the director wanted it
> in the first place. . . . Everything is given a trial: Mr. K.
> is asked to insert an occasional grunt—"oeh!." But "oeh"
> can be said with the most varied nuances. The most
> significant, the most comical "oeh" will have to be found.
> Six different kinds are tried, and in the end perhaps the
> most effective "oeh" has been discovered.[31]

In spite of Brecht's untheoretical approach it is astonishing
that the Berliner Ensemble's splendidly produced publication
on its work, *Theaterarbeit*, discloses that, in the course of a
survey of the views of the members of the company, it became clear that "the majority of the actors showed considerable uncertainty" when asked whether the Berliner Ensemble was using a special style of acting! This is explained as

> probably due to the fact that neither Brecht nor other
> directors of the Berliner Ensemble refer to Brecht's theo-
> retical writings during rehearsals. For certain plays some
> practical hints from these works are made use of, but in
> Brecht's view the present state of the theatre does not
> permit their full application.[32]

Whether Brecht's theories were merely rationalizations of
his intuition, taste, and imagination (which they almost certainly were), or whether they were the results of the application of ice-cold logic and deeply probing sociological analysis
(as he sometimes claimed them to be), they have had a most
stimulating effect in freeing the stage from a narrow and
cramping convention and will certainly continue to play their

part within the much wider movement for the renewal of the theatre.

Brecht, who loved the exotic and the "vulgar," often drew attention to his debt to the Oriental theatre of China, India, and Japan, and the folk theatre of Austria and Bavaria. These exotic and folk influences, however, should not lead one to overlook the large extent to which the Brechtian theatre represents a return to the main stream of the European classical tradition. As Jean-Paul Sartre has pointed out,[33] the *Verfremdungseffekt*, the idea that the playwright should not show characters or situations too familiar to the audience, was one of the basic principles of classical French tragedy. Racine anticipates many of Brecht's ideas in his preface to *Bajazet*:

> Les personnages tragiques doivent être regardés d'un autre oeil que nous ne regardons d'ordinaire les personnages que nous avons vus de si près. On peut dire que le respect que l'on a pour les héros augmente à mesure qu'ils s'éloignent de nous: *major e longinquo reverentia*.[34]

The same is true of the rejection of empathy as the basis of great acting. Diderot in his *Paradoxe sur le Comédien* foreshadows Brecht's demand for critical, "cool" acting by condemning the idea that actors should be able to feel the emotions they portray, or even that they should be people of more than average sensibility.

> C'est l'extrême sensibilité qui fait les acteurs médiocres: c'est la sensibilité médiocre qui fait la multitude des mauvais acteurs; et c'est le manque absolu de sensibilité qui prépare les acteurs sublimes. Les larmes du comédien descendent de son cerveau; celles de l'homme sensible montent de son cœur: ce sont les entrailles qui troublent sans mesure la tête de l'homme sensible; c'est la tête du comédien qui porte quelquefois un trouble passager dans ses entrailles; il pleure comme un prêtre incrédule qui prêche la Passion; comme un séducteur aux genoux d'une femme qu'il n'aime pas, mais qu'il veut tromper; comme un gueux dans la rue ou à la porte d'une église,

qui vous injurie lorsqu'il désespère de vous toucher; ou comme une courtisane qui ne sent rien, mais qui se pâme entre vos bras.[35]

Brecht's most original contribution to the theory of the theatre—but also the most disputable—concerns the reactions of the audience. From Greek tragedy to Gerhart Hauptmann and Ibsen the audience was supposed to be *moved* by what was presented on the stage. Whether they were to believe in the play as real or artificial, to regard the actors as skillful mimics or suffering human beings, they were to feel pity with them and to identify themselves with the experiences of the hero. Towards the end of his life Brecht defended himself against the reproach that he wanted to banish emotion from the theatre altogether. But the emotions he wanted to produce were of an entirely different nature. The "epic" theatre, he said,

in no way renounces emotion. Least of all emotions like the love of justice, the urge to freedom or justified anger: so little does it renounce these emotions, that it does not rely on their being there, but tries to strengthen or to evoke them. The "critical attitude" into which it is trying to put its public cannot be passionate enough.[36]

It is highly doubtful whether such emotions could ever be made to play a more than merely marginal part among the feelings engendered by the theatre. In his rejection of identification between audience and characters Brecht comes into conflict with the fundamental concept of psychology that regards processes of identification as the basic mechanisms by which one human being communicates with another. Without identification and empathy each person would be irrevocably imprisoned within himself. Even the spectators of a sporting contest, whom Brecht so often invoked as the ideal of a critical audience, identify themselves with the contestants. And, of course, the use of the various "estranging" devices in Brecht's theatre shows that he was aware of the constant need to counteract the powerful effect of these tendencies in the audience. In practice, he succeeded at best merely in reducing to some extent the emotional identification of the audience with his characters. He never succeeded in evoking the critical attitude he postulated. The audience stubbornly went on being moved to terror and to pity.

But perhaps it is precisely this contradiction between the author's and director's intention and the audience's natural tendency to react, that creates the peculiar effect of the Brechtian theatre; the conflict between head and heart in the actors and in the spectators, the ambiguity created by the tug-of-war between the intended and the actual reaction of the audience gives depth to two-dimensional characters and sophistication to what was intended as naïve. If the audience were merely repelled by the rascality and baseness of the robber Macheath, they *might* conceivably leave the theatre convinced, as Brecht intended, of the corruption of bourgeois society. But in fact, while they are to a certain extent repelled by Macheath, they also identify themselves with him; while they are made to loathe his sentimentality they also are made to participate in it. And they leave the theatre by no means entirely convinced that bourgeois society is rotten, but having greatly enjoyed a poetical experience. And so Brecht's success lies in his partial failure to realize his own intentions.

Brecht believed that his "non-Aristotelian," "epic" theatre was destined to become the theatre of the scientific age.

In an age whose science is able to change nature to an extent that makes the world appear almost habitable, man can no longer be described to man as a mere victim, the object of an unknown, but unalterable environment. . . . The world of today can be described to the human beings of today only as a world that can be changed.[37]

He thought that the "epic" theatre which aimed at awakening the spectator's critical faculty, which concentrated on showing mankind from the point of view of social relationships, would serve as an instrument of social change, a laboratory of revolutionary enlightenment; in other words, that the "epic" theatre was the Marxist theatre *par excellence*. But the chain of reasoning by which he arrives at this conclusion contains more than one weak link. A narrative theatre, he argues, can

show far more than just the way people act and suffer. It is
not compelled, as the conventional theatre is, to leave the con
clusions entirely to the audience. It can provide sociologica
background material; it can comment on the action. By keep
ing the spectator in a critical frame of mind it prevents him
from seeing the conflict entirely from the point of view of the
characters involved in it and from accepting their passions and
motives as being conditioned by "eternal human nature." Such
a theatre will make the audience see the contradictions in
the existing state of society; it might even make them ask
themselves how such a society might be changed. But there is
nothing in this particular stage convention that in itself would
lead the public to a *Marxist* answer to this question. Of
course, the characters, or the chorus, can be made to advocate
Marxist solutions—but so can the characters in the conven
tional theatre, as innumerable Soviet propaganda plays, ex
cellently acted in the tradition of Stanislavsky, amply prove.
Brecht disliked and despised the openly propagandist play in
the naturalistic convention. In his speech to the Fourth East
German Writers' Congress in January 1956 he ridiculed plays
in which "the new" was being advocated through

> the playwright giving a representative of "the new" so
> much freedom of speech, that his point of view does in
> fact get the better of his opponent's point of view. But
> you must not forget that the representation of militant
> action on the stage, even from a set point of view, does
> not by itself automatically produce a militant effect.
> What we must achieve is the creation of militancy in
> the audience, the militancy of the new against the old.[38]

But there is little evidence that Brecht's own, more subtle
methods ever roused the audience to a militantly Marxist
point of view. The Brechtian theatre is a theatre designed to
arouse indignation in the audience, dissatisfaction, a realization of contradictions—it is a theatre supremely fitted for
parody, caricature, and denunciation, therefore essentially a
negative theatre. That is why Brecht's plays conspicuously
lack positive heroes, why the good characters are invariably
crushed and defeated. Brecht believed that the audience's

indignation with the existing order would necessarily and automatically lead them to support the Marxist alternative. But this belief presupposes a touching faith in the self-evident truth of the Marxist creed. What Brecht says, in effect, is: "Show the world in a critical spirit—and the audience will automatically see the need for a Marxist solution! It is enough to point out the contradictions in the existing state of society to make people clamor for Communism." This is not only a *non sequitur* in theory, but has been shown to be one in practice. The East Berlin audience who followed the adventures of *Mother Courage* and saw poor dumb Katrin raped by the brutal soldiery knowingly compared what they had seen in the theatre with their experiences with the Russian soldiers, and concluded that in fact human nature had *not* changed. . . .

If Brecht believed that the "epic" theatre was the truly Marxist theatre, the authorities of the Communist world certainly did not. The Brechtian theatre still exists only on the fringes of the Communist world, while the doctrines of Stanislavsky, the theatre of identification and illusion, remain the prescribed, official norm for actors, directors, and critics from Vladivostok to Prague.

Brecht's lifelong struggle for the acceptance of his theories as those of the truly Marxist theatre (which is described in Chapter VII) finally led him to abandon the very name of the "epic" theatre. His last theoretical essays, entitled *Dialectics in the Theatre*, foreshadow its substitution by the term "dialectical" theatre. His disciple Manfred Wekwerth describes how he spoke of his theatre as a "dialectical theatre" shortly before he died.[39] But in the introductory note to *The Dialectic on the Stage*, published after his death, Brecht merely says:

The essays that follow suggest that the term "epic theatre" may be too formal for the theatre we mean (and practice—up to a point). The epic theatre may be the underlying basis of these presentations, but it does not fully account for the way they show the productivity and malleability of society, which is the source of most of the enjoyment they provide. The term "epic theatre" must therefore be regarded as inadequate, without our being able to offer a new one.[40]

NOTES

1. Brecht, "Gespraech auf der Probe" (1953), *Schriften zum Theater*, pp. 285–86.

2. Brecht, "Anmerkungen zur Dreigroschenoper" (1931), *Schriften zum Theater*, p. 35.

3. Brecht, "Kleines Organon fuer das Theater" (1948), *Versuche* 12, para. 26, p. 119.

4. Ibid., para. 34, p. 122.

5. Ibid., para. 1, p. 110.

6. Brecht, "Anmerkungen zur Oper *Aufstieg und Fall der Stadt Mahagonny*" (1930), *Schriften zum Theater*, p. 28.

7. Brecht, "Anmerkung zu den Lehrstuecken," *Stuecke* V, p. 276.

8. Brecht, "Kleines Organon fuer das Theater; Vorrede" (1948), *Versuche* 12, p. 109.

9. Brecht, "Anmerkungen zu *Leben des Galilei*," *Stuecke* VIII, p. 205.

10. H. J. Bunge, "Brecht probiert," *Sinn und Form*, Second Special Brecht Issue, 1957, p. 324.

11. Brecht, "Vergnuegungstheater oder Lehrtheater" (1936), *Schriften zum Theater*, p. 63.

12. Ibid., pp. 63–64.

13. Brecht, "Die Strassenszene" (1940), *Schriften zum Theater*, p. 99.

14. "Kleines Organon," *Versuche* 12, para. 48, p. 127.

15. Ibid., para. 47, p. 126.

16. Brecht, "Neue Technik der Schauspielkunst" (1940), *Schriften zum Theater*, pp. 108–9.

17. "Kleines Organon," *Versuche* 12, para. 76, p. 140.

18. Brecht, "Einige Irrtuemer ueber die Spielweise des Berliner Ensembles," *Sinn und Form*, Second Special Brecht Issue, 1957, p. 258.

19. "Kleines Organon," *Versuche* 12, para. 58, p. 131.

20. Brecht, "Die Strassenszene" (1940), *Schriften zum Theater*, p. 96.

21. "Kleines Organon," *Versuche* 12, para. 65, p. 135.

22. Ibid., para. 61, p. 132.

23. Brecht quoted in Wekwerth, "Sechs Punkte zum erzaehlenden Arrangement Bertolt Brechts," *Theater der Zeit*, East Berlin, supplement to no. 11, 1956.

24. "Kleines Organon," *Versuche* 12, para. 67, p. 136.

25. Brecht, "Die Beleuchtung," from "Der Messingkauf," *Schriften zum Theater*, pp. 260–61.

26. Brecht, "Die Sichtbarkeit der Lichtquellen" (1940), *Schriften zum Theater*, p. 262.

27. Brecht, "Die Vorhaenge," *Schriften zum Theater*, p. 260.

28. Brecht, "Der Hofmeister, Episierungen," *Versuche* 11, p. 67.

29. Ibid.

30. Brecht and Neher, *Antigonemodell 1948*.

31. J. Ruehle, *Das gefesselte Theater*, p. 229.

32. *Theaterarbeit*, p. 412.

33. J. P. Sartre, "Brecht et les classiques," *World Theatre*, Paris, No. VII, Spring 1958.

34. Racine, "Bajazet, Seconde Preface," *Œuvres* (Ed. de la Pléiade), vol. I, p. 548.

35. Diderot, "Paradoxe sur le Comédien," *Œuvres* (Ed. de la Pléiade), p. 1041.

36. Brecht and F. Wolf, "Formprobleme des Theaters mit neuem Inhalt," *Theaterarbeit*, p. 254.

37. Brecht, "Kann die heutige Welt durch Theater widergegeben werden?" (1955), *Schriften zum Theater*, p. 8.

38. Brecht, Ausfuehrungen vor der Sektion Dramatik," 1.12.1956. Proceedings of the Fourth East German Writers' Congress, published in *Beitraege zur Gegenwartsliteratur*, 1956/I.

39. M. Wekwerth, "Auffinden einer aesthetischen Kategorie," *Sinn und Form*, Second Special Brecht Issue, 1957, p. 265.

40. Brecht, "Die Dialektik auf dem Theater," *Schriften zum Theater*, p. 174.

Part Three: PITFALLS OF COMMITMENT

CHAPTER VII

BRECHT AND THE COMMUNISTS

> *What meanness would you not commit, to*
> *Stamp our meanness?*
> *If, at last, you could change the world, what*
> *Would you think yourself too good for?*
> *Who are you?*
> *Sink into the mire*
> *Embrace the butcher, but*
> *Change the world: it needs it!*
> BRECHT: *Die Massnahme*

No one could call the author of these lines a starry-eyed idealist who did not realize the complexity of the moral dilemma
that faces the artist and the intellectual who ranges himself
in the Communist camp.

Did Brecht ever actually join the Communist party? Ruth
Fischer, once a leading German Communist herself and the
sister of Brecht's close friend, Hanns Eisler, categorically
states that he joined the party in 1930.[1] On the other hand,
when the chief investigator of the Un-American Activities
Committee in Washington asked him if he had ever applied
for admission to the party, Brecht's reply was equally categorical: "No, no, no, no, no, never!"[2]

This sixfold denial may well have been a sixfold deliberate
lie; it may, in the narrowest, technical sense of the word, have
been the truth. In the case of artists who are unlikely to be
very effective in the organizational work of the party and
whose usefulness in attracting the sympathies of left-wing
and liberal intellectuals is far greater if they are not too

closely identified with the more sordid side of politics, the Communists often advise, or even order, them not to join. But the technical detail of formal party membership hardly matters. What matters is that, with or without a party card, Brecht considered himself a Marxist; that he loyally supported the Communist cause and did all he could to put himself and his great talents at its service. There can be no doubt that he was ready, for its sake, to sink into the mire and to embrace more than one butcher.

Yet, a moralist at heart, despite his outward contempt for all accepted rules of conduct, he remained aware of the delicate balance between ends and means involved in such a risky compromise and of the existence of a limit beyond which such a compromise could not go.

The party, on the other hand, often accepted his support without enthusiasm, and sometimes with an embarrassment bordering on bad grace. The freely offered adherence of an artist of world-wide fame and prestige is too great an asset ever to be lightly cast aside. Yet it is an asset that can all too easily turn into a liability, as in the case of André Gide, and, more than once, in that of Jean-Paul Sartre. Brecht never caused the party such embarrassment; he was only too conscious of the need for discipline and self-denial. But while he had no intention of defecting, he made full and cunning use of the implied threat of possible defection. He carefully selected for himself the most advantageous position within the Eastern orbit, a position that was to secure him the material advantages of Communist patronage while allowing him the maximum freedom of speech and movement.

With a theatre at his disposal in East Berlin, an Austrian passport in his pocket, and the copyright of his plays in the hands of a West German publisher, Brecht could dedicate himself to the pursuit of his political and artistic aims without risking the fate that had overtaken so many of his fellow artists who had been denied the opportunity of striking a bargain like his: Mayakovsky, Meyerhold, Tairov, and Pasternak.

But even after Brecht had succeeded in arriving at this arrangement, his relations with the Communist authorities remained complex and beset with problems and dangers. The story of Brecht's relations with the party, in spite of the deep craving that drove him towards this haven of orthodoxy and certainty, exemplifies the deep, fundamental contradiction between a creative personality ultimately subject to the laws of its own inner being, however willing and loyal, and the party, an apparatus of power constantly shifting its tactics and demands behind a façade of rigidly unchanging dogma.

From his earliest youth Brecht was in revolt against the bourgeois world and the social order that had led to war. But, although he was briefly involved in the Communist uprising at Augsburg at the end of the First World War, his attitude remained that of an anarchist, iconoclast, and radical pacifist, who was against authority of any kind.

Kragler, the soldier from the wars returning in Brecht's second play, *Drums in the Night*, who refuses to risk his life by fighting for the Spartakists, expresses a violently unheroic attitude: "I am a swine and the swine goes home." Rather than fight for the ideals of the revolution he will settle down with his girl, even if she is pregnant by another man. "I'll put on a clean shirt. I still have my skin. I'll grease my boots. The shouting will be all over by tomorrow morning, but I'll be in my bed tomorrow morning, procreating, lest I die out."[3]

As so often with Brecht, it is left unclear whether the author shares his character's view or not. When Brecht published his collected plays shortly before he died, the earlier Western edition contained *Drums in the Night* without comment. But for East Germany he wrote a foreword, later incorporated in the reprints of the Western version, in which he argues that he had in fact intended Kragler as a negative, comic character. "But I did not succeed in making the audience see the revolution differently from the way 'the hero' Kragler saw it. I did not yet have the technique of '*Verfremdung*' at my disposal."[4] Brecht confesses that he thought of suppressing the play altogether. "Only the thought that literature is part of history, and history must not be falsified"[5] kept him from doing so. Instead he strengthened the play by inserting some reference to a more positive revolutionary who did fight for his cause and was killed.

But it is difficult to believe that Brecht had in fact intended Kragler as a negative character. In the first edition of the *Domestic Breviary* there is a poem that shows that Brecht's contempt for fighting of any kind extended even to the Russian Revolution and civil war. This poem, which has disappeared without a trace from later editions of the *Domestic Breviary*, in spite of Brecht's professed conviction that literature belongs to history, and history must not be falsified, is called "The Red Army Soldier's Song." This Red Army soldier—it is left unclear whether he belongs to the Russian or the Communist German Red Army—feels even more bitter than Kragler:

> *Many we saw with tigers' teeth*
> *Behind the red, inhuman flag. . . .*[6]

The civil war was said to be a war for freedom,

> *But freedom, boys, it never came.*[7]

These lines are not quoted here to score a point against Brecht: why should he not have gradually become converted to the Communist cause? But they are important as evidence that he did not, as he later tried to make it appear, and as the official legend now fostered in the Communist world proclaims, support the Russian Revolution from the moment he heard of it. Arnolt Bronnen described how he discussed the problem of Communism with Brecht in the winter of 1922–23. When Bronnen spoke about the need to change the world so that people need not starve any more, "Brecht began to get angry. 'What business is it of yours, if people are starving,' he said. 'One must get on, make a name for oneself, get a theatre to put on one's own plays!' He was not interested in anything else."[8]

When Brecht was converted to Marxism in the late twenties, he was much attracted by its negative aspects. The anti-bourgeois and anarchist in him reveled in so savage and acute a diagnosis of the existing social order. This was Germany after the First World War, with its bloated and ignorant *nouveaux riches*, its stock-exchange gamblers and black marketeers, and all the prostitution and degradation that surrounded them. This was the world that George Grosz depicted in his devastating drawings. And this world Brecht attacked with the weapon of his newly discovered Marxist analysis.

The Threepenny Opera is an essay on Proudhon's famous aphorism *"la propriété c'est le vol,"* and *Mahagonny* shows the capitalist system as a brothel town where everything is for sale and the only capital crime is lack of money. But if the Communist implications of these themes were clear to Brecht, they were not clear to the public, which either enjoyed the plays as rollicking near-pornography or attacked them as such. They were even less clear to the Communists themselves.

Die Rote Fahne, the main organ of the German Communist party, criticized *The Threepenny Opera* for its "lack of social concreteness"[9] while the theoretical periodical of the left-wing intellectuals, *Die Linkskurve*, referred to Brecht, in connection with *Mahagonny*, as "the spokesman of a resigned, sceptical petty bourgeoisie, which tries to cross the void of its own confusion by performing nihilistic balancing acts."[10] And, twenty-five years later, the Marxist author of the bulky East German study of the young Brecht, Ernst Schumacher, also condemned *Mahagonny*: does this opera not err grievously in trying to expose the vices of capitalism by showing them being practiced by lumberjacks—working-class men? It was a grave error on Brecht's part to have suggested that lumberjacks indulge in the capitalist sins of eating, drinking, and lechery. "It may be true," Schumacher explains, "that certain sections of the working class might under capitalism, and especially under imperialism, have an opportunity at times, and briefly, to indulge in 'hedonism'." But nevertheless Brecht should not have demonstrated the aberrations of capitalism on such men, who "may be in possession of money for a while, but are not owners of the means of production."[11]

Brecht soon abandoned his attempt to reform society by holding up to it the mirror of its own vice and lechery. He became fascinated with the problem of discipline. The austere, monastic side of Communism, its practice of self-denial and strict obedience had a magnetic attraction for the self-indulgent anarchist. Here was the rigid framework of order that he instinctively felt he needed to counteract his drift towards amorphous emotions and nebulous formlessness. The nihilist needed a faith. He found it in the stark social logic of Marxism.

In his didactic plays and school operas Brecht grappled with the problem of order, discipline, and submission: discipline within the party, submission to the inexorable laws of history. These were the themes of *The Didactic Play of Baden*, in which a group of transatlantic flyers are made to consent to their own death in the interest of technical progress, and the school opera *He Who Says Yes*. But, again, Brecht had not been specific enough: the critics saw these paeans to discipline and self-denial as expressions of Christian, Buddhist, or even Prussian military ethics, while the left-wing intellectuals were horrified. As one of them said about *He Who Says Yes*: "This school opera cunningly infuses into the souls of young people a view of life containing all the wicked ingredients of reactionary thinking based on senseless authority. . . ."[12] Even the pupils of the left-wing Karl Marx School in Berlin who were to perform the play disagreed with its authoritarian ethics. Brecht, always open to change his mind, turned *He Who Says Yes* into *He Who Says No*. But this did not correspond to his yearning for discipline. And so he returned to the subject in his first real masterpiece, *The Measures Taken*.

Now for the first time he tackled the theme of Communism and Communist discipline itself. The moral problem of the conflict between ends and means is faced boldly and without fear of carrying it to its logical conclusion. The young comrade, whose heart has been too soft, who has failed to resist the temptation of helping the poor when the higher interest of the party lay in ignoring their suffering, must be killed. He sees the need for it himself and begs for death. The story is told and re-enacted by a group of party workers after their return to headquarters: each of them in turn plays the part of the young comrade, for he represents a part of their own nature, the part they have to suppress and kill in themselves. The "control chorus," sitting in judgment on the party workers, approves of their disciplinary measure and praises them for having been hard.

The first performance of *The Measures Taken* was followed a few days later by a public discussion. According to an eyewitness,

> the Communists above all refused to admit that the killing of a comrade was a Communist practice. The Communist way was expulsion from the party, not the physical one of liquidation. The chairman of the meeting pointed out that physical death would be less tragic for the comrade . . . than expulsion.[13]

The party was horrified that Brecht had given the anti-Communist press the occasion of speaking about the "murderous practices" of the Communist party, and the party organs strenuously denied that any such killing could ever happen in reality. *Die Linkskurve* attacked Brecht's lack of revolutionary experience:

> One feels that he does not draw his knowledge from practice, that he is merely deducing from theory. . . . The unreal analysis of the premises leads to a false synthesis of their political and artistic consequences. All this mirrors an abstract attitude towards the manifold and complicated store of knowledge, derived from experience, which the party possesses.[14]

In the light of these criticisms Brecht revised the text. But the second performance still did not satisfy the critics. The *Rote Fahne* admonished him:

> The author of *The Measures Taken* Bert Brecht must be told that knowledge of the theories of Marxism-Leninism is not enough, that the genius and wide reading of a writer cannot take the place of revolutionary experience and detailed day-to-day work in the movement.

But the heaviest attack came from Moscow itself. The cen-

tral organ of the International Association of Revolutionary
Writers, *Literatur der Weltrevolution*, published a long article by the German Communist theoretician Alfred Kurella
entitled "An Attempt with Inadequate Means," in which *The
Measures Taken* was condemned on a number of counts.
Above all, the young comrade would not have been killed
because

> we can quote various examples how the Bolsheviks, and
> above all Lenin, took up the same position as the young
> comrade and acted accordingly: not to stop a sponta-
> neous rising of the revolutionary masses by pointing with
> an air of wisdom to the teachings of the classics but to
> take it in hand and to lead it, even if it was to be as-
> sumed that it would end in defeat.[15]

Brecht also erred because he postulated an opposition between reason and emotion, and therefore fell into the sin of
idealism. "The conflict between reason and emotion is a basic
experience of the bourgeois intellectual, who is about to join
the revolutionary proletariat." In fact, *The Measures Taken*
was "a typically petty-bourgeois, intellectualist piece of
work."[16]

In the end Brecht, who always considered himself a better
Marxist than the party pundits, was vindicated by history
itself. *The Measures Taken*, written in 1930, is an exact and
horrifying anticipation of the great confession trials of the
Stalinist era. Many years before Bukharin consented to his
own execution in front of his judges, Brecht had given that
act of self-sacrifice for the sake of the party its great, tragic
expression. With the intuition of the poet he had grasped
the real problem of Communist discipline with all its far-
reaching implications. To this day *The Measures Taken* remains the only great tragedy on the moral dilemma of Soviet
Communism.

The Measures Taken cannot, of course, be performed in
the Communist world. Ernst Schumacher goes to grotesque
lengths in trying to expose the errors of the play as they appear to a present-day East German critic.

If Brecht's description in *The Measures Taken* corresponded to an objective revolutionary situation it would not be the young comrade who would be in conflict with party discipline, but it would be a historical situation in which the three party workers would have to be removed from the leadership as reformists and opportunists. . . . Such a removal of the three party officials as they appear in *The Measures Taken* would in any case be necessary as they are employing the young comrade for tasks that are obviously beyond him.[17]

In other words, Brecht had liquidated the wrong comrade! Brecht himself reacted to all this in his own peculiar way. His French translator Pierre Abraham describes a conversation with Brecht in 1956 shortly before he died. Brecht spoke about his intention of writing a new preface to his didactic plays, in which he wanted to explain that these plays were not meant to teach anything in particular, but were merely "limbering-up exercises for those athletes of the spirit that good dialecticians must be. The question whether any particular judgment in them is well or ill founded is an entirely different matter, which depends on elements I have not introduced into these discussions at all."[18] Anyone who knows Brecht's love of irony and leg-pulling will feel that he would have written this preface with tongue in cheek. In fact, it was not written. Instead, in volume five of the collected plays, published after his death, we find a very brief "Note on the Didactic Plays" that refers to *The Measures Taken* as follows:

The author has repeatedly refused to permit performances of *The Measures Taken*, as only the actor of the young comrade can learn from it and he only if he has also acted one of the party workers and taken part in the control chorus.[19]

As the notes of the first edition already expressly state that "each of the four actors is to have the opportunity of showing the attitude of the young comrade and therefore each actor is to play one of the main scenes of the young comrade in turn,"[20] his solemn reiteration of his original intention as an argument against performance of the play must surely be considered as an example of typically Brechtian irony and delight in mystification.

Whatever Brecht may have thought about the party's condemnation of *The Measures Taken* in the fifties, in the early thirties he displayed a degree of patience and loyalty truly remarkable in so openly professed a cynic. He continued to devote himself to the Communist cause with all the fervor of a new convert. Only occasionally was he driven to utter a mild criticism of the party's dogmatism. "It is a mistake to believe," he makes his Mr. Keuner say in 1932, "that a stupid thing can be refuted only by a clever argument. Many stupid arguments are put forward merely to refute stupid statements." And Keuner goes on to explain that he feels that the party is frightening people away by knowing the answer to every question. "Could we not, in the interests of propaganda, draw up a list of questions which we consider quite unsolved?"[21] Apart from such mild digs at the party stalwarts, however, Brecht did his utmost to help the cause: he fought like a lion to infuse a more positively Marxist content into the film version of *The Threepenny Opera*. He wrote another film scenario, strictly on party lines, for *Kuhle Wampe*. Above all, he produced a play that carefully embodied all the lessons learned from the party's strictures on *The Measures Taken*. If *The Measures Taken* had been criticized for its lack of concreteness and its remoteness from the daily struggles of the ordinary party member, Brecht's adaptation of Gorky's novel *The Mother* was severely practical, concrete, and historical. Although Brecht did not follow Gorky very closely and continued the story to the eve of the October Revolution, he avoided all abstract argument and presented his audience with a primer of propaganda methods and revolutionary behavior. And on the whole the German Communist Party approved of this effort, in spite of the somewhat patronizing tone of *Die Rote Fahne*:

This is a new Bert Brecht. He has escaped from the desert of bourgeois theatre business; he is fighting for

the revolutionary working class. As yet he has not torn
off all the shackles that bind him to his past. But he will.
He must—soon.[22]

The Mother is Brecht's nearest approach to an orthodox
Communist propaganda play. It is based on an accepted classic of Russian revolutionary literature, and apart from *The
Measures Taken* it is his only play that deals directly with
the Russian Revolution or the Communist party. The reaction of Soviet party circles was therefore of particular interest
to him. When it came, five years after the first performance
of *The Mother*, it took a characteristic form.

In 1937 the Soviet monthly journal *International Literature*—in its English edition—published an article on Brecht
by the Soviet dramatist Sergei Tretyakov. This essay, described as a chapter from Tretyakov's forthcoming book on
banned German authors, gave a vivid sketch of Brecht's personality. It showed him as typical of those German intellectuals who spent their time arguing about abstract problems
while the Nazis were about to take power, described how
Brecht had only gradually freed himself from this bourgeois
attitude, and how he had finally reached a definite proletarian standpoint in *The Mother*. But even this turned out
to be a somewhat backhanded compliment.

> At first sight [Tretyakov wrote] Brecht's *Mother* deals
> with the revolutionary development of Pelageya Vlasova,
> the Tver working woman. But this is misleading. It
> would be wrong to regard it as an historical play about a
> Russian working woman. Such an interpretation involves
> one absurdity after another.[23]

And Tretyakov enumerates a whole list of features of the play
that would be quite unthinkable in Russia. He continues:

> Regardless of whether Brecht likes it or not I must men-
> tion the vividness of the teacher, the house-owner, the
> shopwoman, and the policeman in the play. The workers
> are hard to distinguish from each other; this is a general
> shortcoming of all Brecht's plays, which shows that he

does not know the proletarian milieu intimately (this is a warning to him that he must get to know it so).[23]

Brecht is said to have been infuriated by this article, which managed to imply that *The Mother* was the only good thing he had ever written, thanks to a Soviet model, but at the same time suggested that this model had not been imitated well enough.

Tretyakov's proposed book on banned German writers never seems to have been published; he disappeared without a trace in the great purges. All his writings were banned in the Soviet Union until 1957.

The Mother was Brecht's last play to be performed on the German stage before Hitler came to power. The material and spiritual needs of exile drove Brecht closer than ever to the Communists. On the other hand, the struggle against the Nazis made it much easier to keep in step with them. The Communists became the allies of all anti-fascists, and even anti-Nazi writers with liberal views could rally round them.

It is a sign of Brecht's uncanny shrewdness in these matters that he, an ardent and convinced supporter of the party and eager to participate in its propaganda activities, should have resisted the temptation of settling in the Soviet Union. With Lion Feuchtwanger and Willi Bredel, he accepted the joint editorship of *Das Wort*, published in Moscow. But he performed his duties by mail from Denmark. The story is told—on very good authority—that in 1935 he went to Moscow to have a look at the place and to decide whether he should make it his home. He looked around—and left after a few days. When he was asked why he had not stayed, he would smile and say: "I could not get enough sugar for my tea and coffee."[24]

The play *Galileo*, written in 1938–39, reflects his thinking on this point: Galileo has the choice between a life of relative freedom and hard work by earning his living as a teacher in the mercantile Republic of Venice, or leisure and luxury in the service of the Medici in Florence, where papal influence is strong and he runs the risk of having his research prohibited by the Inquisition. After Galileo has gone to Florence and been forced to recant, his pupils discuss this dilemma: ". . . he should never have left Venice," says one of them. "There he could not have written his book," retorts the other. "And in Florence he could not publish it," replies a third.[25]

This is a dilemma that Brecht faced more than once in his life. His Galileo went to Florence, the totalitarian country where he had the leisure to write his book at the cost of terrible suffering. Brecht stayed in Denmark, where he had to work hard to keep alive and lacked the chance of having his plays performed as he imagined them. It turned out to have been the wiser choice; the large majority of the German Communist intellectuals who had gone to Russia came to grief in the great purges. Brecht's great love Carola Neher, the Polly of *The Threepenny Opera* film, was among those who perished.

By the time he was faced with the need to leave Scandinavia the dilemma had temporarily vanished. In the spring of 1941 the Soviet Union and Nazi Germany were allies. Brecht went to America. In one of his poems he describes his situation in Finland in 1941—

> . . . *with curiosity*
> *I scan the map of Europe. High up in Lapland*
> *Towards the Arctic Ocean*
> *I still see a tiny door.*[26]

As Herbert Luethy has pointed out, if one really looks at the map of Europe one will find that Finland has an immensely long eastern frontier with the Soviet Union. Brecht had not even thought of that country as a possible refuge. What is even more astonishing, he published that poem in the East German edition of his verse in 1951!

Seven years after he decided to go to the United States, Brecht was once more faced with the necessity of making up his mind: should he settle in Switzerland or Austria, an independent artist struggling to get his plays performed according to his own ideas, or should he accept the offer of a theatre all his own in East Berlin, lavishly subsidized but dependent on the good will of an authoritarian state? It was not an easy decision. The long time he took over it and his trial period in Berlin show that he weighed the arguments for and against it most carefully. He even considered settling in Munich, but abandoned the idea when it became clear that he could do so only as a German citizen subject to the U.S. military government. In the end he did accept the East German offer.

And so the eternal rebel became a member of the ruling class of a rigidly organized, hierarchical society, the eternal outsider a member of the establishment. It was an interesting and a dangerous situation. Brecht's experiences provide an illuminating example of the strains and stresses that arise when an intellectual of high standing and strong personality sincerely tries to live and work under a totalitarian system.

To understand his reactions and development in this situation it is, however, important to keep in mind the nature of his own personal brand of Communist beliefs and the motives that had brought him to adopt them.

Contempt for bourgeois society, the bourgeois way of life, bourgeois respectability lies at the root of these beliefs. In Germany more than elsewhere the artistic temperament was driven into opposition to the established way of life. Respectable society was not only stuffy, stupid, and hypocritical, it was, above all, utterly without grace or wit, ugly and unaesthetic. The German intellectuals and artists of the Wilhelmian period used to dream of the wit and gay conversation, the *savoir-vivre* of France, the exquisite manners and beautiful country houses of England. The First World War confirmed the younger generation's contempt for the respectable Germany of their parents, which now stood revealed as not only crude and ugly but incompetent and bankrupt.

Brecht's generation of young poets linked its contempt for this society with an utter rejection of its accepted standards of art and literature. Goethe and Schiller and all the other schoolbook classics filled these young men with disgust. The very language they used to express their idealistic sentiments seemed contaminated. Feuchtwanger describes how Brecht told him one day: "When Horace expresses the most ordinary thought or the most trivial emotion, it looks magnificent. He worked in marble. We work with dirt."[27]

The cheap chauvinism of German patriotic literature turned young people like Brecht into violent antinationalists. Sentiments expressed in such vulgar, graceless language could not but be contemptible.

When the First World War broke out, the ugliness of wartime propaganda and the horrors of physical suffering appeared inextricably linked in the minds of such intellectuals. The Austrian critic Karl Kraus, whom Brecht greatly admired, was their chief spokesman. To him the debasement of its language appeared as the expression of the moral and intellectual debasement of the nation.

If the ugliness of jingoist sentiments turned young Brecht into an antipatriot, the horror of war made him a pacifist, and the vulgarity and crudeness of the German postwar profiteers, the feverish parasites of the inflationary boom, inspired him with loathing for what he thought to be the capitalist system.

So it was for aesthetic reasons that Brecht, like many sensitive German intellectuals of artistic temperament and tastes, was driven into opposition against the existing order of things.

In Germany after the First World War the picture of commercial society was certainly an ugly one. There the bull-necked, bloated financier, in his loud suit, his bowler hat, chewing enormous cigars in dreary nightclubs, listening to vulgar music, and leering at disgusting floor shows, really existed. The horror of this picture left a lasting mark on Brecht's writing. It is the origin of his crude and oversimplified ideas about the nature of all business: again and again he equates finance and industrial enterprise with robbery, fraud, vulgarity, and violence. And this naïve idea of the nature of the capitalist system often mars his efforts to present a serious analysis of the evils of a commercial society, particularly when he transfers his vulgar German black marketeers to London or Chicago, where they become completely unconvincing. But in the very special context of the Germany of the twenties these images did have a meaning.

These were the aesthetic roots of Brecht's furious negation of the existing order of things. He could not endure the ugliness and vulgarity of patriotic cant, the witlessness of respectable society, and the loathsome cynicism of the *nouveaux riches*. And it is clear that his sensitivity was not only aesthetic. He also was basically a puritan and an idealist. When this moral sensitivity was shattered by the horrors of the war and the postwar era, it turned into a violent denial of all values. But in the long run so purely destructive and negative an attitude was bound to lead to disaster. Brecht needed a new core of positive belief.

Marxism, as Brecht understood it, provided such a framework. It allowed all these negative attitudes to crystallize into a positive pattern. And what was even more important to Brecht, it was aesthetically satisfying.

Marxism provided the dramatist in Brecht with a splendid picture of conflict, a ready-made tragic pattern of history. He was so taken with the grandeur of the historical conception of the Marxist classics that he tried to put the *Communist Manifesto* into hexameters on the pattern of Lucretius's *De Rerum Natura*. Although he abandoned the attempt after many years of strenuous effort, a long and impressive fragment was found among his posthumous papers:

Reading history you read of the deeds of great individuals
Rising and falling like stars and the mighty march of their
*   armies,*
Glory and ruin of empires. But to the classics
History is, above all, the history of struggles of classes:
For they see the nations divided and fighting as classes
Riven within themselves: Knights and Patricians, Slaves and
*   Plebeians,*
Nobles, Artisans, Peasants—and now Bourgeois and Proletarians,
Ever maintaining in motion the gigantic machine of production
And distribution of goods, while they are fighting the age-old
Fight to the death, the mighty struggle for power. . . .[28]

For the anarchist Brecht, to whom the world had appeared utterly without sense of purpose, and the individual so completely alone that he made his hero say in *In the Jungle of the Cities*: "The infinite isolation of man makes even enmity an unattainable goal. . . . Yes, so great is this isolation that there cannot even be a struggle,"[29] the discovery of this great and simple pattern and purpose in history must have come as a tremendous relief.

But what excited him even more was the dramatic quality of the Hegelian dialectic. The coexistence of opposites, the merging of thesis and antithesis appealed not only to Brecht's dramatic sense but also to his sense of the comic:

> [Hegel] had the greatest comic talent among all the phi-
> losophers; only Socrates, whose method was similar, was
> his equal. . . . He had such a sense of humor that, for
> example, he could not even conceive of, say, order with-
> out disorder. . . . He denied that one equals one, not
> only because everything that exists is continually turning
> into something else, namely its opposite, but because
> generally nothing is identical with itself.[30]

For Brecht this ambiguity of all things, the idea that noth-ing is really what it seems, constituted the essence of drama and poetry. His ideas about the "epic" theatre antedate his discovery of the dialectic. But it is easy to see how the Marxist dialectic as he understood it must have confirmed and justi-fied these ideas: the actor who impersonates the character and yet remains himself, the stage that represents reality and yet remains a stage, the characters who are themselves but can at a moment's notice be retooled into someone else, like Galy Gay in *Man Equals Man*, they all fell into place within the framework of the Hegelian dialectic.

And if the despair engendered by the seeming absurdity of the human condition had led the young Brecht into a self-destructive attitude of complete moral anarchism, now that the world was seen to have a purpose the force of this despair could be canalized into more positive channels. If the pat-tern and purpose of history were known, it was easy to submit to them. The self-destructive impulses could be turned out-wards. If the heroes of *Baal* and *In the Jungle of the Cities* drifted to self-destruction by yielding to blind impulses within them, the airmen of *The Didactic Play of Baden* who

have to perish are redeemed by the knowledge that their fate
has significance within the process of history:

> But you who consent and agree with the flow of things
> Will not sink back into the void. . . .[31]

The young comrade in *The Measures Taken* still yields to the
impulse of pity, because he cannot endure the suffering inherent in the human condition. But he also knows that he was
wrong to be weak, that the inexorable workings of history
cannot be hurried and therefore consents to his own liquidation.

The horror at the violence of war, which had led Brecht
to despair, turned into the willing acceptance of violence as
part of the workings of necessity. The little Salvation Army
girl of *St. Joan of the Stockyards*, driven to despair by the
human suffering before her, tries to relieve suffering by kindness. But in the hour of her death she comes to the conclusion:

> For only violence helps, where violence reigns
> And only men can help where there are men. . . .[32]

It is easy to see how this austere, poetic version of the Marxist
creed corresponded to the subconscious needs of a young man
of deep sensibility whose world had been shattered by the
spectacle of horrible human suffering. But it is equally clear
that the chief value of this creed to him was that it dissolved
the nightmare of absurdity, that it dispelled the oppressive
feeling that life was ruled by vast impersonal and irrational
forces; in the light of this redeeming creed human suffering
no longer appeared as the outcome of a fate beyond human
comprehension and incapable of being influenced by human
endeavor; if history was merely the outcome of human struggles, and the laws that governed these were known, the fate of
mankind could be controlled. Brecht's aggressive rationalism,
his obstinate refusal to recognize the existence of psychological factors or areas of mystery in nature, is the reaction of a
personality that had felt deeply threatened and disturbed by
the irrationality of the world around it, and that therefore

had to cling to its newly found belief in reason with grim determination. Hence Brecht's fear of emotion in the theatre and his constant insistence on the scientific nature of Marxism and of the "epic" theatre based on it.

This preoccupation with the scientific certainty of the Marxist creed shows to what an extent Brecht really was an idealist of truly religious fervor behind the mask of cynicism and toughness he displayed. He never did much as a practical politician or party worker; during the Hitler period he wrote some anti-Nazi plays and poems for broadcasting, made a few speeches at international congresses of anti-Fascist writers, and even composed one or two pamphlets that were smuggled into Germany. One of these, characteristically, was *Five Difficulties in Writing the Truth* (published behind the title page of a booklet on *Hints for First Aid*), a highly theoretical piece of advice to other writers that reveals moral scruples of all kinds. No wonder that the professional Communists, preoccupied with the techniques of subversion and the exercise of power, thought little of so ineffectual a dreamer. For them the means were all; the ends had been thrust into the limbo of a utopian future. For Brecht the relation between ends and means always remained a vital problem.

That is why the scientific character of Marxism was so important to him. The means are justified only when they are based on the mathematical certainty that they will bring about the ends to be attained. Violence can be accepted only when it is based on an absolutely certain knowledge of the results, freedom can be given up only for a time, when it is certain that the state will really wither away in the end. Brecht had a horror of dogma and therefore insisted that doubt, criticism, and free inquiry, the essential elements of the scientific attitude, must be the basis of Marxism. One of his pupils reports that during the rehearsals of *Galileo* in the last months of his life, whenever he came to the sentence "My task is not to prove that I have been right up till now, but to find out *whether* I have been right," "Brecht regularly used to interrupt the rehearsal and to draw his pupils' attention to the fact that for a Marxist this was the most important sentence in the play."[33]

As long as Brecht could believe in the scientific certainty

of Marxism he was safe. Everything became very simple. Violence and dictatorship could be defended, as old Pelageya Vlasova defends them in *The Mother*:

> With freedom it is rather as it is with your money, Nikolai Ivanovich. Since I have been giving you so little pocket money, you are able to buy much more. By spending less money for a time, you can spend more money later.[34]

That is how clear and simple things became as long as the truth of the doctrine remained inviolate. To one who had been driven to despair by the absurdity and chaos of the world, this certainty was of the utmost importance. That is why for Brecht Communism, as he put it:

> *. . . is not madness, but*
> *The end of madness.*
> *It is not chaos*
> *But order.*
> *It is the simple thing*
> *That is hard to accomplish.*[35]

Yet Brecht was far too lucid and sceptical a person to have any illusions about the true nature of Stalin's regime in the Soviet Union. Brecht's great friend, the critic Walter Benjamin (1892–1940; he committed suicide while fleeing from Nazi-occupied France), has left us a vivid record of conversations he had with Brecht during a visit to Brecht's Danish home in the summer of 1938. On June 28, 1938, for example, Benjamin noted: "Brecht talks about his deeply ingrained hatred of priests, which he inherited from his grandmother. He drops hints that those who have made Marx's theoretical teachings their own . . . will always form a priestly camarilla." On the same day Benjamin reports a conversation on Soviet literature and the bad Soviet poetry which flooded the issues of *Das Wort*, the Soviet German-language periodical, of which Brecht was nominally an editor. "Brecht says, authors over there have a hard life. It is already considered a sign of ill will if the name of Stalin does not appear in a poem."

On July 29, 1938 Benjamin reports that Brecht was preparing an article against György Lukács's views on "socialist realism" and asked Benjamin whether he ought to take the risk and publish it in *Das Wort*. "I told him I could not give him useful advice. 'These are questions of power. You ought to ask someone over there. After all, you've got friends there [i.e. in the Soviet Union].' Brecht: 'To tell you the truth, I have no friends there. And the Moscovites themselves have no friends—like the dead.' "

Benjamin's reports of private conversations with Brecht are fully confirmed by fragments of a book which was published nine years after Brecht died—in 1965—but which dates back to the late thirties: *Me-ti. Buch der Wendungen* (*Me-ti. Book of Twists and Turns*). This consists of brief stories and thoughts, purporting to be the work of an ancient Chinese philosopher (there are echoes here of Confucius, Lao-tzu and the Book of Changes), but clearly referring to Brecht's own political and private experience. The posthumous edition even contains a key to the Chinese names. Lenin appears as Mi-en-leh, Marx as Ka-meh, Stalin as Ni-en, the Soviet Union as Su.

The book of Me-ti leaves no doubt whatever on Brecht's attitude to Stalin: "Mi-en-leh (Lenin) believed before the great revolution that the workers would have to help the citizens to free themselves from the rule of the Emperor. . . . Later the workers, under his leadership, obtained power; but his successor, Ni-en, acted exactly like an Emperor. The backwardness of the country of Su, of which Mi-en-leh had always spoken, did after all show itself in this phenomenon. The great machinery (i.e. technology) was built up not by the citizens under people's rule, but by workers under the rule of an Emperor." In another section Brecht deals with the show trials under Stalin: "Me-ti expressed his disapproval of Ni-en (Stalin) because, in his trials against his enemies in the association [i.e. the Party] he demanded too much confidence from the people. He said: If I am asked to believe something which can be proven (without furnishing me the proof) that is tantamount to my being asked to believe some-

thing that can*not* be proven. Ni-en *might* have benefited th
people by removing his enemies inside the association, but h
did not prove it. By conducting trials without proof he ha
done damage to the people. He ought to have taught th
people to demand proof. . . ."

That Brecht was equally disturbed by Stalin's influence on
the Party and on the Marxist doctrine itself is shown by thi
passage from *Me-ti*: "Under Ni-en's leadership industry with
out exploiters was being built up in Su and agriculture col
lectivised and furnished with machines. But the association
[i.e. Communist Parties] outside Su decayed. It was no longer
the members who elected the secretaries, but the secretaries
who elected the members. The guidelines were issued by Su
and the secretaries were paid from Su. If mistakes were made,
those who had *criticised* the mistakes were punished; but
those who had *made* the mistakes remained in office. Soon the
office holders were no longer the best members but merely
the most servile. . . . Those who issued the orders in Su no
longer learned any facts, because the secretaries no longer reported facts that might not have pleased them. In view of
these conditions, the best (members) were in despair. Me-ti
deplored the decay of the great method [i.e. Marxism]. Master
Ko [i.e. Korsch, Brecht's teacher of Marxism] turned away
from it. . . . Outside Su all those who praised Ni-en's merits,
even those which were undeniable, became suspect of corruption; inside Su all those who uncovered his mistakes, even
those from which he himself suffered, became suspect of
treason."

When Brecht returned to East Berlin in 1948 he was well
aware of the duality, the truly Hegelian contradiction, between his own ideals of Communism and the realities of life
in a Communist country. In the thirties he had watched the
fight against the *avant-gardists* of the Soviet theatre and seen
the acceptance of the Stanislavsky method as the official style
of acting in the Soviet Union. In his earlier theoretical writings he had never concealed his opinion of Stanislavsky's
theatre as the antithesis of what a truly Marxist theatre
should be. Nevertheless he had paid his tribute to the newly

dopted formula of "socialist realism." But it had been a typi-
ally double-edged Brechtian tribute: in the essay *Range and
Variety of the Realist Style* (1938) Brecht used Shelley's
Mask of Anarchy as an example of realism—i.e., progressive
political tendency—that was nevertheless clothed in the form
of fantasy. From it he had drawn the conclusion:

> . . . we see . . . that realism is not a matter of form.
> Nothing is so bad in putting up models as to put up *too
> few models*. It is dangerous to tie the great concept of
> realism to a few names, and to gather together a few
> forms as examples of the only true creative method, how-
> ever useful these forms themselves may be. . . . The
> truth can be concealed in many ways. It can be said in
> many ways. . . .[36]

A few months later Brecht felt that he ought to come out
more clearly against "formalism," but here again he kept his
obeisance to the antiformalist campaign then raging in the
Soviet Union carefully balanced:

> The very salutary campaign against formalism has helped
> the productive development of artistic forms, by proving
> that social content is an absolutely decisive condition for
> such development. Any formal innovation which does
> not serve, and derive its justification from, its social con-
> tent will remain utterly fruitless.[37]

Which means that Brecht, while acknowledging the demand
for social content (which he had never denied), insisted on
his right to continue his experiments with form.

Brecht never concealed his contempt for the artistic standards of Stalinist Russia. Shortly after his return to East Berlin
he created considerable embarrassment among a group of
German actors in the Soviet-run artists' club *Die Moewe* by
declaring in a loud voice that he regarded the performances
of Soviet drama he had seen as downright *Kitsch*. And when
he advised the Swiss journalist Gody Suter to read Soviet

novels, he praised their social attitude but added "As to quality—rather like Gerstaecker or Kellermann"[38]—both authors of highly popular novels whose names are synonymous with *Kitsch* among most German left-wing intellectuals. During his visit to Moscow in 1955 to receive the Stalin Peace Prize, Brecht told the Soviet critic Fradkin that the performances he had liked best among those he had been taken to see were Mayakovsky's *The Bug* and *The Bath* at the Satirical Theatre. Both these plays had been banned since the middle thirties, because they are savage and grotesque satires on Soviet bureaucracy. Fradkin adds that Brecht told him he considered the actor Yachnitski a perfect exponent of the "epic" style, because he left no doubt about the difference between his own personality and that of the character he portrayed.[39] A typically Brechtian way of expressing his contempt for the Stanislavsky method and the official style of the Stalinist era!

Brecht's first postwar visit to East Berlin had been preceded by a performance of *Fear and Misery of the Third Reich* at the Deutsches Theater in January 1948. One of the party's main spokesmen in the field of theatrical criticism, Fritz Erpenbeck, had greeted this sequence of relatively un-Brechtian scenes with shouts of joy that Brecht had at last abandoned his "in our view false theory of the epic theatre and the 'didactic play'," his advocacy of which his friends had considered a tragic aberration in so talented an artist.[40] So it must have been clear to Brecht that he was in for a hard struggle.

The East German authorities regarded the winning over of such a famous playwright as a major propaganda victory against the West; they also made a sincere attempt to win him over to their own—artistic—point of view. They spared no expense to give him what he wanted and argued with him, patiently and at great length. Much of this went on behind closed doors, but sometimes it was found necessary to bring the arguments into the open. In the case of *Mother Courage*, for example, the text has been published of a discussion that Brecht had with the party's favorite playwright, Friedrich Wolf (author of the well-known anti-Nazi play *Professor Mamlock*). Wolf very politely reproached Brecht with leavng the audience to draw its own conclusions from Mother Courage's fate. "How can we activate our people to overcome that fatalistic attitude towards a new war?" Wolf asked, and added, "I should have thought Courage *even more* effective if her words 'Cursed be war!' had found a visible expression in action, if she had drawn the consequences from her experience." In other words, the party would have liked Mother Courage to have been converted to an active political attitude at the end of the play, instead of continuing her old life as a victualler. Brecht's retort was: "If Courage learns nothing—in my opinion the public can learn something by watching her."[41]

From its own point of view the party was right: the East Berlin public regarded *Mother Courage* as a faithful picture of the horrors of war, including those of the Russian occupation. The brilliantly sarcastic things that are said in *Mother Courage* about great generals and field marshals who bask in glory at the expense of the poor devils in the mud apply to the great Marshal Stalin with the same force as to Field Marshal Tilly or King Gustavus Adolphus of Sweden.

But if Brecht was prepared for, and unperturbed by, this kind of criticism, the matter became more serious when his most openly Communist play, *The Mother*, was the target for similar criticism. This was a magnificent production. Helene Weigel gave a great performance and Caspar Neher had designed some highly effective sets. It looked like a great success. But a few weeks after the first night the Central Committee of the party launched a massive attack against it. At the fifth plenary meeting of the Central Committee in March 1951 one of the highest members of the hierarchy, Oelssner, asked:

Is this in fact realism? Are these typical figures shown in typical surroundings? . . . In my opinion this is not theatre. It is a kind of mixture between Meyerhold and Proletkult. If a man as talented as Brecht could write a play that really hangs together, that is really composed, what a work of art we could get! Besides . . . there are scenes that are historically wrong and politically harmful.[42]

Here Brecht was bluntly asked to abandon his own "epic" style. The mention of Meyerhold was ominous in view of what had happened to that unfortunate director of genius. Another high party official, Hans Rodenberg, also reproached Brecht for holding wrong views of Marxism, but asked that Brecht should be reprieved:

Of course, we must give him more time. . . . Brecht is using up his old luggage at the moment . . . he needs time to find his feet. . . . Provided he had felt able to do so, he would surely by now have written a play about our own time. Our real criticism of Brecht will depend on the time it takes him to write this play, and what a play it will be! . . . We must give Brecht some time. We must not stop criticizing him, but we must criticize him as intelligently as he himself is intelligent.[42]

So Brecht was given a reprieve to allow him to write a play on a contemporary East German problem. He never wrote such a play and continued, to the day of his death, to produce his earlier works—the luggage he had brought with him from his exile.

One of these earlier works was *The Trial of Lucullus*, which caused the most widely publicized of Brecht's clashes with the authorities.

The Trial of Lucullus had been written in 1939 as a radio play and had been broadcast by a Swiss station. It shows the trial of the great Roman general after his death by a jury of shades in the underworld. It is a straightforward and very moving poem on the futility of military glory and conquest *sub specie aeternitatis*. Stravinsky is said to have at one time been interested in setting it to music, Roger Sessions based an opera on the English version, but it was Paul Dessau, whom Brecht had met in the United States and who had also gone back to East Berlin, who wrote the music for the new opera, which was to be performed for the first time by the East Berlin State Opera on March 17, 1951.

This was the period of the Korean War, and the Communist authorities were clearly perturbed when they heard that the new work was a condemnation of all war as folly and showed the futility of conquest, a sentiment that might have been appropriate when it referred to Hitler but could scarcely appear very politic in the center of Soviet-occupied Germany. The story goes that the Communist authorities wanted to stop the performance altogether, but because a great deal of money had already been spent on the production, a famous conductor, Hermann Scherchen, had been invited from the West, and the first performance of so important a work had been widely publicized, they decided to permit three performances before a strictly controlled, hand-picked audience of party stalwarts and members of the youth organization.

These young people, however, were not very interested in opera, and many of them sold their tickets to Brecht enthusiasts and intellectuals from East and West Berlin. As a result the plan misfired. Instead of giving the new opera the planned cool reception that would have allowed the production to have been withdrawn as unsuccessful, the first night audience received it with tremendous applause and cheers. The members of the East German government, who had watched the performance with growing consternation, left in a huff, and the two remaining performances that had already been billed were cancelled.

On March 22 the party organ *Neues Deutschland* fired a veritable broadside against Brecht and Paul Dessau. In an article headed "*The Trial of Lucullus*—the Failure of an Experiment of the German State Opera," they were taken to task for having produced a work that

does not correspond to reality. The world peace camp with its 800 million people, led by the Soviet Union, is not a court of shades, but has the very real power to subject all war criminals to a very earthbound kind of justice. What at the beginning of Hitler's war might have been understood as the expression of the uncertain political position of an exiled anti-Fascist writer appears in

1951 as a relapse into doubt and weakness the poet
should have overcome long ago, particularly when, by
the very manner of its staging, it is put forward as an
authoritative comment on the current situation.[43]

Dessau was accused of cheap cabaret effects. A Western
paper had compared his music to that of Stravinsky. And, the
paper pointed out,

Igor Stravinsky, a composer who lives in the U.S.A., is a
fanatical destroyer of the European musical tradition.
Anyone who follows such an example destroys his own
talent. Dessau robs himself of the possibility of arousing
the enthusiasm of the masses against a new war of conquest. A music that pours dissonances and intellectualist
cleverness over its listeners confirms the reactionary part
of the audience in its attitudes, and repels the progressive section. . . .[43]

The fury of this attack against the music of *The Trial of
Lucullus* is reminiscent of the Nazis' campaign against "decadent" music. In a later article in the party organ, directed
this time mainly against the management of the State Opera,
this point was put even more forcefully:

Take *The Trial of Lucullus* and look at the composition
of the orchestra for this work. There are no violins. This
most noble of all instruments, which can produce the
most beautiful tonal patterns, is missing. Instead there is
a piano doctored with drawing-pins and nine different
kinds of percussion instrument, among them drums,
large and small, and metal sheets that are banged with
stones. . . .[44]

Brecht and Dessau were summoned to a discussion with
the party leaders, which is reported to have lasted eight hours.
When Brecht emerged from this marathon he said, with his
usual ambiguity: "Where else in the world can you find a
government that shows such interest in, and pays such attention to, artists?"[45]

But he tackled the rewriting of the text with the good grace of a craftsman who puts in alterations according to the wishes and tastes of his employers. Yet on closer scrutiny these alterations do not amount to much: some passages are omitted for obvious reasons—for example:

> . . . they say, they are recruiting legionaries
> in the taverns by the Tiber, for the war against the West
> which is to be conquered. . . .[46]

Other passages have been inserted to make a distinction between a war of conquest and one of national defense. The shades of Roman soldiers are now made to exclaim:

> If only we had ceased
> Serving the aggressor!
> If only we had
> Joined the defenders![47]

The title was changed from the excessively objective *The Trial of Lucullus* to the more clear-cut *Condemnation of Lucullus*. Dessau revised the music and replaced some of the *Sprechgesang* with arias that could have come from traditional grand opera.

To forestall any criticism that a trial by the shades of the departed was too unrealistic, at the first performance of the revised version on October 12, 1951 an inscription in large letters announced that "the verdict of the court of the dead differs in no way from that of posterity."[48]

But in spite of all these precautions the reception of the *Condemnation of Lucullus* by *Neues Deutschland* was decidedly cool:

> It must be stated that the new version represents a distinct improvement on the original shape of the work, as a number of weaknesses have been eliminated. Nevertheless it must not be overlooked that it still lacks the real dramatic tension that would compel the spectator to participate and take sides. This is due to the fact that the defeat and annihilation of the conqueror takes place

not in living reality, not as part of the real struggle of the
progressive forces of the nations against their blood-
suckers but, as it were, posthumously, in the kingdom of
the dead. . . . This brings the whole conception dangerously near to symbolism. . . .[49]

The music, too, in spite of Dessau's changes, received a severe
rebuke. After a few performances the *Condemnation of
Lucullus* also disappeared from the stage of the State Opera.
It reappeared in the East German repertoire only after
Brecht's death.

Shortly after the revised version failed to win the favor of
the East German authorities, Brecht gave permission for *Lucullus* to be performed in West Germany—in the original
unrevised version and under its original title, *The Trial of
Lucullus!* At the same time he published the text of the opera
in the eleventh issue of his *Versuche*—also in the original
form, with the alterations attached as an appendix.

Friends who met Brecht at the time of the controversy
about *Lucullus* unanimously report that he took to it like a
duck to water and seemed to enjoy it all tremendously. He
cheerfully entered into the intentions of the authorities, gladly admitted his political mistakes—and yet, he did
not make any really important changes, certainly none that
altered the character of the work as a whole. The essential
features that had been singled out as formalistic remained
intact. The decision to publish both versions, and the permission to perform the original version in West Germany,
show Brecht's tactics: cheerful compliance, even subservience,
in his dealings with the authorities on the one hand, stubborn
persistence in his own essential convictions on the other.

There is a passage in *Galileo* that throws a good deal of
light on Brecht's attitude in these matters. One of his friends
is horrified by the groveling tone of the letter in which
Galileo solicits the favors of the Medici. Galileo replies:

You think my letter is too subservient? I ask myself: is it
subservient *enough*? Not too formal, as though I lacked
genuine devotion? . . . A man like me can get into a
moderately dignified position only by crawling on his

belly. And you know I despise people whose brains are
unable to fill their stomachs.[50]

To make up for *Lucullus,* to prove their usefulness to the
regime, Brecht and Dessau followed it up by producing one
of the most blatant pieces of propaganda hack work of their
careers—the choral cantata *Herrnburger Bericht (Report on
Herrnburg),* written for performance by youth groups during
the East German World Youth Festival in the summer of
1951. The theme is an incident from the previous year, when
West German police had tried to stop a large contingent of
Western Communist youths from recrossing the zonal frontier in force. Dessau, who had been accused of failing to write
music of propaganda value, produced a pastiche of folk songs
to the accompaniment of such recognized popular instruments as accordions, guitars, mandolins, etc., and Brecht
manfully tried to express politically acceptable sentiments.

> . . . *Adenauer, Adenauer, show us your hand*
> *For thirty pieces of silver you sell our land,*[51]

is a fair sample of the studied banality of this verse, which
almost makes it appear intentional, as if designed to expose
its absurdity. Yet Brecht no doubt meant it seriously enough.
He was merely too good a poet to be able to write such stuff
to order.

It is significant that *Report on Herrnburg* was never published in its entirety by Brecht in the issues of his *Versuche,*
which appeared at regular intervals till he died, and that he
did not include it in the collected edition of his plays or any
of the various anthologies of his poetry published in his lifetime. Nor has Dessau published any of the *Herrnburg* songs
in his volume of Brecht songs, issued in 1957.[52] On the other
hand, it was certainly for this rather than for *The Trial of
Lucullus* that Brecht received the National Prize for Literature, First Class, from the East German government in 1951.
In the last collected edition of Brecht's works published in
1957 under the auspices of Brecht's literary executors the
Report on Herrnburg was omitted, although it is briefly mentioned in a note as an unimportant "cantata for schools." This

seems to be due to the embarrassment that Brecht's indignation about the West Germans closing of a frontier would cause in a Germany bearing the burden of the Berlin Wall and a frontier closely guarded by the East German regime.

The fact that he was a national laureate and a member of the Academy of Arts did not exempt Brecht from further and even more serious attack. This was the last phase of Stalin's reign, a time of trials, purges, and terror. In the cultural field it was the period of the campaign against "cosmopolitanism." In East Germany this coincided with a return to violent chauvinism, partly to win over the masses who were still largely conditioned by National Socialism, partly to lend weight to the propaganda line that East Germany represented the true spirit of the nation. Brecht had always been nauseated by German chauvinism. He disliked the schoolbook view of the German classics. No wonder that he fell foul of the party line.

In Brecht's view the German people had to make a fresh start and to cut themselves loose from much of their tradition. He began to revive some of the classical plays of the German repertory to show the values they represented in a critical light, and to draw the German public's attention to the moral and material squalor of their own past—*Deutsche Misere* (German miserableness). Already in 1950 he had turned an eighteenth-century play, *The Private Tutor* by J. M. R. Lenz, into a vitriolic attack against the subservience of German intellectuals and schoolmasters to the whims of the rich and powerful. The hero of the play, Laeuffer, finds that his sexual instinct interferes with the performance of his duties as a private tutor, so he castrates himself to show his willingness to serve his master. The regime accepted this performance, one of the most brilliant ever put on by the Berliner Ensemble, with relatively good grace. After all, the mad genius, Lenz, had never been an acknowledged German classic. But when, in the following year, Kleist's *Der Zerbrochene Krug* (*The Broken Jug*) was put on to display the corruption and hypocrisy of rural life and the administration of justice in eighteenth-century Germany, this was considered too much: the honor of the nation was being dragged in the mud. And when Brecht went a step further by producing Goethe's *Faust* in its original form (*Urfaust*) the storm broke. *Neues Deutschland* attacked Brecht's young pupil Egon Monk, who had directed the play, for following in the footsteps of his master:

The director Monk copied models we have already encountered in *The Private Tutor* and *The Broken Jug*. They too were fatalistic and pessimistic pictures of static conditions; they had only one hero: "German miserableness." This expresses an attitude—an attitude in fact directed against Germany's cultural heritage, against Germany's national culture.[53]

What particularly shocked the national feelings of *Neues Deutschland* was the scene in Auerbach's cellar, in which the drunken students bawl out some German folk songs.

Never before have we seen a similar mockery of German folk song on our stage! . . . Abandon your forced primitivism, your artistic economy of means, be not afraid to say yes to the best artistic products of our past and you will produce wonderful, great theatre. We feel we must say that the young members of the Berliner Ensemble, many of whom are very talented, are being led into a wrong direction by the methods and principles applied in the adaptation of the classics by Bertolt Brecht, the artistic director of the Ensemble.[54]

Such an attack was a serious threat not only to Brecht but to the continued existence of the Berliner Ensemble. It coincided with a second and perhaps even more serious threat: the campaign to make Stanislavsky's method the only style of acting permitted in East Germany.

In April 1953 a Stanislavsky Conference was held in East Berlin. Actors and directors from all over East Germany were lectured on the absolute necessity of following the Soviet style: "The Soviet theatre is the most highly developed form of theatre in history," said *Neues Deutschland* in an article on the conference. It went on:

> We are compelled to state here that the reprehensible underestimation of the significance of the Stanislavsky method for the development of a German national theatre is the main reason why the fight against formalism and cosmopolitanism on the stage has not yet reached that sharpness of principle which alone can guarantee a decisive breakthrough towards socialist realism in our theatre.[55]

And if there was still any doubt against whom this was directed, the following passage removed it:

> Are there not—and we all know it, above all in our capital city—performances in which admittedly "great theatre" is produced under the direction of great artists, but in which nevertheless formalism and its twin brother schematism look out from every nook and cranny, starting from the choice of plays, right down to the adaptation, the basic production idea, the production itself, the décor, and the method of acting?[55]

Helene Weigel tried to parry the blow by declaring in the course of the conference debates that there *were* some things in common between the Brechtian theatre and the Stanislavsky method: accuracy of observation, ensemble acting, truthfulness, naturalness, etc. But the party was far too acutely aware of the real situation to be taken in. *Neues Deutschland* replied:

> . . . Helene Weigel . . . may have been right in so far as there is always something of Stanislavsky anywhere in the theatre where work is done conscientiously, with artistic ability and craftsmanship, and on the basis of socialist convictions. . . . But in so far as the Berliner Ensemble tries to put into practice Brecht's theoretical views embodied in *Little Organon for the Theatre* and his other writings, it is undeniably in opposition to every-

thing the name Stanislavsky stands for. The two leaders of the Ensemble must surely be the last people to hide their heads in the sand when faced with these facts.[56]

Such language could not be ignored. Brecht promptly announced that he had already begun to study Stanislavsky. And Western newspapers were already speculating on the imminent demise of the Berliner Ensemble. Their prophecies proved wrong—the party critics themselves had been overtaken by the events. They believed that they were still following the party line. But the party line had already changed. For in the meantime Stalin had died, and the thaw had set in.

Brecht's reaction to the death of Stalin was in character. While the official court poet, Johannes R. Becher, published a poem in which Stalin, now an immortal among immortals, was shown sitting on a bench with Lenin and Thaelmann listening to accordion music, and stalking through the picture gallery of Dresden with the great paintings bowing in reverence before him, and while most of the other members of the German Academy of Arts indulged in similarly fulsome paeans of praise and gratitude, Brecht's contribution was strictly in prose:

The oppressed of all five continents, those who have already freed themselves, and all those who fight for world peace, must have felt their heart-beats stop, when they heard that Stalin was dead. He was the embodiment of their hopes. But the spiritual and material weapons he made exist, and so does the doctrine, to make new ones.[57]

To a casual reader this may appear wholly in praise of Stalin. But on more careful examination it will be noticed that the statement confines itself severely to fact. It does not even say *why* the heartbeats of the millions stopped. To say that Stalin was the embodiment of hopes is an equally factual, and ambiguous, statement, and the last sentence openly stresses the need to develop the Marxist doctrine beyond Stalin. Once again Brecht proved his shrewdness in these matters. When the cult of Stalin was denounced his colleagues had to eat their words. The party pundits who had questioned Brecht's soundness as a Marxist were embarrassed, or in trouble. But he had struck a note that was exactly right.

Stalin's death threw the party authorities in East Germany into confusion and disarray. While the attacks on cosmopolitanism and anti-Stanislavskians continued, some concessions were made to the masses, who had become restive. On June 17, 1953 the people of East Germany rose in open revolt. For a few hours the regime lost control. Then Soviet tanks restored order.

On June 21 *Neues Deutschland* published the following brief item of news:

National Prize Laureate Bertolt Brecht has sent the General Secretary of the Central Committee of the Socialist Unity Party, Walter Ulbricht, a letter, in which he declared: "I feel the need to express to you at this moment my attachment to the Socialist Unity Party. Yours, Bertolt Brecht."

This piece of news was immediately picked up in West Germany, where it aroused a storm of indignation. Many who greatly admired Brecht as one of the outstanding poets of the nation were rightly outraged at seeing him so brazenly support a regime that had called out Soviet tanks to shoot down unarmed workers demonstrating against intolerable living conditions. His message seemed to be couched in such unequivocal terms that there could be no doubt about the meaning of this "telegram," as it soon came to be called. Brecht had clearly lost the claim to be considered anything but an obedient, unthinking follower of the masters who paid for his services by providing him with a theatre and a life of luxury, while the workers starved.

This indignation in West Germany was no doubt justified. For once Brecht had been too clever. He still believed in the Marxist doctrine, he still believed that it could be put into practice in East Germany. He had thought he could use the opportunity for putting forward his criticisms of the methods of the regime in a long and closely argued letter. But, as the Swiss correspondent Gody Suter later reported, of that whole long clever piece of writing only the one sentence, which had been of no importance to Brecht, remained. The red pencil of the party line had destroyed his cunning design and mercilessly exposed the poet, and turned him, in the eyes of the West, into a loyal henchman of the executioners. His independent position, the platform of a kind of "inner opposition," was suddenly revealed as a grotesque illusion; a well-aimed blow by the party's paw had smashed the reputation Brecht had built up for himself in long, patient efforts. It was the only time that I saw him helpless, almost small: when he eagerly pulled the tattered original of that letter, that he had obviously shown to many people, from his pocket.[58]

There can be no doubt that this version of the incident is correct. If any proof were needed it is furnished by an official East German publication. The organ of the German Academy of Arts, the periodical *Sinn und Form*, published a voluminous commemorative number after Brecht's death. This contains an excellent bibliography of Brecht's writings, compiled by Mr. Walter Nubel of New York, but with the obvious cooperation of Brecht's own circle. This bibliography, which lists even the minutest contributions by Brecht to newspapers and periodicals, enters the famous message to Ulbricht, under number C. 370, as follows:

(Bertolt Brecht to Walter Ulbricht.) *Neues Deutschland* (Berlin), No. 143, 21 June 1953. (On the occasion of the Berlin riots of 17 June 1953. *Final sentence of a letter*.)[59]

This, however discreetly it may be done, clearly puts it on record that the party distorted, and thereby virtually forged, the message of loyalty to Ulbricht that earned Brecht the detestation of many of his erstwhile admirers.

On June 23, 1953, two days after the publication of the truncated letter, another declaration by Brecht appeared in *Neues Deutschland*:

On the morning of June 17, when it became clear that

the workers' demonstrations were being misused for war-like purposes, I expressed my attachment to the Socialist Unity Party. Now I hope that the provocateurs will be isolated and their network of communication destroyed, but that *the workers who demonstrated from justified discontent*, will not be put on the same level with the provocateurs, so as not to inhibit the very necessary exchange of views on the *mistakes which have been made on all sides*, from the very outset. (My italics, M.E.)

It is as though Brecht had demanded that his views which had been censored on June 21 should after all be published.

The commemorative issue of *Sinn und Form* contains other unmistakable indications of Brecht's attitude after June 17. It publishes a number of interviews with stagehands and technicians of the Berliner Ensemble who describe their experiences with Brecht. One of them is quoted as saying:

After June 17 we had three workers' meetings. I put forward the view that many party officials had shown little interest in the needs and worries of the workers. I also said that the technicians had too little opportunity to qualify. . . . Afterwards [Brecht] firmly shook my hand and told me that what I had said had been particularly good; that I should have said it much sooner; and that one could not say these things too often.[60]

Even more revealing of Brecht's state of mind after June 17, 1953 is a group of his poems dating from that period, also published posthumously in the special issue of *Sinn und Form*. One of these, headed "Evil Morning," shows a state of deep malaise. The world looks stale and joyless. And why?

Last night I dreamed I saw fingers pointing at me
As at a leper. They were work-gnarled and
They were broken.
"You don't know!" I cried
Guiltily.[61]

Another poem by Brecht that came to light after his death openly attacks the official interpretation of the June uprising. The poem is called "The Solution":

> After the rising of the 17th June
> The Secretary of the Writers' Union
> Had leaflets distributed in the Stalinallee
> In which you could read that the People
> Had lost the Government's confidence
> Which it could only regain
> By redoubled efforts. Would it in that case
> Not be simpler if the Government
> Dissolved the People
> And elected another?[62]

June 17 had revealed the depth of the hatred the masses felt for the regime. It left the party deeply shaken. Mistakes had to be admitted. The way was open for freer speaking and criticism.

For Brecht this was an opportunity to put forward some of the suggestions that had no doubt been contained in the censored letter to Ulbricht. The main target for his attack was the Staatliche Kunstkommission (State Commission for the Arts), the body that had been mainly responsible for the campaign against the Berliner Ensemble.

On June 30 the German Academy of Arts, of which Brecht was one of the most active members, passed a resolution containing a number of sharp criticisms of past cultural policy and putting forward some bold demands:

The artist's responsibility before his public must be restored. The artistic directors of theatres must be able to exercise responsibility for the choice of their repertoire, publishers for the literary output of their authors, juries of artists for exhibitions, etc. State organs should help the arts in every imaginable way, but refrain from administrative interference in matters of artistic production and style. Criticism should be left to the public.[63]

This amounts to a plea for the re-establishment of freedom of artistic expression. Brecht certainly played an important part in drafting this resolution. A few days later he published a satirical poem that openly attacked the members of the State Commission for the Arts, who had attended a session of the Academy where they had practiced the Communist ritual of self-criticism by vaguely admitting that they had made some mistakes:

> . . . But when asked:
> "What mistakes?" somehow they could not remember
> Any particular mistakes, hard as they tried. Anything
> That was brought forward, had
> Not in fact been a mistake, for the commission
> Had, after all, suppressed only worthless things, and even
>   these
> Not precisely suppressed, but only not fostered. . . .[64]

A few days later the same newspaper printed a second poem of Brecht's, similar in style, which took the "Office for Literature" to task for refusing paper for original works:

> Welcome
> Are only works with ideas
> The "Office for Literature" knows from the newspapers.[65]

That these poems were published showed that the government was about to jettison the discredited State Commission for the Arts. On August 12 the party's own organ, *Neues Deutschland*, published a contribution by Brecht that was even more outspokenly critical:

> . . . it cannot be denied that many of our artists were in many essential points opposed to our cultural policy. . . . I see the reason for this in that a great ideology was not put before the artists as a tempting offering, but forced on them like sour beer. The unfortunate ways of the commissions, their dictates, with their poverty of argument, their inartistic administrative measures, their "vulgar-Marxist" language, repelled the artists (even the Marxists among them). . . . No new state can be built

up without confidence in the future . . . but facile optimism is dangerous. . . . Prettification and complacency are not only the worst enemies of the beautiful, but also of political reason. . . . Art must strive to be widely understood. But society for its part must raise the level of the appreciation of the arts by an educational effort. The requirements of the population must be met—but in opposition to the demand for *Kitsch*. From the point of view of the administration and to suit the requirements of the officials available to it, it may be simpler to work out certain schematic patterns for works of art. Then the artists "only" will have to put their (or the administration's?) thoughts into the required form and everything will be "in order." But the cry for living art will then be a cry for living things to fill coffins. Art has its own order.[66]

This was bold speaking and a passionate plea in Brecht's own cause. June 17 had so deeply shaken the party that free speaking had again become possible for a time—and up to a point. Beyond that point irony was still necessary:

We cannot expect to reach the political level of the Soviet Union within a few years, however much its example may help us. But taking our bearings from these models would be fruitless if we did not succeed in modifying them to correspond to our own specific conditions. We have, to put it bluntly, less of the new, more of the old. . . .[67]

And therefore, Brecht argued, there was a need to attack the wrong conceptions of the past—room for a general onslaught on "German miserableness":

Eager to turn to the future, we have too soon turned our backs on our immediate past. But the future will depend on our liquidating the past. . . . Our socialist realism must at the same time be a critical realism.[68]

A number of East Germany's intellectuals joined in this attack on the State Commission for the Arts. Foremost among them was Wolfgang Harich, one of the country's leading literary critics and Professor of Marxist Philosophy at East Berlin University. The Government yielded; the commission was dissolved and replaced at the beginning of 1954 by a newly formed Ministry of Culture, headed by Johannes R. Becher, the former Expressionist poet who had turned himself into a mass-producer of pastiche political folk songs of incredible banality. The Berliner Ensemble could move into its own house, the rebuilt Theater am Schiffbauerdamm.

In spite of his violent feelings about the pettiness and stupidity of the party's cultural bureaucrats, Brecht remained convinced that in theory there was no contradiction between the dictatorship of the proletariat and artistic freedom—at least for Marxist artists of his own stamp.

When Western newspapers gleefully reported his outbursts against the State Commission for the Arts he retorted, in a poem dated 1953 but not published during his lifetime,

> *Even the narrowest minds*
> *That harbor peace,*
> *Are more welcome to the arts than those friends of art*
> *Who are also friends of the art of war.*[69]

For Brecht the Eastern camp was the camp of peace. Like many other German intellectuals who had suffered at the hands of the Nazis Brecht had little faith in a genuine regeneration of the German people or in the creation of a German democracy. That is why he supported the ruthless dictatorship in the Soviet Zone.

> For democracy you need democrats [he told one of his friends]; you can't simply decree or order democracy. . . . In the Kaiser's Germany the democrats sat at the bottom and the authoritarians on top. We have turned the whole structure upside down. Now the democrats sit on top, and the lower down you go the more authoritarian becomes the administration.[70]

In other words, in the Soviet Zone a handful of democrats

(i.e., Communists) had to rule with an iron hand a vast mass of Nazis, to which even the lower echelons of the administration belonged. The shortcomings of the regime could be explained by the presence of Nazis, and the authoritarian spirit, everywhere. In West Germany, on the other hand, the mass of the people *did* have real freedom to choose their leaders, and Brecht was certain that for this reason the Nazi elements *must* be on top in the West, that freedom and democracy could mean only freedom for the militarists there. When, after the Korean War and the creation of an East German army, West Germany also prepared herself to rearm, his worst fears seemed confirmed: he worked indefatigably against West German rearmament and sent appeals to theatre people in the West and to the West German parliament, made eloquent speeches at peace congresses and meetings, and argued heatedly with Western friends.

For this activity he was awarded the Stalin Peace Prize towards the end of 1954. In May 1955 he journeyed to Moscow to receive it in the Sverdlov Hall of the Kremlin. He returned —and deposited a large proportion of his 160,000 roubles of prize money in his Swiss bank account, to the undisguised dismay and fury of the East German party stalwarts.

The abolition of the State Commission for the Arts may have eased the situation for Brecht and his theatre, but in essentials it changed little. The great success of the Berliner Ensemble at the Paris Festival of 1954 and the growing interest in the Brechtian theatre that it engendered throughout Western Europe certainly put its future out of danger; it had become too obvious a propaganda asset and any drastic action against it would have provoked too much adverse publicity. So the Berliner Ensemble was left in relative peace and freedom. Brecht continued to produce his old plays, with an occasional Soviet or Chinese Communist play thrown in, as well as from time to time a local party product. In January 1955, for example, the Berliner Ensemble produced a play by Johannes R. Becher, the new Minister for Culture, *Winterschlacht* (*Winter Battle*), a feeble attempt at putting the Hamlet theme into the setting of Hitler's Russian campaign. But the performance had bad reviews in the party press: the hero had not been shown in a positive enough light. "We have been reproached because young Hoerder was much more radiant in other theatres."[71] Sometimes the official party organ *Neues Deutschland* ignored first nights of the Berliner Ensemble altogether, notably that of *The Caucasian Chalk Circle*. And Brecht's plays were not given a very good showing by the other theatres of the Soviet Zone. At the Fourth East German Writers' Congress in January 1956, Brecht rather bitterly remarked: "The theatres of the German Democratic Republic are—regrettably from my point of view —among the few theatres in Europe that do not perform my plays."[72]

And Brecht was still critical of the continued bureaucratic supervision of literary work:

> Young Dramaturgen [literary editors] of the Berliner Ensemble have adapted plays for amateurs. To make these plays available to amateur groups they must be published. But they cannot be published because the Office for Literature does not grant the financial aid required. This shows an astonishing lack of political instinct—I am not even speaking of artistic instinct. It is a scandal—among others.[73]

In the same speech Brecht returned to the general lack of initiative shown in the Soviet Zone:

> You cannot have your revolutions made by ministries alone. This is a special feature of the *Deutsche Misere* that we still have with us: that people are always looking at others. . . .[74]

By the time Brecht made this speech he had grown visibly weary—weary not only of the constant struggle against bureaucrats like those who tried to prevent the publication of his volume of antiwar photographs and quatrains, *Primer of War*, on the grounds that it was "too pacifist,"[75] but more and more critical also of the ruthless oppression of the common people by the government of the German Democratic Republic. He is known to have been bitterly critical of the administration of justice by the brutal and unsavory woman minister, Hilde Benjamin, that *tricoteuse* of German Communism. He was equally violently opposed to the whole apparatus of secret police, informers, and concentration camps represented by the State Security Service (SSD), the Communist Gestapo. He particularly hated the then deputy head of this organization, Mielke (who has since become Minister of State Security).[76]

But in spite of his dislike for the terror and oppression and the constant arbitrariness of a petty bureaucracy, Brecht remained a Marxist to the end. His touching, almost religious, faith in the truth of the Marxist theory sustained in him the hope, however diminishing a hope this became in the last months of his life after Khrushchev's denunciation of Stalin, that the terrible reality of Communist practice would in the end be superseded by a society based on Confucian friendliness and courtesy.

In conversations with his more intimate friends on the evils of the Eastern and the Western types of society, Brecht used to illustrate his view by a parable. A doctor in a hospital is faced with two patients equally horribly afflicted with venereal disease, equally repulsive from a moral point of view: an old lecher and a pregnant prostitute. If he has only enough penicillin to save one of these two patients, will he not *have* to save the woman, because there still might be a chance that she would give birth to a healthy child? In the same way, Brecht argued, the rotten Ulbricht regime must be regarded as a possible transition to better things and must therefore be supported. At least this was a regime paying lip service to the idea that society must be changed. . . . That was the hope to which he clung.

Wolfgang Harich, the brilliant young Marxist philosopher who had been Brecht's ally in the fight against the party's culture bureaucrats, categorically stated—in his manifesto against Ulbricht that later led to his being sentenced to ten years' penal servitude—that Brecht shared his opposition to the regime:

Bertolt Brecht sympathized strongly with our group up to the time of his death, and saw in it the healthy forces of our party. In our frequent discussions with Bertolt Brecht we could see how bitterly he felt about the existing conditions in the GDR.[77]

From all we know it is certain that this claim is correct. Brecht agreed with Harich's attitude to Marxism and the party:

> We do not intend to break with the Communist party. We don't want to become renegades like, for example, the ex-Communist Koestler. We don't want to break with Marxism-Leninism, but we want to free it from Stalinism and dogmatism and to bring it back to its humanist and undogmatic way of thinking. . . .[77]

Harich's group was ruthlessly dealt with after the Hungarian revolution of October 1956. Would Brecht have been among those who were arrested and tried, like Harich and many of Brecht's pupils and friends? Probably not. He was far too cautious and unheroic to have left any clear evidence of his being implicated with such foolhardy young people. But he escaped the terrible moral dilemma the events in Hungary would have presented to him—a feeling of guilt far deeper than that engendered by the East German uprising of 1953, which had caused him such guilty dreams. For with his usual uncanny sense of timing Brecht died ten weeks before the outbreak of the Hungarian revolution.

Brecht's attitude to the problem of freedom in a Communist society coincided with the views of the Communist intellectuals who supported Gomulka in Poland and those who belonged to the Petoefi circle in Hungary. In the last months of his life Brecht was working on a translation of *Poem for Adults* by the Polish poet Adam Wazyk—a violent attack on the inhumanity of the Stalinist brand of Communism. György Lukács, the great Hungarian Marxist literary critic and philosopher, who played an important part in the Hungarian revolution, was one of the main speakers at the memorial meeting in the Schiffbauerdamm theatre after Brecht's death. And among the obituary tributes published by *Neues Deutschland* we find one from the Hungarian playwright Gyula Hay, one of the leaders of the Hungarian revolutionary intellectuals, whose message already foreshadowed the coming events:

> We Hungarian writers have in recent times had particular occasion to reflect on how far literary progress can be linked with politics in our daily struggles. In my thoughts I have often turned to Brecht and from his works I have gained the conviction that a writer cannot and must not spare himself, when the truth is at stake; and that eventually the truth will not fail a writer who remains loyal to it. Posterity will learn a very, very great deal from him, more than can even be imagined today.[78]

These words sounded harmless enough in August 1956. In the light of subsequent events their meaning is all too clear.

Brecht's irony and amused contempt for the party apparatus made itself felt even after he was dead. Immediately the news became known, the authorities appointed a funeral committee to prepare for a sumptuous ceremony from which they might extract the maximum propaganda benefit. But Rudi Engel, the director of the Academy of Arts, produced a letter of Brecht's, dated May 15, 1955, that frustrated these efforts:

> In the event of my death I don't want to be made to lie in state or to be *exhibited* anywhere. No speeches are to be made at my funeral. . . .[79]

But the speeches had to be made. So the party arranged a special memorial meeting at the Schiffbauerdamm theatre for the day after the funeral. There Ulbricht himself, Becher and many others had their say in spite of Brecht. But Brecht nevertheless had the last word: on the day after the ceremony Karl Kleinschmidt, a Protestant cleric, canon of Schwerin Cathedral—note Brecht's deliberate choice of a clergyman, though a party sympathizer—published his reminiscences of his last conversation with Brecht:

It was a conversation as unsentimental and unpathetic as any I ever had with him and dealt with the obituary I should probably have to write when he died. He regretted, with a smile, that he would be unable to read it and all the other beautiful obituaries, in which posterity would breathe its sigh of relief. . . . "You at least write a candid obituary!" he said. "That will make a very original effect among my obituaries. . . . Don't write that you admire me! Write that I was an uncomfortable person, and that I intend to remain so after my death. Even then there are certain possibilities." These were his last words to me.[80]

Brecht's relations with the Communist party exemplify the dilemma of his generation, the dilemma of so many left-wing intellectuals between the wars. The old social order had collapsed in 1918. Something new, they felt, must be put in its place. The ugliness of the postwar world, in central Europe at least, drove the seekers for aesthetic and moral beauty into the arms of the left. The weakness and poverty of ideas of the liberal and democratic forces in Germany when faced with the menace of Hitler finally confirmed them in their belief that the Communists were the only positive answer to fascism. In Brecht's case the deeper structure of his complex personality also made it imperative that he should find some positive faith—a positive set of beliefs that would be compatible with his antibourgeois, antipsychological, antireligious bias, with his need for a rational, scientific explanation of the world. Once Communism had been made to form the hard core around which his personality had crystallized it became impossible to separate the two again.

And so, while he was fully and intelligently aware of the excesses of Stalinism—and took good care to remain at a safe distance, well out of reach of the terror machine—he had to cling to the ideal image of Marxism he had built up for himself. The Marxist dialectic, with its comforting doctrine that progress proceeds along zigzag lines and that even errors already contain the seeds of their own abolition, made it easy for him to develop the peculiar split mind of the believer who perceives the shortcomings of his idol and yet is happily able to ignore them completely.

Nor can it be said that Brecht's experiences in the West during his exile gave him a real chance to change his opinion on the sterility of bourgeois society and its neglect of the artist. His lack of financial or critical success seemed to confirm his most pessimistic view about the philistinism and contempt for values in a commercial society. Of course, what he blamed the Western world for was his personal lack of success; but can he be expected to have realized that this was largely due to the language barrier and the strangeness of his views and background in countries with an utterly different tradition?

When the East offered him the most lavish means to put his ideas into practice, to work and to experiment to his heart's content, he accepted—after having made elaborate provision for his personal safety and prepared the avenues of retreat in case of necessity.

By accepting the East German government's offer he put himself at the disposal of one of the most cruel and heartless regimes in history and must bear his share of responsibility for it. On the other hand, the factual evidence here quoted also shows that he was opposed to many of the least attractive sides of the regime, and that he actively fought it in his own cautious and unheroic way. His dilemma was the dilemma of the Hungarian writers, the Polish intellectuals, and all the other "liberal" elements within the Communist world. They fight against what they consider distortions of the true ideal of social justice by petty bureaucrats, cancerous growths of the apparatus of power that should have withered away; and they cannot believe that such distortions should not be quite easily corrected. But in fact these features of Communism are not surface blemishes but its essence—and the party itself proclaims them as such by ruthlessly liquidating the elements that dare to suggest their removal. It is the dilemma of Dostoyevsky's parable about the Grand Inquisitor transferred into the setting of another and even more implacable orthodoxy. That Brecht was fully conscious of this problem is shown by his remark, also quoted by Kleinschmidt in his obituary, about the consequences of the Twentieth Party

Congress. He saw in it "the first step towards a regeneration of Marxism from its total *ideologization* towards total *secularization*," which, to translate the purposely esoteric jargon into plain language, means that Marxism must lose its character as a totalitarian orthodoxy and should return to being a practical and empirical way of social change. This view is identical with that we have quoted from Harich's oppositional manifesto, the view that emerges from the writings and speeches of the Polish intellectuals of *Po Prostu* or those of the doomed Hungarian writers. Events have shown again and again that such hopes are of necessity an illusion. But for men as deeply committed with their whole personalities, with their whole past work and achievement, to the Marxist creed to have realized this would have amounted to spiritual and physical suicide.

It is nevertheless remarkable how far Brecht succeeded in keeping the dead hand of orthodoxy and Marxist conformism out of his work. Whenever he failed to do it, he failed as a writer—not only in propaganda hack work he undertook with his tongue in his cheek, but also in more serious experiments of putting Marxism to work as an instrument for the understanding of the real world. In a play that has as many fine passages as *The Roundheads and the Peakheads* the Marxist explanation of Hitler's racial policies fails so lamentably that the whole play is invalidated: the racial theory is explained as a mere trick to deceive the common people, and the rich peakheads in the end fraternize with the rich roundheads. In other words, if this Marxist interpretation of Nazi policy had been correct, the rich Jews would have been spared by Hitler and would in the end have emerged as having been on his side all the time! In *Fear and Misery of the Third Reich* the Marxist interpretation also completely vitiates Brecht's efforts at explaining a totalitarian system. His main charge against Nazism, apart from its military preparations, was that it created hunger and delivered the workers into the hands of the capitalists. In fact, the main strength of Nazism was that it gave the German people a semblance of prosperity in exchange for the loss of their liberties. And in this Hitler's totalitarianism was closely akin to that of the Communists. But in his greatest plays Brecht avoids these pitfalls. And when he deals with human problems on the basis of his marvelously keen eye for human nature and human behavior the sociological bias of his Marxist standpoint only adds spice and interest. The real content of these plays does not spring from the conscious level but from the creative subconscious of a great poet. These great plays may fail as Communist propaganda. They succeed as plays and poetry.

From its own point of view, therefore, the party cannot be blamed for treating Brecht's work with considerable reserve and caution. Brecht believed himself a better Marxist than the party. But the party had very good reasons to think differently.

NOTES

1. Ruth Fischer, *Stalin and German Communism*, Harvard University Press, Cambridge, Mass., 1948, p. 615.
2. *Hearings Regarding the Communist Infiltration of the Motion Picture Industry*, Washington, D.C., 1947.
3. Brecht, *Trommeln in der Nacht, Erste Stuecke I*, p. 188.
4. Brecht, *Stuecke I* (Aufbau Verlag, East Berlin), pp. 6–7.
5. Ibid.
6. Brecht, *Hauspostille*, Berlin, 1927, p. 15.
7. Ibid., p. 16.
8. *Arnolt Bronnen gibt zu Protokoll*, Hamburg, 1954, p. 112.
9. *Die Rote Fahne*, 9.4.1928. Quoted by Schumacher, p. 255.
10. *Die Linkskurve*, Berlin, January 1931. Quoted by Schumacher, p. 279.
11. Schumacher, p. 273.
12. *Die Weltbuehne*, Berlin, 7.8.1930.
13. Thieme in *Hochland*, Munich, February 1932. Quoted by Schumacher, p. 367.
14. *Die Linkskurve*, January 1931. Quoted by Schumacher, p. 367.
15. Kurella, "Ein Versuch mit nicht ganz tauglichen Mitteln," *Literatur der Weltrevolution*, Moscow, no. 4, 1931. Quoted by Schumacher, p. 361.
16. Kurella, *loc. cit.* Quoted by Schumacher, p. 366.
17. Schumacher, p. 365.
18. *Europe*, Paris, January/February 1957, p. 173.
19. "Anmerkung zu den Lehrstuecken," *Stuecke* V, p. 276.
20. *Versuche 4*, p. 361.
21. *Geschichten vom Herrn Keuner*. *Versuche 5*, p. 457. In later

versions of this story the reference to "stupid arguments" is omitted.

22. *Die Rote Fahne*, 1.19.1932. Quoted by Schumacher, p. 432.

23. S. Tretyakov, "Bert Brecht," *International Literature*, Moscow, May 1937.

24. E. W. White in *Life and Letters*, September 1935. The story has been independently confirmed by other, oral sources.

25. *Leben des Galilei, Stuecke VIII*, p. 162.

26. "1941," *Hundert Gedichte*, East Berlin, 1951, p. 307.

27. L. Feuchtwanger, "Bertolt Brecht," *Sinn und Form*, Second Special Brecht Issue, 1957, p. 106.

28. Brecht, "Das Manifest," *Sinn und Form*, 1957/V, p. 293.

29. Brecht, *Im Dickicht der Staedte, Erste Stuecke I*, pp. 291–92.

30. Brecht, "Fluechtlingsgespraeche," *Aufbau*, East Berlin, February 1958, pp. 181–82.

31. Brecht, *Das Badener Lehrstueck, Versuche 2*, p. 145.

32. Brecht, *Die Heilige Johanna der Schlachthoefe, Versuche 5*, p. 453.

33. Kaethe Ruelicke, "Leben des Galilei—Schlusszene," *Sinn und Form*, Second Special Brecht Issue, 1957, p. 284.

34. *Die Mutter, Stuecke V*, p. 84 (this passage is not in the earlier version, *Versuche 7*).

35. Brecht, *Die Mutter, Versuche 7*, pp. 26–27. When Brecht republished this song in East Germany in 1951 the lines about chaos and order had disappeared and been replaced by:

It is not the *riddle*
But the *solution*.

36. Brecht, "Weite und Vielfalt der Realistischen Schreibweise," *Versuche 13*, p. 107.

37. "Ueber Reimlose Lyrik mit Unregelmaessigen Rhythmen," *Versuche 12*, p. 147.

38. Gody Suter, "Brecht," *Tagesanzeiger*, Zurich, 9.1.1956.

39. I. Fradkin, "Bertolt Brecht," *Teatr*, Moscow, January 1956.

40. F. Erpenbeck, *Lebendiges Theater*, Berlin, 1949, p. 281.

41. *Theaterarbeit*, p. 255.

42. Quoted in Ruehle, *Das gefesselte Theater*, pp. 238 ff.

43. *Neues Deutschland*, East Berlin, 3.22.1951.

44. Ibid., quoted in *Deutsche Zeitung*, 1.10.1953.

45. Ruehle, *Das gefesselte Theater*, p. 243.

46. Brecht, *Das Verhoer des Lukullus*, Scene 12, *Versuche 11*, p. 150.

47. Ibid., p. 159.

48. *National Zeitung*, East Berlin, 10.19.1951.

49. *Neues Deutschland*, East Berlin, 10.19.1951.

50. Brecht, *Leben des Galilei, Stuecke VIII*, pp. 53–54.

51. Brecht and Dessau, "Herrnburger Bericht," *Neues Deutschland*, East Berlin, 7.22.1951.

52. Brecht and Dessau, *Lieder und Gesaenge*, East Berlin, 1957.

53. "Weitere Bemerkungen zum Faust-Problem," *Neues Deutschland*, East Berlin, 5.27.1953.

54. Ibid.

55. "Fuer den Sieg des sozialistischen Realismus auf der Buehne," *Neues Deutschland*, East Berlin, 4.17.1953.

56. *Neues Deutschland*, East Berlin, quoted in *Berliner Stimme*, 6.6.1953.

57. *Sinn und Form*, 1953/II, p. 9.

58. Gody Suter, "Brecht," *Tagesanzeiger*, Zurich, 9.1.1956.

59. *Sinn und Form*, Second Special Brecht Issue, 1957, p. 560.

60. "13 Buehnentechniker erzaehlen," ibid., p. 472.

61. "*Unwissende!*" *schrie ich/Schuldbewusst*, Brecht, "Boeser Morgen," ibid., p. 341.

62. Quoted by W. Paul, "Aus Bertolt Brechts spaeten Jahren," *Neue Deutsche Hefte*, Guetersloh, November 1958.

63. "Mitteilungen der Deutschen Akademie der Kuenste," *Sinn und Form*, 1953/III–IV, p. 256.

64. Brecht, "Nicht feststellbare Fehler der Kunstkommission," *Berliner Zeitung*, East Berlin, 7.11.1953.

65. Brecht, "Das Amt fuer Literatur," *Berliner Zeitung*, East Berlin, 7.15.1953.

66. Brecht, "Kulturpolitik und Akademie der Kuenste," *Neues Deutschland*, East Berlin, 8.12.1953.

67. Ibid.

68. Ibid.

69. Brecht, "Nicht so gemeint," *Sinn und Form*, Second Special Brecht Issue, 1957, p. 342.

70. Karl Kleinschmidt, "Wir sind der Mensch von Sezuan," *Neue Zeit*, East Berlin, 8.19.1956.

71. Brecht, "Einige Irrtuemer ueber die Spielweise des Berliner Ensembles," *Sinn und Form*, Second Special Brecht Issue, 1957, p. 253.

72. Brecht, "Ausfuehrungen vor der Sektion Dramatik," 1.12. 1956; *Beitraege zur Gegenwartsliteratur*, East Berlin, January 1956, p. 153.

73. Ibid., pp. 153–54.

74. Ibid.

75. "Brecht beinahe verboten," *Frankfurter Allgemeine Zeitung*, 11.19.1955.

76. This account of Brecht's attitude is mainly based on information contained in a letter from Professor Alfred Kantorowicz to the author.

77. Harich's manifesto quoted by *Frankfurter Allgemeine Zeitung*, 3.21.1957.

78. Julius Hay, "Es ist unfassbar . . . ," *Neues Deutschland*, East Berlin, 8.18.1956.

79. *Neues Deutschland*, East Berlin, 8.17.1956.

80. Karl Kleinschmidt, "Wir sind der Mensch von Sezuan," *Neue Zeit*, East Berlin, 9.19.1956.

CHAPTER VIII

THE COMMUNISTS AND BRECHT

On est contre les formalistes! Moi, je suis aussi contre les formalistes—mais ils ne sont pas les mêmes.

PICASSO[1]

To live in a country without a sense of humor is unbearable; but it is even more unbearable to live in a country where you need a sense of humor.

BRECHT[2]

In the summer of 1956, shortly before Brecht died, the Berliner Ensemble received an invitation to give a number of performances in the Soviet Union.

One of Brecht's Russian acquaintances, Joseph Yuzovski, later described how the same post that brought him Brecht's letter with this news also brought the announcement of his death. Brecht's letter, Yuzovski says, expressed his gratification, that "after his plays had passed across the stages of the world and had aroused such a lively response from millions of spectators and so much passionate discussion among theatre people, they were *at last* coming to Moscow. . . ."[3]

But Yuzovski also detected another note in Brecht's letter:

. . . something that I had already felt in the spring of this year [1956] when I received a crate from Berlin, filled with his plays, books and other literature, together with a letter from him, asking me to acquaint myself with all this—as it was so little known here in Moscow. I understood the hint, the hidden allusion—with its amused kind of puzzlement that was without any reproach, but contained a certain bitterness nevertheless. And indeed! Do we know Brecht's work in all its variety, do we know the writer, who, without exaggeration, can be called the most significant dramatist of our time? Who of us knows him? Let us be honest—don't we really know him very little?[4]

However false the emphasis of this question may sound with its assumed air of innocence, which naïvely seems to suggest that Brecht had been neglected by the Soviet public unaccountably, by some oversight, behind the heavy-handed question there stands a solid fact: until the time of his death Brecht, the most important Communist dramatist, was almost totally unknown in the Soviet Union. As a Soviet periodical put it after Brecht died:

Brecht's dramatic productions have not been fortunate in the Soviet Union. Not one of his plays has ever been performed, save for a (not very successful) showing of The Threepenny Opera at the Kamerny theatre over a quarter of a century ago. It would be wrong to gloss over these facts. . . .[5]

A few of Brecht's more orthodox Communist works had been published in Russian translations and in German in the Soviet Union in the thirties, a few of his poems in praise of the party were known, occasionally his name would be mentioned in the newspapers in connection with some peace appeal he had signed, but his importance as a literary figure and as an innovator in the theatre was certainly not appreciated, even among experts. Boris Pasternak, the great Russian poet, who is the Soviet Union's leading translator of German literature, recently told a West German journalist:

. . . that Bertolt Brecht had asked him to put into Russian the speech of thanks he made when he came to Moscow to receive his Stalin Prize. He had done so without pleasure, and without pleasure had read the volume of

Brecht's poetry which the German dramatist had in gratitude sent him. He had little affinity with poets who were above all else political. It was only when Helene Weigel brought her company to Moscow (in 1957) that he realized that he had translated the speech of a great poet and that because of the selection made in an anthology published in East Germany, he had nearly missed knowing the work of a great poet.[6]

The new edition of the *Great Soviet Encyclopedia*, a monumental publication in fifty-one enormous volumes, mentions Brecht in a short article of only about half a column, thirty three lines to be exact. In the first edition, published in 1927, before he had written even *The Threepenny Opera*, Brecht had been accorded thirty-four lines, one line more than in 1951, when he had become one of the world's leading dramatists. This counting of lines is by no means as childish as it must strike Western readers, unacquainted with the rigidly hierarchical ways of Soviet Russia and with the part the *Great Soviet Encyclopedia* plays in that society as the repository of all officially sanctioned knowledge. When a great man—like the late Lavrenti Beria—falls, subscribers to the encyclopedia are officially asked to excise the pages devoted to him and to replace them by new matter just come to light on the Bering Sea. In such a work the precise number and order of the adjectives after the name of a politician denotes his exact order of precedence in the ranks of the party—and in the same way the fact that Brecht was accorded only thirty-three lines as against seventy-seven for a poet like Aragon, or a full one hundred and twelve lines for the East German party's court poet, J. R. Becher, shows how low his stock stood in the Communist world in 1951, when volume six of the *Great Soviet Encyclopedia* was printed. It is equally significant that the bibliographical note that follows this brief article mentions only one Soviet study of Brecht—an article on German antifascist writers published in a periodical in 1941.

Why should a Communist of Brecht's eminence be treated in such a way? In his obituary article Brecht's Russian friend Yuzovski also asks this question. He wraps up the answer in an account of a conversation with an eminent Soviet director,

-hom he had asked why *he* had never produced any of
Brecht's plays. Without waiting for that eminent man's an-
wer, Yuzovski himself anticipated it:

> I know that you will immediately say: the personality
> cult and its consequences in art! Administrative and bu-
> reaucratic tutelage—suppression of initiative—arbitrari-
> ness that eventually leads to closed minds. . . . That is
> indeed true. But don't you think the time has come
> when we should not merely talk about this state of af-
> fairs but *do* something about it? Were not the revivals
> of *The Optimistic Tragedy* [an *avant-gardist* work by
> Vishnyevsky] and of *The Bath* [Mayakovsky's bitter sat-
> ire on the party that had long disappeared from the
> Soviet stage] great successes after all this time? What
> would you have risked if you had dared to put on Brecht
> —which between ourselves, wouldn't have been such a
> special risk even much earlier![7]

Whether in 1956, when Stalin was safely dead, Yuzovski
thought that putting on a play by Brecht would not have been
such a risk as in Stalin's lifetime matters little. What matters
a great deal for the record, however, is the implied admission that in Stalin's time an eminent director did indeed
think that to perform a play by Brecht was such a risk—or that
at least he felt no desire whatsoever to put the matter to the
test.

There can be no doubt about it: from the early thirties to
the time of his death Brecht's work was virtually suppressed
in the Soviet Union and the whole Soviet orbit except in the
East Zone of Germany, where Brecht served his own very
special purpose in showing that the rickety regime enjoyed
the support of an acknowledged leader of German letters and
as an advertisement for the achievements of German Communist culture to West Germany. Vast populations in the
Communist sphere had to be guarded from contamination
by the works of that selfsame great Communist master. For
rebels and iconoclasts against the established order of things,
like Brecht or Picasso, are considered useful as allies in the
task of undermining it in countries where the Communists

are in opposition. In the Soviet sphere itself, where the es
tablished order of things is a Communist one, such rebel
are highly undesirable.

Brecht's conversion to the Communist cause as the embodi
ment of his hatred of bourgeois society had—ironically enough
—taken place at the precise moment when the Communis
party in the Soviet Union had begun to jettison the motle
crowd of anarchist poets, futurist and abstract painters, and
other reformers of the arts and ethics that it had gathered
around it in the chaotic wake of the revolution. It was a rude
disappointment for many of these intellectuals, not only
among artists but also among champions of progressive edu
cation, believers in open prisons, and social reformers who
preached free love and hundreds of other panaceas and re
garded the party as the ideal instrument for the realization
of their dreams. By the early thirties the revolution had been
consolidated. The party began to rediscover the usefulness of
the traditional supports of any established power. Gradually
epaulettes and dress uniforms for officers were reintroduced,
and officers had to be saluted again. Schoolchildren were de
prived of the right to vote for the dismissal of unpopular
teachers; divorce was made more difficult and free love was
frowned upon. And so was experiment and innovation in the
arts.

In 1934 Stalin's trusted lieutenant, A. A. Zhdanov, told
the First All-Union Congress of Soviet Writers what their
duty was. "Comrade Stalin," he said, "has called our writers
engineers of the human soul." Like any other technicians they
would henceforth have to deliver the products assigned to
them in the plan: concrete results in the field of party propaganda. But to write in the true Communist spirit alone was
not enough. From now on the writers' work must be understood by all. For the masses know what they like, and they
like only what they can recognize. So all art must be true to
life—up to a point:

The truthfulness and historical exactitude of the artistic
image must be linked with the task of ideological trans-

formation, of the education of the working people in the
spirit of socialism. This method in fiction and literary
criticism is what we call the method of socialist realism.[8]

Not realism—*tout court*, but *socialist* realism. The world, if
depicted as it really was in the Soviet Union, might well appear too nasty. Therefore it had to be shown not as it was,
but as it *ought* to be, and perhaps *would* be one day, when
the new society had been successfully established:

> Soviet literature must be able to portray our heroes and
> to see our tomorrow. This will not be Utopian since our
> tomorrow is being prepared by planned and conscious
> work today.[9]

Any work that showed reality in too gloomy a light fell into
the sin of "naturalism." But even more grievous was the opposite fault: formalism. Formalism, like Trotskyism, is extremely difficult to define. According to the *Great Soviet Encyclopedia* it is "the attribution to form, or formal elements,
of self-contained, primary significance to the detriment of
content."[10] Content here obviously means *representational*
content, for even the most abstract painting does not entirely
divorce form from content; even there the artist is concerned
with telling us something—namely what he feels about certain
shapes, colors, or textures. The pseudo-philosophical language
of the *Great Soviet Encyclopedia*'s definition of formalism
can be reduced to much simpler terms: any work of art that
lacks *political* content is condemned as formalist. And so is
any work of art that conveys a political content in a stylized
form. As one East German Communist newspaper once
summed up its whole case against Brecht: Why is it that in
his theatre the trees have no leaves? Or, as the East German
party's top expert on theatre matters put it:

> In [Brecht's] *The Mother* the didactic element becomes
> an end in itself—and that is formalism. The didactic
> element must lie in man, in action, in conflict, in every-
> thing that man on the stage thinks, and feels, and in the
> relations of men to reality and of reality to them, in the

clash of contradictions and in their solution. These things must contain the didactic element, but it cannot be isolated from them.[11]

So even Brecht's most openly political and propagandist pla was condemned as formalist, for the simple reason that did not obey the crude convention of a purely represent tional theatre, where all the political propaganda was neat wrapped up in the plot itself. Brecht detested this kind theatre and all his life's work was devoted to its destructio But the party had decided that the only method of acting an production that was truly Marxist was the Stanislavsk method of the Moscow Art Theatre. Brecht's whole theory based on his conception that the theatre of Stanislavsky, making the audience identify themselves with the character prevents them from seeing the world in a detached, critic spirit and is therefore un-Marxist and reactionary. But th party did not want the audience to be put into a critic frame of mind. It *wanted* them to be hypnotized and mad uncritical by having their emotions fully engaged in favor the positive characters and against the negative ones. Brech wanted to let them draw their own conclusions from a critic reflection on the play. The party wanted the audience to b left in no doubt as to any conclusion they should draw from what they saw. Brecht believed in irony and parody. Th party wanted simplicity—the good characters wholly good, th bad ones wholly bad. But Brecht considered himself a bette Marxist than the party officials.

This was a truly tragicomic conflict—a conflict born from the totalitarian fallacy that each political system must hav its own philosophy in which every element logically follow from one great central principle: the one Communist cree determining its one Communist art, theatre, style of chess playing, or gardening, right down to the most trivial activity As there could only be one correct Communist policy line there could only be one correct way of painting, theatrica production, or chess-playing. Any other style automatically became treason. On the altars of this fallacy the party sacri ficed some of its greatest talents. What good was it to Meyer hold, one of the world's greatest directors, that he was a onvinced and active supporter of the Communist party? talin had decided that only Stanislavsky's kind of theatre as truly Marxist. When Meyerhold persisted in working in is own style, he was denounced, deprived of his theatre, arested, and finally he disappeared. And he was only one mong hundreds of artists who paid with their lives for not onforming to the wishes of the party authorities, while hunreds of others, who were less brave, had to do violence to heir talents and inclinations by slavishly following the offiially prescribed models.

Brecht had been far too shrewd to put himself into any uch situation by accepting a position inside the Soviet Union a the early years of his exile. He knew only too well that he elonged to the same world-wide movement against naturalsm in the theatre as Tairov, Meyerhold, and so many other utstanding Soviet directors. As early as 1907 Meyerhold had dvocated a theatre in which the audience "never forgets for minute that it is seeing actors who are playing and the acors never forget that an auditorium is before them, a stage eneath them and décor all along the sides,"[12] the very priniples of Brecht's anti-illusionist theatre. And it was Meyerold who had demanded a style of acting without tremolo, enseness, and emotionalism, and insisted on "epic" calm, oolness, and ease of delivery[13] long before Brecht formuated the same ideas. So as long as Meyerhold stood condemned as a formalist and his style was proscribed in the Soviet Union, Brecht's ideas too had to be played down. No wonder the Soviet directors and actors who got to know about them shunned his plays like the plague.

The contradiction between the propaganda requirements of the East German regime in its need to impress the West, and the official attitude of the inner core of the Soviet orbit, produced its own curious result: once Brecht's theatre was established in East Berlin to dazzle Western intellectuals it could not be concealed from visitors from the Communist countries. The Berliner Ensemble became a point of attraction for visiting Communist intellectuals, and its ideas began to radiate throughout the Communist world.

It is characteristic that the first breach in the virtual ba‍
on the Brechtian theatre throughout the satellite countrie‍
occurred in Poland, where socialist realism with all its crudity
and dullness had always been most resented. In 1952 the‍
Berliner Ensemble was invited to perform *The Mother* an‍
Mother Courage in a number of Polish cities. Another tou‍
followed in 1954. Some of Brecht's plays were performed i‍
Polish as the thaw gathered momentum after Stalin's death‍
The post-Stalinist renaissance in the Polish theatre is dated
by Polish critics from the first appearance of the Berliner Ensemble in Warsaw.[14] Support for Brecht became synonymous
with opposition to the vulgar creed of socialist realism. The
authorities still uttered warning cries, but they were already
tempered by the recognition of *some* merit, as we can see
from this official directive to a theatre magazine:

> . . . Brecht does not . . . represent the art of socialist
> realism and therefore not even a special approach to-
> wards it, although in its own peculiar way Brecht's work
> has enriched and fructified the theatre of socialist real-
> ism. . . .[15]

And the introduction to a Polish edition of some of Brecht's
plays still warned the readers:

> In Brecht's theatre very different elements of diverse
> value are mixed together: here realism exists together
> with naturalism and both are subject to the influences of
> expressionism.[16]

Both naturalism and expressionism were still regarded as heinous crimes at that time (1953), but the revolt against the
Stalinist categories was already stirring. A Polish Brechtian
critic, Andrzej Wirth, later described the feelings of his
friends about Brecht and the accepted standards of party
aesthetics:

> The falsifiers of socialist realism had canonized a formal
> pattern that had been created by the bourgeois theatre

of the nineteenth century. One need not be surprised that Brecht's art could not be accommodated within this rigid framework. Its formal means suddenly found themselves proscribed. Suitable terms were lacking, and so dreadful epithets had to be applied to it—expressionist, naturalist, symbolist. . . . It is typical that this odd kind of criticism from the left showed complete indifference to the plebeian content of Brecht's work, which one might surely have regarded as the essential element in any progressive play. . . .[17]

Here the Polish Marxist critic has seized the essential weakness of the antiformalists who were so preoccupied with the question of form—the need for trees to have leaves—that they completely neglected the content, so that in fact the standard-bearers of antiformalism stood themselves condemned as worshipers of external formal criteria. In the opinion of this Polish follower of Brecht this kind of criticism simply could not appreciate

. . . the Socratic method, which confines itself to the stating of questions, to undermining the established view of the problem and the awakening of creative doubt. This was a reflection of the general dogmatization of intellectual life that reduced the process of learning to a magical attitude, thereby completely frustrating the dialectical process as a genuine exploration of truth. It also showed complete contempt for the public, the people who were seen as mere consumers of ready-made results rather than as participants in a process of discovery. The Brechtian conception of the educational role of art, based as it is on the conviction that a socialist revolution implies the intellectual activization of the masses, could never come to terms with the educational theory of the vulgarists, who never considered the people as worthy intellectual partners. The criticism of the vulgarists merely noticed the "suspicious" formal aspects and immediately denounced these as having acquired absolute value (of an end in itself) without paying any attention to the function these formal elements had in Brecht's work. The discussion thus circled around the illusory problem, whether a play using expressionist, symbolist, or other means could be socialist. . . .[18]

In spite of the jargon in which all this is wrapped up, it is a devastating attack from the Marxist point of view on the advocates of socialist realism—that is, from that variant of the Marxist point of view that we know to have been Brecht's own. In Poland the revolution of October 1956 meant the collapse of the Stalinist doctrine of art. To many Polish intellectuals Brecht now became a symbol that a true socialist art of a different kind was possible. As Andrzej Wirth put it, in another essay on Brecht written about the same time:

Today, in view of the crisis through which the art of the falsifiers is passing, Brecht's example assumes universal significance: for this experiment, carried out over many years, has proved the connection between progressive trends in art and revolutionary ideas. . . .[19]

So in Poland Brecht became the living proof that Communist art need not necessarily be modeled on Victorian oleographs and melodramas. But then Poland had undergone a second, anti-Stalinist revolution, which may have been cautious in the political field but swept all before it in the arts and literature. In the Soviet Union the recognition of Brecht came far more slowly and was far more reluctant.

The thaw in the Soviet theatre that had set in gradually even before Stalin died had its ups and downs, advances and retreats. The monotonous insistence of the authorities that socialist realism should show only the positive sides of contemporary life had driven all conflict from the stage. Authors were afraid of showing anything in a critical light, lest they be dubbed "naturalists" or "bourgeois wreckers." When this state of affairs led to a virtual boycott of the theatres by the public there were attempts to allow some negative features of

oviet life to be shown. Old satires like Mayakovsky's long
anned plays reappeared, some bold new plays castigated the
hady sides of Soviet life. But when these were felt to have
one too far their authors were severely taken to task. All
hese advances and retreats were closely bound up with the
truggles for power of the post-Stalin era, the fall of Beria,
nd the rise of Malenkov, followed by the fall of Malenkov
nd the rise of Khrushchev. This is not the place to tell that
ntricate and depressing story. But it is relevant here to show
ow these developments appeared to Brecht and his theatre,
vhose future was intimately bound up with their outcome.
)ne of Brecht's most brilliant and loyal young pupils, the
lirector Manfred Wekwerth (born 1929), whose entire out-
ook is based on Brecht's teaching, went to Moscow and
_eningrad with the Berliner Ensemble in 1957. This is
1ow he described the Soviet theatrical scene in an article
)ublished after his return:

Muscovites told us that their theatres had come dangerously close to stagnation around 1953. The repertoire,
the style of acting, the lack of topicality had reached a
stage where it was sufficient to see one theatre to know
what all the others were like. The Moscow Art Theatre
had become the only model. Regardless of whether a
theatre was presenting satire, historical plays, farce, or
propaganda, the only standard was that of the great,
lonely eminence of the Moscow Art Theatre. Only
Obraztsov remained—with his puppets and his own
theory. But all this had left the audience out of account.
A certain theory about the theatre may have appeared
vindicated, but the audience no longer came to the
theatres. They often remained half empty, which means
a great deal considering the Muscovites' proverbial love
of the theatre. The situation changed rapidly towards the
end of 1953. Here as in other fields people in Moscow
talk about "before" and "after." "Before" all theatres
played exactly like the Moscow Art Theatre—only
worse. "After" the Theatre of Satire developed its own
style—within a matter of months. . . . "After" the

lost records of Meyerhold's productions were dug up and edited for study. "After" Meyerhold was mentioned with Stanislavsky. "After" the revolutionary discoveries of Tairov, the performances of the classical drama of the revolution (Vishnyevsky's *Optimistic Tragedy* and *First Cavalry Army*, etc.) were studied and used for new productions. "After" the work of young Eisenstein was again studied. "After" Okhlopkov repeated his famous production of the thirties, *Aristocrats* by Pogodin. . . .[20]

This description of the Moscow theatre in 1957, seen through the eyes of one of Brecht's pupils and published in an East German periodical towards the end of 1957, sums up the feelings with which Brecht himself must have regarded the absolute sway of the Stanislavsky style that prevailed from the middle thirties to the middle fifties, and the relief and hope with which he and his followers watched the thaw. But even in 1957 Wekwerth registered his astonishment that Soviet theatre people knew practically nothing about Brecht's ideas.

About our discussions with Moscow theatre people much could be said. They certainly created a most fruitful confusion . . . the Moscow Dramaturgen who double as theatre critics heard with astonishment that the "epic" theatre does not want to abolish the plot in plays. . . .[21]

In other words, the Moscow theatre experts, who had vaguely heard Brecht condemned as a formalist, imagined that in his theatre form and content had been so completely separated that no plot remained.

By the spring of 1957 a number of articles on Brecht had appeared in Soviet newspapers and periodicals, but most of these were so mealymouthed and dull that one can hardly blame the literary editors of the Moscow theatres for not reading them very carefully.

The first indication that the thaw that had brought back Mayakovsky's satires, Pogodin's *Aristocrats*, and Bulgakov'

Days of the Turbins, and had even made it possible to mention Meyerhold again, extended to Brecht came while he was still alive. In January 1956 the Soviet Union's official monthly of the theatre arts, *Teatr,* published a lengthy article on Brecht by the critic I. Fradkin, who had spent some time in East Berlin and had come into contact with Brecht and his theatre there. This article is rather dry and tedious, accurate as far as it goes, yet not accurate enough to venture a mention of *The Measures Taken.* Its most interesting feature is the half-hearted account of Brecht's theory of the "epic" theatre it gives, constantly hedging with safeguards that make it quite clear that the author of the article understands these views but does not share them:

> In opposing a theatre which saps the intellect and will power of the audience, i.e., the contemporary decadent theatre, Brecht resorts to generalizations that go far beyond his own objective. Calling his "epic" theatre the complete antithesis of the "Aristotelian" theatre Brecht lays himself open to the reproach that he takes an unjustifiedly sceptical attitude towards a significant part of the dramatic heritage and stage tradition of the past. On this point Brecht's position is not entirely clear—in any case this is not the essential feature of his theory: Brecht's main concern is with making the theatre a weapon for influencing the masses in a partisan spirit and teaching them ideas of a progressive revolutionary nature. . . .[22]

That is, Brecht is acceptable in so far as he wants to support Communist ideas and attacks the decadent bourgeois theatre —but not inasmuch as he is against the Moscow Art Theatre style of acting and direction. In this respect his ideas have no relevance to the Soviet theatre:

> To the reader who knows the history of the Soviet theatre and the productions and discussions of the twenties, it is clear that much in the theoretical ideas of Brecht is not new, and in any case already superseded; much of it has

already been tested, some of it accepted, some of it rejected by the experience and practice of the Soviet theatre. . . .[22]

These passages are quoted not so much for their own intrinsic
interest, but as examples of the curiously naïve approach dictated to Soviet critics of undoubted intelligence and taste by
the fears and taboos that surround them even in periods of
thaw. With the utmost caution Fradkin approaches the
dreaded center of the problem, the wholly scholastic and ver-
bal question of whether Brecht can be called a realist:

But is Brecht a realist? In this respect there is some room
for doubt. Can a work be realistic in which the action
happens among people of two imaginary races in a country not to be found on any map? (*Roundheads and Peakheads.*) Is it in accordance with the laws of realism to
present a quarrel between two collective farms, in the
course of which, against all the rules of agricultural co-
operatives and against existing Soviet legal practice, the
dispute is decided with the help of a ballad singer who
tells the collective farmers an ancient legend? (In the
prologue to *The Caucasian Chalk Circle*.) Can there be
a trial of a dead man? (*Lucullus*.) But if these questions
are put, what of such stories or plays as *Gulliver, Faust*,
etc. . . . ?[23]

And with the help of these examples of literature that was not
banned in the Soviet Union even in the period of the most
rigorous enforcement of socialist realism, Fradkin, heaving a
sigh of relief, pronounces Brecht a realist—if only in the spirit
of the eighteenth-century enlightenment:

Just as Voltaire speaks about a Bulgarian army in *Can-
dide*, or of a Princess of Babylon, so Brecht's Caucasus
or his contemporary Setzuan have nothing to do with
these regions in reality. . . .[23]

And as a follower of Swift, Voltaire, and Diderot, all recognized ancestors of revolutionary literature, Brecht just man-

ages to secure the all-important epithet, "realist." In spite of the disavowal of the "superseded" parts of his theories, he had secured something like approval. And so, when the time came for his obituaries a few months later, the Soviet press could in good conscience praise him not only as a staunch supporter of the Communist cause, but as an important dramatist and director.

The visit of the Berliner Ensemble to Moscow and Leningrad was carefully prepared. In March and April 1957 three of Brecht's most important plays were published in translation: *Mother Courage, Galileo,* and *The Caucasian Chalk Circle*—little booklets with introductions and some notes, with a printing of five thousand copies each, not a very large edition by Soviet standards. In April 1957 another important Soviet literary periodical, *Zvezda,* published a long study of Brecht by A. Dymshits. This article, which closely follows the pattern of Fradkin's pioneer effort, starts off with a pointed reference to the party's permission that foreign writers like Brecht could now be studied:

In the message of greetings the Central Committee of the Communist Party of the USSR sent to the Second All-Union Congress of Writers, special stress is laid on how important it is that our artistic workers learn from, and master, the artistic experience of progressive artists in foreign countries. In the ranks of these Bertolt Brecht undoubtedly occupies one of the first places. His work as poet, dramatist, novelist, publicist, theoretician of aesthetics, and director is received with the greatest attention; and his achievement, which constitutes the pride and glory of German democratic culture, must also enrich our literature and our theatre. . . .[24]

An imprecation like this unmistakably shows how conscious the writer still was of the daring of his action, that he had to reassure himself and his readers before he started out to discuss a writer who had been proscribed such a short while ago. This lengthy article also suppresses any mention of *The Measures Taken,* and even, whether by design or by mistake, attributes one of the choruses from that work, *Praise of the*

Party, to *The Mother*—a clear sign that *The Measures Taken*
of which a Russian translation had existed in 1932, was no
longer available in the Soviet Union. And again Brecht's
theory of the "epic" theatre is explained away as having been
developed in opposition to the "bourgeois decadent theatre,"
and therefore hardly relevant to current Soviet practice.

On the eve of the Berliner Ensemble's arrival in Moscow,
Fradkin, as the leading exponent of Brecht in the Soviet
Union, prepared the readers of *Sovietskaya Kultura,* the organ
of the Soviet Ministry of Culture, for what they should expect
—again almost as if to soften the shock awaiting them:

> The directors, designers, and decorators of the Berliner
> Ensemble avoid the illusion of truth to nature and any
> naturalistically accurate rendering of the outward ap-
> pearance of life. In their effort to explain reality cor-
> rectly, in which they firmly occupy the standpoint of a
> determined realism, the Berliner Ensemble turn towards
> symbolism in the field of form (unfinished, suggestive
> décor, masks, etc.), and thus stimulate the imagination
> of the spectator. . . .[25]

And so the Berliner Ensemble came to Moscow. On
May 8, 1957 they opened at the Vakhtangov Theatre with
Galileo. Mother Courage, Drums and Trumpets (Farquhar's
Recruiting Officer), and *The Caucasian Chalk Circle* followed. There was a good deal of applause, speech-making, and
official receptions. The notices in the newspapers were gener-
ous while not displaying overmuch genuine understanding of
what it had all been about, so that praise concentrated
largely on the performances of the protagonists—Ernst Busch
as Galileo, Helene Weigel as Mother Courage, Angelika Hur-
wicz as Grusche. These actors appealed to the Russian public's love for broadly human characterization. But the "epic"
theatre itself clearly made no headway with the authorities.
This was finally made clear in a long review of *The Caucasian
Chalk Circle* by S. Mokulski and B. Rostotski in *Sovietskaya*

Kultura. After praising the progressive tendency of the play and pouring cold water on the genuineness of its Caucasian types, the article finally came to grips with the thorny problem of formalism. In a typically Soviet manner the whole question was made to center on a purely external—formal—element: the use of masks for the negative characters. The two Soviet critics could not let this pass:

> Could not the basic idea of the inhumanity of the governor's wife have been expressed by subtler means? What gives us the right to ask this question is the experience of the Soviet theatre in the twenties and early thirties. We remember the disputes that raged at that time about the theory of the so-called "attitude towards the character" and the practical experiments to put this theory into practice from the theatre of Meyerhold to TRAM.[26] We remember that the device of masks was more than once used in our theatres to express the relationship between the actor and the character he portrayed. The performance of the Berliner Ensemble reminds us of this and shows us once more that many experiments of our theatre have left their traces behind. . . . We must clearly ask ourselves if everything is equally valid and justified in this talented performance. . . .[27]

This article, which was headed "The Contemporary and the Old-fashioned," shows one aspect of the lack of sympathy between Brecht's approach to the theatre and that of Soviet socialist realism. The use of masks obviously lacked realism. But Soviet socialist realism also dislikes an excess of reality. In an essay headed "The Strength and Weakness of Brecht's Theatre—Notes of a Director"[28] Boris Zakhava attacked the "naturalism" of the Berliner Ensemble. Of course, he too began by paying the usual compliments. But while he stressed the thoughtfulness and directness of the productions he had seen, his enthusiasm had a distinctly soured air:

> One might quarrel with it [the Berliner Ensemble], one might not agree with some of the principles professed by

this theatre, but it is impossible not to see that we have before us a theatre with a clearly defined creative personality.[29]

Zakhava, himself a well-known director, objected to the coldness and lack of emotion of most of the performances he had seen:

> . . . recognizing the mastery and talent of Helene Weigel we cannot conceal the fact that for complete satisfaction we would have liked just one moment which would be filled with a powerful emotional upsurge, a creative outburst rising to the heights of great human feelings.[30]

But Zakhava not only disliked the coldness of the Berliner Ensemble's acting, he was appalled by its stress on the sordid side of life:

> Why was it necessary that Ernst Busch who plays the cook in *Mother Courage* should take off his dirty leggings, and sitting right in the foreground should so carefully and with such visible pleasure rub them between his fingers? And why altogether should there be so many bare feet? To my puzzled question about this, one of our German guests replied by putting a counterquestion: "Would you want to put a brassière on the Venus of Milo?" Of course not! We should be indignant if anything prevented us from contemplating the magnificent body of Venus with delight—we despise all sanctimoniousness—but we should also be very much offended if someone wanted to paint the Venus of Milo in flesh colors. Let her stay white![31]

It is clear that this is not just a criticism of details, but a basic divergence of tastes. On the one hand we have the respectable, Victorian sensibility of post-Zhadanov Soviet Russia, and on the other the bitter realism of the West European *avant-garde*. This becomes even more pointed in the Soviet critic's attack against one of the key scenes in *Mother Courage*

—the scene in which poor dumb Katrin, Mother Courage's backward daughter, sacrifices her life to save the city of Halle from destruction. For Brecht the point of this scene obviously lay in the contrast between the dumb girl's inarticulate, almost animal, instinctive reaction and the conventional schoolbook idea of heroism. But the Soviet critic called precisely for this hackneyed, blimpish heroism in its purest form:

> . . . in carrying out this heroic action, the actress Angelika Hurwicz, who plays the part, does not forget to emphasize Katrin's pathological state. And yet to what a pitch of emotion could the audience be raised, if in this scene of self-denying, fearless heroism Katrin's features could have been wholly free from the marks of mental sickness, and if this unhappy creature could have stood before us outwardly and inwardly transfigured.[32]

One might as well ask that Picasso's *Demoiselles d'Avignon* be improved by the addition of faces borrowed from fashion photographs in *Vogue*.

These extracts from Soviet reactions to the visit of the Berliner Ensemble speak for themselves. It is not just a matter of official disapproval—although that element is certainly present—but of the irreconcilability of tastes. It may be that it is the Soviet theatre that is old-fashioned and the Western *avant-garde*, to which Brecht belonged, that is modern; or the Soviet critics may be right in regarding the styles of Meyerhold, Tairov—and Brecht—as reeking of the twenties, and therefore more old-fashioned than their own. But one thing is certain: in spite of all politeness and the sincere desire to understand what Brecht was after, Brecht's attempt to create a Marxist theatre simply could not be appreciated in the Soviet Union, at least among the circles in power in the state —and in the theatre.

In the period of the thaw under Khrushchev, Brecht's plays did reach the Soviet stage, at first in the outlying Baltic republics then, but not until 1959, in Russian, in Moscow, when *The Visions of Simone Machard* were performed at the M. N. Yermolova Theatre. In 1961 M. M. Strauch directed one of Brecht's great plays, *Mother Courage*, at the Mayakov-

sky Theatre. But he conformed to Soviet Russian rather than
Brechtian methods of production by making the play into a
naturalistic historical canvas and letting Mother Courage
die a hero's death in the end, rather than trying to get back
into business as Brecht had conceived the play. Since then
there have been many productions of Brecht in the Soviet
Union; *The Threepenny Opera* particularly has been widely
produced, but the indications are that none of these productions is particularly Brechtian, with the sole exception of those
by Lyubimov at the *avant-garde* Taganka Theatre in Moscow,
where however they are reputed to incur the disapproval of
the authorities.

In the satellite countries Brecht's theatre was allowed to
make greater headway after he died. In 1957 *Mother Courage*
and *The Good Woman of Setzuan* were performed in Hungarian in Budapest—as the papers pointed out, the first performances of Brecht in Hungarian since *The Threepenny
Opera* had been produced there in the early thirties. And in
1958 the Berliner Ensemble went to Prague. On this occasion
a Czech correspondent told East Berlin readers that since *The
Threepenny Opera* had been put on immediately after the
war in E. F. Burian's theatre "D34," "there has been silence
about Brecht for almost ten years. Only the year 1955 brought
a change. Czech theatre people remembered the importance
of his work, and Brecht was rediscovered for the Czech stage."
But in spite of performances of *The Threepenny Opera* and
Mother Courage in Prague, *Puntila* in Brno, and *Galileo* in
Bratislava, the article says "even among theatre artists the
knowledge of Brecht's work is not yet deep enough, let alone
the general public."[33]
  As Brecht was more and more transformed into a Communist saint and an establishment figure by East German propaganda in the years after his death, and as the thaw of the early
sixties made him more acceptable in the Communist-bloc
countries of Eastern Europe and he was more readily performed in Czechoslovakia, Poland, Hungary and Rumania, a
paradoxical change in the public's attitude occurred. The
younger generation, fighting for a new conception of Com-

munism, "Communism with a human face," began to associate Brecht with the official, old-fashioned, neo-Stalinist line.
At the height of the 1968 revolution in Czechoslovakia the
younger generation of Czechs and Slovaks openly rejected
Brecht. This was the bitterest irony of all, for Brecht had
always, behind the façade of Party loyalty he showed to the
world, been a fighter for precisely that Communism with a
human face. That, after all, was the reason why he was denounced as a formalist during the Stalinist and post-Stalinist
period.

In all fairness, from the party's own narrow point of view
Brecht was not only useless but potentially harmful. To the
technicians of power who regard the arts merely as vehicles
for propaganda, Brecht's claim that his work would help the
Communist cause must have appeared absurd. Only two of
his plays have openly Communist subjects: *The Measures
Taken*, which in its frankness about the use of force within the
party was a propaganda catastrophe, and *The Mother*, a play
so starkly didactic that the audience could not associate it with
any real happenings in pre-revolutionary Russia. Such didactic
drama was at best suitable for intellectuals who knew how to
transfer abstract notions into everyday terms for themselves.
Hence the party's attack on *The Mother* as formalism. All
other plays by Brecht may be intended to prove Communist
theses, but in the eyes of the party they must certainly be
regarded as ineffective propaganda. *Mother Courage* and
Lucullus are pacifism pure and simple, and rather embarrass-
ing in times when the Soviet Union is the strongest military
power in the world. *Puntila* and *The Good Woman of Setzuan* describe the deep contradictions of human nature and
the moral dilemma of being good in a wicked world. *The
Caucasian Chalk Circle* preaches that things should be given
to those who make the best use of them—a dangerous doctrine
in any Communist country, where the waste and inefficiency
of the authorities are in constant evidence. Apart from that,
the prologue, intended to show the Confucian friendliness
prevailing among the members of two rival collective farms
in the Soviet Caucasus, is so clearly idealized that the Soviet

critics hastened to protest that life in the Soviet Union was certainly not like *that*. *Galileo* deals with the problem of the freedom of scientific inquiry—also a very touchy problem in any Communist society. And as to the earlier plays—they are immoral, nihilist, and anarchist. Can the party be blamed for having so long discouraged performances of the works of such an author? In East Germany, where Brecht's adherence was a major political asset to the regime, his plays caused constant embarrassment to the authorities by provoking unnecessarily stormy applause at the more revolutionary passages, like the one in *The Mother* where the heroine says:

> *While you are still alive, do not say: never!*
> *The safe things are not safe.*
> *As it is, it will not remain.*
> *When the rulers have spoken*
> *The ruled will speak. . . .*[34]

This rousing poetry is dangerously ambiguous. From the party's point of view any useful propaganda has to be far more specific: such a passage would have to be made to speak not of rulers and ruled, but of wicked capitalists and their down-trodden slaves. Hence the constant nagging by the party authorities that Brecht's work was not *clear* enough, that it was too obscure, too highbrow, and made too many demands on the intelligence of the listeners. It is known that Brecht took these criticisms very seriously indeed. He wanted to be a poet of the people, as widely understood as possible. He constantly tried to make his writing clearer, to elucidate any obscurities. But he succeeded only in making it less clear. For his idea of clarity was entirely different from the party's. A real poet, he simply could not stoop down to pure, unadulterated platitudes and clichés, which are the only really clear language in the eyes of a party used to thinking in ready-made formulas and slogans. When in his *pièces d'occasion* Brecht did comply with the party's demands, his poetic genius vanished without trace. Even then, from the party's point of view, he proved completely useless: they already had a surfeit of bad political hacks. And he never delivered the play on an East German contemporary problem that the party demanded in the hope of extracting a really effective piece of propaganda from him. He is known to have been trying to write such a play—on the theme of the shock worker who is resented by his mates for putting up the norms and lowering their wages. But he never finished it, and from what is known of Brecht's plan it is clear that the party would not have been very happy about it.

From the party's point of view, therefore, there remained only the propaganda value such a poet had in impressing the Western world. The original conception for the Berliner Ensemble, which in the first four years of its existence possessed no permanent theatre of its own, was clearly that of a touring company, designed to spread the prestige of advanced Communist culture in the West. In the tensest times of East-West crisis the Berliner Ensemble could be seen in West Germany, Austria, and France—a shop window in which the Communist camp, as it does so frequently, displayed goods not for sale within its own orbit. Brecht's case closely resembles that of Picasso: Picasso, who proclaims himself a Communist, is held up as proof that the world's greatest talents are in the "progressive" camp; he is even allowed to design a dove of peace, but he is rebuked when he produces a portrait of Stalin that is not a good likeness, and his works were consigned to the cellars of the Soviet museums until very recently. It is no coincidence that Brecht asked Picasso to design the curtain and the main poster for the Berliner Ensemble, nor that Picasso furnished him with highly "formalist" designs. The difference, however, is that Picasso is so successful that he can afford to live and work in the West as his own master. Brecht was never successful enough in the Western world to gain similar independence to work and experiment in complete freedom from financial worries. So Picasso lives and works in France, while Brecht to get the means to work had to accept the invitation to settle in East Berlin. To make effective use of Brecht the party had to give him the means to do his work according to his own ideas. By displaying that work to the West while barring it from its own orbit, the party thought that it was making use of Brecht for its own purpose. By accepting the party's lavish support and stubbornly sticking to his own ideas, Brecht was equally firmly

convinced that he was making use of the party to further his
own artistic and political objectives. And so with mutual
cynicism they mutually used each other. It was a curious ar
rangement. And who can tell which side had the better
bargain?

NOTES

1. Picasso, quoted by Max Frisch, *Tagebuch 1946–1949*, Frankfurt, 1950, p. 300.

2. Brecht, "Fluechtlingsgespraeche: Ueber die Hegelsche Dialektik," *Aufbau*, February 1958, p. 181.

3. J. Yuzovski, "Brecht und sein guter Mensch," *Sinn und Form*,
Second Special Brecht Issue, 1957, p. 204.

4. Ibid.

5. *Inostrannaya Literatura*, Moscow, no. 12, 1956, quoted by
Laqueur and Lichtheim, *The Soviet Cultural Scene 1956–57*, New
York and London, 1958, p. 61.

6. Gerd Ruge, "A Visit to Pasternak," *Encounter*, London, March
1958.

7. J. Yuzovski, "Brecht und sein guter Mensch," *Sinn und Form*,
Second Special Brecht Issue, 1951, pp. 205–6.

8. A. Zhdanov, "Speech to the First All-Union Congress of Soviet
Writers, 1934," *On Literature, Music and Philosophy*, London,
1950, p. 15.

9. Ibid., p. 16.

10. *Bolshaya Sovietskaya Entsiklopediya*, vol. 45, pp. 314–15.

11. Hans Rodenberg in a speech at the 5th Plenary Session of the
Central Committee of the SED, quoted by Schumacher, p. 573.

12. V. Meyerhold in *Vesy*, January 1907, quoted by Gorchakov,
The Theatre in Soviet Russia, Columbia University Press, 1957,
p. 58.

13. V. Meyerhold, *Teatr*, quoted by Gorchakov, (op. cit.), p. 58.

14. Jerzy Pomianowski, "Un Théâtre du Renouveau en Pologne,"
Les Temps Modernes, Paris, July 1958.

15. Official directive to *Pamietnik Teatralny*, published by *Pamietnik Teatralny*, no. 1, 1955, quoted by Wirth, "Beitrag zur Brecht-
Rezeption in Polen," *Theater der Zeit*, East Berlin, December 1956,
p. 6.

16. Alfred Szczepanski, Introduction to three plays by Brecht,
Warsaw, 1953, quoted by Wirth, op. cit.

17. Andrzej Wirth, "Beitrag zur Brecht-Rezeption in Polen,"
Theater der Zeit, East Berlin, December 1956, p. 6.

18. Ibid.

19. Andrzej Wirth, "Ueber die stereometrische Struktur der Brechtschen Stuecke," *Sinn und Form*, Second Special Brecht Issue, 1957, p. 385.

20. Manfred Wekwerth, "Anblick, Einblick, Ausblick. Bemerkungen zum Sowjet-Theater," *Theater der Zeit*, East Berlin, no. 19, 1957, p. 20.

21. Ibid., p. 23.

22. I. Fradkin, "Bertolt Brecht," *Teatr*, Moscow, January 1956.

23. Ibid.

24. A. Dymshits, "Bertolt Brecht," *Zvezda*, Moscow and Leningrad, April 1957, pp. 192 ff.

25. I. Fradkin in *Sovietskaya Kultura*, quoted by *Neues Deutschland*, East Berlin, 5.9.1957.

26. Theater of Working Youth, an *avant-garde* movement condemned by the party.

27. S. Mokulski and B. Rostotski, "Segodnyashnee i proidyennoe," *Sovietskaya Kultura*, Moscow, 5.18.1957.

28. Boris Zakhava, "Sila i Slabost Teatra Brekhta," *Znamya*, Moscow, August 1957, pp. 160–66.

29. Ibid., p. 160.

30. Ibid., p. 163.

31. Ibid., p. 165.

32. Ibid.

33. Zdenek Eis, "Brecht auf Buehnen der CSR," *Berliner Zeitung*, East Berlin, 4.26.1958.

34. Brecht, *Die Mutter*, *Stuecke* V, p. 116.

Part Four: THE REAL BRECHT

CHAPTER IX

THE USES OF COMMITMENT

I have feelings only when I have a headache—
never when I am writing: for then I think.
                                                    BRECHT[1]

Man lives by his head,
His head will not suffice.
You have a try! Your head will not
Feed more than a few lice.
    Because for this existence
    Man has not brains enough. . . .
        BRECHT, *Song on the Inadequacy*
                of Human Endeavor[2]

Brecht was a professed, and aggressive, rationalist. From the
time of his final conversion to Marxism in the late twenties
he endeavored to make his writing a scientific activity, a series
of controlled experiments devoted to the elucidation of social relations and to the transformation of society, by producing strictly calculated, socially useful responses in the audience. The element of emotion was thus excluded both in the
writer and in the public for whom he wrote.

The theory of the "epic" theatre is based on this intention:
the audience is to be confronted with a body of evidence from
which it is to draw its conclusions in a critical, highly lucid
state of mind. The emotions are to be involved only at a further remove; the critical analysis of the social facts, presented
in the concrete form of living pictures, is to produce socially
useful emotions such as indignation at injustice, hatred of

oppressors, or an active desire for the overthrow of the existing social order.

This was Brecht's sincere intention. Yet the long and tangled story of his relations with the Communist party shows that those most qualified to evaluate his efforts in terms of their practical value as Marxist propaganda were far from convinced that he had succeeded in achieving his aim. Nor would most Western observers have wanted to disagree with the Communist authorities. In Munich and Cologne, Paris and London, Brecht's own productions of his plays evoked anything but a wholly cerebral response. On the contrary, their success was due to their deep emotional impact on the audience.

For Brecht this was a tragic paradox. He always seemed to succeed in doing things he had never intended, to hit bull's-eyes on targets he never wanted to aim at, or, like Columbus, to discover continents he had not intended to reach. The plays he had written as ice-cold intellectual exercises contain far more than he himself consciously put into them. Behind the rational, propagandist surface there is always a layer of profound emotion, repressed, but all the more powerfully active. This repressed emotional content communicates itself to the deeper layers of the reader's or spectator's mind and is felt as a *poetic* quality. In fact, the tension between the poet's conscious aim and the subconscious, emotional content of his work of which he himself is unaware is in Brecht's case the source of its poetic power.

Here lies the explanation for the contradictory emotions, the tangle of misunderstandings and misconceptions Brecht has aroused in so many different quarters. The divergence between his subjective intentions and his objective achievement was bound to puzzle and confuse both himself and his public. Those who responded to the poetical power of his work disliked his Communist intentions; those who agreed with his intentions were made uncomfortable by the actual effect. And Brecht himself was often enraged by people who admired his work, and denounced them for liking it for the wrong reasons, while those he intended to please hurt him by rejecting it for reasons he could not understand.

This makes Brecht's case an illuminating example for the often noticed, but rarely so fully documented, phenomenon of the cleavage between an author's professed, conscious intention and its actual impact on the audience—a mystery that lies at the very base of all creative activity. Most writers and poets are aware of the mysterious mixture of conscious and subconscious processes by which their work is produced. The idea of inspiration, the mythic image of the Muse who dictates the finished poem into the poet's pen, are attempts to describe them.

But if a poet like T. S. Eliot wisely acknowledges the mystery behind his own poetic activity, and therefore declines to explain what he *intended* his poetry to mean, Brecht obstinately refused to acknowledge that there was more in what he wrote than the rationally calculated effects he had wanted to achieve. This attitude, which sprang from Brecht's highly complex personality, had very curious results. As he refused even to consider the presence of subconscious emotional factors in his poetry, he could not and did not control it, so that the subconscious elements are, if anything, *more* clearly visible in Brecht's work than in that of poets who understand, and are therefore able to conceal, their subconscious impulses. In fact, as will be shown in the next chapter, the conflict between the rational and the instinctive was itself one of the main themes of Brecht's poetic work. His very denial of the emotional factor is an indication of his constant preoccupation with this subject.

But the most obvious outcome of Brecht's refusal to admit the irrational was his blindness towards the real meaning and content of some of his best work. Unlike Pirandello's characters, who were in search of an author, Brecht was constantly faced with the problem of his characters running away from him and assuming an independent existence of which he strongly disapproved. The most clear-cut example of this curious state of affairs is that of *Mother Courage*.

Mother Courage was meant as a cautionary tale about the inevitable consequences of battening on war. Anna Fierling, called "Mother Courage," is a camp follower who in her small way helps the prosecution of the Thirty Years' War by providing shoes, ale, and comforts for the soldiers. She was, in Brecht's conception, a negative, villainous character. Those who live by war must pay war its due. So Mother Courage loses her three children. Having sacrificed her family to her commercial instinct, she fails to learn her lesson. She continues her trade, and as the final curtain falls she is seen dragging her cart across the stage to catch up with the advancing army.

Brecht wanted this last scene to arouse the spectator's indignation that such blindness and stupidity were possible. The public was to leave the theatre determined that something positive must be done to stop wars.

But when *Mother Courage* was first performed at the Zurich Schauspielhaus with Therese Giehse, an actress of great power, in the title role, the public's response was quite different: they were moved to tears by the sufferings of a poor woman who, having lost her three children, heroically continued her brave struggle and refused to give in, an embodiment of the eternal virtues of the common people.

Brecht was furious. He rewrote the play to emphasize the villainous side of Mother Courage's character. As he put it in a note to the text of the play in the ninth volume of *Versuche*:

> The first performance of *Mother Courage* gave the bourgeois press occasion to talk about a Niobe-tragedy and about the moving endurance of the female animal. Warned by this experience, the author has made some alterations for the Berlin performance.[3]

Having underlined the villainy of *Mother Courage*, Brecht himself supervised the Berlin production, in which his own wife, Helene Weigel, also an excellent actress but far less warm and motherly than Therese Giehse and therefore more in line with Brecht's intention, played the title role. The Berlin production was a triumph. But how did the leading Communist critic, Max Schroeder, describe its impact?

"Mother Courage," he wrote, "is a humanist saint from the tribe of Niobe and the *mater dolorosa*, who defends the life to which she has given birth with her bared teeth and claws. . . ."[4] Again, hardly anyone had noticed the villainy of Mother Courage, the profiteer who battens on war. Brecht himself admitted this but tried to explain it, not by any failure on his part to make himself clear, but by the obtuseness of the spectators who remained the slaves of long-established habits of emotion:

> Numerous discussions with members of the audience and many notices in the press show that many people regard *Mother Courage* merely as the representative of "the little people," who are "involved" in the war and "who can't do anything about it," who are helplessly at the mercy of events, etc. A deeply ingrained habit induces the audience in the theatre to pick out the more emotional aspects of the characters and to ignore the rest. . . .[5]

The East German authorities also noted the lack of propagandist effect. While *Mother Courage* moved people to tears about the horrors of war, if the play had any lesson at all it was that all soldiers are beasts (and the people of East Berlin automatically thought of Russian soldiers when it came to rape and rapine) and that nevertheless "life goes on" and the little man is eternally resilient. This was not a specifically Communist message, and so it was suggested to Brecht that he might make the end of the play more explicit. Mother Courage might make a little speech drawing a more positively Communist lesson, or she might do something that showed she had at last realized that she would have to become politically active.

If Brecht had really been as cold a rationalist and propagandist as he professed, he could easily have yielded to these demands. In fact, he did nothing of the sort. However willing he had previously been to accept advice and suggestions for alterations from practically any quarter, in this case he refused. With a great display of casuistry he argued that it was *better* propaganda to leave Mother Courage unconverted, untaught, and unteachable.

No doubt Brecht himself was convinced that he was arguing on strictly logical and rational grounds. Yet his arguments clearly are nothing but the rationalizations of instinctive responses. With the sound instinct of the creative artist Brecht knew that the suggested alterations would simply have spoiled his play. The suggested change did not make sense to his poetic instinct, and so he was unable to accept it. Yet the deeper needs of his personality made it impossible for Brecht to argue on any lines other than strictly rational considerations of political, or propaganda, expediency. The poet deep within him always had to hide behind the Marxist.

The case of Mother Courage is by no means an isolated instance of Brecht's characters belying their author's intentions. The inhuman Finnish landowner Puntila, whose relapse into human feelings under the influence of drink was to emphasize his heartlessness when sober, conquered all audiences by his humanity and charm, while his hired man Matti, conceived by Brecht as a paragon of proletarian virtue, was disliked as the cold prig he is. Again Brecht fought vainly against this misunderstanding. "In Zurich . . . most spectators had the impression of a sympathetic person with some evil moods when sober. . . . Practically all performances of the play in Germany, before and after the Berlin performance [where Brecht himself had tried to correct this wrong impression], suffered from the same mistake as the Zurich performance. . . ."[6] Galileo, whom Brecht had intended as a villain and coward who made science subservient to the state for centuries to come, was hailed by Soviet critics as a "hero of science" bravely suffering for his convictions.

Not only single characters, however, made themselves independent of their author's intentions. Whole plays conceived as arguments to prove one thing turned out to prove something quite different. The school opera *He Who Says Yes* was hailed by Prussian patriots as a masterly case for the maintenance of the old military virtues.

In the case of *The Measures Taken*, the discrepancy between Brecht's intention and the play's real meaning is even more instructive. Brecht had wanted to write a propaganda tract designed to foster the stern virtues of discipline and unquestioning obedience among party members. In a scene of great poetic power the four party workers divest themselves of their private personalities before entering China, the country where they are to carry out their clandestine activities. As they don their masks, which symbolize the extinction of their private selves, the "control chorus," the party's conscience, intones:

He who fights for Communism must be able to fight and not to fight; to speak the truth and not to speak the truth; to tender services and to refuse services; to keep promises and not to keep promises; to incur danger and to avoid danger; to be recognizable and unrecognizable. He who fights for Communism, has of all virtues only one; that he fights for Communism.[7]

But one of the four party workers cannot abide by these stern principles. His compassion for the suffering Chinese coolies leads him to disobey the party's orders. He is killed by his comrades. The control chorus agrees with the party workers' action and absolves them from all guilt.

The party's angry reaction to *The Measures Taken* has been discussed in a previous chapter. Brecht had intended to write a propaganda tract and had in fact written a somber tragedy of great emotional intensity. The party did not want to admit that its members were faced with such fearful choices and such heavy risks. They denied the truth of the incident Brecht had depicted and asserted that such an occurrence was impossible. Yet Brecht's poetic intuition—as distinct from his understanding of party doctrine—proved itself in the most unexpected manner a few years later at the Moscow trials.

Today, when three decades have passed since Brecht wrote *The Measures Taken*, the play is as powerful, as vital, and as true as ever. And its meaning can be seen to be wholly independent of the author's conscious intention. What was written to boost the morale of Communist party stalwarts in the last years of the Weimar Republic now stands revealed as one of the most powerful statements of the essence of the moral problem of Communism. The play, which is banned in the Communist world, could be performed anywhere outside it as a terrible picture of the party member's moral conflict, a devastating revelation of the tragic dilemma facing the adherents of a creed that demands the subordination of all human feeling to a dry and abstract ideal. The truth of a great poet's intuitive insight has transcended the author's conscious understanding of what he was doing.

This, of course, is by no means an unusual occurrence. Shakespeare, for example, may conceivably have intended Shylock as a piece of anti-Semitic propaganda. If so, his powers of characterization were too strong for his conscious intention. In any case, the immediate motives for which Shakespeare created the character have become irrelevant today, just as the political implications of *Richard II* or *Macbeth*, which may have played a considerable part in Shakespeare's approach to those plays, have lost any relevance for present-day audiences, whose attention is held by their deeper human content.

This relative lack of importance of conscious political purpose in a poet's work, for which Brecht furnishes so many powerful and recent examples, has its bearing on the much discussed problem of whether writers should or should not commit themselves to a political cause.

Of all the major creative writers of his age Brecht probably was the most wholeheartedly committed. Yet if his example shows anything, it shows that there is more to the act of commitment than the mere will, however wholehearted and sincere it may be, to throw in one's lot with a political party.

A really creative writer's power springs from sources that lie far below the sphere of conscious and rational thought. In committing himself, such a writer can commit only a relatively unimportant part of his personality. His commitment will furnish him with an incentive to write and will influence his choice of subject matter. But to the substance of what he has to say, the political ties of a major creative writer will remain relatively irrelevant.

All great writing must be true—that is, it must convey some truth about human nature or some aspect of reality. It must convey a genuine picture of the world as it is seen through the eyes of an important individual. As long, therefore, as the ideology or creed of a writer helps him in uncovering some aspect of the essential nature of reality, his commitment to it will be beneficial to his work. But as soon as the ideology concerned comes into conflict with reality—and most political ideologies, concerned as they are with some isolated and over-simplified aspect of reality, will do so sooner or later—a truly creative writer will have to break out of the narrow limits of the creed to which he has committed himself. By following his own intuition, which is nourished not only from his conscious but also from his subconscious perception of reality, he will inevitably come into conflict with the political ideology. That is why Brecht's characters, though they were intended as black villains, so often emerge as poor struggling human beings who cannot but win the sympathy of the audience.

The narrower a political creed, the less it corresponds to the real complexities of the world and the more difficult it will be for a creative writer to obey its dictates. Marxist dogma, in its mid-twentieth-century Communist form, is so far removed from reality that it is practically impossible to make any literary work aiming at poetic truth conform to it. Hence Brecht's inability to keep his work even remotely in line with the requirements of the party.

On the other hand, Brecht's commitment to Marxism and to the party did have a beneficial effect on his writing: it gave his anarchic and nihilistic tendencies a rigid framework of intellectual discipline. The inner tension created by this discipline, by the effort to repress the amorphous forces of his subconscious mind, gave Brecht's work its own peculiar spell, its tautness, poetic ambiguity, and depth. Had he set out by a conscious effort to make Mother Courage a latter-day Niobe, he would have succeeded only in producing a sentimental character—for Brecht had his sentimental, self-pitying side. But by following his rationalist, behaviorist conception, which denied the very existence of the deeper levels of human character and saw man as merely the product of the social environment he finds himself in at any moment, Brecht made Mother Courage a battlefield of contradictory impulses. Behind the rigid sociological framework the human side constantly reasserted itself; while the politician in Brecht piled on the social villainy, the poet in him drew on the subconscious feeling he had for the archetypal mother-figure, on his fund of pity—and sentiment—and cunningly smuggled these elements into the language, loading it with the subtlest overtones. And so in spite of Brecht's conscious and often declared intention of producing one-dimensional social schemata, the character he created has all the depth of a great tragic figure. And it is to this that the audience responds.

The act of *engagement* in Brecht's case can therefore be seen as having been of considerable importance in the mechanism of his creative process. It gave him the reason, the justification, and the incentive to work. On the other hand, Brecht's commitment to the Communist cause was, paradoxically, of little relevance to the ultimate significance, political or otherwise, of his work. His adherence to a political cause may have helped Brecht to write; it did not make him a very effective supporter of the cause, nor could it decisively influence the real content of his writing.

It is difficult to agree with Herbert Luethy, who argues in his penetrating essay on Brecht that his commitment to the Communist cause amounted to a *sacrificium intellectus* because it decisively impoverished his creative talent.[8] Brecht may have wanted to renounce his perception of the realities of human existence and character, and in that sense to abdicate the use of his own reason; he simply did not succeed in doing so. And even more paradoxically, while Brecht's conscious acceptance of Marxism, which he wrongly regarded as a supreme expression of scientific rationality, was wholly irrational, it allowed him to continue to follow his creative impulse and to produce plays that, based as they are on his intuitive perception of reality rather than his consciously held beliefs, constantly belie the pedantic concepts of Marxism and give the audience a genuine insight into the dilemmas of the human condition.

Brecht's commitment was thus of importance mainly in stabilizing his tumultuous personality. It resolved the deep feeling of nihilism and despair that pervaded his early writings, canalized the destructive forces within him, and allowed him to rationalize his poetic impulse by giving it a purpose.

As long as he could believe that the devastatingly dark picture of the world he painted was helping people to realize the need to change the world, as long as he could believe that such a change was possible and even inevitable, he was safe from despair. Only by committing himself to a rigidly dogmatic faith in the inevitability of social progress could a writer whose perception of the human condition was as pessimistic and devoid of saving grace as Brecht's justify his own creative activity to himself.

If the foregoing analysis of the role of Brecht's commitment within the complex structure of his creative personality is correct, it is clear that any analysis or critical evaluation of his work which does not go beyond the social purpose and political content of his plays will never be able to penetrate to the real springs of its poetic power and undoubted emotional impact. To understand the real significance of Brecht's work it is necessary to go beyond the superficial level of his conscious political intention.

Superficially, most of Brecht's later plays deal with the iniquities of capitalism, the equation of business and crime, the injustice and brutality of a commercial society. But beneath this surface, behind the abrupt changes in style and subject matter between Brecht's earlier and later works, there is a considerable unity in theme and imagery that links the exuberantly anarchic plays of his youth, the austerely didactic school operas and *Lehrstuecke*, to the broader historical or fairy-tale plays of his last phase. On closer analysis the whole of Brecht's work can be seen as reflecting his preoccupation with the same recurring basic problems, the same fundamental contradictions within himself, the same highly personal attitude to the world.

NOTES

1. Quoted by Ruth Berlau, "Wie war Bert Brecht?" *Magazin*, East Berlin, February 1958.

2. *Dreigroschenoper, Stuecke III*, p. 111.

3. *Versuche 9*, p. 79.

4. Max Schroeder, "Verflucht sei der Krieg" (1949), reprinted in *Aufbau*, East Berlin, 1957, no. 1.

5. Brecht, "Der lange Weg in den Krieg," *Theaterarbeit*, p. 230.

6. "Steckels zwei Puntilas," ibid., p. 22.

7. Brecht, *Die Massnahme, Versuche 4*, p. 334.

8. Herbert Luethy, "Vom armen Bert Brecht," *Der Monat*, West Berlin, May 1952. English version in *Encounter*, London, July 1956.

CHAPTER X

REASON VERSUS INSTINCT

The conflict between reason and emotion is . . . the basic experience of the bourgeois intellectual about to join the revolutionary proletariat. In its idealistic approach to the problem [Die Massnahme] is a typically petty bourgeois, intellectualist work.

ALFRED KURELLA[1]

Our arrangement is very simple: on the one hand we have the gooseliver, which [Galileo] insists that he must have, on the other hand is science, on which he also insists. So he sits between his two great vices: science and gluttony.

BRECHT[2]

In one of his early poems, the *Ballad of Mazeppa*, Brecht describes the execution of this Cossack Hetman, who, according to legend, was tied to the back of a wild horse that was let loose in the desolation of the endless Russian steppes and carried him to his death, headlong across the wilderness.

In Brecht's poem Mazeppa's fate becomes an image of the human condition. Helplessly tied to a blind elemental force that carries us along, the conscious part of ourselves is condemned to watch the skies rush past as they change from light to darkness and back again to light, waiting for the inevitable end, while the vultures already circle above.

This poem expresses one of Brecht's fundamental experiences: the helplessness of man, his inability to influence the world around him. It is an experience that recurs in many of his poems and plays. In his early volume, *Domestic Breviary,* it is the basic theme behind the ballad about the boy, Jakob Apfelboeck, who killed his parents and watched them decompose in the cupboard without ever knowing why he had done what he had done or ever feeling any guilt; about the infanticide Marie Farrar, who brought a child into the world without knowing how or why it should happen, and killed it without knowing why. It is also the basic theme of *The Legend of the Dead Soldier,* who is dragged to the wars although he is already dead. And the same image of man, helplessly drifting along in a universe beyond his understanding or control, imbues Brecht's poems modeled on Rimbaud's *Bateau ivre:* ships floating down mysterious rivers, their hulls slowly rotting away, decomposing bodies carried towards the sea. This is the experience of life that Brecht expresses in his first play, *Baal,* whose hero is entirely at the mercy of his uncontrollable impulses and who sees himself flying through space on our planet exactly like Mazeppa on his horse:

> If you lie in the grass at night, you feel it in your bones that the earth is a sphere and that we are flying. . . .[3]

And in *Baal,* too, we find the image of drifting down a river carried along by a current:

> . . . when you are carried along by a torrent, on your back, naked under an orange-colored sky and you see nothing, but the sky as it turns purple and then black, like a hole. . . .[4]

This picture of the human condition is essentially one of passive acceptance; it matters little whether the bodies floating down the rivers are alive or dead, they drift along with equal helplessness. And if the living swimmer's body is not yet in a state of decomposition, it soon will be. The process of nature is seen as one of incessant birth and decay, with human consciousness powerless to break the eternal cycle. In *Baal* it is the privy that is proclaimed the true symbol of the human condition:

> *You see the meaning there of man's estate;*
> *Creatures that eat, while they evacuate. . . .*⁵

Man in fact is merely a vessel in which the process of decay takes place.

In another of his most powerful ballads, *The Ballad of Cortez's Men*, Brecht depicts a party of conquistadors who are literally choked by the luxuriant growth of the jungle that has enveloped their camping place while they slept. Here again the blind forces of Nature smother helpless mankind.

Nature, the forest, and the sky stand for the forces of instinct and uncontrolled emotion that threaten self-control. At a later stage of his development Brecht feared losing himself to nature as he had lost himself in his youth, when his poetry reflected a complete merging of his self in the powerful process of vegetative growth and decay. His later poems often refer to the need to shut out the ecstasy of such feelings from a life that must be devoted to the pursuit of social betterment and the struggle against war and injustice. As Brecht's *alter ego*, Mr. Keuner, puts it: "We must make sparing use of Nature. If you spend your time in Nature without anything to do, you easily get into an unhealthy state—something like a fever comes over you."⁶

In his early plays Brecht was still in the grip of this fever. With a mixture of horror and delight he yielded to the powerful lure of nature and the dark, irrational call of subconscious compulsions. Baal is a poet, and his poetic gift is shown by Brecht as directly derived from his passivity. He is a poet *because* irrational forces are at work within him; his poetry pours from him without conscious effort on his part. And equally he cannot help seducing women; he cannot help becoming emotionally tied to his friend Ekart, the musician. When Ekart betrays him with a woman he cannot help killing him. In this Baal resembles the *poètes maudits*, Verlaine and Villon, whom Brecht so greatly admired. They, too, were vagabonds drifting through life because they were poets—and they were poets because they had to obey the irrational forces within them. There can be no doubt that in writing *Baal* at the age of nineteen Brecht was describing his own experience.

The hero of Brecht's second play, Kragler, in *Drums in the Night*, though no poet, is also in the grip of an experience beyond his conscious control. He has been pressed into the army, has been kept a prisoner in Africa, and has come back to Germany. He is faced with the decision of whether to join the revolutionary Spartakists or to marry his bride, pregnant by another man, and settle down to a life of passive mediocrity. He, too, chooses what instinct dictates rather than what reason would have demanded. He refuses to do anything about changing society and relaxes into a vegetative contentment. Kragler is no longer wholly representative of his author's own attitude. But while Brecht clearly feels some pangs of social conscience, Kragler's choice nevertheless represents a victory of instinct over rational premeditated action.

The two men, who are locked in battle in Brecht's third youthful play, *In the Jungle of the Cities* (the jungle of the great city of Chicago, even more elemental and relentless than the jungle that choked the men of Cortez), are still more completely in the grip of irrational impulses. Their love-hate relationship is wholly motiveless and inexplicable; they are driven along by forces entirely outside their control. And the author begs the audience not even to attempt to understand them: "Do not wrack your brains as to the motive of this fight . . . but direct your attention towards the finish."[7] But the finish of the fight merely brings the recognition of the complete isolation of man and his utter inability to control his own fate.

Self-destruction through his inability to resist subconscious forces within him is also the fate of Brecht's Edward II, who loses his kingdom and his life by his inexplicable infatuation with Gaveston—in Marlowe's original a nobleman but in Brecht's adaptation a vulgar butcher's son devoid of any charm that might make the king's folly more easily understood on rational grounds. Edward also drifts towards his doom like a helpless piece of wood carried along a stream.

The hero of *Man Equals Man*, Galy Gay, an Irish stevedore in a Kiplingesque India, is so passive a character that a trio of brutal soldiers can wipe out his individuality altogether; to replace a member of their platoon whose absence would give them away as temple-robbers, they change Galy

Gay into the soldier Jeriah Jip. Man equals man—and human individuality can be wiped off like a coat of dust from a windowpane. A passport and a soldier's pay-book are more essential parts of a personality than memories or habits. The meek little pacifist Galy Gay is turned into a ferocious fighting machine that terrorizes whole populations. But his very fierceness is merely the outward sign of his passivity; he has been molded like a piece of clay.

Brecht's early poems and the plays of his pre-Marxist phase reveal his basic attitude to life as that of a sensitive personality passively aware of being at the mercy of compulsions beyond conscious control; irrational impulses from within, powerful and inexplicable forces from without: nature, the jungle of the great cities, the social conditions that determine man's character and way of life. And the helplessness of the individual is heightened to nightmare proportions by his inability to communicate with his fellow human beings. As Shlink and Garga, the heroes of *In the Jungle of the Cities*, realize at the end of their fight to the death:

Language is inadequate for communication. I have watched the animals; love, the warmth created by the proximity of our bodies, is the sole mercy in our darkness. But the contact of organs is the only possible contact. It cannot bridge the gulf of language. . . .[8]

This is the side of Brecht's nature that led Feuchtwanger to describe Proeckl, the character in his novel *Success* closely modeled on Brecht, as deficient in social instinct and unable to develop genuine contact with other human beings.

All the characters in Brecht's early plays, not only Shlink and Garga, move through them like somnambulists or victims of post-hypnotic suggestion. But Shlink and Garga are particularly passive and unable to understand what it is that drives them to their ruin. As they cannot understand their own actions they cannot communicate with each other.

What does the fight between these men consist of? It opens with Shlink wanting to buy Garga's opinion about a book, and continues with a series of attempts by Garga and Shlink in turn to gain complete moral ascendancy over the other, to conquer the other's will and bring him to submission. Their strange relationship, which the author himself calls "the inexplicable wrestling match of two men"[9] and which he begs the audience not even to try to understand, is clearly a sexual one. Without knowing it, and probably without the author's knowing, Shlink and Garga are the victims of homosexual passion. But as the motivation of the action is repressed, the play is presented as a series of motiveless events—*actes gratuits*.

It is surely no coincidence that the term *acte gratuit* was first used by Gide, another writer deeply concerned with gaining mastery over, and coming to terms with, inexplicable and forbidden subconscious urges. Loss of contact with reality, inability to control events are neurotic symptoms. They characterize an age of anxiety and neurosis. The visions of Kafka, the automatic writing and painting of the surrealists, the dramatization of the absurd, from Alfred Jarry and Apollinaire to Beckett and Ionesco, are the expressions of such a loss of contact with the real world. The whole of Brecht's early work has close affinities with these writers.

Though it may be significant that three out of Brecht's early plays are concerned with the problem of homosexuality (*Baal, In the Jungle of the Cities,* and *Edward II*) the exact nature of the subconscious urge he sought to suppress is irrelevant. What matters for the understanding of Brecht's development as a writer and his deeply felt need for political commitment is merely the indisputable fact that his whole work is deeply concerned with the problem of the struggle between subconscious impulse and conscious control. In his early period the incomprehensible forces are presented as irresistible and the prevailing image is that of submission and drift.

But Brecht's passive acceptance of incomprehensible emotional forces was counterbalanced by an increasingly strenuous effort at rational, active self-control. Gradually the passive submission to instinct was resisted and gave rise to feelings of guilt and distaste. That is why the spectacle of an audience in the grip of emotional identification with the characters on the stage filled Brecht with feelings of physical disgust at so degrading an exhibition of lost self-control. That is why, as his friend George Grosz put it, Brecht "clearly would have wanted a sensitive electric computer instead of a heart, and spokes like the wheels of a motorcar instead of legs."[10]

To overcome the temptation to let himself drift along passively in the grip of emotion, Brecht had to become active, tough, cynical, and cerebral, to assume the public persona of a wholly rational, impersonal being. It is surely significant that in the whole canon of his hitherto published work there is not a single love poem addressed to a named person. The nearest approach to it—*Erinnerung an Marie A.* (*Memory of Marie A.*)—is a poem that insists that he remembers the girl in question only by virtue of the cloud that passed over them when he lay with her under a plum tree. His feelings are forgotten. The image of a cloud remains. The extreme reticence of all love scenes in Brecht's plays has often been remarked on. In *The Caucasian Chalk Circle* Grusche and her soldier speak to each other in the third person as if afraid to address each other directly. The love scene between Paul and Jenny in *Mahagonny* takes place in a brothel, with a whole queue of men waiting outside and clamoring to be admitted. In *The Threepenny Opera* the love scenes are presented as grotesque parodies of petty-bourgeois sentimentality.

The ostentatious rejection of all sentiment and emotion led Brecht into the displays of arrogant rudeness that characterize his *enfant terrible* period, into his friendship with boxers, his interest in six-day bicycle racing, and his onslaught on oversensitive poets. But ultimately the irrational forces within him needed a stronger and more positive discipline: the discipline of political commitment.

Communism was particularly suitable for this purpose. It was itself supremely tough. It rejected the existing world with all its ugliness, cruelty, and absurdity. It provided a technique of self-control, discipline, and rational thought. It rejected all sentiment or emotion and claimed to be completely scientific. And it gave sense to a world that otherwise appeared devoid of meaning and purpose. That the claims of Communism were themselves basically irrational did not make its acceptance more difficult, but on the contrary easier; a deeply irrational nature could best express itself in clinging to an irrational creed.

The middle phase of Brecht's career reflects the inner struggles inherent in the acceptance of such a creed, the submission of emotional impulses to conscious control according to scientific principles. In Brecht's plays of this period the problem appears as that of *Einverstaendnis* (consent, acceptance) and discipline. The airmen of the *Didactic Play of Baden: On Consent* agree to subordinate their individual instinctive craving for life to historic necessity and are redeemed by dying in the cause of technological progress; the Japanese boy in *He Who Says Yes* accepts the need to die in the interests of his companions; the young comrade of *The Measures Taken* agrees with the party's disciplinary measure and accepts his own liquidation to help the cause. All these are *hard, tough* decisions, brutally unsentimental. On the surface they are diametrically opposed to the passive drift of Baal, Kragler, Shlink, Garga, or Edward II. But on closer reflection the contradiction between the *soft* heroes of the early, exuberant plays and the *hard* heroes of the austere didactic works disappears. They are all brothers under the skin. The heroes of the hard plays are as passive as those of the earlier ones. The airmen of the *Didactic Play of Baden: On Consent* submit and die; the boy of *He Who Says Yes* meekly suffers his sacrifice to ancient custom; and the young Communist of *The Measures Taken* resembles Baal and Edward II in being a victim of his inability to control his emotional impulses. The difference is merely that while the heroes of the early, soft plays drift to their death as casually as they sinned, the young comrade of *The Measures Taken* is deliberately put to death *as a punishment for having been unable to resist his emotional impulse.*

Henceforth the indulgence of one's emotions is linked with feelings of guilt. In *Man Equals Man* the toughest character is the ferocious Sergeant Fairchild, nicknamed "Bloody Five." But this tough and hard character has one weakness:

It is known throughout the whole army that when it rains he falls into a state of sensuality and changes inwardly and outwardly. . . . When it rains Bloody Five, the most dangerous man in the British Army, becomes as harmless as a milk-tooth. When he has one of his fits of sensuality he is blind for everything that happens around him.[11]

To end this unsatisfactory state of affairs and to regain complete self-control and manliness Sergeant Fairchild castrates himself:

It is simple. Here is the solution. Here is a bit of rope. Here is a revolver. I know no mercy. Rebels are shot. . . . Girls will not cost me another penny after this. . . . I *must* do it, to remain "Bloody Five," Fire![12]

And so the cause of the trouble is removed. The root of instinctive impulse is torn out. Reason and self-control are reestablished. Twenty-five years later Brecht returned to the same subject in *The Private Tutor*.

The conflict between subconscious instinct and rational self-control is one of the main themes of Brecht's work. At times it takes the form of violence directed against the instinctive part of man's nature, at others it is mellowed into a gentler mood, like that of Schweik's friend Baloun, who cannot restrain his boundless appetite. But it is always present, even if Brecht's own attitude towards the two warring sides of his nature changes—sometimes it is reason that appears as the positive force and instinctive emotion that is seen as dangerous or evil, sometimes it is reason that is evil and emotion and instinct that are good.

In the bitter didactic play *The Exception and the Rule*, for example, the poor coolie yields to his positive emotion of compassion for a suffering fellow being and offers his water bottle to the thirsty merchant. The merchant, who has reason to believe that the coolie whom he has maltreated hates him, mistakes the gesture of compassion for an attack and kills the coolie. The judge at the trial accepts the evidence. He nevertheless acquits the merchant. To expect a human being to help his fellow creature in the hour of need is *unreasonable*. The merchant could not be expected to think that the coolie did not want to attack him. Kindness and compassion being the exception, inhumanity the rule, the coolie deserved to be killed. He was a victim of his kindly emotion. Reason, cold and hard, rules the world.

In the *Rise and Fall of the City of Mahagonny* instinct and emotion stand for the chaos and wickedness of the self-seeking, greedy capitalist world. The hero Paul proclaims self-indulgence as the supreme law of Mahagonny. The result is intolerable chaos and Paul himself is condemned to death; those who follow the blind impulse of instinct must die.

It is interesting to see how Brecht transformed his own conflict into the struggle between the old and new world order: the mysterious forces of instinct, which had been represented by the image of the luxuriant virgin forest that choked the men of Cortez and later by the jungle of the great city of Chicago, become the symbol of the greedy *laissez-faire* society of capitalism. Against it the forces of discipline and self-control are ranged under the banner of scientific Marxism and Communist party discipline.

The subjugation of one's own irrational impulses requires a violent effort. Self-restraint of this kind, projected outward, turns into violence. And so Brecht, outwardly the mildest and most rigidly self-controlled person, although occasionally prone to violent outbursts, was constantly preoccupied with the need for violence. The victory of reason could, for him, be brought about only by violent means. When chaos had been banished from the world, then there could be friendliness and Confucian courtesy, but first there must be violence; the violence of the Communist party workers in *The Measures Taken* against their young comrade, the violence of the he-donistic self-seekers of *Mahagonny*, and of the gangsters of *The Threepenny Opera*. Even the gentle Joan Dark, the *St. Joan of the Stockyards* who believed in the God of love and Christian nonviolence till events taught her better, dies with the demand for violence on her lips.

Violence is both evil and good; it is evil in the hands of the gangsters of *The Threepenny Opera*, the gold diggers of *Mahagonny*, the tsar of the Chicago meat-packers, Pierpont Mauler, but good in the hands of the Communist party, where it can be defended as being violence serving the end of abolishing violence. Nevertheless those who use violence are

ways seen with admiration by Brecht, just as he preferred
the boxers and six-day bicyclists to the whining bourgeois
poets. It is the admiration for the strong man, the doer as
opposed to the thinker, the Nietzschean hero, that pervades
so much of German literature—an attitude born of the frus-
trations, the deep feelings of impotence of poets and philoso-
phers in a country where intellectuals were traditionally
classed as mere dreamers and excluded from any influence
in the affairs of the real world. Marx's demand that philosophy should cease to be mere theory and enter the field of
practical action springs from the same source—and also natu-
rally involves the use of violence.

But can the world be changed by violence? For Brecht,
struggling to subdue the forces of chaos within him, a positive
answer to this question was a desperate necessity. Violence
would certainly change the world for the worse—why then not
also for the better? Brecht, as usual, tackled the problem
from the negative angle. In his comedy *Man Equals Man*,
written in the middle twenties, three greedy, wicked, and vulgar British colonial soldiers completely transform a harmless
little individual into a ferocious fighting man by methods
that foreshadow the brainwashing techniques of totalitarian
society with an accuracy as uncannily prophetic as that with
which *The Measures Taken* foreshadowed the Stalinist purge
trials. Little Galy Gay is accused of some crime till he feels
an overwhelming sense of guilt, condemned to death in a
mock trial and is induced to believe that he has been executed. Thereafter he willingly accepts his new identity:

. . . *Mr. Bertolt Brecht will prove that one can*
Do whatever one wants to do with a man:
A man will be reassembled like a motor-car tonight in
    front of you—
And afterwards will be as good as new. . . .[13]

In the light of recent research on the techniques of brainwashing Brecht's intuitive anticipation of the essence and the
methods of this process as early as 1924–26 is staggering.
Once again what he intended as an attack on the brutality of
the existing social order turned in fact into a forecast of the

reality of his own brand of totalitarianism. His argument t
if a man can be transformed by such violent methods in
something worse he can also be made into something bet
was put into practice by the Stalinist "social engineers" wi
results as horrifying as those Brecht depicted in his play.

Does Brecht condemn the soldiers who brainwash lit
Galy Gay? Or does he admire them? Does he applaud t
self-mutilation of Sergeant Fairchild? Or is he repelled
it? Here as elsewhere in Brecht's writings it is impossible
give a clear answer. What one part of his personality a
proved, another condemned. The reader or spectator can ta
his choice. Brecht's success as a writer is largely depende
on the ambivalence of the images he uses—and this in tu
is derived from the particularly acute form in which he w
involved in the basic human conflict between reason and i
stinct. Moreover, the ambivalence he displays in his attitu
towards the subject matter of his writing is also reflected
the struggle between the exuberance of the romantic and t
austerity of the classical in the formal aspect of his wor
The alternation between harshness and lyricism, banality a
sublime simplicity, austerity and luxuriant imagery in his p
etry and plays is the hallmark of Brecht. Its most characte
istic expression is his use of parody. For parody in itself
ambivalent—it mocks and imitates at one and the same m
ment. The success of the songs in The Threepenny Oper
for example, is largely attributable to this dual nature of pa
ody. The sentimental ballad of the pimp or the mock lo
duets of Macheath and Polly allow us to laugh at the gi
tesqueness of such emotions in such abject characters; at t
same time they have the genuine force of true sentimer
behind them. Parody enabled Brecht to be sentimental a
to write love lyrics without consciously yielding to his em
tions. It also enables the spectator to feel at once ironical
superior and sentimental.

The ambivalence of Brecht's attitude, which springs fro
the duality of a personality deeply divided within itself, als
provides the clue to the Brechtian style of acting: the deni
of identification between the actor and the character produce
a split image. The actor embodies the character and at t
same time comments on him; in other words, he shows t

ctions of the character and simultaneously presents the critical reasoning that might have stopped him from acting as he does. Brecht wanted the actor to present a picture of man mpelled by his emotions, critically yet helplessly aware of heir irrationality.

The violence of Brecht's early conflicts within himself visibly abated from about the time he finally committed himself o the Communist creed. Communism, or rather his own rand of it, tailored to measure to his personal needs, provided the focus around which he could integrate the forces hat pulled him in so many different directions. The Hegelian dialectic gave an aura of rationality to the most glaringly mbivalent attitudes and emotions; the Marxist claim to cientific certainty made the most blatantly irrational promptings of hatred and violence acceptable, and the Marxist conlemnation of the existing social order allowed him to indulge his blackest nihilistic pessimism without having to give in to lespair. To a personality so deeply aware of human isolation, o hard put to establish contact with others, the standardized magery and collective aims of the party provided a redeeming illusion of being able to share in a great collective experience. As Pelageya Vlasova puts it in *The Mother*, a shared cause provides that "third thing" that enables two human beings to communicate:

> . . . I
> Kept my son. How did I keep him? Through
> The third thing.
> He and I were two, but the third thing
> We had in common, pursued in common,
> United us. . . .
>
> How near were we to each other, when near
> This thing. How good were we for each other, near
> This good cause.[14]

It cannot be coincidence that this mellowing of Brecht's attitude, the reintegration of his violently divided personality, dates from the time when a new type of character ap-

pears in his writing—the mother image. Until then a ve
large proportion of the female characters in Brecht's pla
are whores and bawds, infanticides and ruined girls; the v
lainous brothelkeeper Leocadia Begbick, who appears both :
Mahagonny and in *Man Equals Man*, the women of *Ba*
who are little more than objects of Baal's sexual greed, a
these female characters were seen with a mixture of hatre
and contempt.

The Mother and *St. Joan of the Stockyards* introduce
new type of female character—the female revolutionary. B
while Joan Dark is completely sexless, Pelageya Vlasova ha
the features of a real woman; her motherliness is both emo
tional and rational, and so is her revolutionary attitude, whic
is born of a mother's love for mankind, the desire to sprea
happiness. The same archetypal character, frequently playe
by Brecht's wife, Helene Weigel, reappears in a successio
of Brecht's later plays: in *Mother Courage*, where the mothe
image is overlaid by the camp follower's greed for profit an
her war guilt yet breaks through to the audience with ele
mental force; in *Señora Carrar's Rifles*, where mother-lov
emerges from selfishness with the readiness to sacrifice eve
one's children in the fight against the class enemy; in *Th
Good Woman of Setzuan*, where the only good human bein
is a prostitute but one with motherly feelings, ready to figh
for her offspring; and in *The Caucasian Chalk Circle*, wher
characteristically the mother figure is split in two: the phys
cal mother and the spiritual mother, the woman who love
the child and the one who wants to use it for her own selfis
ends. In trying to prove their claim to the child they are pul
ing it out of the chalk circle in different directions, threater
ing to tear it in half, just as the conflict of reason and instinc
pulls the personality in opposite directions. But characterist
cally in this late play it is emotion, not reason, that wins th
battle. What is more, the foster mother who loves the chil
lets it go so as not to hurt it. It is not violence but yieldin,
that is awarded the prize.

Once Brecht had accepted the discipline of his new creed
and the threat of being overwhelmed by uncontrolled instinc
tive forces had receded, the emotional side appeared in a

ncreasingly sympathetic light. It was as if the guilt feelings
hat had originally been evoked by the temptation to suc-
umb to subconscious urges were now transferred to the other
ide: Brecht now felt guilty at having opted for a coldly ra-
ional and inevitably cruel ideology.

Frequently the conflict between reason and instinct is symbolized by split characters. In the ballet-cantata *The Seven
Deadly Sins*, the heroine Anna appears split into the instinc-
ive, emotional Anna who dances and the rational, practical
Anna who sings. Anna is a dancer who leaves her home in
Louisiana to try to earn enough money for her family to build
a house. The natural instincts of a healthy girl, which, if fol-
owed, would impair her earning power, appear as the seven
deadly sins to her family and her rational self. Her love for a
poor man, which might keep her from selling herself to a rich
over, is the sin of lust, her desire to eat rather than starve
and keep her figure for the strip-tease act is greed, etc. Hav-
ng resisted all these temptations Anna returns home with the
money. In a commercial society instinct has to yield to calculation. Here instinct and emotion are seen as positive, cold
rationality as negative.

This is also the theme of *The Good Woman of Setzuan*.
The gods reward the kind prostitute with enough money to
start a modest business, but to prevent her fellow men from
exploiting her kindly Shen Te has to assume the mask of a
ruthless cousin, who drives the spongers out. Again reason
and emotion appear as separate and contradictory aspects of
the same personality. Since to be wholly good means ruin,
the ruthless, hard-boiled, rational part of human nature must
take command.

In the character of Puntila the rational personality is sober,
while the emotional, kindly side of his nature appears only
when he is drunk. Shen Te is a good human being who has
to be wicked to survive. Puntila is a wicked character who
loses his villainy when he loses his reason. In both cases, as in
The Seven Deadly Sins, reason is equated with the negative
aspect of human nature. Here lies the main difference from
Brecht's early period, in which he tended to reject the emotional side of human nature and called upon the discipline

of cold reason to restore order when the emotions led to
chaos. The change, however, is merely the result of lessened
tension. The emotions, if followed, would still lead to ruin.
In that sense they are still negative. But they are now
seen as basically good rather than uncontrollable urges that
threaten sanity itself. When Brecht was working his way towards the acceptance of Communist discipline he tended to
reject the emotional side of man and to equate it with the
chaos of the existing social order; after he had surrendered
himself to what he regarded as a supremely rational creed, he
depicted the rational side of his characters as an element of
villainy in them—though one that was necessary for their survival in society. He, of course, always argued that after the
victory of Communism this conflict between reason and instinct would disappear. But the fact remains that a practical
approach to the problem of survival and success—such as the
highly realistic tactics of Communism demanded—is consistently shown in a negative light in Brecht's later work.

The conflict of instinct and emotion also colors Brecht's
two most mature works, *The Caucasian Chalk Circle* and
Galileo. In both these great plays one of the chief characters
bears autobiographical features of the author. At last Brecht
had found a way of portraying himself on the stage. The
judge Azdak in *The Caucasian Chalk Circle* is a lecherous
and immoral jester, yet, even if for the wrong reason, he does
good. When civil war and public disorder sweep him into the
seat of judgment, he dispenses justice because he is ignorant
of the law and because he is corrupt enough not only to accept bribes but to cheat those who have bribed him. Because
he follows his emotions he is a villain, but because he follows
his native shrewdness and intuitive understanding of people
rather than listening to the reasoning of lawyers he does good.
Whether he did it intentionally or not, Brecht has here
drawn a masterly portrait of himself: a highly complex and
contradictory character, servile and arrogant, shrewd and foolish, humorous and lewd, humble and conceited, familiar and
yet distant—and a genius. Azdak is a battlefield of the conflict
of instinct and emotion—but instinct wins every time; that
is why Azdak is in the last resort a good man. He seldom

achieves what he has set out to achieve, his plans are defeated by his instincts and intuition—just as Brecht's own poetical talent and intuition always got the better of his rational intentions.

Galileo too, is a genius. He, too, is a lecherous and gluttonous man. But his most powerful instinct is curiosity. His greatest sensual pleasure is the pleasure of discovery. Here Brecht comes to the very core of the problem. The urge for knowledge, the most rational side of human endeavor, science itself, is shown as merely another of man's basic, instinctive urges, just as deeply rooted in the irrational as the instinct for procreation. To be able to indulge this instinct Galileo is prepared to commit the meanest action: he cheats the Venetians by selling them the telescope he has not invented but merely plagiarized—clearly an autobiographical trait. He writes abjectly servile letters to the Medici, whose despotism he despises. And, with the physical cowardice of the sensuous man, he recants his theories. In the earlier version of the play Galileo's action was made to appear excusable as a deliberate act of calculation and cunning; by recanting he saved his life and gained the time to complete his treatise, which was then smuggled out into the free world. But shortly before Brecht died, as he put the final touches to the revised version of the play and conducted the rehearsals of the Berliner Ensemble, he changed his mind—he insisted that Galileo "must be shown as a social criminal, a complete rogue,"[15] and told his actors:

Galileo is shown as a man who is right, one of the great heroes of the following five hundred years, who sweeps away all obstacles, but who then collapses and becomes a criminal. That is one of the great difficulties: to bring out the criminal element in the character of the hero. In spite of all, he is a hero—and in spite of all he becomes a criminal. . . .[16]

Hero and criminal—once again we encounter the duality of the Brechtian character. Galileo becomes a criminal because by his cowardice he has established the tradition of the scientist's subservience to the state—the tradition that, according to Brecht, reached its culmination in the production of the atomic bomb, which science put at the disposal of ordinary, nonscientific men, to serve their power politics. Galileo, the hero of science, is the embodiment of reason in all its splendor, ruined once more by its inability to overcome the base, instinctive, inarticulate side of human nature. The greatest of intellects, the personification of science itself, is just as helplessly tied to the blind instincts of his subconscious nature, as poor Mazeppa is tied to the wild steed that carries him to his doom.

The attempt to banish instinct and emotion and to live as a wholly rational being is foredoomed to failure. Although he strenuously denied it in public, Brecht knew that this was so. In one of his few really intimate, private poems, the magnificent sequence of *Four Psalms* (written early in his life but published only after his death), he confessed it:

> *I am the most practical of all my brethren—*
> *And my head comes first of all!*
> *My brethren were cruel, I am the cruelest—*
> *And I weep in the night!*[17]

NOTES

1. Alfred Kurella, writing in *Literatur der Weltrevolution* (organ of the International Association of Revolutionary writers), Moscow, 1931, quoted by Schumacher, p. 366.
2. Quoted by K. Ruelicke, "Leben des Galilei—Schlussszene," *Sinn und Form*, Second Special Brecht Issue, 1957, p. 287.
3. *Erste Stuecke I*, p. 15.
4. Ibid., p. 28.
5. Ibid., p. 23.
6. "Herr Keuner und die Natur," *Versuche 5*, p. 457.
7. *Erste Stuecke I*, p. 194.
8. Ibid., p. 191.
9. Ibid., p. 194.
10. George Grosz, *Ein grosses Ja und ein kleines Nein*, Hamburg, 1955, p. 181.
11. *Erste Stuecke II*, p. 196.
12. Ibid., p. 281.
13. Ibid., p. 229.

14. Brecht, *Die Mutter, Versuche* 7, p. 48.

15. Brecht quoted by K. Ruelicke, "Leben des Galilei—Schluss-zene," *Sinn und Form,* Second Special Brecht Issue, 1957, p. 292.

16. Ibid., p. 294.

17. Brecht, "Der vierte Psalm," *Sinn und Form,* Second Special Brecht Issue, 1957, p. 141. This passage, though obscure, clearly points to the contrast between the practical head and its connection with cruelty, and the break-through of repressed emotions which erupt in the night in tears.

CHAPTER XI

BRECHT'S WORLD

> *I see the world in a mellow light:*
> *it is God's excrement. . . .*
> BRECHT, *Baal*[1]
>
> *It was very beautiful. . . . Everything.*
> BRECHT, *Baal*[2]

If the analysis attempted in the previous chapter of Brecht's lifelong preoccupation with his own conflict between the forces of reason and instinct is accepted, his inability to conform with the requirements of a narrow political line will be readily understood. And it will be seen that far from being a mere left-wing, conformist *auteur du boulevard* as Eugene Ionesco has described him[3]—surely on the evidence of hearsay rather than from a close reading of his plays—Brecht was as deeply concerned with the predicament of man and the irony of the human condition as James Joyce, Kafka, or the French existentialists.

Brecht's picture of the world has a great deal in common with the somber canvas of the latter school. Like Sartre or Camus, Brecht saw man determined by his social environment, his personality the mere product of changing outside circumstances.

It is, of course, no coincidence that Brecht—and the whole generation of German writers whose foremost representative he is, the only one likely to survive through the force of his language and the intensity of his poetic vision—anticipated the French existentialists of the next generation. If their despair, their decision to "commit" themselves, sprang from the experience of the French defeat of 1940, that of Brecht and his contemporaries was engendered by the German defeat in 1918. In each case the young intellectuals responded to a world in which the comfortable security of bourgeois standards and assumptions had been replaced by terror and violence, in a spirit of grim realism.

This ruthlessly realistic attitude was, in Brecht's case, akin to the ruthlessness born of despair and wounded pride that led other, less sophisticated members of his generation in Germany into the arms of Hitler. On the other hand, that tribal nationalist myth itself constituted the break-through of the forces of man's savage and irrational nature that Brecht so dreaded in himself as well as in society. Yet, being of his time and generation, he sought to meet this threat by countermeasures that were tainted with the same poison: violence to stamp out violence, hatred to eradicate hatred and to pave the way for sweet reason and friendliness, totalitarianism to defeat totalitarianism, evil to drive out evil.

His very failure to extricate himself from this dilemma is at the root of his success, and his significance, as a poet: being so deeply involved in the conflict, so deeply tainted with the evil of his time, he was able to give it full and valid expression. That is why plays like *The Measures Taken* and *Man Equals Man* were not merely prophetic forecasts of things unthought of when they were written but remain the most compelling and concentrated poetic statements of some of the fundamental preoccupations of our time.

Brecht's world is the empty universe through which Nietzsche's cry "God is dead" resounds with terrifying and reverberating echo. "The world is poor, and man is bad,"[4] and "The meanest thing alive, and the weakest, is man."[5] If these two statements sum up Brecht's opinion in his early phase, one of the foolish and impotent gods in *The Good Woman of Setzuan* repeats it in that much later play: "The world is uninhabitable, you must admit that,"[6] and the good woman herself, Shen Te, the motherly prostitute, comes to the same conclusion:

> . . . He who helps the lost
> Is lost himself. For who could long
> Refuse to be wicked, when those die who eat no meat?

And she asks:

> Something must be wrong with your world. Why
> Is there a reward for wickedness, why do the good receive
> Such hard punishment?[7]

That virtue brings no reward and is in fact a sign of stupidity
is a recurring theme. As Mother Courage puts it:

> If there is too much virtue somewhere, it is a sure sign
> that there is something wrong. . . . Why, if a general or
> king is stupid and lands his people in a mess, then they
> need desperate courage, a virtue. If he is too mean and
> recruits too few soldiers, then they have to be as strong
> as Hercules. And if he is slovenly and pays no attention,
> they have to be as clever as snakes, or else they are done
> for. They need special loyalty if he always asks too much
> of them. . . . All virtues that a proper country and a
> good king and general can do without. In a good country
> you need no virtues; people can all be quite ordinary,
> of middling intelligence and cowards, for all it mat-
> ters. . . .[8]

And in that most bitter of all of Brecht's plays, *The Exception and the Rule*, one of the characters proclaims this philosophy:

> Next to you someone is thirsty: quickly close your eyes!
> Plug up your ears: someone is groaning next to you!
> Restrain your foot: someone is calling for help!
> Woe to him who forgets himself! He
> Offers water to a man, and
> A wolf drinks![9]

The poor are mean and the rich are ruthless and cruel.
Repeatedly Brecht demonstrates his thesis that the suffering

poor, if given a chance to get on top, would be as greedy and heartless as the vulgar, rapacious businessmen he so delighted in putting before his audience. War is the natural state in a world peopled by men. And there is no justice. For all his love of courtroom scenes (there is hardly a play by Brecht without one) he denied that man can be an honest judge of his fellow men. The possibility of a Solomonic judgment like that of *The Caucasian Chalk Circle* has to be explained by the very peculiar circumstances that bring a real rogue, Azdak, to act as judge. Only the very young and very simple have something like innocence: the two St. Joans, Joan Dark of the Chicago stockyards and Simone Machard, the little French girl who dreams of saving her country in 1940. And they are doomed because of their innocence and goodness. The only innocent and good character who wins in the end is the servant girl Grusche in *The Caucasian Chalk Circle*, the mellowest of all the plays. But even she is warned against saving the helpless child: "Terrible is the temptation to goodness!"[10] And life continues only because the mothers doggedly and irrationally persist in rearing their young.

This, then, is a vision of the world in the great tragic tradition of pessimism that has inspired so much of dramatic literature from Aeschylus to Seneca, from Shakespeare to the present day. It is a world sullied by the presence of evil, the blind workings of irrational forces, a world without God. In Brecht's plays the place of fate is taken by the inscrutable workings of the social order, which molds the lives of the characters and tosses them into misfortune or happiness. Human personality is no longer an immutable essence but merely the product of the pull of social forces at any given moment. And human will is helpless against them.

That is the negative side of his view of the world. Again and again in his later years, Brecht asserted that this was only half the picture. On the positive side, he claimed, it was counterbalanced by the hope, the virtual certainty, of Communism. But invariably Brecht's plays have an elliptic construction: the negative side is presented at length and the world is shown to be a dreadful place. Sometimes at the very end there is a suggestion that all this must be, and could be, changed. Sometimes it is left entirely to the audience to draw this conclusion for itself. But the positive side is always merely postulated. It is never shown. The most positive play of all, *The Mother*, shows Pelageya Vlasova advancing in the van of the demonstrators of the October Revolution, on the very threshold of the new order, but not a single step is taken inside it. Play after play depicts the horrors of the world *before* the revolution. Only a single scene, the prologue to *The Caucasian Chalk Circle*, is laid inside the promised land —a collective farm in Soviet Russia. And here Soviet critics have angrily disclaimed any resemblance to the real thing and pointed out that the way Brecht's Soviet collective farmers behave is pure fantasy. Brecht wrote *The Caucasian Chalk Circle* in the United States, where, it could be argued, he was out of touch with the realities of the Communist order. But in eight years in East Berlin he was unable to produce a single play on the realities of life in Communist Germany. There he had the experience on his doorstep. The authorities alternately begged and ordered him to try his hand. He did not succeed.

The reason why he did not is only too obvious: the positive side represents not a scientifically demonstrable truth, but merely a pious and touching hope—a hope, moreover, which was constantly belied by Brecht's own experience of the real world. He had escaped despair by attributing all the horror and disgust he felt to the social order of his time, but what he in fact attacked was not human nature under capitalism but his personal experience of human nature itself. Analysis of his language shows that as a rule he is talking about *man, the world*, when he paints this pessimistic picture; only occasionally is there a qualifying clause: "man in these circumstances," "the world under this system," etc. Even then the truth of the proposition that the world can be changed for the better is never demonstrated. "Change the world: it needs to be changed!" is an exhortation that runs through Brecht's plays like a refrain. But he never succeeded in convincingly demonstrating *what* he wanted the world to be changed into and *how* it could be changed. "The Truth is concrete" was the slogan he displayed to his visitors in his workrooms in Denmark and Hollywood. It is an aphorism that contains the essence of the dramatist's objective and justifies his labors.

For science or philosophy can only generalize. The dramatist can put the truth in the only wholly convincing form because he creates a completely individual, concrete picture of reality. That is why it is, in Brecht's own terms, irrelevant what his political convictions were *outside* his work. The truth can be contained only within the concrete action of his plays themselves. But these *never* give concrete evidence of the feasibility, or even the nature, of the utopian state he aimed at. They are wholly negative, attacks upon the existing order.

In this, of course, Brecht was a genuine Marxist. Marx and Engels themselves never presented a concrete picture of the world order they wanted to create. They, too, were essentially critics. They criticized the social system of their day in brilliant, witty, copiously documented and often unfair terms; they analyzed the shortcomings of mid-nineteenth-century capitalism and proved to their own satisfaction that it was doomed to end in catastrophe. But when it came to defining the new order that was to take its place, their prophetic vision became a virtual blank. Brecht, too, was mainly a critic, brilliant in demonstrating the predicament of man, the iniquity of his institutions, somewhat naïve in exposing the details of the workings of business or high finance. But he had nothing concrete to offer when it came to showing how a better system would work. The very violence of his demand for a change, his recurrent assertion that things cannot, must not, go on as they are at present, springs from this failure.

If we extract the meaning contained in his plays in the concrete, three-dimensional form of the artist's re-creation of reality, the result belies the facile optimism of Brecht's professed, and monotonously asserted, eschatological hope of a Marxist earthly paradise. For he constantly shows the weakness of man, his inability to deal with his problems rationally, his subjection to instinct and blind passion. Poverty, he never tired of demonstrating, breeds meanness and selfishness. But the rich too are mean and selfish. Why? Because they thrive on a wicked system to which they, too, have to conform. Therefore the system must be changed. But, in Brecht's view, it cannot be changed slowly and gradually; only violence can bring about a really fundamental change. But violence is wicked. And wicked methods, as Brecht shows again and again, make wicked people. Brecht's creative power puts the proof of each of these propositions before us concretely and convincingly. And he was unable to suggest a way of breaking this vicious circle:

> Would you deny that the use of force debases him who resorts to it?
> No, I do not deny that.[11]

This brief exchange, which occurs in Brecht's last completed play, *The Days of the Commune*, sums up his dilemma. He could not solve it and was far too deeply imbued with the instinctive integrity of a real poet to bluff his way out with the empty rhetoric of a purple passage. After showing that the revolutionaries of the Paris Commune failed because their leaders were too idealistic, too tenderhearted to apply the terror in its ultimate ruthlessness, he could not deny that violence itself is evil and begets evil. Whether Brecht was aware of the implication or not, it is clearly there. Lenin, who *did* learn the lesson of the Paris Commune and did not shrink from violence, landed on the other horn of the dilemma. And this is not the dilemma of capitalism. It is the dilemma of human nature.

Brecht's work fails, as the Communists rightly felt, in conveying the message of hope in man's redemption by a radical change in the social order that he so earnestly and persistently sought to put into it. Yet the final effect of Brecht's negative picture of the human condition is not entirely one of despair. Again and again the hopelessness of man's lonely and senseless struggle is made bearable by its very acceptance by humble people who battle against the terrors of the universe in resignation and simplicity: Joan Dark, Simone Machard, Mother Courage, Schweik, Shen Te, Grusche—they all redeem themselves by their courage in the face of overwhelming odds.

One of the projects that occupied Brecht's mind but that he never completed was an opera, *Die Reisen des Gluecks-gotts* (*The Travels of the God of Fortune*), in which the Chinese god of fortune was to come into the ruined cities after a great war to urge the people to fight for their happiness. He comes into conflict with the authorities and is condemned to death.

> And now the hangmen try their arts on this little god of fortune. But the poisons they administer taste delightful to him, his head, which is cut off, immediately grows again, he executes a dance of contagious hilarity on the gallows, etc. It is impossible to kill humanity's yearning for happiness.[12]

Paul Dessau, who was to write the score, reports: "Happiness means Communism."[13] But again this identification, which Brecht certainly believed in, remains an abstract one, confined to the author's private convictions, and does not appear to have been put into concrete terms. What the opera would once more have put before the audience was the apparatus of force and authority at grips with the unquenchable desire of humanity for redemption from the evils of the world.

The little god who cannot be subdued by the hangman is also an image of nonviolence: he shows that executions and coercive measures are bound to fail. Here Brecht, in sympathy with the Chinese god of fortune whose tiny statuette he treasured, accepted the stoicism of the Orient. It is an attitude that recognizes the senselessness, the unreality of the world, but, having done so, reconciles itself to life and its everyday tasks. Long before he had discovered Confucianism and Taoism, Brecht had expressed similar sentiments; for example, in his early *Great Hymn of Thanksgiving*:

> *Praise the cold, the darkness and death down here,*
> *Look up from the ground:*
> *You are of no account*
> *And can die without fear.*[14]

This Taoist attitude of yielding to the flow of things, while recognizing its absurdity, in Brecht's mind coexisted with, and underlay, the doctrine of the class struggle and the gospel of the violent transformation of the world. This in fact is the passive attitude, the yielding to emotion, the abandonment of reason he so feared in his youth, transformed into a mellow and profound philosophy.

And so Brecht, the prophet of rational planning by violent methods, is also the author of a poem like *The Legend of the Origin of the Book Tao Te Ching during Lao Tzu's Journey into Exile*, where he preaches the wisdom of patient nonviolence. For,

> . . . *the movement of the softest water will*
> *Conquer in time the powerful hard stone.*
> *You understand: hard things are overcome.* . . .[15]

And in one of his late, epigrammatic poems Brecht speaks of the Japanese mask of an evil demon on his wall, whose distorted features show

> . . . *how strenuous it is to be evil.*[16]

Behind the loud, frenzied demand for violent change, dictated by the ruthless, cold process of scientific reasoning, there always lay a yearning for the quiet, passive acceptance of the world as it is, with all its harshness and absurdity. The more he forced himself into the strait jacket of discipline and purposeful activity, the more deeply he longed for the warmth of self-oblivion and self-abandon. Brecht's work as a director called for a style of relaxed ease. He abhorred the cramped features and strenuous movements of violent acting. The favorite image of his early poems is that of the swimmer who is carried down the river, gently drifting. But such was his nature that his passive moods gave way to yearnings for self-control and self-domination by discipline and strenuous activity. Powerful attractions and revulsions propelled him in different directions, and his poetry is the result of this highly complex parallelogram of forces. No wonder that it does not move in the direction his lucid, calculating intellect had planned.

This is the reason for the bewildering complexity of Brecht's artistic impact. Behind a surface of deceptive simplicity his work reveals layer after layer of surprising intricacy and depth. The Polish critic Andrzej Wirth has spoken of the "stereometric" construction of Brecht's plays, which always move on several levels of time, space, and narrative method at once. But the real secret of this three-dimensional effect lies not in any formal principle of construction but in the inner tensions and contradictions within the author's mind, conscious and subconscious. It seems that such deep conflicts within a personality are among the conditions without which major creative work cannot be produced, that such work must spring from the constant and painful clash between the different levels of the artist's personality. Only thus can there be more in a work than its creator consciously put into it. Only thus can it mean different things to different men and reveal new aspects to each succeeding generation.

But to Brecht himself, who could not suffer the idea that he was not wholly in control of his own activity, the obvious divergence between his intentions and the effect of his work on the public must have been truly tragic.

He wanted to be a writer for the common people, as easy to understand as fair-ground comedians, but the simpler he tried to be, the more complex his work became, so that only intellectuals could appreciate it; he wanted to serve the cause of the revolution, but was regarded with suspicion by its recognized standard-bearers, who reviled him as a formalist and banned him as a dangerous, defeatist influence; he wanted to arouse the critical faculties of his audience, but only succeeded in moving them to tears; he wanted to make his theatre a laboratory of social change, a living proof that the world and mankind could be altered, and had to see it strengthen his public's faith in the enduring virtues of unchanging human nature. He had to witness his villains acclaimed as heroes and his heroes mistaken for villains. He sought to spread the cold light of logical clarity—and produced a rich texture of poetic ambiguity. He abhorred the very idea of beauty—and created beauty.

Yet such is the paradox of the creative process that, had he succeeded in his objectives, he would have been merely a flat and boring party hack. He failed—and became one of the most puzzling, one of the most hotly debated, but also one of the most important writers of his age.

NOTES

1. *Erste Stuecke I*, p. 80.
2. Ibid., p. 98.
3. Eugene Ionesco, "The Playwright's Role," *The Observer*, London, 6.29.1958.
4. *Die Dreigroschenoper, Stuecke III*, p. 62.
5. *Mann ist Mann, Erste Stuecke II*, p. 272.
6. *Der Gute Mensch von Sezuan, Stuecke VIII*, p. 389.
7. Ibid., p. 402.
8. *Mutter Courage, Stuecke VII*, p. 88.
9. *Die Ausnahme und die Regel, Stuecke V*, p. 226.
10. *Der kaukasische Kreidekreis, Stuecke X*, p. 174.
11. *Die Tage der Kommune, Stuecke X*, p. 417.
12. Brecht, "Bei Durchsicht meiner ersten Stuecke," *Stuecke I*, East Berlin, p. 9.
13. Brecht and Dessau, *Lieder und Gesaenge*, East Berlin, 1957, p. 20.
14. Brecht, "Grosser Dankchoral," *Hauspostille*, Berlin, 1927, p. 62.
15. Brecht, "Legende vom der Enstehung des Buches Taoteking auf dem Wege des Lao Tse in die Emigration," *Hundert Gedichte*, East Berlin, 1951, p. 112.
16. Brecht, "Die Maske des Boesen," ibid., p. 309.

Part Five: FOR REFERENCE

A SHORT CHRONOLOGY OF BRECHT'S LIFE

1898	February 10. Born at Augsburg.
1904–8	Elementary school, Augsburg.
1908–17	Realgymnasium, Augsburg.
1914	August 17. Brecht's first contribution to a newspaper, a short prose sketch, published in *Augsburger Neueste Nachrichten*.
1917	Starts reading medicine and natural science at Munich University.
1918	Called up for military service as a medical orderly. Writes his first play, *Baal*.
1919	Continues his studies at Munich University, while acting as drama critic of *Der Volkswille*, Augsburg.
1920	"Dramaturg" at the Munich Kammerspiele.
1922	September 29. First night of *Drums in the Night*, Munich.
	November 3. Marries Marianne Zoff in Munich.
1923	May 9. First night of *In the Jungle*, Munich.
	December 8. First night of *Baal*, Leipzig.
1924	March 18. First night of *Edward II*, Munich.
	Autumn. Moves to Berlin.
1926	September 26. First night of *Man Equals Man*, Darmstadt.
1927	*Domestic Breviary* published.
	Summer. First version of *Mahagonny* (setting

of poems from *Domestic Breviary* by Kurt
Weill) performed at Baden-Baden.

November 22. Divorced from Marianne Zoff.

1928   January 23. First night of *Schweik*, adapted by
Gasbarra, Leo Lania, and Brecht, in Piscator's
production.

August 31. First night of *The Threepenny
Opera* at the Theater am Schiffbauerdamm.
Marries Helene Weigel.

December. Awarded first prize in *Berliner Illustrirte* short story competition for *The Beast*.

1929   Summer. First performance of *Flight of the
Lindberghs* and *Didactic Play of Baden* at
Baden-Baden Music Week.

August 31. Failure of *Happy End*.

1930   March 9. First night of *Rise and Fall of the
City of Mahagonny* at Leipzig.

October 17 and 20. Hearings of Brecht's lawsuit against the company producing the film
version of *The Threepenny Opera*.

December 10. First performance of *The Measures Taken* by Arbeiterchor Grossberlin.

1932   January 15. First performance of *The Mother*.
March. Brecht's film *Kuhle Wampe* banned.

1933   February 28. Leaves Germany.

Spring. Vienna, Switzerland, France.

June. *The Seven Deadly Sins* at Théâtre des
Champs-Elysées, Paris.

Settles in Denmark.

1935   June. International Writers' Congress, Paris.

November. Visits New York to attend performance of *The Mother* by the Theatre Union at the Civic Theatre.

1936   Becomes co-editor of *Das Wort*, Moscow.

November 4. First performance of *The Roundheads and the Peakheads*, Copenhagen.

1937   October 17. First performance of *Señora Carrar's Rifles*, Paris.

1938   May 21. First performance of *Fear and Misery*

of the Third Reich (seven scenes under the title "99%"), Paris.

1939	Summer. Leaves Denmark for Stockholm.
1940	Moves to Finland.
	April 19. First night of *Mother Courage* at Zurich.
1941	May 3. U. S. Consul at Helsinki issues visa for the United States.
	June 11. Leaves Vladivostok aboard a Swedish ship.
	July 21. Arrives San Pedro, California.
1942	May. Performance of five scenes from *Fear and Misery of the Third Reich* by refugee actors at New York.
	Film: *Hangmen Also Die.*
1943	February 4. First night of *The Good Woman of Setzuan* at Zurich.
	September 9. First night of *Galileo* at Zurich.
1945	Co-founder of German publishing house Aurora Verlag at New York.
	June 7. *The Private Life of the Master Race* (English version of *Fear and Misery*), first performance at Berkeley, California.
	June 12. *The Private Life of the Master Race* opens at New York with Albert Bassermann.
1947	July 30. English version of *Galileo* with Charles Laughton opens at Coronet Theatre, Hollywood.
	October 30. Brecht before the Un-American Activities Committee, Washington.
	November. Returns to Europe.
	December 7. *Galileo* opens in New York.
1948	February. *Antigone* at Chur (Coire), Switzerland.
	June 5. First night of *Mr. Puntila and His Hired Man, Matti*, Zurich.
	October 22. Arrives in Berlin to prepare production of *Mother Courage* at Deutsches Theater.

1949	January 11. *Mother Courage* opens at Deutsches Theater. Spring. Returns to Zurich. Autumn. Foundation of Berliner Ensemble. Brecht settles in East Berlin. November 8. Berliner Ensemble opens with *Puntila*.
1950	April. Application for Austrian nationality granted. October. Produces *Mother Courage* at Munich.
1951	March 17. *The Trial of Lucullus* withdrawn after one performance at Berlin State Opera. October 12. Revised version of *Lucullus*—*The Condemnation of Lucullus*—at Berlin State Opera. November 8. *Mère Courage*, produced by Théâtre Nationale Populaire at Paris.
1952	The Berliner Ensemble tours Poland: Warsaw, Cracow, Lodz, etc.
1953	June 17. Outbreak of East German uprising. June 21. Publication of Brecht's "message of loyalty" to Ulbricht (First Secretary of SED).
1954	March. Berliner Ensemble takes over the renovated Theater am Schiffbauerdamm. June 15. First night of *The Caucasian Chalk Circle*, ignored by party organ, *Neues Deutschland*. July. Berliner Ensemble in *Mother Courage* at Paris International Festival.
1955	May 26. Receives Stalin Peace Prize in Moscow. June. Berliner Ensemble in *The Caucasian Chalk Circle* at Paris International Festival.
1956	August 14. Dies of coronary thrombosis.

A DESCRIPTIVE LIST OF BRECHT'S PRINCIPAL WORKS

POEMS

The principal volumes of poetry or cycles of poems published individually in Brecht's lifetime are:

Augsburger Sonette. Only ten poems from this cycle of *juvenilia* have been preserved in private hands. Brecht himself, when asked about these poems, laughingly replied: "Just pornography."

Bertolt Brechts Taschenpostille (published 1926; reprinted East Berlin, 1958).

Bertolt Brecht's Pocket Breviary, privately printed in an edition limited to only twenty-five copies, is, except for one poem, identical with

Bertolt Brechts Hauspostille (published 1927). A German critic once called this *Domestic Breviary* the devil's prayer book. It is divided into five sections of "Lessons": (1) Intercessions; (2) Spiritual Exercises; (3) Chronicles; (4) Mahagonny Songs; (5) Little Book of Hours of the Departed. Three more personal poems are appended as a final section "Of Poor B.B." There are fifty poems in the book. Some of these Brecht had already used in his first plays, others appear in later plays. They include the ballads of *Baal, The Legend*

of the Dead Soldier, which is sung in *Drums in the Night,*
many of the songs in *Mahagonny* and *The Threepenny Opera,*
etc. The poetry of *Hauspostille* derives from the folk ballad
and the French cabaret *chanson* as well as from more strictly
literary models like Villon or Rimbaud. Its mood is one of
passive acceptance of nature with its sensuous beauty and its
horror, and of pity for all poor and helpless creatures.

Lesebuch fuer Staedtebewohner (published in *Versuche* 2,
1930). Described as "texts for gramophone records," the ten
poems in this *Primer for City-dwellers* deal with the loneliness
and lovelessness of the individual lost in the stone jungle of
the great cities.

Die Drei Soldaten (published in *Versuche* 6, 1932). *The
Three Soldiers,* a "children's book" with twenty-five illustrations by George Grosz, consists of fourteen stories in verse.
Three soldiers of the First World War refuse to die and return
to the cities. They want to help the poor and downtrodden.
But to accomplish this aim they *kill* all those poor people
who suffer from the consequences of the postwar crisis. They
want thus to induce the poor and downtrodden to cease to
accept unbearable conditions. The three soldiers are eventually revealed to be personifications of "Hunger," "Accident,"
and "Cough." When they get to Moscow, where there are
neither poor nor downtrodden people, they themselves are
killed. The book is intended "to provoke the children to ask
questions."

Gedichte, Lieder, Choere (published Paris, 1934), a collection of poems and songs that were set to music by Hanns
Eisler. In addition to the choruses and songs from *The Mother*
and *The Measures Taken,* it contains mainly political poems
written at the height of the economic crisis and the struggle
against Hitler.

Svendborger Gedichte (published London, 1939), a collection of poetry written in the years of exile in Denmark. It
includes a good deal of political verse of an ephemeral na-

ture (*Kriegsfibel*—antiwar quatrains; *Deutsche Satiren*—satirical poems written for broadcasting), but also some of Brecht's most outstanding narrative poems: *Der Schuh des Empedokles* (*The Shoe of Empedocles*); *Legende von der Entstehung des Buches Taoteking auf dem Weg des Laotse in die Emigration* (*Legend of the Origin of the Book Tao Te Ching during Lao Tzu's Journey into Exile*); *Gleichnis des Buddha vom Brennenden Haus* (*Buddha's Parable of the Burning House*), etc., as well as Brecht's most significant personal statement: *An die Nachgeborenen* (*To Posterity*).

Chinesische Gedichte (published in *Versuche 10*, 1950), nine poems from the Chinese, seven of them based on English versions by Arthur Waley, the two others being based on modern Chinese poems by Mao Tse-tung and Kuan Chao.

Studien (published in *Versuche 11*, 1951), eight "studies" in sonnet form, which elucidate—or debunk—literary masterpieces ranging from Dante's *Beatrice* and Shakespeare's *Hamlet* to Kant's *Metaphysics of Manners*.

Die Erziehung der Hirse (published 1951). *The Nurture of Millet*, a long poem of fifty-two stanzas, is based on a Soviet propaganda story of how an old Tartar peasant, following the precepts of Michurin and Lysenko, so improved the yield of millet that he made a vital contribution to the Soviet victory in the Second World War. One of Brecht's rare attempts to write a propaganda poem in the Soviet tradition and to extract the lyrical possibilities from the statistics of increased yields per hectare. Paul Dessau has set the poem to music.

Buckower Elegien (published in *Versuche 13*, 1954), six short poems written at Brecht's country retreat at Buckow, some of them in his late epigrammatic manner, modeled on the Japanese *haiku*. The cycle is, however, known to consist of a larger number of poems than the six published in *Versuche 13*.

Gedichte aus dem "Messingkauf" (published in *Versuche 14*,

1955), didactic poems on the theory of the "epic" theatre. (See below under "Essays and Theoretical Writings.")

A number of posthumous poems were published in *Sinn und Form*, Second Special Brecht Issue, 1957. They include some autobiographical poems from the thirties, among them the remarkable sequence

Vier Psalmen (Four Psalms), written in the middle thirties, four prose poems in Biblical language with a surrealist imagery quite unlike any of Brecht's other writing and reminiscent of St. John Perse.

Equally impressive is a group of Brecht's last poems:

Aus Letzten Gedichten, which includes his melancholy reflections from the time of the East German uprising (1953).

Three volumes of Brecht's selected poetry are easily obtainable. These are:

Hundert Gedichte (East Berlin, 1951; fifth amended edition, 1958). This selection is heavily biased towards Brecht's political output and does not do justice to his full range as a poet.

Brecht: Gedichte (Reclam, Leipzig, 1955), another East German selection in the famous cheap paperback series of Reclams Universalbibliothek (no. 7996/97). This, too, is a politically biased selection. Some of the poems have been ruthlessly mutilated or altered.

Bertolt Brechts Gedichte und Lieder (Frankfurt, 1956). Edited by Brecht's friend and publisher Peter Suhrkamp, this is by far the best anthology of Brecht's poetry available.

PLAYS AND OTHER STAGE WORKS

BAAL
Written: 1918.
First performance: Leipzig, December 8, 1923.
Baal, a loosely constructed sequence of twenty-two (in another version twenty-one) scenes, preceded by the ballad *"Choral vom grossen Baal"* ("Hymn of Great Baal"), tells the story of an ugly, asocial, vagabond poet. Baal is an amoral being who blindly follows his instincts. He has a fatal attraction for women, whom he ruthlessly discards when he is tired of them. He spends his life in a variety of Bohemian occupations (cabaret artist, owner of a merry-go-round), but mostly in taverns, where he sings his songs to the guitar. He acquires a friend, the composer Ekart. When he finds Ekart making love to a waitress he kills him in a fit of jealous rage. He flees from the police into the forests of the north, where he dies among the woodcutters.

Baal is a chaotically brilliant play in the tradition of German *Sturm und Drang*, Buechner and Wedekind. Its magnificently exuberant language expresses a passionate acceptance of the world in all its sordid grandeur.

TROMMELN IN DER NACHT (Drums in the Night)
Written: 1918.
First performance: Munich, September 29, 1922.
A comedy in five acts.
Berlin 1919: Kragler, a soldier returning from the war after years of captivity in Africa, finds his fiancée engaged to a repulsive profiteer. During the engagement party, held at the Piccadilly Bar, while the shooting of the Spartakus uprising can be heard from the street, Kragler appears like a ghost from the past and demands his girl back. Anna, who is pregnant by the shady profiteer, still loves Kragler but cannot bear to tell him what has happened and sends him away. As the drums of the doomed revolutionary uprising reverberate through the night, Kragler wanders through the streets, pur-

sued by Anna, who does not want to lose him after all. Kragler is about to join the Spartakists when Anna finds him, confesses her disloyalty, and asks forgiveness. Kragler hurls abuse at her but then nevertheless decides that he prefers a comfortable life with his bride, however shopworn she may be, to death as a revolutionary, however heroic. "Every man feels best in his own skin," he says. "I am a swine and the swine goes home!"

Drums in the Night is to be played with simple sets, over which the backdrop of the city appears. A huge red moon hangs like a Chinese lantern from the flies and symbolizes the atmosphere of doom that pervades the play. The auditorium is to be decorated with antiromantic slogans.

Drums in the Night was one of the first of a long line of plays about returning soldiers. It is still one of the best.

In the collected edition of his plays, published after Brecht's return to East Berlin, Brecht tried to offset the anti-revolutionary cynicism of his hero by introducing some references to a young revolutionary who does fight for the cause and dies a hero's death. But hardly anyone would have noticed this amendment if Brecht had not specially drawn the readers' attention to it in his introduction. The play remains a violent rejection of all heroic cant, whether militarist or revolutionary.

IM DICKICHT DER STAEDTE (In the Jungle of the Cities)
Written: 1921–23.
First performance: Munich, May 1923.
Eleven scenes, subtitled: "The Struggle of Two Men in the Giant City of Chicago." An earlier version was called *Im Dickicht* (*In the Jungle*). This is an attempt to write a play about a fight without motive. The public is especially asked not to wrack its brains about the motives of the wrestling match it is about to watch, but to savor it like a sporting contest and to concentrate on the *style* of the opponents.

Chicago 1912: Shlink, a middle-aged, well-to-do timber merchant, a Malay from Yokohama, becomes obsessed with a desire to dominate the will of young Garga, a clerk in a lending library. Garga refuses to sell his opinion about a book, and from this opening move the strange duel between the two men develops. Shlink seeks to gain possession of

Garga's soul. Garga refuses to be bought, cajoled, or even to be won over by gratitude when Shlink makes him a gift of his thriving business. He revenges himself by concluding a fraudulent deal in Shlink's name that must lead to Shlink's disgrace as a swindler. But when Shlink is about to be arrested, Garga to shame him takes the blame and goes to prison himself. He deposits a letter with a newspaper, to be opened shortly before his release is due, that accuses Shlink of the rape of Garga's sister (who is in fact deeply in love with Shlink) and is certain to lead to his being lynched. As the lynching mob approaches, Shlink and Garga face each other and realize that man's loneliness is so great that not even a fight like theirs can establish real contact between human beings. "If you crammed a ship full of human bodies till it burst, the loneliness inside it would be so great that they would turn to ice . . . so great is our isolation that even conflict is impossible."

This strange play anticipates the plays of Beckett, Ionesco, and Adamov, which it resembles by its insistence on the impossibility of communication. Garga recites passages lifted from Rimbaud's *Une Saison en enfer*, and in many ways the relationship between him and Shlink resembles that of Rimbaud and Verlaine. The setting is a fantastically exotic dream-America, and there are a number of complicated side plots involving Garga's sister and wife and a number of Chicago gangsters.

In the Jungle of the Cities is one of Brecht's most difficult but also one of his most intriguing creations.

LEBEN EDUARDS DES ZWEITEN VON ENGLAND (Life of Edward II of England)

Written (in collaboration with Lion Feuchtwanger): 1923–24.

First performance: Munich, March 18, 1924.

A history, after Marlowe.

Marlowe's *Edward II* very freely adapted. The plot has been concentrated and coarsened so that the relationship between Edward and Gaveston, which Marlowe treats with a certain amount of discretion, becomes an openly homosexual infatuation. The effect aimed at is that of the crude vitality of an old broadsheet ballad or a historical "panorama" as it was displayed at country fairs. Captions giving the place and exact (though freely invented) date of the action and other devices of the "epic" theatre are used. The language of the play is a rough, highly irregular form of blank verse of great vigor and poetic impact.

The story of Edward II's love for Gaveston, his war with the barons, his capture and execution, and the revenge of his young son upon his murderers is, however, told without any political or social moral, but merely as an illustration of the futility of human ambition and the blind turnings of the wheel of fortune.

GOESTA BERLING

The Prologue to a planned stage version of Selma Lagerloef's novel was published in the periodical *Das Kunstblatt*, Potsdam, January 1924. It is described as based on an adaptation of the novel by E. Karin and is written in rhymed couplets. Other fragments of this adaptation are preserved in the Brecht Archive in East Berlin.

DIE HOCHZEIT (The Wedding—later renamed DIE KLEINBUERGER HOCHZEIT, The Petty Bourgeois Wedding)

Written: 1919.
First performance: Frankfurt, December 11, 1926.
Unpublished.
A one-act play in the slapstick tradition of Bavarian folk comedy. The wedding reception is in the newly married couple's apartment. The bridegroom boasts that he has made the furniture himself. But he has made it badly. As the veneer of gentility fades from the proceedings and the guests lose their party manners, one piece of furniture after another collapses. The resulting recrimination reveals that all is not as it seems. The bride is already pregnant, the bridegroom suspects her of infidelity, etc. But as the guests depart peace is re-established. The lights go out and as the curtain falls the bridal bed is heard to collapse with a mighty crash.

This unpretentious play, which was a complete failure at its performance in Frankfurt, also foreshadows the "pure" theatre of the fifties.

DER BETTLER ODER DER TOTE HUND (The Beggar or The
  Dead Dog)
Written: 1919.
This one-act play, which has never been performed, consists,
according to Schumacher, of a dialogue between a king and a
blind beggar. The beggar hurls abuse at the king and dis-
concerts him by revealing the loathing of the common people
for the meaningless antics of the mighty. For the blind beggar
a dead dog is more important than the mighty king and all
his futile activity.

ER TREIBT EINEN TEUFEL AUS (He Exorcises A Devil)
Written: 1919.
Another one-act play in the style of Bavarian folk comedy. A
village wooing is constantly disturbed by the girl's parents.
The lovers in their attempt to elude these intrusions end up
on the roof of the house.

LUX IN TENEBRIS (Light in Darkness)
Written: 1919.
The last in this group of early one-act plays deals with hypocrisy in matters of sex. In a brothel street, Paduk, a shady entrepreneur, has set up an exhibition on venereal disease,
which, though it pretends to be intended to combat immorality, is in fact visited by a clientele no less prurient than that
of the brothel opposite. The brothelkeeper, Madame Hogge,
reveals that Paduk himself is a former *habitué* of her establishment and seeks revenge for having been thrown out. In
the end Paduk, after making a vigorous speech against vice, is
won over by an invitation to avail himself of the facilities of
Madame Hogge's institution, becomes a partner in it, and
closes his antivice exhibition.

KALKUTTA, 4. MAI (Calcutta, May 4)
Feuchtwanger's play *Warren Hastings, Gouverneur von In-
dien* (written 1915, published 1916), revised by Feucht-
wanger and Brecht in 1925. English translation: *Warren
Hastings* (in *Feuchtwanger: Two Anglo-Saxon Plays*) by
Willa and Edwin Muir. Martin Secker, London, 1929.
A colonial history in four acts.

Warren Hastings appalls the Commissioners of the East India Company, sent out to investigate his conduct, by the ruthlessness and cynicism of his methods. But though he is cruel and corrupt, he is not out for personal gain but to fulfill his civilizing mission. Brecht's hand can be seen clearly only in the song "Surabaya Johnny" (sung by Warren Hastings's mistress, Lady Marjorie Hike), which he used again in *Happy End*.

MANN IST MANN (Man Equals Man)
Written: 1924–25.
First performance: Darmstadt, September 26, 1926.
A comedy.
The transformation of the porter Galy Gay in the military barracks of Kilkoa in the year 1925. The scene is a fantastical India based on Kipling's *Barrack-Room Ballads*. Galy Gay, an Irish dockworker in the port of Kilkoa, a mild little man who cannot say no, goes out to buy a fish for supper. He encounters three British soldiers who have been trying to rob a pagoda and have lost the fourth member of their squad in the process. They would be discovered as the wanted temple thieves if they failed to produce the fourth man, so they decide that Galy Gay must be transformed into the soldier Jeriah Jip. One man, they argue, is as good as another and human personality can be taken apart and reassembled like a motorcar. With the help of the canteen landlady, Leocadia Begbick, the great transformation scene is set in motion. As each phase is announced like a circus act, poor Galy Gay is first involved in an illicit business deal, made to feel guilty, apprehended, sentenced to be shot, put through a mock execution, and as he reawakens from his faint his mind is such a blank that he consents to pronounce the funeral oration for Galy Gay. Having been persuaded that he is Jeriah Jip, the soldier, he takes part in the campaign against Tibet and captures the frontier fortress singlehanded. A side plot shows the consequences of being too attached to one's personality: Sergeant Fairchild, nicknamed "Bloody Five," is a fierce warrior and great disciplinarian. But whenever it rains he succumbs to his sensuality and cannot resist the seduction of

women. To avoid disgracing himself and to keep his honorable nickname he castrates himself.

Man Equals Man marks the turning point in Brecht's development from the anarchic nihilism of his youth to social awareness and didacticism. The theme of the play is the malleability of man, the possibility of social engineering. With amazing intuition Brecht grasped the essence of later brainwashing techniques.

DAS ELEPHANTENKALB (The Baby Elephant)
Written: 1924–25.

An interlude for performance in the foyer during the interval of *Man Equals Man*. This short surrealist extravaganza is an attempt at creating a kind of sideshow based on pure clowning. The actor of Galy Gay appears as a baby elephant accused of having murdered its mother. Although the mother is proved to be alive, and the baby elephant is proved not to be her child, the case against it is found proven.

This short play also anticipates the "antitheatre" of thirty years later. Moreover, being the outcome of almost completely free association, it gives a fascinating insight into Brecht's subconscious mind.

DIE DREIGROSCHENOPER (The Threepenny Opera)
Written: 1928.
First performance: Berlin, Theater am Schiffbauerdamm, August 31, 1928.
Ballad opera.
Music by Kurt Weill.

This free adaptation of John Gay's *Beggar's Opera* with ballads inspired by Villon and Kipling is the only play by Brecht that has achieved real popular success.

Although it has been transferred into a fantastic late nineteenth-century Soho, the main line of Gay's plot has been kept. Polly, the daughter of Peachum, the king of the beggars, still marries the robber Macheath. Peachum, who disapproves of the match, still wants his son-in-law to be hanged. But the chief of police is now called Brown, nicknamed Tiger Brown, and has served with Macheath, "Mac the Knife," in the Indian Army. Being in Macheath's pay, and his friend, Tiger

Brown has to be blackmailed into having him arrested by the terrible threat that hordes of disgusting beggars will otherwise mar the coronation of a young queen that is about to take place. Macheath is warned to leave London, but the force of habit is so strong that he cannot give up his usual Thursday afternoon with the whores of his favorite brothel at Turnbridge [sic]. He is arrested, but escapes with the help of Lucy, Brown's daughter, another of his bigamous wives. Again he goes to the brothel, and again he is arrested. This time there is no escape. Already he stands on the scaffold, the noose round his neck. But this is opera, not real life. A mounted messenger arrives with the queen's pardon, the award of a country house, and a pension of £10,000 per annum. Lest we forget, however, that such things do not happen in real life, the play ends with a solemn chorus imploring mankind to forgive all malefactors.

HAPPY END
Written (in collaboration with Elisabeth Hauptmann): 1928–29.
First performance: Berlin, Theater am Schiffbauerdamm, August 31, 1929.
A musical play.
Music by Kurt Weill.
This attempt to cash in on the success of *The Threepenny Opera* was billed as an adaptation of an American short story by "Dorothy Lane," which never existed.

Set in Chicago before the First World War, *Happy End* describes the efforts of a Salvation Army girl, Lilian Holiday, to save a group of gangsters, led by a mysterious lady in gray, "The Fly." To win the gangsters' confidence Lilian has to conform to their tastes, to sing seductive songs, and to lure one of the gangsters into a *tête-à-tête* in order to prevent him from taking part in a robbery. Eventually the gang, who are being hotly pursued by the police, decide to join the Salvation Army.

This musical play, which contains some of Brecht's most effective jazz lyrics, was a complete failure. The plot is curiously similar to that of the American musical *Guys and Dolls*, based on Damon Runyon's story, *The Idyll of Sarah Brown*, which first appeared in *Collier's* (1933).

DER FLUG DER LINDBERGHS (The Flight of the Lindberghs
—later renamed DER OZEANFLUG, The Atlantic Flight)
Written: 1928–29.
First performance: Baden-Baden Music Week, Summer 1929.
Published: *Versuche 1*.
Didactic radio play for boys and girls.
Music by Kurt Weill and Paul Hindemith.
Lindbergh (who is impersonated by a chorus, to avoid any
suggestion of individual hero-worship) describes his famous
flight, while the American newspapers discuss his chances of
success; fog, snowstorms, and weariness try to defeat him. He
meditates on the significance of his adventure: it is a battle
against the primitive forces of nature and will sweep the idea
of God from the heavens. When he arrives at his destination,
his achievement is greeted as a triumph of the forces of enlightenment.

FATZER 3
Written: *c.* 1930.
Two scenes from an uncompleted play, *Untergang des Egois-
ten Johann Fatzer (Downfall of the Egoist Johann Fatzer)*.
This curious fragment deals with the efforts of Fatzer, the
leader of a group of army deserters in the last stage of the
war, to secure a quantity of black-market meat for them. He
persuades a soldier to let him have part of an army consign-
ment of beef, but when the soldier appears at the meeting
place they have agreed on, Fatzer fails to turn up. The other
members of Fatzer's group cannot recognize the soldier. One
of the members of Fatzer's band is Keuner, the hero of
Brecht's anecdotes, *Geschichten vom Herrn Keuner*. The
Fatzer fragment is followed by a poem, entitled *Fatzer, Komm*
(probably "Commentary on Fatzer"), which deals with the
need to change the social order.

AUFSTIEG UND FALL DER STADT MAHAGONNY (Rise and Fall
of the City of Mahagonny)
Written: 1928–29.
First performance: Leipzig, March 1930.
Published: *Versuche 2; Stuecke III*.

Music by Kurt Weill. Opera.

Unlike *The Threepenny Opera*, which is a ballad opera, *Mahagonny* was designed for performance in opera houses, although Weill wrote it for an orchestra of only about thirty "specialists."

A group of shady characters on the run from the police towards the gold fields of the north decide that it would be more profitable to establish a business that takes money from the gold miners than to dig for gold themselves. Led by the widow Leocadia Begbick, the canteen landlady from *Man Equals Man*, they build the city of Mahagonny, where the hard-working men of the world will be able to buy any pleasure they may desire.

Four such men, woodcutters who have spent seven years in Alaska, arrive: Paul (called Jim Mahoney in an earlier version), Heinrich, Jakob, and Joe. But they are not happy. There are still too many restrictions and regulations. In a moment of terror, when an approaching hurricane is almost certain to bring death and destruction to Mahagonny, Paul has an inspiration. He discovers the real principle of happiness: the abolition of *all* restrictions. Everything must be permitted. When the hurricane mysteriously spares Mahagonny, Paul's discovery becomes its supreme law: love-making, eating, fighting, and drinking become the sole duties of the citizens. But self-indulgence leads to ruin: Jakob, the glutton, eats himself to death; Joe, the fighter, is killed in a boxing bout; Paul, who has found fleeting love in the arms of the prostitute Jenny, spends all his money on drink and incurs a large debt. He is arrested and tried on a number of charges. Of most of these he is acquitted. But for the greatest crime of all he is sentenced to death: lack of money. In the electric chair he realizes that the society he has created was founded on greed: "The joy that I bought was no joy and freedom for money was not freedom." As he dies processions of the inhabitants march and countermarch across the stage, carrying posters that proclaim the helplessness and chaos of such a society. The final chorus is a cry of despair: "We cannot help ourselves— or you—or any man."

Mahagonny is a powerful symbol of the *laissez-faire* society of the late twenties and its feeling of helplessness in the face of the great economic crisis. It also proclaims Brecht's conviction that art should not just sell pleasurable emotion but serve the improvement and instruction of man.

DAS BADENER LEHRSTUECK VOM EINVERSTAENDNIS (The Didactic Play of Baden: On Consent)
Written: 1928–29.
First performance: Baden-Baden Music Week, Summer 1929.
Published: *Versuche 2, Stuecke III.*
A short oratorio with an interlude of clowning.
Music by Paul Hindemith.
Four airmen who have tried to cross the Atlantic have crash-landed. They do not want to die and ask mankind for help. The two choirs ("skilled choir" and "mass choir") debate the question: "Does man help man?" The evidence produced in the course of the debate includes pictures of men killing men in this century and a scene between three clowns. A giant clown, Herr Schmitt, complains that various parts of his body hurt. The two other clowns cure his ailments by sawing off the limbs in question, until in the end, with arms and legs and even his head torn off, Herr Schmitt is completely dismantled. The conclusion: man does not help man. The four airmen will have to die. The pilot refuses to accept the necessity of his extinction. The three mechanics, however, accept the choirs' instruction that death can be overcome only by consenting to the inevitable necessities of history. The pilot who has clung to his individual desire for life and glory is annihilated. The three mechanics are redeemed, for "you who have consented to the flow of things will not sink back into nothingness." Violence and death cannot be overcome by palliatives. Only when a just world order is established will violence disappear.

An obscure but significant work.

DER JASAGER (He Who Says Yes)
Written: 1929–30.
First performance: Berlin, 1930.
School opera. Based on the Japanese Nō-play *Taniko*, translated by Arthur Waley.
Music by Kurt Weill.

A remote village. The schoolteacher is about to leave for a journey across the mountains. He has to bring back medicine to fight an epidemic. A boy whose mother is ill joins the party: he wants to consult the doctors in the town about her ailment. During the journey the boy falls ill. The expedition will have to be abandoned if the boy is not to be left by himself in the wilderness. According to an ancient custom he is asked whether he consents to being left behind. He answers yes, but asks to be killed rather than to suffer a slow death. He is thrown into the abyss.

DER NEINSAGER (He Who Says No)
Written: 1930.
A revised version of *Der Jasager*, in deference to criticisms made by pupils of schools that had performed that opera. The teacher's expedition is no longer a journey to obtain medicine against an epidemic, but a journey of exploration. Nor is the need to kill the boy when he falls ill the outcome of circumstances. An old custom demands that anyone abandoned in that spot *must* be thrown into the abyss. This time, however, the boy refuses to consent to die. He rejects the old custom: "I see the need for a *new* custom, which must be established at once: the custom of thinking afresh in every new situation." The teacher and his party recognize the force of this argument and turn back, taking the boy with them.

DER BROTLADEN (The Bread Shop)
Written: 1929–30.
This unfinished play, a forerunner of *St. Joan of the Stockyards,* deals with helpless humanity overwhelmed by the elemental force of economic crisis, which strikes like a hurricane. Meininger, the owner of the bread shop, asks his caretaker, the widow Queck, to order a load of firewood for him. When his bank forecloses his mortgage, Meininger disowns his order and the poor woman is faced with ruin. A Salvation Army girl, Miss Hippler, and a Communist, Washington Meyer, try to help her, while a chorus of unemployed comments on the action.

The Bread Shop treats of trivial events in heroic language, particularly during a scuffle involving the unemployed, which is presented in Homeric idiom as "the Battle of the Bread Shop."

DIE HEILIGE JOHANNA DER SCHLACHTHOEFE (St. Joan of the Stockyards)

Written: 1929–30.

First performance: Berlin radio, April 11, 1932. First stage performance: Hamburg, April 30, 1959.

This long play, which contains a good deal of parody of German classical drama (Schiller's *Maid of Orleans*, Goethe's *Faust*, etc.), tells the story of Joan Dark (i.e., d'Arc), a simple girl belonging to "The Black Straw Hats," an evangelical organization modeled on the Salvation Army. Trying to alleviate the misery of the working people in the stockyards of Chicago, she learns that unemployment and misery are caused by the machinations of Pierpont Mauler, the canned-meat king, who is waging a life-and-death struggle with his competitors. Joan seeks him out, recognizes him—as St. Joan recognized the Dauphin—and tries to persuade him to help the suffering masses. Mauler is strangely touched by the girl's innocence. But he wants to show her that the poor are wicked and not worthy of her efforts. Joan is shown the wickedness of the poor, but realizes that they are wicked only because of their poverty. The meat-packers want to use "The Black Straw Hats" to divert the attention of the unemployed from their plight. Joan drives them out of the temple, but is expelled from "The Black Straw Hats." She decides to share the sufferings of the unemployed until Mauler consents to reopen the canning plants. The Communists want to persuade the other workers of the city to join them in a general strike. They send out messengers. Joan offers to carry one of the letters. But when she realizes that the Communists will not hesitate to use violence, she has doubts and fails to deliver her letter. The strike collapses. Mauler has smashed his competitors and is reopening the factories. But Joan, worn down by the privations she has taken upon herself, is dying; with her last breath she proclaims her newly found conviction that the world cannot be improved without violence. But the meat-packers and "The Black Straw Hats," who want to use the touching story of Joan's martyrdom for their pious propaganda, drown her last words with their pseudo-religious claptrap (modeled on the final scene of the second part of Goethe's *Faust*), by which she is canonized as the valiant little St. Joan of the Stockyards.

Although the long scenes of stock-exchange intrigues give a grotesquely naïve picture of the workings of capitalism, *St. Joan of the Stockyards* is one of Brecht's finest achievements.

DIE MASSNAHME (The Measures Taken)
Written: 1930.
First performance: Berlin, December 10, 1930, by the Arbeiterchor Grossberlin (Greater Berlin Workers' Choir). Music by Hanns Eisler.

Labeled by Brecht a "didactic play," *The Measures Taken* is a dramatic cantata performed by four soloists (one woman, three men) and chorus. The chorus represents the conscience of the Communist party (hence: *Kontrollchor*—control chorus). The four soloists are a group of party workers (agitators) who have returned from an illegal mission in China (the time is the 1920s) and report the liquidation of a member of their group. The "control chorus" invites them to act out what has happened, before it can pronounce judgment on *the measure* they felt compelled to take. The four agitators then report the incidents that led to their decision in dramatic form, playing all the parts—with *each* taking *the part of the young comrade*, who was killed, *in turn*.

At the last party house before the frontier the four agitators asked for a guide who knew the country. The young comrade was assigned this task. Before they started on their journey the party workers solemnly pledged themselves to efface their previous personalities. This descent into anonymity, a solemn, almost religious act ("the extinction"), is symbolized by the masking of their faces.

Inside China the young comrade's inability to control his emotion has four times endangered the illegal party work of the agitators: instead of exploiting the hardships of the coolies pulling the rice boats on the river, he found a way of alleviating their plight and thereby delayed their revolt; unable to bear seeing another man arrested for distributing illegal leaflets for which he himself was responsible, he attacked a policeman, alerted the authorities, and frustrated the party's propaganda work; sent to negotiate with a local capitalist who might become an ally in the fight against the imperialists, he was so revolted by the man's vileness that he broke off the talks; and lastly, he could not bear to see the sufferings of the starving unemployed, and in defiance of the party's order he led their premature uprising and thereby disclosed his identity as an emissary of Moscow. This is symbolized by his tearing off his mask.

The agitators, whose continued illegal work depended on their not being recognized, had to protect themselves. The young comrade had to disappear without a trace. He himself saw that there was no other way out, confessed his errors and asked to be liquidated. So they shot him and threw his body into a chalk pit, where the quicklime was sure to obliterate its traces.

Having listened to this account, the control chorus acquits the four agitators of any guilt and signifies its approval of the measure they have taken in the interest of the party.

The Measures Taken is a work of severe purity, grimly austere but without doubt one of Brecht's best works. Years before the great Soviet purge trials it expressed the essential nature of Stalinist Communism. Owing to Brecht's uncannily penetrating intuitive grasp of the realities of the problem of totalitarianism, the play transcends its author's conscious intention and becomes a classical statement of its basic dilemma.

DIE AUSNAHME UND DIE REGEL (The Exception and the Rule)
Written: 1930.
First performance: Paris, 1947 (in French).
Music by Paul Dessau.
This short didactic play tells the story of a merchant who is trying to cross a desert in Asia at great speed in order to beat a competitor. He ruthlessly drives his coolie porter. In the waterless desert, when their supplies are running low, the kindly coolie offers the merchant some water he has secretly hoarded in his flask. The merchant mistakes the gesture for

an attack upon his life and kills the coolie. At the subsequent
trial it is established that the coolie only wanted to help. The
judge, however, finds that the coolie had every reason to hate
the merchant, so that the latter could not expect an act of
kindness from him and was justified in interpreting the
coolie's gesture as an attack. The merchant is acquitted as
having acted in legitimate self-defense. In our world an act
of kindness is an exception, hatred and violence the rule, by
which alone we can regulate our conduct.

DIE MUTTER: Leben der Revolutionaerin Pelagea Wlassowa
aus Twer (The Mother: Life of the Revolutionary Pelageya
Vlasova from Tver)
Written: 1930–32.
First performance: Berlin, January 12, 1932.
Music by Hanns Eisler.
This very free adaptation of Gorky's novel, which continues
Gorky's story that ends in 1905 to the eve of the October
Revolution of 1917, intentionally neglects the psychological
and sentimental aspects of the characters. It is intended as a
primer of revolutionary method and gives a wealth of practical demonstrations of effective action and propaganda. Pelageya Vlasova at first disapproves of her son's revolutionary
work, but gradually, to protect him, she is drawn into it: she
learns to read and write, converts the neighbors, carries the
message of the party into the countryside. Her son is shot. But
she continues the good work. On the eve of the October Revolution she marches in the van of the striking munitions
workers.
   The Mother is written in a dry, puritanical style; even the
songs and choral passages are strictly didactic. But the central
figure nevertheless emerges as a human being: dignified, sly,
stubborn, and heroic.

DIE RUNDKOEPFE UND DIE SPITZKOEPFE (The Roundheads
and the Peakheads)
Written: 1932–34.
First performance: Copenhagen, November 4, 1936.
Music by Hanns Eisler.
A long parable play about Hitler's race theories, based on the

plot of Shakespeare's *Measure for Measure*. The land of Yahoo is threatened by an uprising of the poor tenant farmers. The Viceroy is persuaded to meet the crisis by handing over power to Angelo Iberin, a demagogue, who promises that he will deal with the situation. He proclaims the racial superiority of the Roundheads over the Peakheads, and thus confuses the clear-cut social distinction that lies between rich and poor. The rich landlord De Guzman has seduced the daughter of his tenant, the peasant Callas. As a Peakhead he is accused of having ruined the honor of a Roundhead and is sentenced to death. But when the father of the girl claims his rights as a Roundhead and takes possession of a team of horses belonging to De Guzman, the laws of property are upheld by the court. Isabella, De Guzman's sister and a novice in a convent, learns that she might save her brother's life by spending the night with the commandant of the concentration camp where her brother awaits his execution. She pays Nanna Callas, who has become a prostitute, to take her place. De Guzman's lawyers persuade old Callas, who is in debt to his landlord, to take De Guzman's place under the gallows. The Viceroy returns and uncovers the substitutions: despite the race theory the poor among the Roundheads are still at a disadvantage, being poor. But the racial issue has diverted the attention of the poor and led to the defeat of the revolutionary movement. The country can now safely plan an attack against the land of the Squareheads.

DIE SIEBEN TODSUENDEN DER KLEINBUERGER (ANNA ANNA)
(The Seven Deadly Sins of the Petty Bourgeois [Anna Anna])
Written: *c*. 1933.
First performance: Paris, June 1933, by "Les Ballets 1933."
Music by Kurt Weill.
Choreography by George Balanchine.
Ballet cantata.
The story of two sisters, both called Anna, who are aspects of the same personality. Anna I (the singer) represents her rational self, Anna II (the dancer) her emotional, instinctive nature.

Anna leaves her home in Louisiana to earn enough money for the building of a house for her family. As the ballet proceeds the house gradually rises in the background and the family is seen and heard admonishing Anna to work harder. Anna is a dancer. To make money she has to avoid committing the seven deadly sins of commercial society, which in fact represent the healthy instincts of her nature: she must not eat (greed), lest she grow fat; she must not love the man she wants (lust) but the one who pays; she must overcome her pride and exhibit herself in strip-tease shows, etc. Having resisted these temptations Anna can return to Louisiana, where the money she has earned has given her family a home.

DIE HORATIER UND DIE KURIATIER (The Horatians and the Curiatians)

Written: 1934.

First performance: Halle, April 26, 1958.

Music by Kurt Schwaen.

Didactic play.

This short and rather arid piece deals with dialectics and tactics. To distract their people's attention from internal social conflicts, the Curiatians attack the Horatians. As in Chinese classical theatre, whole armies are represented by single actors, who carry little flags on their shoulders to symbolize their strength. Each time a unit is destroyed, a flag is discarded. The course of the struggle demonstrates the principles of Marxist dialectics (identical actions have different values in differing circumstances) and of Marxist tactics (the weaker Horatians tire their attackers by hasty retreat and then beat their three detachments one by one. "The flight was an attack.")

FURCHT UND ELEND DES DRITTEN REICHES (Fear and Misery of the Third Reich)

Written: 1935–38.

First performance: Selected scenes under the title "99%" in Paris, May 1938. An English version (*The Private Life of the Master Race*) (17 scenes) by Eric Bentley at Berkeley, California, June 7, 1945, New York, June 12, 1945.

Twenty-eight scenes of varying length, four of which have never been published, describing various aspects of life in Hitler's Reich: the brutality of the concentration camps, the struggle of the Communist underground movement, anti-Semitism, Goebbels' propaganda, etc. Among the most effective episodes are "*Rechtsfindung*" ("Justice"), in which a judge is at a loss how to decide a case of robbery in a Jewish shop; "*Die juedische Frau*" ("The Jewish Wife"), in which a Jewish woman decides to leave her non-Jewish husband to save his career; "*Zwei Baecker*" ("Two Bakers"), a short scene in a prison yard where one baker is in prison because he has adulterated his bread, the other because he *failed* to adulterate his under a new Nazi law; "*Der Spitzel*" ("The Informer"), in which a schoolboy's parents are terrified because they cannot trust the boy not to report some anti-Nazi remarks of theirs, etc.

These playlets are written in a rather un-Brechtian, naturalistic convention. They show his ability to write in a conventional style, but also his limitations outside his personal manner.

DIE GEWEHRE DER FRAU CARRAR (Señora Carrar's Rifles)
Written: 1937.
First performance: Paris, October 1937.
Play in one act, based on Synge's *Riders to the Sea*.
Teresa Carrar's husband, an Andalusian fisherman, has been killed in the Asturian uprising. Now, at the height of the Spanish Civil War, she is determined to keep her son Juan out of the fighting. Señora Carrar's brother, a worker who is in the Republican Army, comes to ask for a cache of rifles hidden in the house by her late husband. She violently defends her decision to keep out of the war. But one cannot remain neutral: fishermen bring the body of her son, who has been machine-gunned while fishing. A Nationalist gunboat fired at him, merely because he wore a workman's cloth cap. Teresa Carrar herself goes out to fight against Franco.

Brecht notes that this play is written in the "Aristotelian" convention. It is effective theatre and gives great opportunities to the actress playing Señora Carrar.

MUTTER COURAGE UND IHRE KINDER (Mother Courage and
    Her Children)

Written: 1939.

First performance: Zurich, April 19, 1941.

A chronicle of the Thirty Years' War.

Music by Paul Burkhard (for Zurich performance); by Paul
    Dessau (for Berliner Ensemble).

Mother Courage is a character in Grimmelshausen's seventeenth-century picaresque writings, but Brecht has used only
the name. Anna Fierling, nicknamed "Mother Courage," is an
itinerant trader who follows the Swedish and Imperial armies
with her covered wagon, selling the soldiers shoes, shirts,
brandy, etc. She has three children, each from a different father: two sons—the daring Eilif and the slow but honest
Schweizerkas ("Swiss Cheese")—and one daughter—Katrin,
who has been dumb and mentally retarded since a soldier hit
her as a child, but who nevertheless is a motherly, tenderhearted creature.

Mother Courage lives by the war, so she must pay the war
its due. One by one she loses her children. Schweizerkas becomes paymaster in a Swedish regiment. When the Imperialists overrun its camp he hides the regimental cashbox. Too
honest to betray his trust, he has to die. Mother Courage
could save him, if she sold her wagon. But she haggles too
long about the price. Schweizerkas is shot. Eilif has become a
hero, because he requisitioned a herd of cattle during a siege.
He repeats his exploit during a brief period of armistice and
is executed as a looter. Poor dumb Katrin, disfigured by the
assaults of lecherous soldiers, overhears a plan to take the
town of Halle by stealth. She cannot bear the thought of
women and children being killed, rouses the town by beating
a drum, and is shot by the soldiers. Mother Courage is left
alone. Determined to continue trading, she wearily pulls her
cart to catch up with the army.

Written in the forceful, coarse language of its period,
Mother Courage is rich in brilliantly observed characters: the
Protestant chaplain, who escapes capture by disguising him-
self as Mother Courage's tapster and handyman and dis-
courses in elevated language; the Dutch cook, who lives with
Mother Courage for a while, offers to marry her when he in-

herits a tavern in Utrecht, but leaves her when she insists on taking her dumb daughter with her; the harlot Yvette, who ends up as the wealthy widow of an Austrian colonel, etc.

Brecht insisted that Mother Courage herself was a negative character, a profiteer who sacrifices her children to her commercial instinct and cannot learn from her experience. But the audience never fails to be moved by her fate.

DAS VERHOER DES LUKULLUS (The Trial of Lucullus)
Written: 1939.
First performance: As a radio play, Beromuenster, Switzerland, 1940. As an opera, with music by Paul Dessau: first version, Berlin, March 17, 1951; second version, under the title *Die Verurteilung des Lukullus* (*The Condemnation of Lucullus*), Berlin, October 12, 1951.
The Roman general Lucullus has died. A judge and jury of the nether world examine him to decide whether he should be admitted to live on among the shades or be condemned to complete extinction. He points to his fame and achievement as a victorious soldier. But of all this nothing has remained except the suffering he caused. Only his cook testifies for him: he has introduced the cherry tree into Europe. But that is not enough.

The first version of the opera was banned by the Communist authorities because it condemned all wars without distinction. The second version includes passages that make it clear that war waged against aggressors is laudable and heroic.

LEBEN DES GALILEI (Galileo)
Written: 1938–39. English version (in collaboration with Charles Laughton), 1947. Third, revised version (in German), 1954.
First performance: Zurich, September 9, 1943. Second version, Beverly Hills, July 30, 1947. Third version, Cologne, April 1955.
Music by Hanns Eisler.
In the final version the play has fifteen scenes, but in the Berliner Ensemble performance the last scene is cut.

1609: Galileo, aged forty-five, lives with his daughter Virginia, his housekeeper Mrs. Sarti, and her little son Andrea, already a promising pupil of the master. He earns a meager living in the service of the Republic of Venice as a lecturer at the University of Padua. Galileo is an unscrupulous and sensuous man who does not hesitate to claim that he has invented the telescope when he has merely copied a Dutch invention. As the Venetians pay him badly and allow him no time for research he accepts the invitation of the Grand Duke of Florence to move to his domain. Though the freedom of Venice may be lacking there, at least he will have leisure to pursue his observation of the stars through his new telescope.

Galileo has proved that the earth is not the center of the universe. But although the Pope's own astronomer, Clavius, confirms his findings, the Inquisition forbids him to publish them. For eight years Galileo is silent. When a new Pope, Urban VIII, a mathematician known as an enlightened mind, ascends the throne, Galileo sees a chance that the new science will be accepted. But the Grand Inquisitor persuades the Pope that such discoveries would undermine the basis of the Church's authority. The Pope agrees that Galileo be shown the instruments of torture.

June 22, 1633: Galileo's pupils, among them Andrea Sarti, grown to manhood, refuse to believe that Galileo will recant his teaching. The tolling of the bells anounces that he has recanted. He enters, a broken man. Andrea cries out: "Pity the country that has no heroes!" Galileo replies: "No. Pity the country that needs heroes!"

Years later: Galileo lives in the country, under close surveillance by the Inquisition. His daughter, whose fiancé has broken off their engagement because of Galileo's views, is now an old maid who nags him incessantly. Galileo, nearly blind, obsequiously spends his time listening to readings from pious tracts. Andrea Sarti, disgusted at the old man's cowardice, visits him before leaving for Holland. When Galileo hands him the completed manuscript of his *Discorsi*, which he has written secretly, Andrea's contempt changes into admiration. Now he understands why Galileo recanted—to gain the time to complete his great work. But Galileo will not accept this view. He sees himself as a criminal, whose cowrdice has set the pattern for centuries to come. He has made science the servant of authority rather than asserting its right to transform the world for the benefit of mankind.

Andrea smuggles the *Discorsi* across the frontier.

Brecht's masterpiece shows the scientist Galileo as a sensualist, for whom even the quest for knowledge is a pleasure of the senses. The representatives of the Church are drawn as brilliantly intelligent men who argue their case with consummate skill. The other characters—Galileo's daughter Virginia, who loves her father, becomes an old maid because of his addiction to science, yet cannot understand him; his motherly old housekeeper, Mrs. Sarti; her son Andrea; and a large cast of minor figures—are finely observed and presented in the round with a wealth of detail.

DER GUTE MENSCH VON SEZUAN (The Good Woman of Setzuan)

Written: 1938–40.
First performance: Zurich, February 4, 1943.
A parable play, set in modern China.
Music by Paul Dessau.

Three gods have come to earth to look for a really good human being. Unless at least one can be found, the world cannot continue to exist. They are weary from their fruitless search. As they enter the town of Setzuan they ask Wang the water-seller to find someone who will give them shelter for the night. The hardhearted and selfish people of the town refuse to take them into their houses. Only Shen Te, a prostitute, offers them a place to rest their weary limbs. She even sends away a customer to keep her room free for them. In the morning the gods reward her with a gift of money, sufficient to enable her to buy a small tobacco shop.

But as soon as the news spreads that the kindly Shen Te has come into a fortune, an army of parasites, would-be relatives and debtors descends upon her. To protect herself she assumes the personality of a ruthless male cousin, Shui Ta. This brash and brutal young man drives the spongers away.

Shen Te meets an unemployed airman, Yang Sun, and saves him from suicide. She falls in love with him; they plan to get married. But when Yang is alone with the ruthless Shui Ta, he admits, speaking as man to man, that he is after her money. He wants it for bribes to get a job as a mail pilot and is not going to marry her. Having lost her fiancé, Shen Te is also about to lose her shop, when she learns that she is pregnant.

Shui Ta reappears. Shen Te is said to be away on a journey, and so her ruthless cousin can restore her fortunes. He starts a tobacco factory and employs the ex-airman Yang, who soon becomes a foreman because he, too, is ruthless and astute in exploiting the workpeople and making them toil harder.

Wang the water-seller, whom the gods have asked to keep them informed on the fortunes of the one good human being they have as yet encountered, is worried about Shen Te's long absence. He suspects Shui Ta of having murdered her. Shui Ta is arrested and the gods themselves appear to act as judges at the trial. Shui Ta reveals that he is Shen Te in disguise. Only under the mask of ruthlessness and greed could the good woman of Setzuan ever hope to provide for herself and her unborn child. For the good cannot live in our world and *stay* good.

The foolish and ineffectual gods are relieved that the good human being they have found is still alive. When Shen Te draws their attention to her dilemma they avoid the issue. Somehow or other, they say, she will manage. Having convinced themselves that they have after all found one good soul in the world they float away into the heavens. And yet, the epilogue insists, a world where the good cannot live surely ought to be changed.

HERR PUNTILA UND SEIN KNECHT MATTI (Mr. Puntila and His Hired Man, Matti)

Written: 1940–41.

First performance: Zurich, June 5, 1948.

Music by Paul Dessau.

Folk play based on Finnish folk tales and the draft of a play by Hella Wuolijoki.

A folk play (*Volksstueck*) in the tradition of Austrian and Bavarian popular drama. Although the action is laid in Finland the speech of common people used is a South German idiom.

Mr. Puntila is a rich farmer. Like the millionaire in Chaplin's *City Lights*, he overflows with good humor and kindness when he is drunk, but reverts to a "reasonable" attitude, mean and businesslike, when he is sober.

Mr. Puntila is about to marry his daughter to an attaché in the diplomatic service, a degenerate fop. But when he gets drunk he scolds Eva for even contemplating such a match merely for money, and draws her attention to the manly figure of his driver and handyman, Matti. Eva herself does not relish the idea of her engagement to the attaché, and induces Matti to compromise her by being seen emerging from a bathing hut with her. But the attaché is too mean to worry about so trivial a matter.

The morning of the engagement party, four girls of the neighborhood to whom Puntila proposed during the night, when he was drunk, appear. Now he is sober, he turns them away. But as the engagement party progresses he gets drunk again and keeps on insulting the attaché, till even he notices that he is not wanted. Puntila wants Matti to take the attaché's place and marry Eva. Matti has his doubts; he puts her through an examination to see if she is qualified to be a workman's wife. She fails. Matti decides the time has come when he must leave: friendship or family ties between a landowner and a hired man can end only in disaster.

Puntila is marred by some tactless pinpricks against the anti-Communist Finns, but it contains some masterly scenes. Puntila himself is a great character; his transitions between his sober and drunken selves are brilliantly managed. Very much against Brecht's own intention, Puntila steals the play. Matti, who has some witty speeches of Schweikian wisdom in the opening scenes, turns out rather a prig when he refuses the girl who loves him for very arid and pedantic reasons.

DER AUFHALTSAME AUFSTIEG DES ARTURO UI (The Resistible Rise of Arturo Ui)
Written: 1941.
First performance: Stuttgart, November 1958.
A very long play (seventeen scenes) in mock-heroic blank

verse. It attempts to transfer the story of Hitler, from his beginnings to the occupation of Austria, into the world of gangsters of Chicago. This ambitious project, however, with its studied parallels to Shakespeare's *Richard III*, fails: the parallels between Hitler's dealings with the German capitalists and the connection between Chicago gangsters and businessmen (vegetable dealers) are labored and unconvincing. Brecht knew Hitler; he knew very little about Chicago.

DIE GESICHTE DER SIMONE MACHARD (The Visions of Simone Machard)
Written (in collaboration with Lion Feuchtwanger): 1941–43.
First performance: Frankfurt, March 8, 1957.
Another play on the subject of St. Joan: Simone Machard, an adolescent girl, works as a servant for the *patron* of a hotel, gas station, and transport business in central France. It is June 1940; the Germans are advancing. Simone is worried about her brother, who is serving in a front-line army unit. She has been reading the story of Joan of Arc. In her dreams her brother keeps appearing as an angel, calling upon her to save France.

In the confusion, greed and selfishness of panic and collapse, Simone alone tries to help the starving refugees, to prevent supplies from falling into the hands of the Germans and to save her country's dignity and honor. In her dream-world Monsieur le Maire has become King Charles VII, and the owner of the hotel, the Connetable, his miserly mother, Queen Isabel. The Germans occupy the village, and the *patron's* mother is collaborating with them. Simone learns that she is about to sell their secret hoard of gas to the Germans and sets fire to it. In her visions she is tried and sentenced to death. In the real world she is certified insane and taken to a mental home.

The charm of this play lies in the skill with which the dreams and visions of the little girl show history through the eyes of a naïve and simple person—with a touching mixture of anachronisms and unsophisticated clichés. At times the language of the dream dissolves into a Joycean idiom.

SCHWEIK IM ZWEITEN WELTKRIEG (Schweik in the Second
  World War)
Written: 1941–44.
First performance: Warsaw (in Polish), January 17, 1957.
  Erfurt (in German), March 1958.
Music by Hanns Eisler.
The immortal good soldier is here transferred to German-
occupied Prague. He still meets his friends in the same bar,
Zum Kelch (The Goblet). But this now has an attractive
landlady, Mrs. Kopecka, a young widow and ardent Czech
patriot. The informer Bretschneider is now a Gestapo agent.
Schweik's friend Baloun still has an insatiable appetite, and
the plot revolves around Schweik's attempts to satisfy it, lest
Baloun feels compelled to join the German Army for the sake
of a square meal. Asked to steal a certain handsome dog,
wanted by an S.S. leader for his wife, Schweik eventually
lands in the German forces himself.

The action is interrupted by interludes, during which the
Nazi leaders appear as figures of more than life size (except
Goebbels, who is less than life size) and proclaim their faith
in the undying readiness of the small man to die for them. In
the final scene of the play Schweik, the embodiment of the
small man, meets Hitler on the snow-covered battlefield of
Stalingrad, and shows himself entirely unconcerned about the
latter's fate.

Brecht's pastiche of Hašek's language and characterization
is most successful. There are also a number of beautiful songs.

LEBEN DES KONFUTSE (Life of Confucius)
Written: Before 1944.
Only one scene of this curious play has been published posthumously. It deals with the life of Confucius and is written
to be acted by children. "It might appear that it would be impossible to do justice to the high theme if it were entrusted to
children. But one might reply that for children only the highest themes are high enough." Besides, having the life of the
great philosopher performed by children will increase the
"distance" between the actors and the public. The short scene

itself shows Confucius in his early youth instructing some playmates. He teaches them how to subdue their instincts by the self-control of perfect manners.

DER KAUKASISCHE KREIDEKREIS (The Caucasian Chalk Circle)

Written: 1944–45.

First performance: In English, Northfield, Minnesota, 1948. In German, Theater am Schiffbauerdamm, Berlin, June 1954.

Music by Paul Dessau.

Based on the old Chinese play, *The Circle of Chalk*, which was successfully adapted by Klabund in Germany in the 1920s.

Prologue. Towards the end of the Second World War members of two collective farms in Soviet Georgia are in dispute about a tract of land that used to belong to the goat-breeding collective before it had to be abandoned to the advancing Germans. The neighboring collective farm, specializing in fruit- and wine-growing, has planned an irrigation scheme for which the land in question would be essential. After discussion it is decided to let the fruit farmers have the land; their plan is likely to make it more productive. To illustrate the ethics of this decision a Georgian folk singer is invited to sing the old legend of the circle of chalk.

In feudal Georgia a long time ago, there once lived a rich Governor with his wife and little son. On an Easter Sunday the barons rose in revolt against the Grand Duke and murdered his Governor. In the panic the Governor's wife fled, leaving her little son behind. A kitchen maid, Grusche Vakhnadze, saved the child and took it with her into the mountains. To conceal its identity and to give it shelter and a name Grusche consented to marry a rich peasant in the last stages of a fatal illness. But after the wedding the dying man revived. He had only pretended to be ill to avoid being recruited for the army. Now the war was over. Simon the soldier, Grusche's fiancé, returned from service and found Grusche married and mother of a child. Before she could explain the situation, soldiers seized the little boy. The Governor's wife was claiming it back and had taken the case to law.

But to understand the trial that followed we must know more about the judge who decided the case. His story takes us back to that same Easter Sunday when the barons rose against the Grand Duke. That night Azdak, a drunken village scribe, gave shelter to a beggar whom he later recognized as the Grand Duke in person. Azdak felt that his unwitting rescue of the rascally ruler was a crime, forced the village constable to arrest him, and take him to the city to be tried for it. In the city, however, there was no judge left; the soldiers, who were the only power in the land, were so amused by Azdak's jests that they made him the judge to replace the one whom the people had just hanged. For two years Azdak sat in judgment over the people of Georgia. He took bribes and was a lecherous man. But he favored the poor and downtrodden.

When Grusche and the Governor's wife appeared before Azdak, however, he was about to be hanged. Now that the Grand Duke was back in power, there was no place for him. The noose was already around his neck when a messenger arrived from the Grand Duke himself, who had appointed the man who saved his life to be judge over the city. So Azdak heard the case. Having listened to the pleas of the two women, he drew a circle of chalk on the ground, put the child in the center, and told them to try and drag it out of the circle. The Governor's wife pulled it towards her with violence. Grusche let it go. Azdak awarded the child to Grusche because her gentleness showed that she loved it more. In the dancing and rejoicing that followed this judgment Azdak disappeared and was never heard of again.

The meaning of the story, the singer concludes, is that things should "belong to those who are good for them: the children to those who are motherly . . . and the valley to those who will irrigate it and make it fruitful."

With its poetry, its use of narrators, its two-pronged construction, its stylized action—the negative, wicked characters are masked—*The Caucasian Chalk Circle* is the outstanding example of the technique of the "epic" drama. It is one of Brecht's greatest plays.

DIE ANTIGONE DES SOPHOKLES (The Antigone of Sophocles)
Written: 1948.
First performance: Chur, Switzerland, February 1948.
An adaptation, based on Hoelderlin's translation. A prologue relates the play to the period after the Second World War. Two sisters in Berlin during the final phase of the war find their brother outside their home, hanged as a deserter by the S.S. The version of the play itself, which treats Hoelderlin's brittle language with great freedom, emphasizes Creon's character as that of a power-drunk tyrant.

DIE TAGE DER KOMMUNE (The Days of the Commune)
Written: 1948–49 at Zurich.
First performance: Chemnitz (Karl-Marxstadt), November 7, 1956.
Music by Hanns Eisler.
The Days of the Commune was written as an answer to Nordahl Grieg's, the Norwegian playwright's play, *The Defeat*. It uses some of the characters and situations of that play to give Brecht's view on the reasons for the defeat of the Paris Commune.

The personal story of a group of inhabitants of a corner of Montmartre is seen against the background of the activities of the Paris City Council, with brief glimpses of the enemies of the Commune, Thiers and Bismarck. The simple faith and staunch common sense of the people are contrasted with the moral scruples and hesitations of the leaders: in their doctrinaire liberalism they fail to use violence, restrain the masses from marching to Versailles and sweeping away Thiers' government; they leave the Bank of France untouched because they are hypnotized by the idea of legality; they neglect to impose discipline and unified command upon their forces because of their antimilitarism, etc. As a result the simple people of Montmartre die in the fighting, while from a hill overlooking the city Thiers and a group of aristocrats watch the spectacle of burning, defeated Paris.

The Days of the Commune is an ambitious play. It has many felicitous touches, but is not wholly successful. The good characters are unduly sentimentalized, while Thiers and Bismarck are savage caricatures. The problem of violence and discipline is stated, but remains unsolved.

DER HOFMEISTER (The Private Tutor)
Written: 1950.
First performance: Berlin, April 15, 1950.
An adaptation of a play by Jacob Michael Reinhold Lenz (1751–92), one of the mad geniuses of eighteenth-century German literature. To pillory the spinelessness and lack of civic courage of German intellectuals under Hitler, Brecht revived this savage portrait of a German schoolmaster. Laeuffer, the poor private tutor, is seduced by Gustchen von der Burg, the daughter of his employers, whose fiancé is away at the university. Gustchen becomes pregnant. Laeuffer is chased by her enraged family and seeks refuge in the house of a village schoolmaster. But here too the sex instinct gets the better of him. Rather than disgrace his benefactor's innocent godchild and thus ruin his career as a teacher for the second time, Laeuffer castrates himself. Nevertheless he marries the girl who drove him to this desperate expedient, and though childless lives happily ever after—an image of the emasculated German pedagogue.

HERRNBURGER BERICHT (Report on Herrnburg)
Written: 1951.
First performance: East Berlin, Summer 1951.
Published: *Neues Deutschland*, East Berlin, July 22, 1951.
Choral cantata.
Music by Paul Dessau.
Written for the Communist World Youth Festival, *Report on Herrnburg* deals with an incident following the previous year's Communist Youth Rally. West German youths who had attended it were stopped on trying to re-enter the territory of the Federal Republic. Police tried to prevent them from marching through West Germany in closed formation, wanted to take down their names, etc. This is presented as a horrid

attack upon human rights and the idea of freedom. The text, consisting largely of witless and abusive doggerel, is one of the low points of Brecht's literary career.

DER PROZESS DER JEANNE D'ARC ZU ROUEN 1431 (The Trial of Joan of Arc at Rouen 1431)
Written: 1952.
First performance: Berliner Ensemble, November 23, 1952.
Based on a radio drama by Anna Seghers which made use of the protocols of the actual trial of Joan of Arc.

DON JUAN
Written: 1952.
First performance: Berliner Ensemble, November 16, 1953.
A fairly close adaptation of Molière's play.

CORIOLAN (Coriolanus)
Written: 1952–53.
Published: *Stuecke XI.*
Brecht was working on the preparations for the production of this play at the time of his death.

PAUKEN UND TROMPETEN (Trumpets and Drums)
First performance: Theater am Schiffbauerdamm, 1956.
Music by Rudolf Wagner-Regeny.
Published: *Stuecke XII.*
An adaptation of Farquhar's Restoration comedy *The Recruiting Officer* by Brecht, Elisabeth Hauptmann, and Benno Besson. The time of the action is transferred to the period of the American Revolution, which gives an opportunity for numerous barbed references to imperialism and colonial conquest. The songs are weak imitations of those of *The Threepenny Opera*.

TURANDOT ODER DER KONGRESS DER WEISSWAESCHER (Turandot or The Congress of Whitewashers)
An uncompleted play, written during Brecht's stay in East Berlin. Set in a mythical China, it attacks Western intellectuals who try to whitewash capitalism.

NARRATIVE PROSE

Novels

DREIGROSCHENROMAN (Threepenny Novel)
Published: 1934.
The *Threepenny Novel* developed from Brecht's rejected story outline for the film version of the play. It is, however, very far removed from the original. The Marxist element, which was only hinted at in *The Threepenny Opera*, has become dominant. The scene of the action is London during the Boer War. Macheath, no longer a dashing and elegant gangster but a middle-aged businessman, runs a chain of cheap multiple shops, the B-stores, that exclusively sell stolen goods. The theft of these is organized on a mass-production basis. Macheath and Polly are no longer romantic lovers. Polly merely marries him because she has become pregnant by another man. The conflict between Polly's father, the beggar king Peachum, and Macheath is a purely business affair. It revolves around the rivalry between a number of similar stolen-goods chain stores and a project for the sale of unseaworthy hulls to the Admiralty as troop transports for the war. The only sympathetic character is George Fewkoombey, a veteran soldier who has lost a leg in South Africa and has found employment with Peachum. After Macheath and Peachum have happily settled their differences in a profitable merger of their respective enterprises, Fewkoombey is hanged for a murder committed by Macheath.

The *Threepenny Novel* is an uneven work. Flashes of Dickensian gusto and Swiftian satire alternate with tedious would-be descriptions of the workings of capitalism and high finance as a system of frauds and thefts. The last chapter, Fewkoombey's dream about a trial of a figure resembling Christ charged with having misled the poor by giving them false hopes, has a blasphemous grandeur of its own.

DIE GESCHAEFTE DES HERRN JULIUS CAESAR (The Business
Deals of Mr. Julius Caesar)
Published: 1957.
This unfinished novel is intended to show a great man
through the eyes of his contemporaries: Caesar's banker
Mummlius Spicer and his private secretary, the slave Rarus.
Caesar is revealed as a debt-ridden puppet of moneylenders,
his political career and rise to power as a series of desperate
expedients to evade his creditors. Roman life is modernized
by the use of present-day terminology of finance and politics
(in the manner of Feuchtwanger and Robert Graves). But
despite some witty passages the novel fails to convince.

Short Stories

In his early years Brecht wrote a considerable number of short
stories to make money. He thought little of them, and they
were not reprinted in his lifetime. Among the more characteristic of these stories are:

"Bargan laesst es sein" ("Bargan Lets it Be"). Published in
Der Neue Merkur, Munich, 1921.
This story, which seems to be the germ of the play In the
Jungle of the Cities, describes the infatuation of a pirate
captain, Bargan, with an utterly worthless, clubfooted mem-
ber of his crew, which eventually leads to Bargan's ruin.

"Der Kinnhaken" ("The Hook to the Chin"). Published in
Scherls Magazin, Berlin, January 1, 1926.
A boxing story. A boxer who has lost confidence in himself
through his manager's constant anxious efforts to keep him
from drinking loses the fight. He realizes that his attempts to
keep himself from drinking have sapped his morale. One
should always do what one feels like doing. This foreshadows
the principle of self-indulgence proclaimed in Mahagonny.

"Eine Pleite-Idee" ("An Idea for Lean Times"). Published in
Uhu, Berlin, September 12, 1926.
A down-and-out financier meets a destitute individual who is
so emaciated and miserable in appearance that nobody would

give him more than a few days to live. The financier feeds this man till he looks healthy, insures his life for a large sum, lets him starve till he regains his desperate looks, and takes him to the insurance company, who are so alarmed at his appearance that they offer to buy the policy back for a considerable sum. This process is repeated with several insurance companies. The financier, who uses the profits from this scheme to start a prosperous business, is hurt because the poor man is not grateful to him, who has fed him so well for such a long time.

"Die Bestie" ("The Beast"). Published in *Berliner Illustrirte Zeitung*, December 1928.
This story, which won Brecht the first prize of three thousand marks in a short-story competition, deals with the problem of reality versus theatrical illusion. A Soviet film producer making a film on a prewar pogrom needs a man who resembles the notorious Governor of the province, Muratov, who organized that bloodbath. An old man who bears a striking resemblance to Muratov is found, but when he acts the scene his appearance and manner are far too gentle for so bloody a villain. The producer takes the part away from the old man —who is Muratov himself.

KALENDERGESCHICHTEN (Calendar Tales)
Published: 1948.
A volume of short stories, some of Brecht's narrative verse and a selection of the Keuner anecdotes (see below). The short stories, written in a highly compressed, terse style modeled on the *Novellen* of Heinrich von Kleist, are:

"Der Augsburger Kreidekreis." The plot of the Caucasian chalk circle transferred to Augsburg in the period of the Thirty Years' War.

"Die Zwei Soehne" ("Two Sons"). The final phase of the Second World War: a peasant woman in Thuringia is struck by the resemblance of one of the Russian prisoners-of-war, working on her farm, to her own son away at the front. When her son, an S.S. man, suddenly returns, having abandoned his unit, it is decided that the Russian prisoner, who would denounce him as a member of the S.S. when Russian troops occupy the village, must be killed. The peasant woman lets the prisoner escape and hands her own son to the Russians to keep him from continuing the senseless fight. She thus saves both her son's and the Russian prisoner's life.

"Das Experiment" ("The Experiment"). Francis Bacon dies as a consequence of his experiment with a chicken stuffed with snow and teaches the little boy who helps him the meaning of the scientific method.

"Der Mantel des Ketzers" ("The Heretic's Coat"). Giordano Bruno, fighting for his life against the Inquisition, is desperately anxious to pay a poor tailor the money he still owes him for an overcoat.

"Caesar und sein Legionaer" ("Caesar and His Legionary"). The lives of the dictator Julius Caesar, his secretary Rarus, and a poor old veteran of Caesar's army are strangely intertwined on the eve of the Ides of March. This story is an early stage of the novel *Die Geschaefte des Herrn Julius Caesar*.

"Der Soldat von La Ciotat" ("The Soldier of La Ciotat"). A shell-shocked French soldier has acquired the ability of standing absolutely motionless. Painted with a bronze color, he exhibits himself at the fair-ground of La Ciotat as the living statue of the unknown soldier.

"Der Verwundete Sokrates" ("Socrates Wounded"). Based on a play by Georg Kaiser, *Der gerettete Alkibiades* (*Alcibiades Saved*). Determined to run away during the battle of Delion, Socrates gets a thorn into his foot and is immobilized. Surrounded by Persians and unable to escape, he utters loud cries, suggesting the presence of a whole Greek army, and causes the defeat of the Persians. He is carried home in triumph, but eventually he summons up the courage to tell Alcibiades what really happened. Admitting one's cowardice is the greatest of all possible acts of courage.

"Die unwuerdige Greisin" ("The Unworthy Old Woman").
Brecht's grandmother abandons the narrow conventions of
petty bourgeois respectability after her husband's death.

GESCHICHTEN VOM HERRN KEUNER (Anecdotes of Mr.
    Keuner)
Written: c. 1930–c. 1956.
The Keuner anecdotes are, as Brecht put it, "attempts to
make gestures quotable." Keuner is Brecht's *alter ego*, and
each anecdote expresses one of his basic personal attitudes,
ranging from the need to be punctual to more profound problems, such as his approach to religion, violence, friendship,
etc. These anecdotes are very short (from about twenty to a
few hundred words) and are among Brecht's most remarkable
achievements: witty, concise, paradoxical, and profound, they
are a modern equivalent to the work of the great French
moralists, lying somewhere between the maxims of La Roche-
foucauld and the characters of La Bruyère.

GESICHTE (Visions). A cycle of dreamlike prose sketches and
parables of remarkable power. They include: "Der Disput,"
published in *Pariser Tageszeitung*, Paris, March 12–13, 1939;
"Der Staedtebauer" in *Berthold Viertel: Dichtungen und
Dokumente*, Munich, 1956; "Parade des Alten Neuen," "Die
Niederkunft der Grossen Babel," and "Der Kriegsgott," in
Brecht, Ein Lesebuch fuer Unsere Zeit, Weimar, 1958.

FLUECHTLINGSGESPRAECHE (Refugee Conversations). A series
of dialogues between two German refugees (written c. 1940).
The idea is clearly taken from Goethe's *Unterhaltungen
Deutscher Ausgewanderter* (*Conversations of German Ex-
iles*), but the main character, Ziffel, resembles Schweik and
Brecht in his deadpan humor.

ME-TI. BUCH DER WENDUNGEN (Me-ti. The Book of Twists
    and Turns)
Written between 1934 and 1950. A collection of short prose
pieces—anecdotes and reflections, very much in the style of
the Keuner stories, but with an ancient Chinese setting
which, however, very thinly disguises Brecht's own political

and personal preoccupations. Brecht himself appears as Kin, Kin-jeh, Ken-jeh or Kien-leh (all clearly derived from Keuner), Stalin as Ni-en, Lenin as Mi-en-leh, the Soviet Union as Su, etc. The book not only gives most revealing insights into Brecht's reactions to the Stalinist terror, the backwardness of the Soviet Union, etc. but also contains some of Brecht's most personal writings about his love for, and relationship with a woman, Lai-tu (presumably Ruth Berlau). These are among the most tender love poems and poetic prose pieces Brecht ever wrote.

DER TUI-ROMAN (The Tui Novel)

Fragments of a novel, written in the thirties and forties, which was to become an indictment of the intellectuals, renamed in the inversion by which Brecht transformed Western names into Chinese ones, *Tellekt-Uell-In*, abbreviated by the opening letter of each section into Tui. Set in a mythical Imperial China, the book was to be a Swiftian satire against intellectuals who live by selling their opinions to the highest bidder. Brecht used much of this material for the play *Turandot or the Congress of Whitewashers*.

ESSAYS AND THEORETICAL WRITINGS

Brecht's voluminous theoretical writings about the theatre are assembled in the latest collected editions in five volumes of the paperback, two of the thin-paper hardcover version. They are divided into *Writings on the Theatre* which run to about thirteen hundred pages of text, *Writings on Literature and Art*, and *Writings on Politics and Society*.

The most important titles of longer works among his theoretical essays on the theatre are:

DER MESSINGKAUF (The Purchase of Brass). Written 1937– 1951.

A compendium of views on epic theatre, which remained unfinished, but was conceived as a series of Platonic dialogues interspersed with poems and short illustrative scenes.

KLEINES ORGANON FUER DAS THEATER (Little Organon for the Theatre). Written 1948.
A terse and concise summary of Brecht's view on epic theatre in seventy-seven gnomic paragraphs.

MODEL BOOKS

Brecht believed that exemplary productions of the "epic" theatre should be recorded and used as models for subsequent productions of the play concerned, giving the new producer a basis on which to work without tying him down in every detail. Every phase of such productions was photographed during an actual performance. The pictures, together with copious notes, were collected in "model books." Some of these have been published:

Antigonemodell 1948. Published 1949, reprinted 1955.
Brecht's production of *Antigone* at Chur.

Die Gewehre der Frau Carrar. Published 1952.
Photographs of productions of this play at Paris, Copenhagen, and Greifswald.

Aufbau einer Rolle, Galilei (*Building Up A Part, Galileo*). Published 1958.
The production with Charles Laughton in California and the performance of Ernst Busch with the Berliner Ensemble.

Couragemodell 1949 (*Mother Courage*). Published 1958.
The Berlin production of 1949.

Photographs from model books of three productions, a full account of three others, and a wealth of material on the Brechtian theatre, written by Brecht and his associates, are contained in:

Theaterarbeit, 6 Auffuehrungen des Berliner Ensembles (6 Performances of the Berliner Ensemble), Dresden, 1952.

A magnificent picture book. The six productions described in detail are: *Puntila*, *Vasa Zheleznova* (Gorky), *Der Hofmeister*, *Die Mutter*, *Biberpelz/Der Rote Hahn* (Hauptmann), *Mother Courage*.

MISCELLANEOUS PUBLICATIONS

Kriegsfibel (*Primer of War*). Published 1955.
A picture book: photographs covering the period from the Spanish Civil War to the end of the Second World War collected by Brecht from Scandinavian and American newspapers and magazines, each accompanied by a quatrain. A grim but impressive piece of pacifist propaganda. He intended to supplement it by a second volume, *Friedensfibel* (*Primer of Peace*), which remained unfinished.

TRANSLATIONS:
Together with Margarete Steffin, Brecht translated the childhood memoirs of the Danish writer, Martin Andersen-Nexoe: *Die Kindheit*, Zurich, 1945. The translation is prefaced by a dedicatory poem by Brecht.

Brecht made a German adaptation, based on a translation by Ernst Hube, of Sergei Tretyakov's play *Ich will ein Kind haben* (*The Pioneers*).

FILMS

Brecht wrote a number of film scripts, most of which never reached the production stage. He had a hand in the following completed films:

Robinsonade auf Asuncion. Written in collaboration with Bronnen, 1922.
A group of characters stranded on a deserted island, which, unlike the island of Robinson Crusoe, contains a giant, modern city—completely abandoned by its inhabitants. The story

published in *Berliner Boersen Courier*, November 1922, as
he winning entry of a film competition) was used as the basis
f a silent picture. It was, however, so far removed from the
uthors' original intentions that they disowned it. The com-
leted film had the title *Die Insel der Traenen* (*The Isle of
ears*) (see *Arnolt Bronnen gibt zu Protokoll*, p. 115).

Die Dreigroschenoper, 1931. Directed by G. W. Pabst.
Brecht's own story outline for the film *Die Beule* (*The Lump
n the Head*) is published in *Versuche* 3. Pabst did not ad-
ere to it, and Brecht disliked the resulting film intensely.
Made in parallel German and French versions, this is never-
heless the most Brechtian of all Brecht films.

Kuhle Wampe, 1932. Script by Brecht and Ernst Ottwalt. Mu-
ic by Hanns Eisler. Directed by Slatan Dudow.
Life among the unemployed in pre-Hitler Berlin. A working-
class family is shown in the throes of the economic crisis. The
on, out of work, commits suicide. The family are evicted
rom their tenement and move into a shack in an allotment
area, Kuhle Wampe. The daughter and her fiancé quarrel because he agrees to marry her only from a sense of duty when
he learns that she is pregnant. The lovers are eventually rec-
onciled during a big Communist party sporting gala, which
symbolizes the forward-looking hope of the new, revolutionary
generation. The film was shown in the United States under
the title *Whither Germany?*

Hangmen Also Die, 1942. Directed by Fritz Lang. Music by
Hanns Eisler.
'I sold a story to a Hollywood firm but I did not write the
screenplay myself" (Brecht at the hearing of the Un-American
Activities Committee). The assassination of the Nazi Gov-
ernor Heydrich by Czech patriots.

Herr Puntila und sein Knecht Matti, 1955. Directed by
A. Cavalcanti.
The script was written with Brecht's advice.
Made in Vienna, this color film of *Puntila*, with Curt Bois in
the name part, is an interesting experiment that fails. The nat-

uralism of the photography and the realistic background de
stroy the stylized convention in which the play is written
proof that Brecht's ideas only worked on the stage. This may
be the explanation why, in spite of his love for the cinema
Brecht was always unhappy about filmed versions of his work

Mutter Courage (started 1954, uncompleted).
A Cinemascope production in color. Originally to be directed
by Wolfgang Staudte, later by Erich Engel. Disputes about
the casting between Brecht and Staudte and interference by
the authorities have until now prevented the completion of
this ambitious project.

A completely new film version, in black and white *Total-
vision* was directed by Peter Palitzsch and Manfred Wekwerth, 1959–60. This film uses the cast of the Berliner Ensemble and sticks closely to the play.

SECTION C

BIBLIOGRAPHY

The list of books and articles that follows does not aim at completeness. Only works that have actually been quoted or otherwise extensively used are listed. Nor is it possible to cover the literature on the large variety of wider subjects that form the background to the present work: German language and literature, Marxism, the history of the theatre, the art of acting, etc.

For more exhaustive bibliographies of works by, and on, Brecht the reader is referred to the following publications:

NUBEL, WALTER. "Bertolt-Brecht-Bibliographie," *Sinn und Form*, Second Special Brecht Issue, 1957.
  This admirable bibliography lists writings by and on Brecht in German, published up to the end of 1956.
NELLHAUS, GERHARD. "Brecht-Bibliographie," *Sinn und Form*, First Special Brecht Issue, 1949.
  A much shorter bibliography, but it also lists translations of works by Brecht and articles on Brecht in English. Not completely accurate.
PETERSEN, KLAUS-DIETRICH. "Bertolt-Brecht-Bibliographie," Bad Homburg v.d.H., Berlin, Zurich, 1968.
RAMTHUN, HERTA. "Bertolt Brecht Archiv/Bestandverzeichnis des literarischen Nachlasses, Band I: Stuecke," Berlin and Weimar, 1969.
  The first volume of a catalogue of Brecht's literary remains in the Brecht Archive in East Berlin.

Very full details about translations of works by Brecht into

English and French are given in *The Theatre of Bertol*
Brecht by John Willett (see below).

BRECHT'S WRITINGS

Brecht's numerous writings first appeared scattered through
out an immense number of separate books, periodicals
anthologies, newspapers etc. The bibliographies listed abov
contain details of these.

Listed below are the principal *collected editions* of Brecht'
works:

Brecht: Versuche, nos. 1–7, 1930–32; nos. 9–15, 1949–57
no. 8 was never published.
The earlier series is out of print and very rare. But a reprin
of all the numbers, including the hitherto unpublishe
number 8, is now available in two volumes. The postwa:
series is published in parallel editions in West Germany
(Suhrkamp) and East Germany (Aufbau Verlag). The
East German series contains an additional—special—num
ber (Sonderheft) that reprints *Die Gewehre der Frau*
Carrar, the short story *Der Augsburger Kreidekreis*, and
the poems *Neue Kinderlieder*.

Another collected edition remained incomplete and is practically unobtainable today:

Brecht: Gesammelte Werke, vols. I and II, Malik Verlag,
London, 1938.
This edition does not contain the plays that precede *Mann*
ist Mann and ends with *Die Gewehre der Frau Carrar*. It
was printed in Prague, although the place of publication
is given as London. The two further volumes planned were
lost after the German occupation of Prague.

An edition which began to be published in Brecht's own
lifetime (1953) by Suhrkamp Verlag in Frankfurt and Auf-

au Verlag—under license from Suhrkamp—in East Berlin, omprises:

tuecke (Plays), 14 volumes.
ʒedichte (Poems), 9 volumes.
ʒchriften zum Theater (Writings on Theatre), 7 volumes.
ʒrosa (Narrative Prose), 5 volumes.
ʒchriften zur Literatur und Kunst (Writings on Literature and Art), 3 volumes.
ʒchriften zur Politik und Gesellschaft (Writings on Politics and Society), 1 volume.

This edition grew rather haphazardly, has few notes and also contains many omissions and repetitious overlaps (the same poems appear several times, the same notes on plays can be found in the volume containing the play itself and then again in the Writings on Theatre). To meet growing criticism, Suhrkamp Verlag, Frankfurt, reassembled Brecht's works in a new collected edition which appeared in 1967—on the eve of Brecht's seventieth birthday. This edition, which still contains some very noticeable gaps, like the suppression of *Herrnburger Bericht*, must nevertheless be regarded as the most complete now—and probably for a long time to come—available. This is:

Bertolt Brecht, Gessamelte Werke.

The edition was issued in two forms: 8 thin-paper, hardcover volumes or 20 pocket-size paperbacks. But the pagination and indexing are identical in both forms.

They are arranged as follows:

Vol. I (corresponds to vols. 1 and 2 of the paperback version)
STUECKE 1 (Plays 1):

Baal/Trommeln in der Nacht/Im Dickicht der Staedte/ Leben Eduards des Zweiten von England/Mann ist Mann /Die Dreigroschenoper/Aufstieg und Fall der Stadt Mahagonny/Der Ozeanflug [i.e. Lindberghflug]/Das Badener Lehrstueck vom Einverstaendnis/Der Jasager/Der Neinsager/Die Massnahme/Die heilige Johanna der Schlachthoefe/Die Ausnahme und die Regel/Die Mutter

Vol. VIII (corresponds to vols. 18, 19, and 20 of the paper-
  back version)
  THEORETICAL PROSE 2:
  Writings on Art and Literature/Writings on Politics and
  Society

Additional volume (two additional volumes in the paperback
  version)
  Screenplays and other writings for the Cinema

The editorial principle on which this collected edition is
based—use of the latest version approved by Brecht—is in
itself doubtful (as it presents early works unhistorically in
versions adapted to suit the political expediency of Brecht's
life in East Berlin), but the omission of significant variants
makes it even less valuable for the serious student of Brecht.
To make up for these deficiencies Brecht's West German publishers are issuing paperback volumes of single plays with
variants, edited by reputable scholars. Those at present available are:

Bertolt Brecht, *Baal. Drei Fassungen*, ed. Dieter Schmidt,
  Frankfurt, 1970. Contains the texts of the versions of 1918,
  1919, and 1926 with variants and critical apparatus.

Bertolt Brecht, *Baal. Der boese Baal, der Asoziale*, ed. Dieter
  Schmidt, Frankfurt, 1968. The last version (1955) with
  variants and details of earlier texts.

Bertolt Brecht, *Im Dickicht der Staedte. Erstfassung und
  Materialien*, ed. Gisela E. Bahr, Frankfurt, 1968. First version of the play (1922) with variants and other critical
  apparatus.

Bertolt Brecht, *Leben Eduards des Zweiten von England.
  Vorlage, Texte und Materialien*, ed. Reinhold Grimm,
  Frankfurt, 1968. Marlowe's play in the translation Brecht
  used, variants, and other critical apparatus.

Bertolt Brecht, *Der Jasager und Der Neinsager. Vorlagen,*

Fassungen und Materialien, ed. Peter Szondi, Frankfurt 1966.

Bertolt Brecht, *Der Brotladen. Stueckfragment. Buehnenfas sung und Texte aus dem Fragment,* Frankfurt, 1969. Tex of the version of this uncompleted play as performed by the Berliner Ensemble, 1967, with additional scenes.

TRANSLATIONS INTO ENGLISH

There are numerous translations of Brecht's works scattered in periodicals and editions which have become difficult to obtain today. Details of most of these can be found in John Willett's *The Theatre of Bertolt Brecht* (see below in the bibliography of books on Brecht). The principal translations now current are:

Bertolt Brecht, *Collected Plays,* Vol. I, ed. John Willett and Ralph Mannheim. The first volume of a comprehensive edition which will eventually extend to Brecht's Poems and Prose Writings as well. This edition will be published by Methuen in London and Pantheon in New York. The translations, not necessarily the same in the British and American editions, will be by different hands. Vol. I contains: *Baal/Drums in the Night/In the Jungle of Cities/ The Life of Edward II of England/*and the One-Act-Plays: *A Respectable Wedding/The Beggar and the Dead Dog/ Driving out the Devil/Lux in Tenebris/The Catch*

Bertolt Brecht, *Plays,* 2 vols. London: Methuen, 1960 and 1962. Contains: Vol. 1: *The Caucasian Chalk Circle/The Threepenny Opera/The Trial of Lucullus/The Life of Galileo;* Vol. 2: *Mother Courage/St. Joan of the Stockyards/The Good Person of Szechwan*

Seven Plays by Bertolt Brecht, edited and with an introduction by Eric Bentley, New York, Grove Press, 1961. Contains: *In the Swamp/A Man's a Man/St. Joan of the*

*Stockyards/Mother Courage/Galileo/The Good Woman of
Setzuan/The Caucasian Chalk Circle.*

Grove Press also publishes a paperback edition of Brecht's
under the general editorship of Eric Bentley. The following
volumes are available:

Baal, A Man's a Man, and *The Elephant Calf*
The Jewish Wife and Other Short Plays (contains three
    sketches from *Furcht und Elend des Dritten Reichs:*
    "The Jewish Wife," "In Search of Justice," "The Informer";
    also: "The Elephant Calf," "The Measures Taken," "The
    Exception and the Rule," and "The Salzburg Dance of
    Death")
Mother Courage
Parables for the Theatre (*The Caucasian Chalk Circle* and
    The Good Woman of Setzuan)
Jungle of the Cities and Other Plays (also contains *Drums
    in the Night* and *Roundheads and Peakheads*)
Galileo
The Visions of Simone Machard
The Threepenny Opera
Edward II
The Mother

Collections of Poems
    Bertolt Brecht, *Selected Poems,* translation by H. R. Hays,
        New York, Grove Press, 1959.
    Bertolt Brecht, *Manual of Piety* (*Die Hauspostille*), bilin-
        gual edition, translations by Eric Bentley.

Prose
    Bertolt Brecht, *Tales from The Calendar,* translated by
        Yvonne Kapp and Michael Hamburger, London, 1961.
    Bertolt Brecht, *Threepenny Novel,* translated by Desmond
        I. Vesey and Christopher Isherwood, New York, 1956,
        London, 1958.
    Brecht on Theatre, translated by John Willett, London,
        1964, New York, 1964.

Bertolt Brecht, *The Messingkauf Dialogues*, translated b
John Willett, London, 1965.

BOOKS ON BRECHT

BENJAMIN, W. *Versuche ueber Brecht*, Frankfurt, 1966.
CHIARINI, P. *Bertolt Brecht*, Bari, 1959.
The first book on Brecht in Italian.
DEMETZ, P., ed. *Brecht, A Collection of Critical Essays*, En
glewood Cliffs, N.J., 1962.
ENGBERG, HARALD. *Brecht på Fyn*, 2 vols., Odense, 1966
Brecht's life in Denmark.
ESSLIN, M. *Bertolt Brecht*, New York and London, 196ç
(Columbia Essays on Modern Writers, No. 42).
EWEN, FREDERIC. *Bertolt Brecht. His Life, His Art and Hi:
Times*, New York, 1967; London, 1970.
FASSMANN, KURT. *Brecht: Eine Bildbiographie*, Munich,
1958.
Brecht's life-story told in pictures.
GRIMM, REINHOLD. *Bertolt Brecht, die Struktur seines
Werkes*, Nuremberg, 1959.
———. *Bertolt Brecht und die Weltliteratur*, Nuremberg,
1961.
HAAS, WILLY. *Bert Brecht* (Koepfe des xx, Jahrhunderts, Bd.
7), West Berlin, 1958.
A brief monograph, containing some vivid personal im-
pressions, but also many inaccurate statements.
HECHT, W., BUNGE, J.-J., RUELICKE-WEILER, K. *Bertolt
Brecht. Sein Leben und Werk*, East Berlin, 1969.
HINCK, WALTER. *Dei Dramaturgie des spaeten Brecht* (Vol.
229 of "Palaestra," Untersuchungen aus des deutschen und
englischen Philologie und Literaturgeschichte), Goettin-
gen, 1959.
A thorough and scholarly analysis of Brecht's dramatic
technique.
HULTBERG, HELGE. *Die aesthetischen Anschauungen Bertolt
Brechts*, Copenhagen, 1962.

HERING, HERBERT. *Bertolt Brecht und das Theater*, Berlin, 1959.
A short essay followed by 64 illustrations.

ENDREIEK, H. *Bertolt Brecht. Drama der Veraenderung*, Duesseldorf, 1969.

KESTING, MARIANNE. *Bertolt Brecht in Selbstzugnissen und Dokumenten*, Hamburg, 1959.
A short paperback monograph based on autobiographical passages from Brecht's work. Illustrated.

KLOTZ, VOLKER. *Bertolt Brecht, Versuche ueber das Werk*, Darmstadt, 1957.
A lucid and penetrating study of Brecht's style and poetic method.

MANN, OTTO. *Mass oder Mythos: Ein kritischer Beitrag ueber die Schaustuecke Bertolt Brechts*, Heidelberg, 1958.
An attack on Brecht from the point of view of the traditional conception of the German classical drama.

MAYER, HANS. *Anmerkungen zu Brecht*, Frankfurt, 1965.
———. *Bertolt Brecht und die Tradition*, Pfullingen, 1961.

MITTENZWEI, WERNER. *Bertolt Brecht. Von der Massnahme zu Leben des Galilei*, East Berlin, 1962.

MUELLER, KLAUS-DETLEF. *Die Funktion der Geschichte im Werk Bertolt Brechts*, Tubingen, 1967.

NIESSEN, CARL. *Brecht auf der Buehne*, Cologne, 1959.
A detailed and profusely illustrated catalogue of an exhibition of pictures and documents relating to the stage history of Brecht's plays, arranged by the Institute of Theatre Studies of Cologne University and held at Munich in the fall of 1959.

REICH, B. *Brecht* (in Russian), Moscow, 1960.
———. *Im Wettlauf mit der Zeit* (Memoirs), East Berlin, 1970.

RISCHBIETER, HENNING. *Brecht*, 2 vols., Velber bein Hannover, 1966.

RUELICKE-WEILER, KAETHE. *Die Dramaturgie Brechts*, East Berlin, 1966.

SCHMIDT, DIETER. *'Baal' und der junge Brecht*, Stuttgart, 1966.

SCHUHMANN, KLAUS. *Der Lyriker Bertolt Brecht 1913–1933*, East Berlin, 1964.

SCHUMACHER, ERNST. *Die dramatischen Versuche Berto Brechts 1918–1933*, East Berlin, 1955.

A voluminous study of the early Brecht from a strictl Marxist point of view. Contains a wealth of valuable fa tual material but also demonstrates the effect of the rig Marxist orthodoxy on the critical faculties of an acute i telligence: the plays are most predictably judged accordin to their political content.

——. *Bertolt Brechts 'Leben des Galilei' und andere Stueck* East Berlin, 1965.

——. *Der Fall Galilei. Das Drama der Wissenschaft*, Ea Berlin, 1964.

SERREAU, GENEVIEVE. *Brecht*, Paris, 1955 (Les Grand Dramaturges no. 4).

SPALTER, MAX. *Brecht's Tradition*, Baltimore, 1967.

STERNBERG, FRITZ. *Der Dichter und die Ratio. Erinnerunge an Bertolt Brecht*, Gottingen, 1963.

SZCZESNY, GERHARD. *Das Leben des Galilei und der Fa Bertolt Brecht*, Frankfurt, 1966.

WILLETT, JOHN. *The Theatre of Bertolt Brecht*, London an New York, 1959.

WINTZEN, RENÉ. *Bertolt Brecht* (Poètes d'aujourd'hui, n 43), Paris, 1954.

A brief study, followed by an anthology of extracts from Brecht's works in French translation.

ZWERENZ, GERHARD. *Aristotelische und Brechtsche Drama tik*, Rudolstadt, East Germany, 1956.

A plea for a compromise between the Brechtian and th "Aristotelian" drama. The author has since fled to th West.

SPECIAL BRECHT ISSUES OF PERIODICALS

Adam & Encore, London, Autumn 1956. A joint Brecht is sue of the literary magazine *Adam* and the theatre quar terly *Encore*.

Cahiers du Cinéma, Paris, No. 114, December 1960.
The Drama Review, New York, Fall 1967.
The Drama Review, New York, Winter 1968.
Europe, 35e année, nos. 133–34, Paris, January/February 1957.
Sinn und Form, East Berlin, Sonderheft Bertolt Brecht, 1949.
Sinn und Form, East Berlin, Zweites Sonderheft Bertolt Brecht, 1957.
  This "Second Special Brecht Issue" of *Sinn und Form* contains a wealth of excellent contributions and much interesting material by Brecht.
Théâtre Populaire, Paris, No. 11, January/February 1955.
The Tulane Drama Review, New Orleans, September 1961.

OTHER BOOKS AND ARTICLES
CONTAINING REFERENCE
TO BRECHT

(a) General studies, biographical material and reminiscences

ABRAHAM, PIERRE. "Renier le passé ou preparer l'avenir?," *Europe*, Special Brecht Issue, 1957.
ARENDT, HANNAH. "Der Dichter Bertolt Brecht," *Die Neue Rundschau*, 1950/no. 1.
BENTLEY, ERIC. "Brecht, Poetry, Drama and the People," *The Nation*, July 31, 1943.
  "A Century of Hero Worship," 2nd edition, New York, 1957.
BERENDSOHN, WALTER A. *Die humanistische Front. Einfuehrung in die Emigrantenliteratur*, Erster Teil, Zurich, 1946.
BERLAU, RUTH. "Brecht und die Kinder," *Das Magazin*, East Berlin, August 1957.
  "Wie war Bert Brecht?" *Das Magazin*, East Berlin, February 1956.
BORNEMAN, ERNEST. "Epitaph fuer Bertolt Brecht," *Sinn und Form*, Second Special Brecht Issue, 1957.

"The Real Brecht," *Encore*, no. 15, July/August 1958.

"Credo quia Absurdum. An Epitaph for Bertolt Brecht, *The Kenyon Review*, Spring 1959.

These three articles are largely versions of the same original text, but the *Sinn und Form* version omits any critical references to Brecht.

"Two Brechtians," *The Kenyon Review*, Summer 1960.

BRECHT, BERTOLT. "Aus dem Arbeitsbuch: Der Aufhaltsam Aufstieg des Arturo Ui," *Sinn und Form*, Second Special Brecht Issue, 1957.

"Augsburger Theaterkritiken," *Sinn und Form*, Second Special Brecht Issue, 1957.

"Ausfuehrungen vor der Sektion Dramatik, IV. Deutsche Schriftstellerkongress (January 1956)," *Beitraege zu Gegenwartsliteratur*, East Berlin, 1956/no. 1.

"Briefe des jungen Brecht an Herbert Ihering," *Sinn und Form*, 1958/no. 1.

"Kleiner Beitrag zum Thema Realismus," *Sonntag*, East Berlin, 1958/no. 6.

(Brecht's encounter with the censor of *Kuhle Wampe*.)

"Kulturpolitik und Akademie der Kuenste," *Neues Deutschland*, East Berlin, 8.12.1953.

"Notizen zur Barlach-Ausstellung," *Sinn und Form*, 1952/no. 4. (In defense of the "formalist" sculptor Barlach.)

BRONNEN, ARNOLT. *Arnolt Bronnen gibt zu Protokoll*, Hamburg, 1954.

"Bertolt Brecht und Berlin," *Berliner Zeitung*, East Berlin, 2.9.1958.

BRYHER. "Bertolt Brecht," *Life and Letters Today*. May 1942
Deutsches Theater, Bericht ueber 10 Jahre, East Berlin, 1957.

(An illustrated account of the first ten postwar years of the Deutsches Theater.)

"Dreizehn Buehnentechniker erzaehlen," *Sinn und Form*, Second Special Brecht Issue, 1957.

(Impressions of stagehands and technicians of the Berliner Ensemble.)

EISLER, HANNS. "Bertolt Brecht und die Musik," *Sinn und Form*, Second Special Brecht Issue, 1957.

EISNER, LOTTE. "Sur le procès de l'Opéra de Quat' Sous," *Europe*, Special Brecht Issue, 1957.

EMMEL, FELIX. *Das Ekstatische Theatre*, Prien, 1924.

ESSLIN, MARTIN. "Bert Brecht's Difficulties," *Encounter*, London, December 1958.

"Brecht's Missing Verse," *Encounter*, London, June 1959.

FEUCHTWANGER, LION. "Bertolt Brecht, dargestellt fuer Englaender," *Die Weltbuehne*, 9.4.1928.

"Bertolt Brecht," *Sinn und Form*, Second Special Brecht Issue, 1957.

Erfolg (Novel), 2 vols., Berlin, 1930.

FISCHER, RUTH. *Stalin and German Communism*, Cambridge, Massachusetts, 1948.

FRISCH, MAX. "Brecht ist tot," *Die Weltwoche*, Zurich, 8.24. 1956.

Tagebuch 1946–1949, Frankfurt, 1950.

GARTEN, HUGO F. "The Origins of Brecht," *Adam & Encore*, Brecht Number, 1956.

GREENBERG, CLEMENT. "Bertolt Brecht's Poetry," *Partisan Review*, March–April 1941.

GROSZ, GEORGE. *Ein kleines Ja und ein grosses Nein*, Hamburg, 1955.

Little Yes and A Big No, New York, 1946.

HAAS, WILLY. *Die Literarische Welt, Erinnerungen*, Munich, 1957.

Hearings Regarding the Communist Infiltration of the Motion Picture Industry, Washington, 1947.

HAUPTMANN, ELISABETH. "Notizen ueber Brechts Arbeit 1926," *Sinn und Form*, Second Special Brecht Issue, 1957.

HOOK, SIDNEY. "A Recollection of Berthold Brecht," *The New Leader*, October 1960.

IHERING, HERBERT (ed.). *Theaterstadt Berlin, Ein Almanach*, East Berlin, 1948.

"Der Volksdramatiker," *Sinn und Form*, First Special Brecht Issue, 1949.

JAHNN, HANS HENNY. "Vom armen BB," *Sinn und Form*, Second Special Brecht Issue, 1957.

JARRELL, RANDALL. "In All Directions," *Partisan Review*, July–August 1942.

KAHN, GORDON. *Hollywood on Trial*, New York, 1948.

KERSTEN, HEINZ. *Der Aufstand der Intellektuellen*, Stuttgart, 1957.

KLEINSCHMIDT, KARL. "Wir sind der Mensch von Sezuan," *Neue Zeit*, East Berlin, 8.19.1956.

KOEHNE, DR. "Das Mitbestimmungsrecht des Urhebers des zur Verfilmung gelangenden Werks am Drehbuch des Films," *Archiv fuer Urheber-Film-und Theaterrecht*, vol. IV, no. I, Berlin, 1931.

KOESTLER, ARTHUR. *The Invisible Writing*, London, 1954.

KRACAUER, SIEGFRIED. *From Caligari to Hitler*, Princeton, 1947.

KRAUS, KARL. "Kerrs Enthuellung," August 1929. Reprinted in *Widerschein der Fackel, Glossen*, Munich, 1956.

LASKY, MELVIN J. "Berliner Tagebuch," *Der Monat*, West Berlin, January 1955.

LEISER, ERWIN. "Nach dem letzten Mal," *Sinn und Form*, Second Special Brecht Issue, 1957.

LUETHY, HERBERT. "Vom armen Bert Brecht," *Der Monat*, West Berlin, May 1952. Also in *Encounter*, London, July 1956.

"Leben und Dichten des unsteten Bert Brecht," *Die Zeit*, Hamburg, 8.23.1956.

MAYER, HANS. "Gelegenheitsdichtung des jungen Brecht," *Sinn und Form*, 1958/no. 1.

MUENSTERER, H. O. "Ich, Bertolt Brecht, bin aus den schwarzen Waeldern. Erinnerungen an Brecht im Jahr 1919 in Augsburg." *Panorama*, Munich, vol. III, 8 (August 1959).

NEHER, CASPAR. "Dem Gedaechtnis meines Freundes," *Sinn und Form*, Second Special Brecht Issue, 1957.

PAUL, WOLFGANG. "Aus Bertolt Brechts spaeten Jahren," *Neue Deutsche Hefte*, Guetersloh, November 1958.

POLGAR, ALFRED. *Handbuch des Kritikers*, Zurich, 1938. *Ja und Nein*, Hamburg, 1956.

POZNER, VLADIMIR. "bb." *Europe*, Special Brecht Issue, 1957. "bb," *Sinn und Form*, Second Special Brecht Issue, 1957.

REICH, BERNHARD. "Erinnerungen an den jungen Brecht," *Sinn und Form*, Second Special Brecht Issue, 1957.

ROZENEL, NATALYA. "Lunacharskii i Bertolt Brekht" (Lunacharsky and Bertolt Brecht), *Teatr*, Moscow, 1957/no. 8.

"Brecht und Lunatscharsky," *Neues Deutschland*, East Berlin, 2.8.1958.

(Translation of above with omission of certain anti-German passages.)

RUEHLE, JUERGEN. *Das gefesselte Theater*, Cologne/Berlin, 1957.

(A history of the vicissitudes of *avant-gardist* theatre under Communism.)

SCHOOP, GUENTHER. *Das Zuercher Schauspielhaus im Zweiten Weltkrieg*, Zurich, 1957.

STRITTMATTER, ERWIN. "Besuch bei Brecht — heute," *DDR-Revue*, 1957/no. 9.

(A description of the Brecht archive.)

SUESKIND, W. E. "Bert Brecht" in *Die Grossen Deutschen, Deutsche Biographie*, vol. v, West Berlin, 1957.

SUTER, GODY. "Brecht, Pinselstriche fuer ein Portraet," *Tagesanzeiger*, Zurich, 9.1.1956.

THOMPSON, LAWRENCE. "Bert Brecht," *Kenyon Review*, Summer 1940.

"Der Tod des Bertolt Brecht," *Der Monat*, West Berlin, October 1956. (A survey of obituaries.)

TRETYAKOV, SERGEI. "Bert Brecht," *International Literature*, Moscow, May 1937.

TYNAN, KENNETH. "The Theatre Abroad: Germany," *The New Yorker*, Sept. 12, 1959.

VALENTIN, KARL. *Karl Valentins Lachkabinett* (ed. G. Pallmann), Munich, 1950.

VIERTEL, BERTHOLD. "Bertolt Brecht," *Kenyon Review*. Summer 1945.

WEISENBORN, GUENTHER. "Zuercher Tagebuch," *Sinn und Form*, Second Special Brecht Issue, 1957.

WEISKOPF, F. C. *Unter Fremden Himmeln, Ein Abriss der deutschen Literatur im Exil*, East Berlin, 1947.

WEKWERTH, MANFRED. "Auffinden einer Kategorie," *Sinn und Form*, Second Special Brecht Issue, 1957.

(A visit to Brecht shortly before he died.)

WHITE, ERIC WALTER. "Bertolt Brecht," *Life and Letters*, vol. XIII, no. 1, September 1935.

WINGE, HANS. "Brecht en privé." *Europe*, Special Brecht Is-
    sue, 1957. Also in *Act*, Winter 1956–57.

(b) The Berlin Theatre before 1933

IHERING, HERBERT. *Die zwanziger Jahre*, East Berlin, 1948.
    Von Reinhardt bis Brecht, vol. 1, East Berlin, 1958. Vol.
    2, East Berlin, 1959.
KERR, ALFRED. *Die Welt im Drama*, Cologne and Berlin,
    1954.
    Was wird aus Deutschlands Theater, Berlin, 1932.
PEM. *Heimweh nach dem Kurfuerstendamm*, West Berlin,
    1952.
PISCATOR, ERWIN. *Das politische Theater*, Berlin, 1929.
STERN, ERNST and HERALD, HEINZ. *Max Reinhardt und seine
    Buehne*, Berlin, 1918.
Die Weltbuehne, Berlin, ed. Siegfried Jacobsohn till 1926,
    thereafter by Carl von Ossietzky (*passim* 1922 to 1933).

(c) The Theory of the "Epic" Theatre

ADLER, HENRY. "Bertolt Brecht and Epic Theatre," *The Lis-
    tener*, London, January 26, 1956; also *The Nation*, New
    York, September 8, 1956.
    "Bertolt Brecht's Theatre," *The Twentieth Century*, Lon-
    don, August 1956.
BENJAMIN, WALTER. "Was ist episches Theater." Reprinted
    in *Schriften*, vol. II, Frankfurt, 1955.
BENTLEY, ERIC. "Bertolt Brecht and His Work" (Postscript
    to *The Private Life of the Master Race*), London, 1948.
    The Playwright as Thinker, New York, 1946.
    In Search of Theatre, New York, 1953.
BUNGE, HANS-JOACHIM. "Brecht probiert," *Sinn und Form*,
    Second Special Brecht Issue, 1957.
    "Der Streit um das Tal," *Theater der Zeit*, East Berlin,
    1956/no. 11 (Beilage). English translation in *Tulane
    Drama Review*, Winter 1959.

(Commentary on the Prologue to *The Caucasian Chalk Circle*.)

ERPENBECK, FRITZ. *Lebendiges Theater*, East Berlin, 1949.

FULLER, EDMUND. "Epic Realism, an Analysis of Bert Brecht," *One-Act Play Magazine*, April 1938.

GARTEN, H. F. "The Drama of Bertolt Brecht," *German Life and Letters*, London, January 1952.

Modern German Drama, London, 1959.

GORELIK, MORDECAI. *New Theatres for Old*, New York, 1940; London, 1947.

"Epic Realism." *Theatre Workshop*. April–July 1937.

HECHT, WERNER. "Die Entwicklung von Brechts Theorie des epischen Theatres 1918–1933," *Theater der Zeit*, East Berlin, 1958/no. 12 and 1959/no. 3.

HOFMANNSTHAL, HUGO VON. *Das Theater des Neuen, Eine Ankuendigung*, 1926. Reprinted Vienna, 1947.

MELCHINGER, SIEGFRIED. *Drama zwischen Shaw und Brecht*, Bremen, 1957.

RUELICKE, KAETHE. "Brecht und Obraszow," *Sinn und Form*, 1955/no. 4.

"Leben des Galilei–Schlusszene," *Sinn und Form*, Second Special Brecht Issue, 1957.

SARTRE, JEAN-PAUL. "Brecht et les classiques," *World Theatre*, Paris, vol. VII/no. 1, Spring 1958.

SCHROEDER, MAX. *"Aufsaetze ueber Brecht," Aufbau*, East Berlin, 1957/no. 1.

WEKWERTH, MANFRED. "Sechs Punkte zum erzaehlenden Arrangement Bertolt Brechts," *Theater der Zeit*, East Berlin, 1956/no. 11 (Beilage).

WIRTH, ANDRZEJ. "Ueber die stereometrische Struktur der Brechtschen Stuecke," *Sinn und Form*, Second Special Brecht Issue, 1957.

(d) *Brecht in the Soviet Union*

ANIKST, A. "Zametki po povodu teatra Brekhta" ("Notes on Brecht's theatre"), *Teatr*, 1957/no. 8.

BACHELIS, T. "Voinstvoyushchaya mysl i ee teatralnaya forma" ("Militant thought and its theatrical form"), *Teatr*, 1957/no. 8.

Bolshaya Sovietskaya Entsiklopediya, first edition, vol. VII, 1927, article "Brecht."

Bolshaya Sovietskaya Entsiklopediya, second edition, vol. VI, 1951, article "Brecht."

Bolshaya Sovietskaya Entsiklopediya, second edition, vol. XLV, 1956, article "Formalism."

BRECHT, BERTOLT. *Kavkazkii melovoi krug* (*The Caucasian Chalk Circle*), translated by S. Apt, postscript by Bernhard Reich, Moscow, 1957.

Mamasha Kurazh i ee deti (*Mother Courage*), translated by S. Apt, postscript by Bernhard Reich, Moscow, 1957.

Zhizn Gaileya (*Life of Galilei*), translated by L. Kopelev, postscript by Bernhard Reich, Moscow, 1957.

"Bertolt Brekht o teorii i praktike revolyutsionnogo teatra" ("Bertolt Brecht on the theory and practice of the revolutionary theatre"), introduction by I. Fradkin, translated by L. Kopelev, *Teatr*, 1957/no. 5.

(A severely selective translation of extracts from *Kleines Organon* and other theoretical writings.)

DYMSHITS, A. "Bertolt Brekht," *Zvezda*, Moscow and Leningrad, April 1957.

FRADKIN, I. "Bertolt Brekht," *Teatr*, 1956/no. 1.

"O khudozhestvennom svoeobrazii dramaturgii Bertolta Brekhta" ("Artistic character of Bertolt Brecht's dramaturgy") *Voprosy Literatury*, Moscow, December 1958.

GAYEVSKII, V. "Zhestokie pritchi Berlinskogo Ansamblya" ("The Cruel Parables of the Berliner Ensemble"), *Teatr*, 1957/no. 8.

GOLOVASHENKO, YURII. "Berliner Ensemble in Leningrad," *Theater der Zeit*, East Berlin, September 1957.

GORCHAKOV, NIKOLAI A. *The Theatre in Soviet Russia*, New York and London, 1957.

LAQUEUR, W. Z., and LICHTHEIM, G. *The Soviet Cultural Scene 1956–57*, New York and London, 1958.

LUTSKAYA, E. "Khudozhniki Berlinskogo Ansamblya" ("The Designers of the Berliner Ensemble"), *Teatr*, 1957/no. 8.

MATSKIN, A. "Politika i Poeziya" ("Politics and Poetry"), *Teatr*, 1957/no. 8.

MOKULSKII, S., and ROSTOTSKII, B. "Segodnyashnee i proidennoe" ("The Contemporary and the Old-fashioned"), *Sovietskaya Kultura*, 5.18.1957.

SURKOV, E. "Pervie Vpechatleniya" ("First Impressions"), *Sovietskaya Kultura*, 5.11.1957.

Teatr i Dramaturgiya, 1935/no. 1. A special issue devoted to Tairov's Kamerny Teatr, which contains a photograph of Tairov's production of *The Threepenny Opera* in 1930. Sets by V. and G. Stenberg.

WEKWERTH, MANFRED. "Anblick, Einblick, Ausblick. Bemerkungen zum Sowjettheater," *Theater der Zeit*, East Berlin, 1957/no. 10.

YUZOVSKII, Y. "Bertolt Brecht und sein guter Mensch," *Sinn und Form*, Second Special Brecht Issue, 1957.

"Na spektalyakh Berlinskogo Ansamblya" ("After the performances of the Berliner Ensemble"), *Teatr*, 1957/no. 8.

ZAKHAVA, B. "Sila i Slabost teatra Brekhta" ("Strength and Weakness of Brecht's Theatre"), *Znamya*, Moscow, 1957/no. 8.

ZHDANOV, A. A. *On Literature, Music and Philosophy*, London, 1950.

(e) *Brecht in Poland*

POMIANOWSKY, JERZY. "Un Théâtre du Renouveau en Pologne," *Les Temps Modernes*, Paris, July 1958.

WIRTH, ANDRZEJ. "Beitrag zur Brecht-Rezeption in Polen," *Theater der Zeit*, East Berlin, 1956/no. 12.

SECTION D

BRECHT IN AMERICA

PRODUCTIONS OF BRECHT'S PLAYS
IN AMERICA UP TO THE TIME OF
HIS DEATH

Since his death, Brecht has been a good deal performed on the British and American stage, even though not in the West End or on Broadway: it becomes increasingly difficult to keep track of all this Brechtian activity.

There is, however, a remarkable story which can be pretty well defined, and that is the story of Brecht production in the United States during the author's lifetime. By a curious paradox, Brecht seems to have been performed more in the great country of capitalism than anywhere else except West (not East) Germany.

The following list of Brecht productions which took place in the United States while the author was still alive was compiled by Walter Nubel and is printed here with his permission. Brief accounts of the earlier part of this story were given by Eric Bentley in two articles: "Brecht on the American Stage: Three Notes," in Bulletin: National Theatre Conference, Cleveland, July 1948, and "Brecht auf der amerikanischen Buehne," in Theater der Welt: Ein Almanach, edited by Herbert Ihering, Berlin 1949.

In a letter to Eric Bentley dated November 12, 1949, Brecht wrote: "I prefer the university productions to the commercial ones."

LINDBERGH'S FLIGHT (The Flight of the Lindberghs)
  Translated by George Antheil
  Music by Kurt Weill
  Academy of Music, Philadelphia, Pa.
  Opening date: April 4, 1931
  Producer: The Philadelphia Orchestra Association
  Conductor: Leopold Stokowski

THE THREEPENNY OPERA
  Translated by Gifford Cochran and Jerrold Krimsky
  Music by Kurt Weill
  Empire Theatre, New York, N.Y.
  Opening date: April 13, 1933
  Producer: John Krimsky and Gifford Cochran
  Director: Francesco von Mendelssohn and Zeke Colvan
  Settings duplicated by Cleon Throckmorton from the de-
    signs by Caspar Neher

THE YEA-SAYER (He Who Says Yes)
  Translated by Alice Mattulath
  Music by Kurt Weill
  Grand Street Playhouse, New York, N.Y.
  Opening date: April 25, 1933
  Producer: Music School of Henry Street Settlement
  Director: Sanford Meisner
  Conductor: A. Lehman Engel
  Designs: R. A. Jones

THE MOTHER
  Translated by Paul Peters
  Music by Hanns Eisler
  Civic Repertory Theatre, New York, N.Y.
  Opening date: November 19, 1935
  Producer: The Theatre Union
  Director: Victor Wolfson
  Settings: Mordecai Gorelik

THE INFORMER (One scene from Fear and Misery of the
    Third Reich)
  Translated by Ruth Norden

SENORA CARRAR'S RIFLES
  Translated by Keene Wallis
  Green Street Theatre, San Francisco, Calif.
  Opening date: February 3, 1939
  Producer: San Francisco Theatre Union
  Director: George Altman

THE PRIVATE LIFE OF THE MASTER RACE
  English version by Eric Russell Bentley
  University of California, Wheeler Auditorium, Los Angeles, Calif.
  Opening date: June 7, 1945
  Producer: Little Theatre & Dept. of Dramatic Art, University of California, Berkeley, Calif.
  Director: Henry Schnitzler

THE PRIVATE LIFE OF THE MASTER RACE
  English version by Eric Russell Bentley
  Music by Hanns Eisler
  Pauline Edwards Theatre, New York, N.Y.
  Opening date: June 12, 1945
  Producer: Theatre of All Nations
  Director: Berthold Viertel
  Settings: Leo Kerz

THE THREEPENNY OPERA
  Translated by Desmond Vesey
  Music by Kurt Weill
  University of Illinois, Lincoln Hall Theatre, Urbana, Ill.
  Opening date: November 15, 1946
  Producer: Illini Theatre Guild
  Director: Charles Shattuck

THE TRIAL OF LUCULLUS
  Translated by H. R. Hays
  Music by Roger Sessions
  University Theatre, University of California, Berkeley, Calif.
  Opening date: April 18, 1947
  Producer: Dept. of Music and Dramatic Art, UCLA

Stage Director: Henry Schnitzler
Musical Director: Roger Sessions
Settings: Warren C. Lounsbury

GALILEO
Translated by Charles Laughton
Music by Hanns Eisler
Coronet Theatre, Hollywood, Calif.
Opening date: July 30, 1947
Producer: T. E. Hambleton
Director: Joseph Losey
Settings: Robert Davison

GALILEO
Translated by Charles Laughton
Music by Hanns Eisler
Maxine Elliot's Theatre, New York, N.Y.
Opening date: December 7, 1947
Producer: The Experimental Theatre
Director: Joseph Losey
Settings: Robert Davison

THE THREEPENNY OPERA
Translated by Desmond I. Vesey
Music by Kurt Weill
Northwestern University Theatre, Evanston, Ill.
Opening date: February 3, 1948
Producer: Northwestern University Theatre
Director: Claudia Webster
Settings: Herbert Philippi

THE GOOD WOMAN OF SETZUAN
English version by Eric and Maja Bentley
Music by John G. Flittie
Hamline University Theatre, St. Paul, Minn.
Opening date: March 16, 1948
Producer: The Hamline Players
Director: James R. Carlson

THE CAUCASIAN CHALK CIRCLE
English version by Eric and Maja Bentley
Music by Katherine Griffith
Nourse Little Theatre, Northfield, Minn.
Opening date: May 4, 1948
Producer: The Carleton College Players
Director: Henry Goodman

THE CAUCASIAN CHALK CIRCLE
English version by Eric and Maja Bentley
Music by Marc Bucci
Hedgerow Theatre, Moylan, Pa.
Opening date: August 20, 1948
Producer: Hedgerow Theatre
Director: Eric Bentley
Scenery: Henry Goodman and Michael de Beausset

THE GOOD WOMAN OF SETZUAN
English version by Eric and Maja Bentley
Music by F. Karl Grossman
Eldred Theatre, Cleveland, Ohio
Opening date: November 2, 1948
Producer: The University Players & The Elder Players,
    Western Reserve University
Director: Nadine Miles
Settings: Henry Kurth

THE GOOD WOMAN OF SETZUAN
English version by Eric and Maja Bentley
Music by Paul Dessau
University of Minnesota Theatre, Minneapolis, Minn.
Opening date: November 26, 1948
Producer: University of Minnesota
Director: David W. Thompson
Settings: Orville K. Larson

THE GOOD WOMAN OF SETZUAN
English version by Eric and Maja Bentley
University of Hawaii, Farrington Hall, Honolulu, T.H.
Opening date: April 1, 1949

Producer: The University of Hawaii Theatre Guild
Director: Earle Ernst
Settings: Earle Ernst

THE GOOD WOMAN OF SETZUAN
English version by Eric and Maja Bentley
Music by Paul Dessau
Vassar College, Poughkeepsie, N.Y.
Opening date: April 27, 1949
Producer: The Experimental Theatre of Vassar College
Director: Charles H. Shattuck
Settings: Doris Lande

THE CAUCASIAN CHALK CIRCLE
English version by Eric and Maja Bentley
Music by Marc Bucci
Alfred University, Alfred, N.Y.
Opening date: May 19, 1949
Producer: The Footlight Club & the Dept. of Dramatics
Director: C. Duryea Smith, III

THE CAUCASIAN CHALK CIRCLE
English version by Eric and Maja Bentley
Music by Marc Bucci
Hedgerow Theatre, Moylan, Pa.
Opening date: June 3, 1949
Producer: Hedgerow Theatre
Director: Jasper Deeter
Settings: Michael de Beausset

THE GOOD WOMAN OF SETZUAN
English version by Eric and Maja Bentley
Music by Paul Dessau
Carnegie Theatre, Pittsburgh, Pa.
Opening date: November 15, 1949
Producer: Dept. of Drama, Carnegie Institute of Tech-
    nology
Director: Lawrence Carra
Settings: Paul Trautvetter

THE GOOD WOMAN OF SETZUAN
English version by Eric and Maja Bentley
Music by Paul Dessau
University of Illinois, Lincoln Hall Theatre, Urbana, Ill.
Opening date: March 29, 1950
Producer: The Illini Theatre Guild
Director: Charles H. Shattuck
Settings: Warwick Brown

THE CAUCASIAN CHALK CIRCLE
English version by Eric and Maja Bentley
Music by Marc Bucci
The Hamline University Theatre, St. Paul, Minn.
Opening date: May 10, 1950
Producer: Dept. of Speech and Dramatics, Hamline University
Director: James R. Carlson

THE GOOD WOMAN OF SETZUAN
English version by Eric and Maja Bentley
Music by F. Karl Grossman
The University of Wyoming, Laramie, Wyoming
Opening date: August 22, 1950
Producer: The Perry-Mansfield Players
Director: Charlotte Perry
Settings: William Kinzer

THE GOOD WOMAN OF SETZUAN
English version by Eric and Maja Bentley
Music by Paul Dessau
Mount Holyoke College, South Hadley, Mass.
Opening date: November 27, 1951
Producer: The Laboratory Theatre
Director: Phyllis Ann Tatt

THE GOOD WOMAN OF SETZUAN
English version by Eric and Maja Bentley
Music by Ynez Lynch and Hazelle Wilson
Little Theatre, Stanford University, Calif.
Opening date: January 30, 1952

Producer: Stanford Studio Players
Director: Nancy Langston
Settings: Hugo Melchione

THE GOOD WOMAN OF SETZUAN
English version by Eric and Maja Bentley
Lewisburg High School Auditorium, Lewisburg, Pa.
Opening date: January 11, 1952
Producer: Cap and Dagger, Bucknell University, Lewisburg, Pa.
Director: Harvey M. Powers, Jr.
Settings: C. Willard Smith and Carroll Barnes

A MAN = A MAN
English version by Gerhard Nellhaus
The Arts Theater Club, Ann Arbor, Michigan
Opening date: August 24, 1952
Director: Strowan Robertson

THE GOOD WOMAN OF SETZUAN
English version by Eric and Maja Bentley
Music by Tom Nichols
The Playmakers Theatre, University of North Carolina, Chapel Hill, N.C.
Opening date: February 26, 1953
Producer: The Carolina Players
Director: Kai Jurgensen
Settings: William I. Long

THE CAUCASIAN CHALK CIRCLE
English version by Eric and Maja Bentley
Music by Marc Bucci
Central High School, Charlotte, N.C.
Opening date: March 25, 1953
Producer: Drama, Music and Art Depts., Central High School
Director: Bristow Hardin, Jr.

THE CAUCASIAN CHALK CIRCLE
English version by Eric and Maja Bentley

Music by Kent McPherron
University Theatre, University of Chicago
Opening date: May 1, 1953
Producer: University Theatre
Director: Otis Imboden
Designs: Stanley Kazdailis and Zohra Alton

THE CAUCASIAN CHALK CIRCLE
English version by Eric and Maja Bentley
Playwrights Theatre Club, Chicago, Ill.
Opening date: June 23, 1953
Producer: David Shepherd
Director: Paul Sills
Settings: John Holabird

THE THREEPENNY OPERA
Translated by Desmond Vesey and Eric Bentley
Music by Kurt Weill
Playwrights Theatre Club, Chicago, Ill.
Opening date: 1954
Producer: David Shepherd
Director: Paul Sills
Settings: Stanley Kazdailis

THE THREEPENNY OPERA
English adaptation by Marc Blitzstein
Music by Kurt Weill
Theatre de Lys, New York, N.Y.
Opening date: March 10, 1954
Producer: Carmen Capalbo and Stanley Chase
Director: Carmen Capalbo
Settings: William Pitkin
Musical Director: Samuel Matlowski

THE CAUCASIAN CHALK CIRCLE
English version by Eric and Maja Bentley
Music by Myron Fink
Lincoln Hall Theatre, Urbana, Ill.
Opening date: January 12, 1955

Producer: The University Theatre, University of Illinois
Director: Charles H. Shattuck
Settings: Wilford Leach

THE PRIVATE LIFE OF THE MASTER RACE
English version by Eric Bentley
Granville Opera House
Opening date: January 19, 1955
Producer: Ace Morgan Studio Theatre
Director: Elizabeth Osborn and Sally Lashar

THE GOOD WOMAN OF SETZUAN
English version by Eric and Maja Bentley
Allegheny College, Meadville, Pa.
Opening date: March 23, 1955

THE TRIAL OF LUCULLUS
Translated by H. R. Hays
Music by Roger Sessions
McCarter Theatre, Princeton, N.J.
Opening date: April 29, 1955
Producer: The Princeton Symphony Orchestra
Director: Kurt Graff
Settings: Hugh Hardy

THE EXCEPTION AND THE RULE
English version by Eric Bentley
Music by Paul Dessau
Dartmouth College, New Hampshire
Opening performance: May 28, 1955
Director: David Glasser
Designer: Alan Sklar

THE CAUCASIAN CHALK CIRCLE
English version by Eric and Maja Bentley
Olga Keith Literary Society, Houston, Texas
Opening date: 1955
Producer: The Rice Players
Director: Sandy Havens

THE THREEPENNY OPERA
  English adaptation by Marc Blitzstein
  Music by Kurt Weill
  Theatre de Lys, New York, N.Y.
  Opening date: September 20, 1955
  Producer: Carmen Capalbo, Stanley Chase and Lucille
    Lortel
  Director: Carmen Capalbo
  Musical Director: Samuel Matlowski
  Settings: William Pitkin

MOTHER COURAGE
  English version by Eric Bentley
  Music by Paul Dessau
  Marines Memorial Theatre, San Francisco
  Opening date: January 17, 1956
  Producer: Actor's Workshop of San Francisco
  Director: Herbert Blau
  Musical Director: Wendell Otey
  Settings: Ernest Baron

THE PRIVATE LIFE OF THE MASTER RACE
  English version by Eric Russell Bentley
  The Open Stage Theatre, New York, N.Y.
  Opening date: January 30, 1956
  Producer: The Open Stage
  Director: Norma Frances
  Designs: Vincent Sorrentino

THE THREEPENNY OPERA
  English version by Eric Bentley and Desmond Vesey
  Music by Kurt Weill
  Community Arts Theatre Group, Champaign, Illinois
  Opening performance: March 1, 1956
  Director: Wilford Leach

THE CAUCASIAN CHALK CIRCLE
  English version by Eric and Maja Bentley
  Goucher College, Towson, Md.

Opening performance: March 1956
Director: Marion Robinson

THE PRIVATE LIFE OF THE MASTER RACE
   English version by Eric Bentley
   Queen's College, Flushing, N.Y.
   Opening performance: March 1956

THE GOOD WOMAN OF SETZUAN
   English version by Eric and Maja Bentley
   Music by Stefan Wolpe
   Silvermine School of Art, Norwalk, Conn.
   Opening performance: June 1956
   Director: Basil Burwell

INDEX* TO WORKS OF BRECHT

---

* This index lists all references to Brecht's writings mentioned in the text. The type of work listed is indicated by the following abbreviations: S (Stage works); N (Narrative prose); E (Essays and theoretical writings); F (Films); P (Poems) and CP (Collections or cycles of poems); M (Model books). No separate references to characters in plays and fiction are given. They can be found by referring to the titles of the works in question.

GENERAL INDEX